D1616947

LESSONS IN CENSORSHIP

Lessons in Censorship

*How Schools and Courts Subvert
Students' First Amendment Rights*

CATHERINE J. ROSS

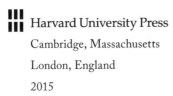
Harvard University Press
Cambridge, Massachusetts
London, England
2015

First printing

Publication of this book has been supported through the generous
provisions of the S. M. Bessie Fund.

Library of Congress Cataloging-in-Publication Data

Ross, Catherine J., author.
   Lessons in censorship : how schools and courts subvert students'
First Amendment rights / Catherine J. Ross.
      pages cm
   Includes bibliographical references and index.
   ISBN 978-0-674-05774-6
1. Freedom of expression—United States. 2. Educational law and
legislation—United States. 3. High school students—Civil rights—
United States. I. Title.
   KF4163.R67 2015
   342.7308'5—dc23   2015002585

For Jon

Contents

LESSONS IN CENSORSHIP

Introduction

Strangling the Free Mind

> That [Boards of Education] are educating the young for citizen-
> ship is reason for scrupulous protection of Constitutional freedoms
> of the individual, if we are not to strangle the free mind at its
> source and teach youth to discount important principles of govern-
> ment as mere platitudes.
>
> —West Virginia State Board of Education v. Barnette (1943)

"You lose all constitutional rights once you enter a school building," a school official in Suffolk County, New York, proclaimed in the spring of 2012. "You are not allowed to do this," she asserted as she confiscated fliers from an indignant student who was protesting her friend's five-day suspension. Layering censorship upon censorship, the episode had a surreal quality to it: The student whose plight prompted the pamphlets had been punished for voicing her opposition to bullying in a way the school deemed inappropriate.[1]

The seizure was as clueless as it was surreal. The official's confidence that the Constitution stopped at the schoolhouse door contradicted decades of jurisprudence recognizing that minors too have constitutional rights, even in school. Unfortunately, the incident was hardly an aberration. A mix of ignorance about, indifference to, and disdain for the speech rights of students permeates society; parents, teachers, school boards, and even some judges exhibit these attitudes.

The speech at the core of *Lessons in Censorship* involves war and peace; civil rights; rights for lesbian, gay, bisexual, and transgendered ("LGBT") students; the Confederate flag; abortion; evangelical proselytizing; immigration; teasing and verbal bullying; sexting; personal prayer in public spaces; pushback against courses in tolerance that sometimes verge on thought reform; and more. No ideological or philosophical camp has been immune

1

from censorship. Schools have stripped conservatives and progressives, secularists and the pious, of their right to speak. Disputes over the constitutional problem of student speech that lead to refinements of legal doctrine also capture an important dimension of everyday life in our schools, told in the stories of real students.

Lessons in Censorship aims to make sense of these controversies and of the constitutional law that governs them. In the process, it will become clear that the courts have left many critical questions unanswered, abandoning educators who need legal guidance. I propose ways of thinking about the law that would forcefully protect free expression without disrupting education. This book is addressed to lawyers, judges, and legal scholars. To make it accessible to other readers, including parents, teachers, school administrators, librarians, concerned citizens, and high school students, I have explained legal conventions and have tried to avoid unnecessary legal terminology.

Three dramatic stories weave through my analysis of the troubled state of student speech rights in public schools today: the entanglement of law and culture wars, divisions on the Supreme Court over jurisprudence, and the frequent failure of schools to perform the critical function of fostering the free exchange of ideas so essential to preserving a vital democracy.

The first story chronicles the intrusion of the nation's most volatile racial, religious, and sexual disagreements into the heart of our elementary, junior high, and senior high schools. Such battles go far beyond the state's curricular choices about evolution, sex education, and ethnic studies that have garnered so much attention. The charged nature of these conflicts encourages school officials to censor expression to avoid controversy.

Consider just a sampling of such infringements. A high school student in Indiana who wanted to express support for U.S. troops overseas in 2005 was told he could not wear a T-shirt showing the Marines' M-16 rifle and the text of the "Creed of the Marines," an ode to the rifle. In Vermont, a middle school student was disciplined for wearing a T-shirt critical of President George W. Bush.[2] Schools promoting tolerance have silenced religious students whose most profound spiritual beliefs compel objection to homosexuality. Officials have even told students they cannot talk about their religion together or study the Bible in their free time. Other schools prevent students from forming support groups for LGBT peers or wearing T-shirts declaring their sexual orientation.

Mirroring fierce divisions in communities, heated fights over the proper balance between liberty and authority among Supreme Court Justices and other federal judges animate the second story. The central drama here has been the retreat from the judiciary's expansion of the rights of children during the period from World War II through the war in Vietnam and the Supreme Court's subsequent creation of an often incomprehensible taxonomy of rules that give different levels of protection to student speech depending on several variables.

The Supreme Court's 1943 ruling in West Virginia State Board of Education v. Barnette provides both the opening scene of this legal drama and the title for this Introduction. In *Barnette*, the Court ruled that students have the right to decline to salute the flag and summarized the important principles behind free speech in inspirational terms. The high point of the movement to guarantee students the protections of the Speech Clause—and a critical moment in this book—came a quarter century later in Tinker v. Des Moines Indepdent Community School District, a 1969 case in which the Supreme Court held that students have the right to express their own views in school if their speech doesn't cross specific lines. *Tinker* provided a special framework for evaluating when schools violate students' affirmative right to speak that balances the constitutional rights of individuals with society's need for schools that can fulfill the many demands we place on them.

In recent decades, successive Supreme Court benches, guided by increasingly conservative Chief Justices and composed of increasingly conservative majorities, have carved out a series of exceptions to *Barnette*'s principles and *Tinker*'s rules. First, the Court removed an undefined swath of "lewd" speech from *Tinker*'s protection. Second, and most powerfully, the Court allowed schools virtually unlimited discretion to censor speech it called "school-sponsored." Finally, it granted schools dispensation to censor speech that appears to promote the use of illegal substances, which many readers will recognize as the "Bong Hits 4 Jesus" case.

The multiplying categories of student speech, each of which has its own level of constitutional protection, have led some judges and law professors to question whether anything remains of *Tinker*'s robust vision of First Amendment rights for students. Even when schools and courts agree about which Supreme Court decision governs a controversy, the law may depend on where the student lives if the Supreme Court has not resolved the particular question at the heart of the dispute and the appellate courts disagree about what the Constitution requires. (A map of the United States showing the geographical division of the federal appellate courts appears on page 302 as an Appendix).

Given this complex series of tests for school speech, it should not surprise anyone that even judges sometimes seem a bit confused by the array of standards and exceptions. Judges too often conflate concepts and fact patterns that should be disaggregated because they raise different legal questions. While the law is not as straightforward as it might be, neither is it as incomprehensible as some commentators have suggested.

If federal judges can misunderstand the law, it seems only to be expected that teachers, principals, and school board members should fail to understand legal intricacies, which brings us to our third story: the failure of schools to fulfill their role of fostering constitutional values. This failure has many dimensions.

Public schools, their employees, and elected school boards susceptible to community pressure are arms of the government, subject to the Constitution. As a result, they are bound by the First Amendment in ways that private persons or institutions, including independent and sectarian schools, are not. And so when I use the term "schools," I am referring to public schools, including charter schools, grades K through twelve.

In truth, educators often lack the most rudimentary familiarity with constitutional demands. Barely half of the top twenty-five graduate programs in education offer a single course on education law, and some of the available courses do not list speech rights among the topics covered. Only two of the top twenty-five programs require students who plan a career in educational administration to complete a course on school law. Too often, mid-career training about students' rights is imposed as a penalty on teachers who have already violated them rather than being offered as information all educators should master.

Moreover, school administrators sometimes exploit the protections of "qualified immunity," a unique defense available to public officials when they are named as defendants in lawsuits alleging violations of constitutional rights. Essentially, the doctrine gives such officials a pass unless the law was so clear that they had to know they were violating the Constitution. The doctrine serves sound social policy goals by allowing public servants to make "reasonable" mistakes when circumstances demand snap decisions. But the lenient treatment of confusion also creates disincentives to learn more about the constitutional rights. The undeniable complexities in identifying clear rules about student speech rights, determining which legal standards govern, and applying the various legal tests to an endless variety of facts have only expanded the opportunities to manipulate the defense. Since 2000, judges have granted qualified immunity in response to student speech claims roughly twice as often as they denied it.

Widespread ignorance and confusion about the law encourage censorship, whether by preventing expression before it is shared or by punishing words that have already been uttered. The infringements I write about are hardly anomalies. I have culled controversies from hundreds of judicial opinions as well as from press accounts and the websites of reputable public interest organizations. Such reported cases are likely "only the tip of the iceberg," as constitutional scholar and former appellate judge Michael W. McConnell has said about conflicts over religion in schools.[3] The obstacles to challenging a school district's penalties—ranging from an imbalance of power and resources to the ongoing need to interact with the school system and the community—prevent many cases from moving forward. And even when families pursue legal remedies, only a small proportion of court cases survive long enough to yield a published judicial opinion rather than a private negotiated settlement. Those lawsuits and remedies are usually hidden from public view.

Much of the litigation stems from efforts to eradicate the penalties schools impose for speech infractions. Discipline may follow even minor breaches of a school's speech code, accounting for the vast majority of school suspensions around the country, as I will show in Chapter 3. The codes often prohibit constitutionally protected expression that could not be punished outside of school. Yet the minimum penalties for violating school rules about speech begin with serious blemishes on students' permanent records. More serious penalties, such as suspensions and expulsions, can follow. Most disturbing, discipline for violations of school rules governing speech sends a large number of children into the juvenile justice system each year. Many of them drop out of school and even end up in prison.

Meanwhile, school districts waste scarce financial resources defending indefensible positions in court; they even refuse to reverse disciplinary decisions based on speech that they subsequently concede was constitutionally protected. Schools that deprive students of expressive rights not only must pay their own attorneys and costs, they often must also pay the injured student's attorneys' fees and expenses as well as damages.

Education's role in fostering the culture of free expression and debate enshrined in the First Amendment and essential to the maintenance, renewal, and vigor of a self-governing democracy lies at the heart of the third story—and of the larger perspective that drives this project. Schools that strip students of the right to speak, to express their central religious, political, and cultural views, or to question received wisdom and popular ideology teach implicit lessons about society's lack of commitment to civil liberties.

Understanding that free expression is a bedrock of democratic governance reveals why the other stories matter. It is the starting point and the end point of all of the episodes in this book. In short, this is a story about the very meaning of democracy, not as an empty incantation but as a vibrant part of daily life.

Educators continually teach students the opposite lesson: that the First Amendment is a sham, something for the ages, but not for them. These counter-lessons register when a school superintendent prevents high school reporters from publishing a story about an environmental lawsuit pending against their school district, a matter of public record. And they register when a high school suspends a gifted art student and demands that she submit to a psychological examination after she displays a poster with the fictional theme "who killed my dog?"—part of a common pattern in which schools punish students for the content of fictional stories and poems. The idea of an all-powerful state is further reinforced when schools suspend students for sharing criticisms of teachers, coaches, or staff members with friends or for muttering a single curse word that is inaudible to peers. Increasingly, educators have extended their reach beyond the school into students' private lives and even their homes, punishing students and referring them to law enforcement authorities based on digital communications sent from students' own computers outside of school, including adolescent antics and web postings labeled as jokes.

The role of the schools as incubators of civic virtue has deep and varied roots in American history. The United States has long assigned schools a central role in preparing children for the rights and responsibilities of adulthood, including both the ability to be self-supporting and the skills needed for active citizenship. Nearly 90 percent of children in the United States attend public schools: No other government domain offers such an expansive and regular face-to-face interaction between citizens and the state. Schools have a unique opportunity and obligation to demonstrate the importance of fundamental constitutional values as an integral part of preparing students to participate in a robust, pluralist democracy. And the best way of transmitting values is by modeling them—showing how the principles that govern us work in action.

First Amendment scholar Vincent Blasi and philosopher Seana Shiffrin observe that the school years are "the primary time and place" for developing "the moral, civic, and intellectual virtues, virtues essential to the functioning of a democratic society." A host of diverse political theorists—including Amy Gutmann, Steven Macedo, Eamonn Callon, Rob Reich, and James Fleming and Linda C. McClain—have fleshed out the various tasks that make up that mission: transmitting foundational values that prepare students for work and citizenship, including commitments to liberty, equality, and freedom of speech; preparing students to exercise the rights and responsibilities of citizenship by teaching them how to think critically; and encouraging them to subscribe to fundamental ideals, such as respect for diversity.[4] Although the Constitution bars schools from promoting standardized beliefs at the expense of individual liberty, whatever social cohesion we aspire to achieve has its best chance of taking hold in public schools.

Within the array of critical tasks assigned to schools, instilling reverence for freedom of speech in each new generation looms especially large. It is hard to imagine how life, liberty, and the pursuit of happiness are possible if people do not have the freedom to explore and debate ideas. Without the freedom to speak, how does one develop personal autonomy, search for identity, or explore the meaning of life?

But the First Amendment does not just protect individual liberty. As Justice Breyer underscores in his book *Active Liberty,* the Speech Clause promotes "a conversation among ordinary citizens that will encourage their informed participation in the electoral process" by sustaining "the exchange of information and ideas necessary for citizens themselves to shape the 'public opinion which is the final source of government in a democratic state.'" Such a government is open to "'all the citizens, without exception,'" including, I would add, the youngest.[5]

The effort to instill intolerance for intolerance in elementary and secondary schools confronts an inherent tension. In order for schools to "reproduc[e] the regime of toleration," political theorist Michael Walzer has observed, the state must foster behavior that conflicts with the illiberal messages some children receive in their homes and religious and cultural communities. Moreover, young people of every age commonly campaign at school on behalf of less inclusive values often learned at home. This "competition" between viewpoints, Walzer argues, provides valuable lessons: "The children presumably learn something about how toleration works in practice and . . . something also about its inevitable strains."[6]

The very character of liberal democracy in the United States imposes limits on how we carry out civic education. The Constitution reins in educators' powers to inculcate because the state must also respect divergent views held by students, their families, and their communities. Schools can expose students to cultural preferences, but they may no more insist that every student sub-scribe to the same viewpoints than they may demand that all worship the same God or no god at all. And the First Amendment doesn't permit schools to silence or punish students for what they say merely because their opinions differ from the school's preferred values. As a result, whether the principal instructs a student about empathy for others or imposes a penalty that remains on the student's permanent record makes a great deal of difference. Exhortation is generally permissible, but penalties may infringe on constitutional rights.

All three of these themes weave through and unify the book's three parts.

Part I examines the emerging interpretation of the Speech Clause in the first half of the twentieth century, showing that the expressive rights of students were an integral part of that doctrinal development. It analyzes the five Supreme Court decisions from 1943 to 2007 that define and govern student speech rights. Chapter 1 introduces readers to the two Supreme Court cases that stand for a robust vision of student speech rights: *Barnette* and *Tinker*. Chapter 2 examines the three subsequent cases in which succes-sively more conservative Supreme Court benches cut back on the earlier expansive rhetoric and reality of rights by creating a series of exceptions: Bethel School District v. Fraser, which held that schools may censor lewd speech; Hazelwood School District v. Kuhlmeier, which held that schools may control school-sponsored speech; and Frederick v. Morse, which allows censorship of speech advocating the use of illegal drugs. These three cases limited the reach of the earlier doctrines and established a taxonomy of student speech rights in which the level of protection speech received would depend on how it was categorized. The question of which labels to attach, and which legal tests to apply, remains critical.

Parts II and III move from the general doctrine set out in Supreme Court opinions to the experience and administration of school speech on the ground—in the schools and in the lower courts. That record is replete with what lawyers call "easy cases," in which the law is so clear that there is no excuse for the intrusions on students' rights. But I also consider more diffi-cult controversies, disputes in which the school's position is justified or the trade-offs between restraint and expression are more closely balanced. This is the case-by-case approach through which the Speech Clause is under-stood and perfected regardless of the setting.

Part II takes a closer look at how contemporary schools interpret the first two exceptions to the general doctrine. *Fraser* and *Hazelwood* granted school officials increased authority to censor and punish student expression, but not nearly as much discretion to silence students as school authorities subsequently claimed. Chapter 3 returns to *Fraser*, showing how schools have abused their authority by stretching the limited opening the Court gave educators to inculcate civility to reach all manner of impertinence far beyond the limited circumstances the Court considered. Chapter 4 reveals an even more alarming expansion of the "school-sponsored" speech that *Hazelwood* gives educators discretion to censor. School officials assert that speech of all sorts needs to be silenced or punished lest observers erroneously attribute it to the school, sometimes including what students themselves say in classrooms and in their private writings. And they too often censor every variety of school-sponsored speech to ward off controversy or criticism, which violates the Constitution even in school.

The four chapters of Part III delve deeper into *Tinker*. It may seem contrarian to take that apex of student rights out of chronological order. But it is impossible to fully grasp the important role *Tinker* continues to play today without understanding the ways in which subsequent judicial decisions diminished its reach but never extinguished its spark. This last part of the book explicates *Tinker's* original and contemporary meanings and reveals its continued vitality.

Chapter 5 analyzes the boundaries of the first prong of the *Tinker* test: Schools may not limit student expression unless they can establish a reasonable apprehension that the speech will cause material disruption. I make clear that *Tinker* doesn't stop schools from keeping students and teachers safe, but overreaction to potential dangers has supported aggressive, inappropriate, and unlawful restrictions on protected student expression. Schools repeatedly silence even core political expression without pausing to ask whether a risk of disruption exists or on grounds courts later label flimsy at best.

Chapter 6 unravels the meaning of the rarely invoked second prong of the *Tinker* test, which suggests schools can constrain speech that collides with the "rights of others." I show that the rights of others concept has never been found to justify silencing speech unless a court also found a risk of material disruption. Increasingly, schools have sought to silence insults based on group attributes and verbal bullying directed to individuals. They repeatedly succumb to the understandable temptation to protect listeners from hurtful words and ideas, even though the First Amendment protects racist and anti-LGBT sentiments, the symbolism of the Confederate flag, and bullying words. In violation of every principle of free speech, schools have muzzled and exiled students whose unpopular statements led *other* students to disrupt the school environment or to threaten the speaker's safety. I propose a new "infringement matrix" for measuring whether disparaging or hostile speech directed to specific individuals is sufficiently aggressive that it materially disrupts the target's education, arguably allowing the school to intervene.

The final chapters apply the messages of the earlier chapters to two emerging areas of law. Chapter 7 rebuts recent claims that schools should be able to discipline students for what they say outside of school, including in online communications. I examine online bullying, sexting, and other novel problems in light of the balance of authority between parents and educators. Chapter 8 analyzes the relationship between speech rights and religious expression. Misunderstanding the Establishment Clause as well as the Speech Clause, educators often silence personal religious speech that the Constitution protects. The chapter also examines how a federal statute enacted to protect the speech rights of religious students has been used to protect speech by advocates of tolerance and rights for LGBT persons, creating an unanticipated alliance for expressive rights.

As I pursue these various cultural and constitutional skirmishes, I clarify the existing judicial interpretations of the law, identify the many legal questions the courts have left unanswered, and show where schools and judges have strayed from both the letter and spirit of the First Amendment. I repeatedly distinguish the conceptually distinct patterns that schools and courts have often run together. In the process, I propose better ways to preserve both liberty and order.

The profusion of cases and patterns, confusions and holdings, exceptions and limitations too often obscure the clarity of *Tinker*'s wisdom. It remains a lodestar for protecting young people's rights to express both their most profound beliefs and their less exalted thoughts. Even if the speech that school officials silence sometimes seems silly or offensive—full of adolescent humor, poor judgment, and gross insensitivity to others—the constitutional principles that protect such expression are not. The Speech Clause embraces even "'the freedom to speak foolishly and without moderation.'"[7]

None of the doctrinal developments since the 1940s has diminished the grandeur of Justice Jackson's recognition in *Barnette* that "educating the young for citizenship" is essential to preserving a robust democracy. So is respecting the rights of the young. Nowhere, he insisted, is "scrupulous protection of constitutional freedoms" more important than in the nation's schools "if we are not to strangle the free mind at its source and teach youth to discount important principles of government as mere platitudes."[8]

PART I

The Emergence of Free Speech Doctrine

CHAPTER 1

Think as You Will
and Speak as You Think

Those who won our independence . . . believed liberty to be the
secret of happiness and courage to be the secret of liberty.

—Whitney v. California (1927) (Brandeis, J., concurring)

Freedom of speech did not begin to develop into a clear legal
doctrine until the 1920s and 1930s. The Supreme Court had no occasion to
interpret the meaning of the Speech Clause until the twentieth century
because, after the short-lived Sedition Act of 1798, the federal government
did not enact a single law restraining or punishing speech for more than a
century. Like the rest of the Bill of Rights, the First Amendment adopted
in 1791 initially applied only to the federal government, though the Supreme
Court eventually held that it restricted the acts of state and local government as well.

Shortly after it began parsing the Speech Clause in the early 1920s, the
Supreme Court extended speech rights to schoolchildren in the landmark
1943 case of West Virginia State Board of Education v. Barnette. The Court
returned to the problem of free speech in public schools in the 1960s in
Tinker v. Des Moines Independent Community School District, where it
began to carve out a distinct set of principles to govern speech in school even
as it reiterated the robust vision of citizenship and liberty embedded in
Barnette two decades earlier.[1]

The Speech Clause Emerges

The brilliance of the Speech Clause lies in its conciseness. Embedded in
the Constitution's First Amendment, it states, "Congress shall make no
law . . . abridging the freedom of speech." Our understanding of the Speech
Clause has developed through what lawyers call the "common law method,"

a case-by-case approach in which law is clarified in the light of specific questions and facts that arise in concrete controversies. That approach explains why the Supreme Court has never attempted to craft a unified theoretical framework for the Speech Clause, fashioning instead different standards and tests depending on where the speech takes place and in what medium it appears. If this approach at its best offers robust flexibility, it also impedes the development of categorical rules that provide clarity and comfort. These same strengths and drawbacks are evident in the jurisprudence governing student rights in schools.

The Espionage Act of 1917, which criminalized criticism of the government and dissent during World War I and led to 1,900 prosecutions, generated the first round of cases about freedom of speech to reach the federal courts. A handful of those convictions reached the Supreme Court. All the cases involved opposition to U.S. entry into the war or to military conscription.[2] During this period, the Court took a cramped view of speech rights; it never ruled for the individual who challenged the power of the state.

Justices Holmes and Brandeis—early champions of free expression—repeatedly found themselves at odds with the majority of their colleagues on the bench. Cosigning each other's opinions, they launched their string of dissents about speech rights in the 1919 case of Abrams v. United States, the fourth Espionage Act case the Court heard. Abrams and three other left-wing Russian immigrants who were his codefendants had thrown leaflets off a rooftop on the lower east side of Manhattan, urging a general strike in opposition to the U.S. decision to send troops into Russia following the Bolshevik revolution. The government claimed this small-scale pamphleteering undermined the United States in its conflict with Germany.[3]

Justice Holmes found it ludicrous that "a silly leaflet by an unknown man, without more" could threaten American interests. He was convinced that Abrams and his codefendants had been convicted purely for their unpopular beliefs, not because they threatened national security.[4]

Holmes's eloquent dissent introduced the concept now known as the "marketplace of ideas." Like John Stuart Mill, who argued in *On Liberty* that even false arguments may contain partial truths that help society test ideas, Holmes insisted that "the best test of truth is the power of the thought to get itself accepted in the competition of the market." This test of truth carried a profound corollary and an implicit warning: The best response to "bad" speech is more and better speech, and so "we should be eternally vigilant against attempts to check the expression of opinions that we loathe and believe to be fraught with death."[5]

Not long after the Supreme Court began its interpretive foray into the Speech Clause, it held that the clause applied to all levels of government, including states and localities.[6] That decision was a prerequisite for finding that freedom of expression applies in public schools. Since then, the majority of speech cases considered by the Supreme Court have involved challenges to state and local laws or the way in which the representatives of state and local governments—a group that includes all those who run or work for public schools—carry out the law.

Despite this advance, the Court remained largely unresponsive to the speech claims of individuals for another decade, as Brandeis and Holmes continued to press for a loftier view of the Speech Clause. Although in 1927 Brandeis agreed with the majority in upholding a fifteen-year prison sentence imposed on Anita Whitney, a socially prominent Californian who helped found the Communist Labor Party of California, he wrote separately to argue that the Speech Clause is not limited to concerns about robust journalism, national security, or political activity. The Founders, he stressed, were courageous dissenters themselves who "valued liberty as both an end and a means" in which "the final end of the state was to make men free to develop their facilities." Liberty, in the Founders' view, was not limited to the formalities between citizens and government: They "believed liberty to be the secret of happiness and courage to be the secret of liberty."[7]

Joined by Justice Holmes, Brandeis went on to explicate Holmes's "marketplace of ideas" and explain the essential role of free speech in democracies. In what many consider the best summary ever written about why freedom of speech matters, Brandeis recounted that the Founders

> believed that freedom to think as you will and to speak as you think are means indispensable to the discovery and spread of political truth; that without free speech and assembly discussion would be futile; that with them, discussion affords ordinarily adequate protection against the dissemination of noxious doctrine; that the greatest menace to freedom is an inert people. . . . Recognizing the occasional tyrannies of governing majorities, they amended the Constitution so that free speech and assembly should be guaranteed.[8]

Brandeis and Holmes were not destined to remain in the minority. Indeed, the groundwork laid in their separate opinions remains the dominant view of the Speech Clause and its constitutional significance today. That reversal of positions offers a classic example of the powerful role that dissents and concurring opinions can play in crafting a coherent alternative that ultimately triumphs.

Tellingly, just four years after it decided Whitney v. California, the Supreme Court for the first time overturned a statute on the ground that it violated the Speech Clause, initiating a new era more protective of speech rights. That same year, 1931, the Supreme Court enunciated one of the first major principles of Speech Clause doctrine: It rejected prior restraint of speech in all but "exceptional cases."[9] This means that under the rare circumstances when the government may inhibit speech, the "marketplace of ideas" almost always requires that the speech be allowed to flow, even if the Constitution allows the state to punish the speaker after the fact.

The Court was following Sir William Blackstone, the esteemed British legal commentator, who had argued that the crux of liberty of the press lay in "no *previous* restraints upon publications, and not in freedom from censure" afterward where publication violated the law, a view incorporated in the First Amendment. Suppression prior to publication, the Supreme Court has made clear, "is of the essence of censorship."[10] The distinction remains important in the school setting because school officials inhibit student speech both when they engage in prior restraint and when they punish students for what has already been communicated.

Turning Point: *Barnette* and the Menace of "Village Tyrants"

Even as the Supreme Court worked to flesh out the meaning of free speech, it recognized that speech rights extend to schoolchildren. West Virginia State Board of Education v. Barnette, decided in 1943, had a profound impact on the jurisprudence, if not the practical reality, of student rights.[11] *Barnette* pitted reflexive patriotism against the rights of students who refused to mouth sentiments they did not believe.

West Virginia had expelled the Barnette sisters from school for refusing to salute the flag and say the Pledge of Allegiance. As Jehovah's Witnesses, the girls explained, the pledge requirement offended their religious beliefs. The state asserted the expulsion served "national unity" and "security."[12]

The state's assertions had triumphed in a series of earlier Supreme Court decisions, culminating in Minersville School District v. Gobitis, handed down in 1940 as World War II was breaking out in Europe. The Court had consistently rejected claims that young Jehovah's Witnesses had a constitutional right to religious exemptions from reciting the Pledge of Allegiance. The Court's deference to school districts rested less on its view of the legitimacy or wisdom of the pledge requirements than on a reluctance to supervise education, a preference for limited judicial review, and a vain hope the state legislatures and school authorities would reconsider their position on the mandatory pledge and do the right thing by allowing children to remain in school.[13]

Dissenting in *Gobitis,* Justice Stone urged the Court to acknowledge the children's free speech rights. The mandatory pledge law, he stated, "does more than suppress freedom of speech, and more than prohibit the free exercise of religion" in violation of the First Amendment. The state "seeks to coerce these children to express a sentiment which, as they interpret it, they do not entertain." Echoing both Holmes and Brandeis, Stone elaborated: "The guaranties of civil liberty are but guaranties of freedom of the human mind and spirit and of reasonable freedom and opportunity to express them. They presuppose the right of the individual to hold such opinions as he will and to give them reasonably free expression, and his freedom, and that of the state as well, to teach and persuade others by the communication of ideas. The very essence of the liberty which they guaranty is the freedom of the individual from compulsion as to what he shall think and what he shall say, at least where the compulsion is to bear false witness to his religion."[14]

Subsequent events showed the futility of the *Gobitis* majority's hopes that the states would take a less draconian approach to Jehovah's Witness children. Instead, the *Gobitis* decision encouraged a spate of new pledge requirements in states and localities and emboldened strict enforcement of compulsory pledge laws. Throughout the country, thousands of Jehovah's Witnesses were expelled from public schools. The American Bar Association reported that some of the children "get piecemeal education from their parents; some are sent away to a distant sectarian school; others are torn from their homes and committed for the rest of their adolescence to institutions for juvenile delinquents."[15]

Parents who couldn't afford to pay for private schools were at risk of being prosecuted for violating compulsory education laws. Mobs, egged on by the American Legion in some locales, attacked the Witnesses, outraged by their oddity and their refusal to say the pledge or serve in the military. The vigilantes, who sometimes included local law enforcement officers, beat

Witnesses, poured castor oil down their throats, destroyed their cars, burned their homes, and in one instance publically castrated a Witness.[16]

In an unusual somersault, the *Barnette* Court reversed its decision in *Gobitis* after only three years. The Court's turnabout could not be attributed to the different facts in *Barnette* and *Gobitis*. The cases were virtually indistinguishable. The Barnette children, whose faith equated a salute to any image (including the American flag) with idolatry, refused to participate in a school flag salute required under West Virginia law. After rejecting a compromise statement of respect used by Witnesses all over the country, the public school expelled the children for "insubordination." The children could not return to school until they agreed to participate in the pledge ceremony. As in other states around the country, West Virginia's schools expelled "great numbers" of Jehovah's Witnesses, effectively preventing them from receiving a public education.[17]

In part, the about-face reflected changes in the Court's composition. President Roosevelt had elevated Justice Stone, who had been the sole dissenter in *Gobitis*, to Chief Justice. Roosevelt had also appointed two new Justices, including Robert Jackson, who wrote the majority opinion in *Barnette*. The events of the intervening years had convinced three Justices who had joined the *Gobitis* majority that they had made a mistake.[18]

Justice Jackson was especially attuned to the plight of the Witnesses. He had served as President Roosevelt's attorney general until 1941 when Roosevelt appointed him to the Supreme Court. As attorney general, he had authority over the FBI's investigations into attacks on Jehovah's Witnesses. He had publicly criticized *Gobitis* as a "deviation" from the Court's "admirable vigilance" in protecting the "free dissemination of ideas."[19]

Signaling the gravity of the issues, Justice Jackson read the Court's decision aloud from the bench. And he did so on Flag Day, a day on which teachers and patriotic groups focus on the flag's meaning.

Writing for the Court in *Barnette*, Justice Jackson dismantled the *Gobitis* opinion point by point. He began by asking a question *Gobitis* had not even considered: Does the state actually have the power "to impose the flag salute discipline upon school children in general"? The *Barnette* majority concluded it does not. "The sole conflict" before the Court, Justice Jackson stated, "is between authority and the rights of the individual." Building on Justice Stone's *Gobitis* dissent, Justice Jackson distilled the problem as "a compulsion of students to declare a belief." The state "requires the individual to communicate by word and sign his acceptance of the political ideas it thus bespeaks," and this it cannot do.[20]

"[C]oerced" communication, wrote Justice Jackson, raises an old problem "well known to the framers of the Bill of Rights." He reminded readers that "early Christians were frequently persecuted for their refusal to participate in ceremonies before the statue of the emperor or other symbols of imperial authority. The story of William Tell's sentence to shoot an apple off his son's head for refusal to salute a bailiff's hat is an ancient one. The Quakers, William Penn included, suffered punishment rather than uncover their heads in deference to any civil authority."[21]

It might have been tempting to limit the scope of the decision to students whose objections to the pledge were based on their religious views. Instead, the Court took a much more ambitious path. Jackson pegged the decision to freedom of speech and personal autonomy, not to religious freedom. Indeed, the opinion emphasizes that although religion motivated the Barnette children, "many citizens who do not share these religious views hold such a compulsory rite to infringe constitutional liberty of the individual."[22] This treatment initiated a much broader vision of the Speech Clause than seen in previous Supreme Court opinions, which were largely limited to the rights of the press or the protections due to political radicals. The right to decline to avow patriotism rests in the individual's conscience and does not depend on the precepts of any organized religion. It is available to all citizens and all schoolchildren.

Barnette takes as its starting point that "the flag salute is a form of utterance." The flag, like other symbols including the crucifix, is "a short cut from mind to mind." Relying on the 1931 case in which a speech claim had its first victory in the Court, Jackson noted that if displaying a red flag (symbolizing socialism) is protected speech that the government cannot legally prohibit, then demonstrations of loyalty to the American flag are also speech. The Court found that the state had failed to present any justification for requiring children to salute the flag that would excuse "an effort even to muffle expression." It is impossible, the Court concluded, that "a Bill of Rights which guards the individual's right to speak his own mind, left it open to public authorities to compel him to utter what is not in his mind."[23]

Summing up, Justice Jackson anticipated patriotic objections: The decision is a "difficult" one, he conceded, "because the flag involved is our own." Ending with a rhetorical flourish, the opinion offers principles to guide us whenever we consider the meaning of individual liberty, words the

Court itself quoted some forty years later and called "deserving of frequent repetition": "[F]reedom to differ is not limited to things that do not matter much. That would be a mere shadow of freedom. The test of its substance is the right to differ as to things that touch the heart of the existing order." Continuing, the Court exhorts, "If there is any fixed star in our constitutional constellation, it is that no official, high or petty, can prescribe what shall be orthodox in politics, nationalism, religion, or other matters of opinion or force citizens to confess by word or act their faith therein. If there are any circumstances which permit an exception, they do not now occur to us."[24]

Barnette stands as a bedrock of First Amendment rights in general and of students' expressive rights in particular. The Court held for the first time that the Speech Clause limits the state's ability to foster and perpetuate "the ideals, principles and spirit of Americanism" in public schools. It laid the foundation for understanding why students have speech rights and why it is essential to the vitality of our democracy that their rights are recognized and exercised.[25] *Barnette* places beyond dispute the principle that the inhibitions on government power and the guarantees of individual liberty contained in the First Amendment bind every government official without exception. It establishes that the Constitution protects children even when they are in a public school and that speech is among the rights to which they are entitled. And it contains some of the Court's most stirring and frequently quoted language about liberty.

Barnette categorically states that the Bill of Rights "protects the citizen against the State itself and all of its creatures—Boards of Education not excepted." There are simply no functions, no matter how important, that state and local officials "may not perform within the limitations of the Bill of Rights." The Court warns that "small and local authority may feel less sense of responsibility to the Constitution" and be less likely to be held to account for violations than authorities at the national level.[26] It is hard to think of a smaller or more local elected authority than a school board.

While the Court doesn't seek to supplant or second-guess local school boards, the opinion left no doubt that the federal judiciary stands ready to constrain any "village tyrants" who imperil civil liberties. "The very purpose of a Bill of Rights," Justice Jackson explained, "was to withdraw certain subjects from the vicissitudes of political controversy, to place them beyond the reach of majorities and officials and to establish them as legal principles to be applied by the courts." Only the judiciary has the power to protect "non-conformist beliefs"—the beliefs *Gobitis* had referred to less respect-fully as "crochety."[27]

Justice Jackson understood that the Constitution asks a lot of average citi-zens when it demands they tolerate ideas that seem to strike at the heart of social cohesion and order. Responding to a compliment on the *Barnette* opinion, Justice Jackson reflected, "I had anticipated a good deal more criti-cism of it than has taken place. Perhaps the American people have a stronger appreciation of what liberty is and of its value than we sometimes think."[28]

In *Barnette*, the Supreme Court resisted the temptation to treat a question involving the rights of schoolchildren as less significant than other contro-versies. On the contrary, the Court emphasized that if we were forced to create a hierarchy of rights in which some citizens had stronger claims than others (which there is no reason to assume), we should be more concerned about the lessons children learn in school about our nation's commitment to liberty and tolerance than we are about any other group of citizens or set-ting. Justice Jackson insisted that this was no trivial dispute—an exhorta-tion echoed by many contemporary judges who chastise school officials for trampling student rights but ignored by some of their colleagues on the bench.

The future of democracy, Justice Jackson insisted, rests on the protection of First Amendment liberties in public schools. By refusing to distinguish between the rights of schoolchildren and the rights of adults, *Barnette* artic-ulated a coherent vision of the role of the First Amendment in preserving liberty, self-actualization, and democracy for all of us, including the unpop-ular or "crotchety" nonconformist of any age.

Rights on Both Sides of the Schoolhouse Gate

The Supreme Court did not revisit the constitutional rights of schoolchil-dren outside the domain of school integration for a quarter of a century. During that time, the Court made great strides in refining the meaning of the Speech Clause and the modes of analysis that courts must use in assessing government infringements on freedom of expression. Most of the general principles that guide application of the Speech Clause today were clearly established by the time the Court issued its next ruling on student speech rights in 1969.[29] During this same period, the Court had also issued several watershed opinions recognizing the constitutional rights of the young—particularly in the arena of juvenile justice.

In the decades after *Barnette*, the Supreme Court added to its canon of free speech principles beyond the presumption against prior restraint. Most critically, it established that restrictions on speech based on either its content (that is, subject matter) or its viewpoint (the position a speaker takes with respect to a subject) are presumptively unconstitutional. As succinctly stated later, "above all else, the First Amendment means that government has no power to restrict expression because of its message, its ideas, its subject matter, or its content."[30]

The Supreme Court also reinforced protections for speakers by instructing the state to control agitated listeners. When protected speech provokes listeners to a hostile response, the crowd should not be allowed to mute the speaker. This scenario—known as the "heckler's veto"—requires authorities to discipline or remove the heckler rather than silence the speaker.[31]

These developments did not prohibit all content-based regulation. The Court acknowledged that some subject matter is so lacking in value that the Speech Clause does not protect it and it remains subject to reasonable government regulation. The unprotected categories of speech include libel, fighting words, words that incite to imminent violence, "true threats," and obscenity. The often-changing definition of obscenity, which the Court considered and reconsidered thirteen times between 1957 and 1973, reflects the difficulty of defining the speech that is unprotected.[32]

Nor did the expansion of speech rights strike down all regulation of speech that does not fall into one of the very few unprotected categories. Protected speech may be subject to "reasonable time, place and manner" regulations that do not prefer one kind of content to another. For example, a city may bar the use of amplifying equipment on residential streets after midnight.[33]

Doctrinal changes since 1969 have not superseded these essential principles save for one major development, the concept of "strict scrutiny," the key test we use today to analyze violations of the Speech Clause. Strict scrutiny means any effort by the government to regulate protected speech based on its content—preventing it or punishing it after the fact—must overcome the presumption that it has violated the Speech Clause.

Even before strict scrutiny, these various notions—prior restraint, content and viewpoint discrimination, heckler's veto—powerfully reinforced the claims of free speech. This cluster of principles, however, did not provide clear guidance. As Yale law professor Thomas Emerson warned in his 1970 treatise on the Speech Clause; the lack of a coherent doctrine had "left the lower courts, public officials, and private citizens in a state of confusion over the applicable rules."[34]

The lower courts were all over the place. According to Emerson, "the lower federal courts and the State courts usually apply the ad hoc balancing test. Yet as late as December 1967 the Attorney General of the United States . . . said: 'Restrictions on freedom of speech are governed under the doctrine [developed by Justice Holmes] of 'clear and present danger.'"[35] It was this "urgent" need, a "clear and present danger," posed by the children's refusal to say the pledge, that the Court found lacking in *Barnette*.

One additional development in law would fortify the claims of children when the Court returned to the free speech claims of public school students in 1969. In the single decade of the 1960s, the Supreme Court transformed the federal due process rights of minors in the juvenile justice system. Nobody played a more powerful role in this part of the rights revolution than Justice Abraham Fortas, who authored the two seminal decisions in this domain shortly after he joined the Court in 1965 and would speak for the Court when it next considered student speech.

The 1966 ruling in Kent v. United States vacated a decision transferring sixteen-year-old Morris Kent from juvenile court to criminal court and subjecting him to onerous penalties: Instead of the maximum five-year sentence available to the juvenile court for housebreaking and robbery, he received a sentence of thirty to ninety years. Kent had lost the presumed advantages of juvenile court without so much as a hearing.[36]

Kent's taming of the unbridled discretion of the juvenile courts culminated in In re Gault the following year. Fifteen-year-old Gerald Gault was arrested for making a prank phone call that offended the recipient, though it did not harm her. The Court described Gault's remarks as "of the irritatingly offensive, adolescent, sex variety." Neither Gerald nor his parents learned what he was charged with until the hearing, and he didn't have a lawyer. The juvenile court sent him to a reformatory for six years, even though an adult convicted of the same offense could not have been jailed for longer than two months.[37]

The Supreme Court found in favor of young Gault. It assumed the outcome would have been much different if a lawyer had represented him. The lack of due process and the disproportionate penalty offended fundamental notions of fairness as they had in *Kent*. *Gault* held the Constitution required greater procedural protections and revolutionized the juvenile justice system by holding that minors accused of behavior that could lead to confinement have constitutional rights to safeguards including, among other things, representation by a lawyer, notice of charges, and protection from exposure to double jeopardy.

The Court held that the paternalistic juvenile justice system, which rested on the state's presumed good faith, had resulted in "kangaroo courts" and disproportionate penalties for minor offenses. Underneath its dramatic language, Justice Fortas's opinion for the majority sought middle ground that protected children while safeguarding society from delinquents. The Court did not hold that procedural rights of minors are identical to those of adults charged with crimes. Children, for example, still lack the right to a jury trial under federal law. In addition, juvenile courts retain enormous discretion in crafting penalties under the rationale that juvenile justice balances rehabilitation with punishment even if that results in longer periods of institutionalization. Children could be treated differently in juvenile court, the Court held, but they had basic rights that the government could not trample without violating the Constitution.[38]

Kent and *Gault* recognized that minors have constitutional rights and limited the discretion of authorities to disregard those rights. The opinions in both cases focus on the elusive quality of fundamental fairness and seek to rein in judicial discretion. Like *Kent, Gault* envisioned a juvenile justice regime that would provide procedural rights to the country's youngest residents and keep society safe without imposing draconian sentences on minors.

The Turmoil of the 1960s Reaches the Schools: Tinker v. Des Moines

This is where the broad outlines of the doctrine governing freedom of speech and the rights of minors in the justice system stood in 1968 when the Justices confronted the black armbands of John Tinker and his associates. In December 1965, as domestic rancor over the war in Vietnam escalated, four children from the Tinker family—John, age fifteen; Mary Beth, age thirteen; Hope, age eleven; and Paul, age eight—along with Christopher Eckhardt, an eleventh grader, and two other students met at the Eckhardt home and hatched a plan for their antiwar protest. They would show up in school on December 16 wearing black armbands—a well-recognized symbol of protest against the war—and continue the protest until the New Year. The young people intended their actions to support Senator Robert Kennedy's call for a Christmas truce in Vietnam that would extend into the next calendar year. Because it bore on a national debate about the war, the protest was clearly political, a form of speech that many judges and scholars regard as at the heart of the First Amendment's protections.[39]

School officials learned about the plan and, just two days before the protest was to begin, the district adopted a new policy: Any student who wore an armband to school and refused to remove it would be suspended. As many as sixty young people had initially planned to participate. Faced with the risk of suspension, most of them withdrew from the protest. At least two young men who abandoned their plan to wear armbands wore dark suits to school to signal their support for the protesters.[40]

John Tinker, who had been attending meetings of the Society of Friends on his own for four years, did not immediately don his armband. He was hoping to meet with the school board to explain his position. The president of the school board, however, failed to provide a model for civic discourse. He declined to meet with John and other students until the next regularly scheduled board meeting, which would not take place until after the date on which the students intended to end their protest. John explained that he put his armband on only after he read in the newspaper that the school board president had referred to the demonstration as "trivial." "I thought," John testified, "that he could at least listen to us and hear what we were going to try to say. And when it came out that he wouldn't even listen to us . . . I decided to wear it."[41]

A guidance counselor displayed much the same attitude as the school board president, telling fifteen-year-old Christopher Eckhardt to take off his armband because he was "too young and immature to have too many views." The counselor's dismissive attitude toward Christopher's beliefs ignored his participation without his parents two years earlier in a thirty-mile civil rights march from Ames, Iowa to Des Moines.[42]

True to their word, school officials suspended the middle school and high school students who wore armbands to school. Like the Barnette sisters, the protesters couldn't return until they complied with the district's conditions. They had to give up their armbands and, with them, their silent protest. Because the suspensions occurred shortly before the December school vacation and the young people had planned to end their protest on New Year's Day, they were able to return without further incident after the break. Had the protest been open-ended, they would have faced a choice between conscience and obedience that might have deprived them of an education—just as had once happened to Jehovah's Witnesses who refused to voice what they did not believe. The Tinkers and Eckhardts sought an injunction against the schools to restrain the disciplinary actions and to expunge the students' disciplinary records.

At first, the school system justified its ban on black armbands as "reasonable." That standard asserted virtually unlimited sway over children's expression, the kind parents have over their minor children. It tacitly belittled the students' liberty interests in speaking. The federal trial court recognized the armbands were protected speech but accepted the schools' claim that its regulation was reasonable and that reasonableness satisfied the Speech Clause. When the students appealed, the Eighth Circuit considered the case en banc, an unusual form of review reserved for doctrinally significant cases in which all the judges in the appellate circuit hear the appeal together or sit together to review the decision of a panel of three appellate judges. The judges of the Eighth Circuit were equally divided, and the district court opinion stood.[43]

As the litigation proceeded, the school district offered additional defenses. It asserted that it had broad powers to prevent schools from sliding into chaos, "the type of demonstration that has been witnessed throughout the country in the past two or three years," referring to the social, cultural, and political tumult of the 1960s that had largely emanated from universities. Finally, the district argued that it had acted out of concern that it would be unable to control the reactions of other students to the protest, although no official had expressed this concern before the schools banned the armbands.[44]

The Supreme Court heard arguments in Tinker v. Des Moines Independent Community School District in November 1968, the week after a tumultuous presidential election in which both Richard Nixon, the Republican candidate, and George Wallace, the segregationist running as an independent, assailed permissiveness and the decline of "law and order." The country was shaken by antiwar demonstrations on and off campus, the recent assassinations of Robert Kennedy and Martin Luther King Jr., the hippie revolution and cult of drugs, long-haired boys and short-skirted, braless girls. More than a few Americans thought the country close to disintegration as the nation divided into hostile tribes, one celebrating untrammeled rights, the other affirming authority and obedience to rules.

This was the charged environment in which the Supreme Court first considered an affirmative claim by minors that they too had the right to speak their minds. *Barnette* had proclaimed that the Constitution protects even schoolchildren, but it did not address whether students had the same right as adults to—in Justice Brandeis's words—"think as you will and to speak as you think." In more concrete terms, the question faced by the Court in *Tinker* was, did students have a constitutional right to express their own views in school? To answer it, the Court had to venture into the difficult terrain "where students in the exercise of First Amendment rights collide with the rules of school authorities."[45]

Chief Justice Earl Warren assigned the task of crafting the majority opinion in *Tinker* to Justice Fortas, who was well positioned to appreciate the arguments made on behalf of the students. Long before he wrote the Court's opinions in *Kent* and *Gault*, as a young lawyer Fortas had worked on the American Bar Association's *amicus curiae* brief to the Supreme Court in *Barnette* in support of the proposition that age posed no bar to constitutional rights. Conceding that many of the criticisms of *Gobitis* were found in law review notes "written by young men and women studying in law schools," the brief argued that "they are none the less important for being the thoughts of youth. . . . All of them wrote in 1940 and 1941 with the knowledge that they might soon be required to risk their lives in the defense of the nation."[46] We don't know who authored that part of the brief, but Fortas was among those who signed it.

The seven Justices who joined Justice Fortas's *Tinker* opinion ruled for the Tinkers. Students, the Court underscored, "are 'persons' under our Constitution. They are possessed of fundamental rights which the State must respect. . . . [S]tudents may not be regarded as closed-circuit recipients of only that which the State chooses to communicate. They may not be confined to the expression of those sentiments that are officially approved. In the absence of a specific showing of constitutionally valid reasons to regulate their speech, students are entitled to freedom of expression of their views."[47]

The Court roundly rejected the school system's insistence that "schools are no place for demonstrations." *Tinker* made clear that children have constitutional rights in school just as they do in court. It reiterated *Barnette*'s message that courts will not permit village tyrants to exercise unrestrained powers over students whose freedom of expression is at stake. It underscored that "the classroom is peculiarly the 'marketplace of ideas.'" Lest there be any doubt about the scope of the student speech right, the Court extended the freedom to speak beyond the "classroom hours" to the cafeteria and the "playing field," anyplace students find themselves "during authorized hours," because expression of ideas is not only protected by the First Amendment, it is "an important part of the educational process."[48]

At first glance, *Tinker* might seem to violate the logic of the Court's ruling just one year earlier in Ginsberg v. New York, which held that unprotected speech could be defined more broadly for children than for adults. That was the gist of Justice Stewart's *Tinker* concurrence in which he rejected what he took to be "the Court's uncritical assumption that, school discipline aside, the First Amendment rights of children are co-extensive with those of adults." Stewart reminded his colleagues that in *Ginsberg* the Court upheld a statute that barred the sale of nonobscene but racy materials to minors, adopting the theory of "variable obscenity" under which some material is obscene for minors even if it is not obscene for adults. The doctrine allows states to restrict the availability of quasi-erotic materials to underage purchasers unless their parents provide it. *Ginsberg* is widely understood as confirmation that the "First Amendment rights of children are different and, in a sense, less than those of adults."[49]

Yet Stewart was reading *Ginsberg* too broadly. Justice Brennan, a strong supporter of First Amendment rights who wrote the majority opinion in *Ginsberg,* conceded that minors have fewer rights than adults under the Speech Clause. But he defined the scope of restrictions on minors' speech rights quite narrowly—"what sex material they may see or read" without facilitation by their parents. Under *Ginsberg,* parents can override the state's judgment about what is good for their children and decide when their children are ready to handle sexual materials that may be titillating but do not meet the legal definition of obscenity for adults. Moreover, in contrast to unprotected obscene speech, where the Constitution requires only that governmental restraint be rational, the Tinkers' speech was political and fell squarely within the First Amendment's protected sphere.

On the most important aspects of *Tinker,* however, Justice Stewart agreed with the majority: that speakers were young or were students did not diminish their First Amendment protections; and because the First Amendment applied to the black armbands, a standard more demanding than mere reasonableness was required to suppress them.

"Reasonable" rules, the Court rebuked the Des Moines school district, are not sufficient to overcome the constitutional presumption against silencing speech. "[I]n our system," the Court explained, "undifferentiated fear or apprehension of disturbance is not enough to overcome the right to freedom of expression. Any departure from absolute regimentation may cause trouble. Any variation from the majority's opinion may inspire fear. Any word spoken, in class, in the lunchroom, or on the campus, that deviates from the views of another person may start an argument or cause a disturbance." "But," the Court stated starkly, "our Constitution says we must take this risk."[50]

The majority opinion made clear that the Des Moines schools had crossed other bright lines in their treatment of the armbands. Administrators had silenced the protesters based on the content of the message they intended to communicate. Officials hadn't treated all symbolic speech in the same way but chose favored and disfavored viewpoints: The schools ignored buttons about national political campaigns and even the "Iron Cross, traditionally a symbol of Nazism," that some students wore before and after the antiwar protest. School authorities singled out for condemnation a particular student viewpoint: speech opposing the war. Far from being "reasonable," the schools' rule violated two basic premises of the Speech Clause by engaging in both content and viewpoint discrimination, and the after-the-fact rationale that other students might respond badly smacked of allowing hecklers to veto unpopular speech.[51]

Stating that the students' expression was protected was only the first step. The Court had to identify a standard for evaluating the schools' defenses and apply it to each of the justifications the school district offered for banning the armbands.

The Court concluded that student speech on campus required a unique constitutional standard, one that would balance the need for order with the right to free speech. From the outset, the opinion evaluated restrictions on student speech in light of the "special characteristics of the school environment." These included the school's "uniquely important role in training young people to assume the mantle of citizenship" and the requirement that students "must respect their obligations to the State."[52]

In identifying the point of equilibrium between rights and order, Justice Fortas adopted a special standard crafted by the Fifth Circuit when it considered the constitutionality of school suspensions in the deep South imposed on African American students who voiced their support for voting rights. Under this approach, now known as the *Tinker* test, students have the right to free expression, including expressive conduct and demonstrations, so long as their speech does not violate two rules: It must not "materially and substantially interfere with the requirements of appropriate discipline in the operation of the school" and it must not collide "with the rights of other students to be secure and let alone." This formulation built directly on the observation in *Barnette* that the Witnesses' refusal to participate in the flag ceremony "does not interfere with or deny rights of others to do so" and that the dissident children were "peaceable and orderly." Intervening decisions in federal courts had also protected student rights when the students weren't disruptive.[53] In *Tinker*, too, the touchstone was the silent, passive nature of the expression, which did not interfere with anyone.

Justice Black read a vitriolic dissent aloud from the bench. This puzzled observers because Black was a strong advocate for free speech and was one of only two Justices remaining on the Court who had participated in *Barnette;* he and Justice Douglas had both signed Justice Jackson's opinion and had dissented, along with Justice Fortas, from *Ginsberg.*

Black had staunchly defended speech rights for adults even before a reliable majority coalesced around that stance. In a 1941 dissent, he proclaimed, "I view the guaranties of the First Amendment as the foundation upon which our governmental structure rests and without which it could not continue to endure as conceived and planned. Freedom to speak . . . is as important in the life of our government as is the heart to the human body."[54]

But Black was also a firm believer in social order, and the culture wars of the 1960s had only reinforced that belief. In essence, Justice Black characterized the majority opinion as handing the asylum over to the inmates.

Tinker was not the first case in which Justice Black opposed what he saw as Justice Fortas's determination to expand rights. In 1965, Black had dissented from the opinion Fortas authored in Brown v. Louisiana. Five young black men had attempted to integrate a small public library by quietly requesting a book and remaining in the library's public space for about fifteen minutes. They were arrested and convicted of disturbing the peace. The Supreme Court reversed the convictions. In terms that anticipated his *Tinker* opinion, Justice Fortas emphasized that the protesters' "deportment . . . was unexceptionable. They were neither loud, boisterous, obstreperous, indecorous nor impolite." They neither intended nor caused "disorder," and "no other users were disturbed."[55]

Black feared that today's calm would become tomorrow's disorder: "[T]he crowd moved by noble ideals today can become the mob ruled by hate and passion and greed and violence tomorrow." He compared the existing political strife to the French Revolution in which the state succumbed to "rule by successive mobs until chaos set in." He also attacked what he regarded as Fortas's attempt to craft a new constitutional right—a right to protest in a variety of public spaces other than the traditional street corners that are known in First Amendment parlance as "public forums." Public forums are spaces open by tradition to speech and demonstrations, like Hyde Park Corner in London. Justice Black predicted that *Brown* would lead to states being "paralyzed with reference to control of their libraries for library purposes, and I suppose that inevitably the next step will be to paralyze the schools."[56]

He wasn't wrong, at least on one count: The schools followed the libraries to the Court the very next year. In *Tinker* Black was ready to double down on the concerns he had voiced in *Brown*. He disagreed with the Court about the facts of the case and disagreed too with the entire premise of the Court's opinion. Disparaging the importance of expression to young people—especially while they are in school—and elevating order over liberty in schools were both central to Justice Black's dissent. Order remains important to those who continue to cite him approvingly, including Justice Clarence Thomas, who has vowed to overturn *Tinker*.[57]

Justice Black discounted the liberty interests of students with an attitude that children should be seen and not heard: "[A]t their age they need to learn, not teach." The Court's holding, he opined, was an open invitation to disorder because the purpose of any protest in a school was to disrupt or at least "to distract." Justice Black also disagreed with the *Tinker* majority about the nature of disruption in a school. He argued that because the protesters wanted to be noticed, they intended to "divert" other students from the work at hand and cited student jibes and verbal exchanges as evidence that they succeeded.[58]

Justice Black also questioned whose speech was really at stake. *Tinker* was argued and decided on the grounds that the students' actions represented their own beliefs and political commitments. He emphasized that Paul, the youngest protesting Tinker, was only eight years old and in the second grade. (Paul's school did not discipline him, and he was not a party to the lawsuit.) The children, Black thought, were pawns for their parents' beliefs. The families had participated in civil rights demonstrations around the country, and the Tinker parents and Christopher Eckhardt's mother were peace activists. A meeting of the parents and other adults preceded the children's decision to wear armbands to school. Christopher testified that his family discussed the Vietnam War at home, though his parents neither encouraged nor discouraged him from wearing the armband to school.[59]

Reading the *Tinker* facts more sympathetically, it could be argued the parents had successfully inculcated their children with their values, just as society and the law expect them to do. As the families' lawyers explained, the young people's decision to protest "reflected the religious, ethical and moral environment in which they were raised."[60]

Why did the Court's leading First Amendment absolutist depart from his usual solicitude for speech rights? Personal considerations may have played a part. According to his biographer, Justice Black was worried about his grandson, Sterling Black Jr., who, shortly after the oral arguments in *Tinker*, was suspended from high school for his role in creating an underground newspaper that attacked school officials. Black's letter to Sterling's mother reads almost like a draft for his opinion in *Tinker*: "[C]hildren cannot run the school which they attend at government expense." Concerned that Sterling's father, a prominent liberal and president of the New Mexico branch of the ACLU, was standing up for his son and considering suing the school district, Black admonished him not to bring "any lawsuit against the school for doing its duty."[61]

Wandering far beyond the facts the case presented, Justice Black's *Tinker* dissent painted a parade of horribles based primarily on disorder at the nation's universities: "[S]tudents all over the land are already running loose, conducting break-ins, sit-ins, lie-ins, and smash-ins."[62] They have "violently attacked earnest but frightened students who wanted an education."[63] The Court's opinion, he predicted, would expose "all the public schools in the country to the whims and caprices of their loudest-mouthed, but maybe not their brightest, students" to whom the Court is now "surrender[ing] control."[64]

Black's colleagues were by turns shocked and puzzled at his outburst. Reading the page proofs for Justice Black's dissent, Fortas stopped short at Black's statement that "Uncontrolled and uncontrollable liberty is an enemy to domestic peace." In the margin, Fortas scribbled, "Hugo Black!!" and just below that, "Therefore deprive them of liberty."[65]

Chief Justice Warren mused, "Old Hugo really got hung up in his jock strap on this one."[66]

Meanwhile, editorial writers and school administrators around the county applauded Black and excoriated Fortas for opening a "Pandora's box." Citizens who wrote to Fortas called him a communist; one forwarded a hostile editorial with the handwritten comment: "SHAME—SHAME—I PRAY GOD HAS MERCY ON YOUR SOUL—!" A school principal in Richmond, Indiana, undermined the Court's authority by calling "'free speech for high schoolers' a 'lot of hogwash'" and dismissing the ruling as "'unclear and muddled.'"[67]

Tinker, however, was not nearly as radical as its critics feared. Just as *Gault* preserved the juvenile court as a separate entity that denied children the full panoply of procedural protections available to adults charged with crimes, *Tinker* distinguished between the speech rights of students and adults. It erected a unique standard applicable only in the special environment of the public school. Under *Tinker*, schools do not violate the First Amendment when they inhibit student expression if they can show that the speech created a reasonable apprehension of material disruption or collided with the rights of others.

The *Tinker* decision fashioned a middle ground in a second way. To fully grasp it requires a brief venture into the thicket of "strict scrutiny." *Tinker's* standard is widely regarded as "relaxed"—or easier to satisfy than strict scrutiny—a concept the Supreme Court first identified later the same year it decided *Tinker* in a case about the right to travel between states. The Court soon applied strict scrutiny to other fundamental rights, including free speech.[68]

The standard is demanding: The state must demonstrate that it has a compelling interest when it regulates protected speech based on its content; next it must establish that inhibiting speech is necessary to achieve the government's goal; finally, it must show that the regulation is "narrowly tailored" to avoid impinging on more speech than necessary to realize the government's purpose. Strict scrutiny is so hard for the government to satisfy that it is often referred to as "strict in theory, fatal in fact," in Gerald Gunther's famous formulation.[69]

How different is *Tinker's* rule from the outcome under strict scrutiny? A compelling interest can be very hard to establish. But *Tinker* takes for granted that schools can legitimately prevent disorder that materially interferes with education; it simply demands that a school anticipate material disorder and that the expectation of disruption be reasonable and based on more than speculation or the desire to avoid controversy. The insurmountable problem for the Des Moines school district was that officials had no basis for fearing material disruption. Today, the looser material disruption standard continues to preempt strict scrutiny in school speech cases. Lower courts routinely find a threat of material disruption without engaging in the rigorous inquiry mandated when the state claims a compelling interest in silencing speech outside the school setting.

Because the Des Moines school system could not justify a fear of disruption, the *Tinker* Court had no need to rule on whether a school that reasonably feared material disruption would also have to convince a judge that its method of controlling the speech satisfied the First Amendment. No subsequent Supreme Court decision has filled in that gap. The Court's premise that whatever speech rights children have outside of school aren't lost when pupils pass through the schoolhouse gates left the precise extent of those rights and many related questions unresolved.

The effort to strike a balance characterized all the major opinions Justice Fortas authored about the rights of minors. *Tinker* perfectly rounded out his work in juvenile justice, supplementing the procedural safeguards of *Kent* and *Gault* with the substantive rights announced in *Tinker*. That trinity positions him as the architect of a coherent vision of constitutional rights for juveniles based on their status as persons under the Constitution. The opinions coalesce around the premise that age should not be used to deprive minors of the constitutional rights that protect adults.

Still, Fortas recognized the ways in which children differ from adults. He entertained adjustments to the specific demands of the Bill of Rights in the settings of criminal justice and schools. Acknowledging the school as a special environment, he adapted constitutional doctrine to ensure that education did not suffer and that schools performed the important functions entrusted to them. Fortas balanced children's rights with competing societal goals by proposing specially tuned measures of constitutionality for institutions that serve the young.

The Legacy

Barnette and *Tinker* remain significant today for their holdings, their commitment to children's rights, and their hortatory vision of the relationship between free speech and democratic governance. *Barnette* continues to hold school officials to their constitutional duties and to elucidate the importance of respecting the constitutional rights of the young, especially in the public schools where children are supposed to be learning how to participate as citizens in a pluralist democracy. And *Tinker* continues to provide the starting point for analyzing student speech rights, hemming in schools' ability to regulate student speech or to punish students for expressing their opinions.

Tinker reached the Supreme Court at the end of an era. Chief Justice Warren and the newly elected President Nixon had a long history of enmity. Warren knew as soon as Nixon won that he would resign from the Court by the end of the 1968–1969 term. Fortas would also soon be gone from the

Court, forced to resign only months after writing the *Tinker* opinion in the face of lingering questions about his integrity after Senate hearings on his nomination to become Chief Justice.[70] When Fortas resigned, young people lost one of their most forceful judicial champions.

As Chief Justice Warren's retirement neared, his grandson Jeffrey wrote to him from the University of California at Berkeley, an institution in turmoil in the late 1960s and, as his own alma mater, close to Warren's heart. Jeffrey begged his grandfather to stay on at the Court in light of the urgency of events. The Chief Justice responded, "Of course I can understand the feelings of youth. . . . I can appreciate the anxieties . . . the Vietnam War, the draft, the arms race, the exhaustion of our resources on military expenditures to the starvation of our domestic problems of poverty, slums, education, environmental pollution, etc." But, he said, the solution to these problems lay with the next generation. "I really believe, Jeff, that what our country needs now is the youth of America—not to destroy what is but to build—to insist on righting the wrongs of society and during its years of stewardship implement the ideal of Lincoln for 'a government of the people, by the people, and for the people' so that it will not 'perish from this earth.'"[71]

The Court's configuration changed dramatically almost as soon as Chief Justice Warren retired. Had *Tinker* reached the Court a year later, it is unimaginable that the outcome would have been the same. It would not survive long as the sole measure of student speech rights.

CHAPTER 2

A Taxonomy of School
Censorship Takes Form

The Court today . . . erects a taxonomy of school censorship,
concluding that *Tinker* applies to one category and not another.

— Hazelwood School District v. Kuhlmeier (1988)
(Brennan, J., dissenting)

Tinker v. Des Moines hardly eradicated what a 1974 study
called the "insidious and enduring" problem of censorship in schools. That
inquiry into the conditions of student journalism lamented, "even [school]
officials who are well aware of court decisions supporting a free high school
press are prone to either ignore the court-approved standards for guidelines
or apply them in such a way as to censor the paper."[1] When students turned
to the federal courts to enforce their rights, however, judges steadfastly upheld
the standard the Supreme Court had established: Students have the right to
form their own thoughts and to express their views at school unless their
speech would threaten to materially disrupt the educational process. This
comparative golden age for student expression lasted less than two decades
after *Tinker*. A counterattack by the proponents of order gained traction and
made significant inroads into the doctrine governing student speech rights.

Realignment

In the years after *Tinker,* the Supreme Court became more conservative as
its composition changed. Presidents Nixon and Reagan pledged to remake
the federal courts, and they did. Nixon, who had campaigned promising
"law and order," appointed four Justices, President Reagan three. As a series
of new Chief Justices took the reins, the Court moved substantially right-
ward. The Burger, Rehnquist, and Roberts Courts each carved out successive exceptions to *Tinker*'s single standard. Moving forward, the level of

protection student speech received would depend on how the court characterized the speech and its function.[2] This new complex framework would prove hard to understand, harder to administer, and prone to abuse. It would severely undermine the solicitude for the liberty of young people that *Barnette* and *Tinker* mandated.

The cultural divisions of the 1960s continued in the years following the *Tinker* decision. Shifting gears as the war in Vietnam ended, disputes focused on approaches to criminal justice, child rearing, and education, among other things. Evangelical Christians mobilized in the late 1970s, entering the political arena in force; their political engagement has not diminished since. Coordinated at the national level, the religious right aimed many of its activities at local schools, pressing to reinstate school prayer (which the Supreme Court had ruled unconstitutional in 1962) and opposing progressive education, including textbooks and sex education it found morally offensive. It accused educators of undermining parents by "teaching the child 'how to think, not what to think.'"[3]

A resurgent secular right shared this preference for authority over individual freedom. The groups joined forces in opposing what they regarded as liberal judicial activism that had led to a proliferation of newly recognized or expanded rights at the expense of communal norms and obligations. They supported conservative politicians who would seek to transform the federal courts.

This was the setting in which the Supreme Court began its retreat from a robust vision of student speech rights. In Bethel School District v. Fraser in 1986 and Hazelwood School District v. Kuhlmeier in 1988, the Court sliced away at *Tinker*'s guarantees. In 2007, the Roberts Court further eroded the school speech framework in Frederick v. Morse by carving out a special niche for censoring expression that appeared to undermine schools' anti-drug messages. Added to *Barnette* and *Tinker*, these cases complete the legal quintet that governs student expression today.

Even before the Supreme Court revisited student speech, it trimmed back the procedural due process rights for juveniles the Warren Court had set out. At first glance, the 1975 decision in Goss v. Lopez appeared to mirror the approach seen in In re Gault. It held that states cannot deprive students of access to education by suspending them for more than ten days without notice and a hearing, with the specific requirements calibrated to the offense and the potential penalties. The details, however, were less reassuring. Suspensions of less than ten days required "*some* kind of notice and *some* kind of hearing," which could be satisfied in a number of ways, including an informal conversation with the disciplinarian, often "less than a fair-minded school principal would impose upon himself in order to avoid unfair suspensions." Just two years later, the Court held that neither notice nor a hearing was required before a school official delivered a paddling. If the paddling proved excessive, the Court suggested a student could pursue a civil lawsuit. It didn't consider the possibility that a student might not have committed the offense for which discipline was imposed. As a result of that ruling, in 2014 corporal punishment by school disciplinarians remained legal (and was regularly administered) in nineteen states.[4]

Similarly, in 1985, the Court ruled in New Jersey v. T.L.O. that the Fourth Amendment's prohibition of unreasonable searches and seizures applied in school but then announced a unique, more permissive standard to "ensure that the interests of students will be invaded no more than is necessary to achieve the legitimate end of preserving order in the schools." That goal might seem to have a great deal in common with the approach in *Tinker*. The new rule the Court announced in *T.L.O.*, however, allowed officials to search students and their possessions based on "reasonable" suspicion that the student had violated the school code. The standard fell far short of the "level of probable cause" that the subject of the search had broken the law that is generally required for a constitutionally sustainable search. The Court did not decide in *T.L.O.* whether individualized suspicion was required at school, though it subsequently dispensed with that foundational Fourth Amendment principle for school searches as well.[5] The fruits of school searches are not only used to justify discipline imposed at school but can be turned over to law enforcement officials who can use them as a basis for charges and prosecution.

The Burger Court then turned its attention to student speech.

"The Shared Values of a Civilized Social Order": Bethel v. Fraser

The events that led to Bethel School District v. Fraser started with what might easily have been dismissed as a mix of juvenile humor and miscalculation about adult tolerance. Matthew Fraser, a high school senior in the state of Washington, delivered a nominating address for a friend who was running for school office to six hundred of his peers at a school assembly on April 26, 1983. An honors student, Fraser was also a champion debater who had twice earned the "Top Speaker" award for the school in statewide competition. He went on to coach debaters at Stanford University for more than twenty-five years.[6]

When Fraser spoke, students had reason to expect a good show, and they got one. Speaking of his friend Jeff Kuhlman, Fraser made the most of double entendre in his short speech:

> I know a man who is firm—he's firm in his pants, he's firm in his shirt, his character is firm—but most . . . of all, his belief in you, the students of Bethel, is firm.
>
> Jeff Kuhlman is a man who takes his point and pounds it in. If necessary, he'll take an issue and nail it to the wall. He doesn't attack things in spurts—he drives hard, pushing and pushing until finally—he succeeds.
>
> Jeff is a man who will go to the very end—even the climax, for each and every one of you.
>
> So vote for Jeff for A.S.B. vice-president—he'll never come between you and the best our high school can be.[7]

The day after Fraser spoke in the assembly, the school punished him for violating a rule modeled on the *Tinker* standard. The rule provided: "Conduct which materially and substantially interferes with the educational process is prohibited, including the use of obscene, profane language or gestures."[8] Similar language is found in many contemporary school codes.

Before acting, the school had consulted William Coats, the district's attorney, who apparently didn't understand the governing law. He never advised school officials that the First Amendment protected Fraser's speech unless it disrupted the school day. As Coats recalled years later, "I got a phone call from a school official saying, 'We had a student give a lewd speech before a student assembly. Can we discipline him?' I said 'yes.'"[9]

The principal suspended Fraser for three days and removed his name from the list of candidates for commencement speaker in the upcoming student election.

Fraser filed a lawsuit seeking an injunction ordering the school to allow him to speak at graduation. He won in district court and delivered the commencement address. The Ninth Circuit affirmed the decision. As Fraser's litigation progressed, the school never seriously claimed that it had anticipated material disturbance, offering only the notion that there was some hooting and gesturing from that audience and that a few of the younger students were "bewildered and embarrassed," which hardly amounts to an invasion of their rights (the alternative test under *Tinker*).[10]

The lower courts concluded that *Tinker* deprived schools of the authority to discipline *Fraser* because his speech had not created a reasonable anticipation of substantial disruption, as the school district essentially conceded. Mentioning disruption as part of a rule did not insulate the school from having to establish that it was justified in fearing material disorder. The Ninth Circuit refused to give schools the "unbridled discretion" the school district sought to be the arbiter of decency and "to determin[e] what is acceptable and proper speech and behavior in our public schools."[11]

The Supreme Court disagreed. The new majority appeared to welcome the opportunity to limit *Tinker's* scope. In 1986, when the Court reviewed the school's appeal, only Justices Brennan, White, and Marshall remained of the Justices who had been on the Court when it decided *Tinker;* all of them had joined the *Tinker* majority. The rest of the Justices serving in 1986 had been appointed by either Nixon or Reagan. Chief Justice Burger authored the Court's opinion, which six other Justices joined. The decision came out on the last day of the Court's term, a day normally reserved for important and difficult cases. It was the last opinion the Chief Justice wrote before retiring. If *Tinker* amounted to a revolution, *Fraser* launched the restoration of the old order.

Burger began by brushing Fraser off as "this confused little boy." He belittled the value of Fraser's expression as "indecent" and "an elaborate, graphic, sexual metaphor." The Court ignored Fraser's suggestion that his nominating speech be treated as political expression entitled to enhanced protection.[12]

Perhaps most telling, the *Fraser* majority was firmly aligned with the ideal of obedient youth that animated Black's *Tinker* dissent. It agreed with Black's take on what *Tinker* got wrong: The Constitution does not "compel[ ] teachers, parents, and elected school officials to surrender control of the American public school system to public school students."[13]

The *Fraser* majority emphasized that children in public schools simply do not get "the same latitude" as adults in other settings. Echoing Black's anxieties about a world in which children neither knew their place nor respected the "fundamental values of 'habits and manners of civility,'" the Chief Justice underscored that teaching the "shared values of a civilized social order" was part of the "basic educational mission" of schools.[14] True enough, but habits of civility are at most one aspect of a complex range of educational aspirations. *Fraser* offers no hint of the intellectually curious if "disputatious" student preparing for life and citizenship who animated *Tinker*.

The *Fraser* Court set the record straight about what the current bench thought *Tinker* meant (or should mean). Burger chastised the lower court for what he characterized as a misreading of *Tinker* to "preclud[e] any discipline of Fraser for indecent speech and lewd conduct in the school assembly," even if there was no reason to think the lewd speech would cause substantial disruption.[15] The Court failed to acknowledge the critical distinction between teaching civility (through modeling civil language and behavior, lectures, lessons, and exhortation) and bringing the state's coercive power to bear in punishing a manner of speech authorities conclude transgresses "shared values" as school officials define them after the fact.

Crucially, the Court never stated what legal standard school administrators and lower courts should apply to restrictions of lewd speech or penalties aimed at "inappropriate" language. The Chief Justice's reasoning was hardly pellucid. He jumped from what amounts to "civilized adults just know this sort of thing is wrong" to concern about the sensitivities and morals of audience members. The opinion neither applied *Tinker,* the only test that existed for student speech at the time, nor announced an alternative test. Instead, it deferred to the judgment of educators on the front lines in the nation's schools to determine what amounted to lewdness and to rout it out.

Fraser allows schools to prohibit and punish speech based on the speaker's choices about *how* to communicate his ideas. The school did not object to nominating speeches in general but, rather, invited them. Nor did it object to Fraser's viewpoint—that is, his support for his friend, Jeff. The school authorities objected solely to what they regarded as his poor judgment about the *manner* in which he promoted his friend's candidacy.

Here we should distinguish the advice we might give our own children if they asked us to review a draft of a speech (for example, you think that's funny, but it is a terrible idea for a formal assembly) from what a school should be allowed to punish, especially where it is unclear if any legal limits rein in the school's judgments. The Constitution does not limit parents' power to squelch or punish their children's expression.

School officials are sometimes viewed as exerting quasi-parental authority during the school day, in part as an extension of the ancient doctrine of *parens patriae* under which the nation protects the vulnerable. Among other things, this doctrine justifies compulsory education laws and allows society to intervene when parents are neglectful or abusive. But the government is not a parent, even when it claims to stand in the place of parents during the school day. Educators exert authority over children only within temporal and geographical constraints, at school during the school day. Because the First Amendment applies within the school's zone of authority, it limits the state's efforts to inculcate the use of polite language. Yet *Fraser* renders school administrators virtually immune from judicial review so long as they base censorship on the manner in which students present ideas (the choice of words, similes, and metaphors) and not on the ideas themselves. As I will show in the next chapter, the distinction between the manner of speech and the ideas the speaker wishes to convey is often elusive in practice.

The Court viewed the students who attended the assembly as a captive audience, building on a suggestion in *Ginsberg* (the case that created a variable obscenity standard for minors) that because minors lack the "full capacity for individual choice which is the presupposition of First Amendment guarantees," they may be likened to a captive audience when confronted with "uninvited views."[16]

While those who apply the captive audience argument to the young generally mean it metaphorically, it may also be literally true, especially in school. Schools are different from other venues that attract listeners—whether the political rally in a park that is a mainstay of First Amendment analysis or the contemporary online site. The most important distinction is that students are required to attend school for the precise purpose of receiving the important messages the state delivers in the curriculum. Students at Bethel High School were allowed to skip the assembly, but once they showed up in the auditorium, they were not free to leave even if they were offended or became bored and restless. Today, after hip-hop, *South Park,* Sarah Silverman, and other developments in popular culture, Fraser's speech seems very tame. At the time, however, no one could have been misled into thinking that Fraser's metaphor adopted the school's preferred mode of discourse.

But the concept of a vulnerable audience may be hard to contain. As First Amendment scholar Harry Kalven pointed out, the notion of a vulnerable audience may be used to argue that the public at large is "simply not ready" to exercise rights and was in fact used to justify laws making it illegal to teach slaves to read. The argument that young people need protection from certain kinds of speech because they are not mature enough to handle the speech or defend themselves against the offensive nature of the speech has led to many statutes aimed at restricting the speech available to all of us, and the Court has overturned every such effort—including federal statutes aimed at regulating telephone sex, content on cable channels, controversial speech on the Internet, and a California statute restricting the sale of violent video games.[17]

Adults are normally free to walk away from offensive speech by not listening or not reading. In different contexts, the Court has observed that "averting" one's eyes from the offensive message or the "short, though regular, journey from the mail box to the trash can . . . is an acceptable burden . . . so far as the Constitution is concerned."[18]

The majority opinion also overlooked concerns about whether Fraser had adequate warning that his metaphor could get him in serious trouble. Under what is known as the "vagueness doctrine," a regulation on speech will be void if it is so vague that the speaker does not realize that expressive words or conduct will violate the rules (or criminal code) exposing her to penalty.

Fraser had shown his speech to three teachers. Two teachers indicated either that it was "inappropriate" or that it would likely "raise eyebrows." None of them told him it would violate the school code and expose him to discipline. As Justice Stevens observed in his dissent, the fact that Fraser consulted adults suggests he understood that the speech might "provoke an adverse reaction, but the teachers' responses certainly did not give him any better notice of the likelihood of discipline than did the student handbook itself."[19]

Justice Stevens reminded his colleagues that even Congress needs guidance from a manual written by Thomas Jefferson that bars "offensive" speech. "If a written rule is needed to forewarn a United States Senator that the use of offensive speech may give rise to discipline," Justice Stevens wryly commented, "a high school student should be entitled to an equally unambiguous warning."[20] We need only consider twenty-first-century rudeness during President Obama's 2009 State of the Union address—a Supreme Court Justice shaking his head "no" at the President and a Congressman shouting, "You lie"—to see why Jefferson's manual remains indispensable.

Of the three Justices who remained on the Court from the time when it decided *Tinker,* only Justice White joined the *Fraser* majority. Justice Brennan did not sign the Court's opinion, but concurred in the result, because he agreed that schools must be able to teach students "to conduct civil and effective public discourse."[21]

Brennan wrote separately to emphasize that the majority opinion failed to define precisely what manner of speech a school may treat as "inappropriate" without infringing on students' rights. He found no common ground with the Chief Justice's characterization of Fraser's talk. It was "difficult to believe," he wrote after reviewing the transcript, "it is the same speech the Court describes." Brennan insisted that Fraser's speech was not obscene even using the unique standard of obscenity that applied for materials available to minors. His concerns about the lack of boundaries around the incivil speech schools could censor would be borne out by subsequent developments.[22]

Dissenting, Justice Marshall, who agreed with Brennan's portrayal of Fraser's speech, emphasized that the Court had not tethered its opinion to existing legal doctrine. The school had not met its burden to prove disruption under *Tinker,* and the majority did not come close to suggesting that the facts at Bethel High School satisfied the *Tinker* test. Speech, he insisted, is not like "forms of conduct" where schools "must be given wide latitude." "Where speech is involved," he insisted, "we may not unquestioningly accept" the school's "assertion that certain pure speech interfered with education."[23]

Justice Stevens, newer to the Court, also dissented vigorously. He compared the adults' concerns about Fraser's presentation to the hoopla surrounding Clark Gable's "Frankly, my dear, I don't give a damn" in *Gone with the Wind,* which created a stir in 1939. He wisely opined that young people themselves might be the best judges of what speech would offend their peers and urged that "a strong presumption in favor of free expression should apply" in this kind of controversy.[24] Fraser's protracted metaphor had not offended too many of his peers. His candidate, Jeff, won a resounding victory at the polls. Then student voters registered their displeasure with the principal's decision to punish Fraser by using a write-in ballot that garnered sufficient votes to elect him commencement speaker.

To date, the Court has neither defined the range of speech covered by *Fraser* nor set out any principle that would limit officials' discretion to punish speech they deem inappropriate. In 2007, Chief Justice Roberts exacerbated the confusion about what the case stands for, stating cryptically, "[T]he mode of analysis in *Fraser* is not entirely clear."[25]

Speech the School Owns: Hazelwood v. Kuhlmeier

From the start, *Fraser* had limited impact because it was confined to one manner of presentation—lewd speech. It didn't declare that *Tinker* was no longer the guiding legal rule, and it didn't offer an alternative rule. But it opened the door to the idea that *Tinker* did not govern the entire universe of student speech. In doing so, it set the stage for a broader incursion on the vision of *Barnette* and *Tinker.*

The frontal attack on the *Tinker* regime came quickly. In 1988, the Court used Hazelwood School District v. Kuhlmeier as an opportunity to define a much broader new category of student speech and remove it from *Tinker*'s sway. Changes in the Court's composition provided the necessary conditions for that shift. Chief Justice Warren Burger retired immediately after writing the Court's opinion in *Fraser.* President Reagan named Sandra Day O'Connor (the Court's first woman Justice), Anthony Kennedy, and Antonin Scalia to the Court. Most critically, he promoted Associate Justice William F. Rehnquist to Chief Justice.

Reagan had been a fierce public partisan in the culture wars of the 1960s, and he had singled out disrespectful students who didn't follow authority as a special danger. In 1966 he launched his political career and his successful race for governor of California with attacks on the student protesters at the University of California campus at Berkeley, home of the Free Speech Movement. Reagan called the politically active students "spoiled" and promised to "throw them out" of college. One of his first acts as governor was to fire Clark Kerr, the university's chancellor, for failing to clamp down on the students.[26]

The theme continued when Reagan ran for President in 1980. In an address to the National Association of Evangelicals during the 1980 election season, he echoed the Moral Majority's language and endorsed school prayer as a cure-all: "If we could get God and discipline back in our schools, maybe we could get drugs and violence out."[27]

The man Reagan made Chief Justice had a more pervasive conservative philosophy than his predecessor. Appointed to the Court by Nixon in 1972, Rehnquist had regularly favored the government against individuals asserting their rights.

Although Rehnquist had clerked for Justice Jackson in the 1951–1952 term after graduating from Stanford Law School, he did not share Jackson's fervor for individual rights. Indeed, Rehnquist stands out among former Supreme Court clerks in his reluctance to attribute lessons about the law or his role as a judge to "his" Justice.[28] Their views on minors as conscious beings and treating rights as what Jackson condemned as "platitudes" in public schools could not have been more at odds.

Since joining the Court, Rehnquist had authored or signed opinions that set forth what education professor Ronald Hyman construed "as a narrow and limited view of what constitutes an education. The emphasis on basic skills, inculcation, a selective presentation of ideas by the teacher, and the orderly exposure to relevant information—relevant as the teacher determines it—indicate[d] a willingness to support those who wish to control tightly what students will study and learn."[29]

Shortly after Rehnquist became Chief Justice, the Supreme Court accepted the *Hazelwood* case for review, undoubtedly aware that it presented an opportunity to reinterpret the law about freedom of speech in schools. Unlike Fraser's antics, the facts in *Hazelwood* transparently raised significant issues about free speech and censorship. A high school principal had deleted two full pages from the school newspaper to avoid publishing two potentially controversial articles.[30]

Hazelwood East High School in St. Louis offered two courses on journalism in 1982–1983. After completing Journalism I, in which students studied the principles and skills needed to publish a newspaper, students could enroll in Journalism II, which produced Hazelwood East's school newspaper, *Spectrum*. Students received grades and course credit for both courses. Students in Journalism II chose the topics for each issue of *Spectrum*, researched and wrote the articles, and prepared the layout, illustrations, and other details preliminary to publication, all under the supervision of a faculty advisor. The faculty advisor, and ultimately the principal, routinely reviewed the issues before they were printed.

One accident of fate proved significant. Robert Stergos, the journalism teacher, resigned to take a private-sector job just weeks before the last issue of *Spectrum* went to press. A less experienced teacher filled in for the remainder of the term. This development meant that the students lacked a practiced advocate as the controversy unfolded, and the principal lacked an advisor he presumably trusted based on their shared history of getting the paper out.

The last issue of the school year originally included two articles that the principal reflexively deleted when he reviewed the page proofs on the eve of publication. The first story contained "'personal accounts of three Hazelwood East students who became pregnant.'" Each of the pseudonymous students had completed a written questionnaire and had agreed to be discussed and quoted. The second story concerned the effects of divorce on children. It also included quotes, attributed by name, from students at the high school. In order to excise these two articles, the principal deleted two full pages from the paper—including three related articles that were on the same pages.[31] This was not only classic prior restraint, it violated yet another maxim of free speech: On the rare occasions when regulation of protected speech is constitutionally permissible, the government must use a scalpel, not a saw.

The journalism students were shocked when the paper appeared missing two whole pages. No one had informed them of the principal's decision, much less given them a chance to defend their work or revise it to assuage the principal's concerns. The principal's rationales for shelving the story kept changing: Readers might think the school endorsed teenage pregnancy; the article was inappropriate for students in the age group (a claim the school later disavowed); the girls who consented to be interviewed and were quoted pseudonymously were identifiable; and the story violated the privacy of the babies' fathers and the girls' families.[32] His argument that readers would conclude that the school endorsed teen pregnancy is so patently absurd that none of the judicial opinions dignified it with discussion.

The remaining rationales all dissolve in the light of additional facts. Virtually everyone in the school knew who the pregnant girls were and who the fathers were. The three girls quoted in the article all remained in school during their pregnancies. "Terri" was already seven months pregnant, visible to all her peers, and intended to return to school after giving birth. The other two informants had already given birth. "Julie" commented that she "was fairly open" about her condition and that "people seemed to accept it." The fathers were also readily identifiable. All of the pregnancies resulted from long-term public relationships. One of the girls had already married the baby's father, a second was planning a wedding after graduation, and the third explained that she and her boyfriend would wait to marry until they had the financial resources to live independently. This widespread knowledge meant that neither the girls' parents nor the babies' fathers had any continuing expectation of privacy. Indeed, none of them, the pregnant girls, their partners, or their parents, ever asserted their own privacy interests.[33]

Clearly, the students knew that peers got pregnant. They were not so sheltered and immature that the material would have been inappropriate. Moreover, the article served an important public good. It "showed that sexual activity has serious consequences. It . . . demonstrated that not just 'bad girls,' but also typical, 'normal' students become pregnant," as an amicus brief authored by Martha Minow, now the Dean of Harvard Law School, and submitted on behalf of Planned Parenthood and other organizations explained. "All three teens in the interview thought that pregnancy would not happen to them. These facts could jolt young people out of their complacency—out of the illusion . . . that only 'bad girls' get pregnant." The article offered this information in the way most calculated to get students' attention—through the voices of peers, and of peers many of them knew personally.[34]

After consulting with Stergos, the paper's original advisor who had told them to call the ACLU, *Spectrum*'s layout editor, Cathy Kuhlmeier and two other students in the Journalism II class sought vindication of their First Amendment rights in federal court.[35]

The school conceded that the censored articles did not pose a risk of material disruption or collide with the rights of other students. Instead, it urged the court to regard *Spectrum* as a part of the curriculum, not as a forum in which students could express their own ideas. The district court agreed that the newspaper was part of a course, the faculty controlled the content, and *Spectrum* was a school-sponsored publication. The trial judge dismissed the case on the basis that press freedoms did not extend to students in a course for which they received academic credit as opposed to a student-initiated journal. He ruled that authorities could "prevent publication" of articles in official school publications as long as their actions were "reasonable"—an assertion the *Tinker* court had roundly rejected as insufficient where speech rights are at issue.[36]

The Court of Appeals disagreed on every score and reinstated the students' lawsuit. After reviewing *Spectrum*'s policy statements and the district rules, the Eighth Circuit panel reasoned that *Spectrum* was curricular but was also something more: "[I]t was a public forum established to give students an opportunity to express their views while gaining an appreciation of their rights and responsibilities under the First Amendment."[37]

Writing while *Tinker* remained the only standard for evaluating restrictions on student speech as *Fraser* was wending its way to the Supreme Court, the appeals court concluded that the school had failed to justify its censorship. It held that the two articles deleted because of their content had not been reasonably likely "to materially disrupt classwork, give rise to substantial disorder, or invade the rights of others." The censorship violated the Speech Clause.[38]

The risk of disruption had even been subjected to a clinical trial. The students photocopied and distributed the articles that had been deleted from *Spectrum* with no untoward results. The court noted that, as so often happens, "the controversy . . . served only to ensure that the offending articles were secured and widely read."[39]

The school's judgment was tested a second time in February 1985 when the *St. Louis Globe Democrat* published the unabridged pregnancy story. That decision by the editors of a respected paper dispelled any doubts about whether the articles satisfied the standards of professional journalism in terms of fairness, fact-checking, and so forth.[40]

The Supreme Court was not impressed by these results, by the appellate court's deference to *Tinker*, or by the vision of student rights that animated it. The majority ruled against the students.

The majority could have confined itself to the very limited question it acknowledged the case presented: To what extent may educators "exercise editorial control over the contents of a high school newspaper produced as part of the school curriculum?"[41] But the Court was in a judicially expansive mood. The majority seized an opportunity to push back against what it saw as the excesses of Warren-era rights talk.

The majority opinion written by Justice White went far beyond the curricular publication that had brought the dispute before the Court. It announced a new category of speech—"school-sponsored"—and a new highly deferential standard for evaluating censorship of that kind of speech.[42]

Before it got down to business, however, *Hazelwood* began by diminishing *Tinker*. First, it made clear that *Tinker* would no longer provide the *only* rubric for evaluating student speech claims. Then *Hazelwood* proceeded to circumscribe *Tinker*'s reach and its power.

The *Hazelwood* majority picked up where *Fraser* left off, presenting its own reframing of what *Tinker* meant. In the process, the *Hazelwood* majority distorted the principles the case stands for. *Hazelwood* interprets *Tinker* as asking whether the Constitution required schools to "tolerate . . . personal expression that happens to occur on school premises."[43]

This framing is misleading in several ways. The armbands in *Tinker* didn't just "happen" to appear at school. The students had designated the school as a site for the expression of their most deeply held political views. John Tinker testified, "I wanted to wear it as many days in school as I could."[44]

More critically, *Tinker* did not insulate the classroom and the curriculum from free speech principles. On the contrary, it insisted that students must be free to disagree about ideas even in classrooms because the young are not "closed-circuit recipients of only that which the State chooses to communicate."[45] It protected the student who challenges the conventional wisdom that Benedict Arnold was a traitor, though she remains vulnerable to receiving a low grade on an exam if she refuses to give the preferred answer.

Hazelwood also misleadingly implied that *Tinker* did not suffice to secure control of the learning environment. White's focus on educators' responsibility "to assure that participants learn whatever lessons the activity is designed to teach" suggested that *Tinker* had discounted the purpose of schooling. As the paper's publisher, White wrote, the school could eliminate "speech that is . . . ungrammatical, poorly written, inadequately researched, biased or prejudiced, vulgar or profane, or unsuitable for immature audiences."[46] Nothing in *Tinker* suggested otherwise.

Tinker no more scanted schools' authority over the curriculum than it discounted the importance of nonnegotiable conditions in which learning would flourish. Under *Tinker* students have no constitutional right to read Latin poetry aloud when asked to recite in Spanish class or to choose their own math book when completing homework assignments. Core curricular speech—the material the school communicates in required and elective courses for credit like the class that produced the East Hazelwood school newspaper—is the government's own speech. The First Amendment doesn't apply where the state—represented by the school board or school administration—is the speaker.[47]

The *Hazelwood* Court briefly considered and rejected a second argument it attributed to the students: "whether the First Amendment requires a school affirmatively to promote particular student speech." This formulation misconstrued the students' objection to classic censorship as a spoiled demand that the school "lend its name and resources to the dissemination of student expression" at the whim of student authors as opposed to allowing students to speak freely in an organ the school had already established for expressive activities.[48]

These basic precepts alone would have resolved the narrow question in *Hazelwood* once the Court expressly found that the school had not invited students to indulge their ideas in *Spectrum* but had reserved the newspaper for "a supervised learning experience" comparable to the syllabus in other classrooms.

Instead, the majority offered its own approach that would encompass far more speech than the "personal expression" it reserved for *Tinker*. *Hazelwood* defined the new category of school-sponsored speech broadly to include all student expression in activities with an educational goal and faculty supervision. In the Court's words, school-sponsored speech "may fairly be characterized as part of the school curriculum, whether or not [expressive activities] occur in a traditional classroom setting, so long as they are supervised by faculty members and designed to impart particular knowledge or skills."[49] School sponsorship spread its tentacles as far as it could, bringing many arenas for expression under a restored regime of deference to authority.

Hazelwood imposed one limitation on a finding of school sponsorship that might have proven significant: The speech must appear to bear the school's imprimatur. By emphasizing *perceptions,* however, the Court gave a great deal of power to uninformed observers: "students, parents, and members of the public [who] might reasonably perceive [the expression] to bear the imprimatur of the school."[50] Moreover, the Court did not ask officials to minimize the risk of mistaken impressions, for instance, by posting disclaimers in bold type that the views were the students' own. Nor did *Hazelwood* require that the reasonable observers who attribute student speech to the school be well informed or that courts assume they knew the facts and the context for the speech. On the contrary, as the doctrine developed, *Hazelwood* allowed school officials to silence speech on the chance that observers might mistakenly attribute the expression to the school, without imposing responsibilities on outside critics to seek out the facts or on the officials themselves to minimize the risk of misunderstanding.

The majority then awarded school authorities almost unlimited discretion to censor school-sponsored student expression, "so long as their actions are reasonably related to legitimate pedagogical concerns." Elsewhere the opinion stated, "school officials were entitled to regulate the contents of *Spectrum* in any reasonable manner."[51] "Reasonableness" is the most deferential judicial review available.

In fact, Justice White had originally wanted to go even further in expanding school officials' authority. A draft opinion he circulated among the Justices would have permitted censorship unless it was "wholly arbitrary—for example, when school officials give no reason for refusing to disseminate" protected student speech. The proposal to grant schools virtually unreviewable power to censor was such a radical departure from existing law that Justice Blackmun's clerk (knowing that Blackmun planned to dissent) informed him the draft "goes even further than I feared."[52]

But to forge his majority, White had to accept the revisions a wavering Justice Stevens sought: The judiciary will not intervene when a school censors school-sponsored speech unless the censorship "has no valid educational purpose." White merely flipped Stevens's phrasing from negative to positive—censorship must be "reasonably related to legitimate pedagogical concerns." The effect was the same: The standard insulated all censorship premised on broadly defined curricular concerns from judicial scrutiny.[53]

The Court has never explained precisely what boundaries the phrase "reasonably related to legitimate pedagogical concerns" might set around censorship. But the almost identical phrasing the Supreme Court used in a decision just one year earlier is suggestive. In Turner v. Safley (a case involving prisoners' right to marry), the Court ruled that prison regulations barring inmates from marrying would be upheld so long as they are "reasonably related to legitimate penological objectives." Under *Turner,* prison regulations that burden fundamental rights would not be upheld if they were based on "exaggerated response[s]" to institutional concerns. *Hazelwood* simply substituted one institution and its goals for another in this formula: "pedagogical" for "penological."[54]

It is axiomatic that pedagogy is a school's purpose, but in *Hazelwood* the Court ignored critical distinctions between what is "legitimate" in penal environments or other government sites and in educational institutions. Prisoners sacrifice some of their rights when they commit the acts that lead to their confinement. In the realm of speech, the government may close a federal warehouse or military base to speakers because it owns the building, which is dedicated to a government function, not open to the public. Government ownership, however, is not the dispositive fact about schools. Rather, the school—unlike a government warehouse, military base, or prison—is primarily a site for learning. If we understand the purpose of education as *Barnette* and *Tinker* described it, then the flow of ideas and the ideal of demonstrating how rights work are as important as anything else that happens at the site.

In contrast to *Tinker, Hazelwood* almost always functions as the equivalent of a "get out of jail free" card for administrators. *Hazelwood* stands in stark contrast to *Tinker's* solicitous protection of student speech, its understanding of what lessons schools should be teaching, and the role schools play in perpetuating active citizens.

Justice Brennan was hardly about to allow this restoration of the authoritarian regime slip by without chastising his brethren. Justice Powell once scribbled, "No one is kinder or more generous than [Justice Brennan] until he takes up his pen in dissent." Powell could have had in mind Brennan's biting dissent in *Hazelwood*, which Justices Marshall and Blackmun joined. Brennan heaped scorn on the majority's acceptance of what he saw as an entirely "illegitimate" goal: the "pedagogical interest in shielding the high school audience from objectionable viewpoints and sensitive topics" based on both content and viewpoint.[55]

He pointedly tackled the new doctrine that diminished student rights. The journalism students at Hazelwood East, Brennan fumed, expected a "civics lesson" when they signed up to work on *Spectrum*, "but not the one the Court teaches them." It is illegitimate, he charged, to shield students from "unsuitable" or "sensitive" topics. *Tinker's* mandate is "not a general warrant to act as 'thought police' stifling discussion of all but state-approved topics and advocacy of all but the official position."[56]

Brennan wasn't content to remain on the generalized level of doctrine. Point by point, he demolished the Court's application of its new standard to the facts at hand. At every turn, he found that Hazelwood East lacked any legitimate pedagogical rationale for its censorship. Using the heightened scrutiny First Amendment jurisprudence demands, Brennan rigorously took apart the principal's shifting rationales.

Brennan pounced on the fact that the principal had not objected to a different article about teenage sexuality focusing on a legislative proposal to require notice to parents when teenagers sought contraceptives. Brennan accused the principal of preferring parental consent laws to a discussion of pregnancy that "might have been read (as the majority apparently does) to advocate 'irresponsible sex.'" Such distinctions normally violate the Speech Clause. The facts in *Hazelwood*, Brennan argued, "aptly illustrate how readily school officials (and courts) can camouflage viewpoint discrimination as the 'mere' protection of students from sensitive topics."[57]

The profound impact *Hazelwood* would have on students' freedom of expression was immediately apparent. A class of third graders from a New York City suburb (presumably with some adult assistance) wrote Justice Blackmun, one of the dissenters: "We have very strong feelings about this ruling. We think you have violated the First Amendment. You have taken away freedom of the press from school newspapers. . . . [S]tudents should be allowed to freely write about controversial issues. If students can't write about things that bother them, we feel nothing will be done about them."[58]

The proliferation of categories of student speech that receive varying levels of constitutional protection would prove very cumbersome for school officials and lower court judges to understand and use. After *Hazelwood*, school officials had to first figure out what kind of speech it was before they could evaluate how much discretion they had to limit it. Was it personal student speech governed by *Tinker*, "inappropriate" speech governed by *Fraser*, or school-sponsored speech governed by *Hazelwood*? This complex approach requires officials to understand the nuances of legal definitions when they need to make on-the-spot disciplinary decisions, so that even the highly motivated and well-intentioned administrator makes mistakes. The growing number of exceptions to *Tinker* undermines its instructions to judges to approach justifications for curtailing school speech with a healthy dose of skepticism.

These developments substantiated Brennan's fears about what would happen when students' expressive rights became contingent on the school's characterization of their speech as "personal expression" or as expression observers might reasonably perceive as bearing "the imprimatur of the school." *Hazelwood* upended the respect for the rights of minors that had been in place since *Barnette* nearly half a century earlier. "Today," Justice Brennan presciently lamented, the Court "erects a taxonomy of school censorship."[59]

"What about the Bill of Rights?" Frederick v. Morse

At first glance, Frederick v. Morse arose from facts as inconsequential as those in *Fraser*. When the Olympic torch passed through Anchorage, Alaska, in 2002, a high school principal released the students early so they could watch from the sidewalks across from the school. A group of students, including Joseph Frederick, unfurled a banner that proclaimed, "Bong Hits 4 Jesus." Principal Deborah Morse grabbed the banner and "crumpled it up" because she thought the words "bong hits" referred to marijuana. The students maintained that their slogan was nonsense and that they made it up hoping to appear on national television. Frederick did more: He asked the principal, "What about the Bill of Rights and freedom of speech?"

The principal suspended him for ten days, later reduced to eight. Frederick sued the school and the principal herself, alleging that Morse had violated his speech rights by punishing him for his slogan and by retaliating against him for asserting his constitutional rights. Joseph was not the only member of his family to face retaliation. His father Frank worked for the insurance company that wrote the policy covering the school district for liability in lawsuits, and the company leaned on Frank to tell his son to abandon his claims. When Frank told his boss the matter was out of his control because Joe was eighteen, the company first demoted and then fired him. Douglas Mertz, the solo practitioner who had taken Joe's case, also successfully represented Frank in a wrongful termination case; a jury awarded Frank damages.[60]

Legal wrangling in the lower courts over Joe's free speech claim reflected the widespread confusion over the legal rules governing student expression. The trial judge applied one standard and the appellate court another, and the test each applied signaled differing outcomes. The trial court ruled for the school after applying *Fraser* as principal Morse urged, reasoning that *Fraser* reached every form of "inappropriate" speech, not just lewd speech, and is broad enough to restrain every form of speech that undermines the school's mission.[61]

Reversing, the Court of Appeals for the Ninth Circuit held that the trial judge had erred by invoking *Fraser,* which only extends to "sexual innuendo." The court reminded the litigants that *Tinker* continued to provide the only legal framework for students' personal expression and that it protected students who criticize the war against drugs no less than those who challenged the war in Vietnam. The school district had not presented evidence that *Tinker* would allow it to silence Frederick's sentiments. The appellate court rejected the school's broad assertion that it could, in the court's words, "punish and censor non-disruptive" speech, even off-campus speech, "because the speech promotes a social message contrary to the one favored by the school." "Under controlling, long-existing precedent," the court scolded, the answer to the district's assertion of power is plainly "no." Expressing its irritation with Principal Morse, the court emphasized that her actions did not fall in an ambiguous area. "This is no case of ignorance. The law was clear, and Morse was aware of it."[62]

The clarity of the law mattered a great deal because principal Morse had asserted a "qualified immunity" defense. Qualified immunity protects public officials from being named as individual defendants in civil rights litigation unless the law was so clear at the time of the violation that the court can presume they knew their actions were unconstitutional. As I mentioned in the Introduction, the doctrine serves sound social policy by protecting public servants who make "reasonable" mistakes; it allows them to make the snap choices that are often necessary. In *Morse,* the Ninth Circuit ruled that the law was so obvious Morse wasn't entitled to qualified immunity. Frederick could sue her personally for damages.

The Ninth Circuit was right about where the law stood when it decided *Morse.*

In 2007, the Roberts Court modified the student speech regime yet again and reversed the Court of Appeals by a vote of five to four.[63] Energized by its increasingly activist conservative wing, the Supreme Court held that schools do not offend the Constitution when they suppress student speech that a reasonable observer would understand to promote the use of illegal drugs. Chief Justice Roberts wrote for the majority, and four other Justices also wrote opinions, including two of the dissenters. As in *Hazelwood,* a majority of the Justices declined to apply any of the established tests for student speech.

The accompanying commentaries significantly muddied the waters. As one federal judge mildly observed, the "five separate opinions in *Morse* illustrate the complexity and diversity of approaches to this evolving area of law." Constitutional scholar Frederick Schauer regards *Morse* as the epitome of the Court's recent "abdication" of its "guidance function"—the role it plays in "issuing a clear, general, and subsequently usable statement" of its reasoning that "officials and citizens" can rely on "as they plan their actions."[64]

Despite the obfuscation, taken together the *Morse* opinions stand for three general propositions. The first concerns the geographical boundaries of the school's authority. A majority of the Justices agreed that the school could assert authority over an eighteen-year-old who had not signed into school that day for what he said on a public street because his speech occurred at a "school-sponsored, school-supervised" event.[65] This was perhaps the only point on which a majority agreed. Justice Alito, who provided the crucial fifth vote for this proposition, said he would not accept claims to off-campus authority that pressed further than these facts, which included teacher supervision on a sidewalk opposite the campus during the school day.

Second, in creating yet another special exception to the *Tinker* doctrine, the Roberts Court expressly confirmed "that the rule of *Tinker* is not the only basis for restricting student speech."[66] That statement signaled that the special rules governing student speech may continue to evolve in ways that extend educators' discretion to silence and punish. And it raised the possibility that new categories of student speech may continue to proliferate if the existing definitions don't allow the Court to reach the results it wants to achieve in any given case—a topsy-turvy view of the rule of law. The operational premise of a legal system based on precedents is that judges first identify the applicable law and then apply it to the facts in the case they are adjudicating; they are not supposed to choose the outcome they would like to see in the case and then craft a legal rule that will permit the result they desire.

Third, the decision inadvertently admitted that the content of expression—including expression protected by the Speech Clause—may determine how much liberty the speaker has to voice it, at least in school. A majority of the Justices exhibited a visceral dislike for Frederick's speech. It didn't strike them as amusing, seemed to promote drug use, and used the name of Jesus in a disrespectful manner. That distaste may have encouraged what law professor Lee Epstein and her coauthors have referred to as "opportunistic behavior" leading to different results in speech cases that depend on the Justices' inclination to favor or disfavor a speaker's position.[67]

In *Morse*, bias against young people who use recreational drugs may have led five Justices to overcome their disagreement on the basic precepts that apply to student speech and enticed them to disregard existing precedents. None of the Court's prior cases established a framework under which the school could suppress Frederick's banner, the result a majority of the Justices apparently wanted to reach. So they identified a new category of student speech—pro-drug speech—that schools could censor virtually at will.

The Justices who joined Roberts's opinion characterized the category of speech the case addressed slightly differently. In their view, the banner wasn't just objectionable because it undermined preferred social mores. It encouraged a specific, dangerous type of criminal conduct: using illegal substances. Under either framing, *Morse* endorses a very targeted form of viewpoint discrimination: Schools may regulate and punish student speech that appears to promote drug use. Not only are drugs dangerous, the Court explained, but if Frederick's sign meant what they thought it might, it challenged the school's educational efforts to stem the use of illegal substances.

The Chief Justice's stance conflicts with a condition attached by two Justices who helped make up the five-person majority. Justice Alito, joined by Justice Kennedy, stated his understanding that *Morse* does not permit schools to censor speech that does not threaten material disruption unless that speech "advocates" drug use. "Advocacy" is a term that usually signals a debate or political dialogue, which would normally imply the speech should have greater protection, not less. The Court's treatment of drug advocacy builds on the Court's diminution of students' Fourth Amendment rights in earlier cases where schools had a diffuse rather than a specific fear of drug use.[68]

New Jersey v. T.L.O., the case about school searches discussed at the beginning of this chapter, and its progeny all involved efforts to ferret out illegal drugs. Later decisions allowed schools to search for legal substances the school code banned from campus, including over-the-counter medications, as long as the search was "reasonable." The Supreme Court immediately began to cite these inapposite Fourth Amendment cases to justify narrowing the definition of student speech rights, even though the precedents used to assess constitutionality under one amendment are generally not used to analyze another except by analogy. Lower courts followed that lead and continue to rely on cases that slice away at students' Fourth Amendment rights when analyzing students' claims about freedom of expression.[69]

Morse did not change the basic framework governing students' expressive rights, but it exacerbated what was already considerable confusion about which standards apply to different facts. Read narrowly, as I have done here, *Morse* applies only where student advocacy of illegal drugs lacks a clear political component. On those facts, schools may censor and punish student speech. Strictly speaking, and we should speak strictly about limitations on constitutional rights, this is the most convincing reading of the Chief Justice's opinion. And it means, among other things, that the holding has very little practical significance because less than a handful of student speech cases in courts before or since have involved students whose advocacy of drug use was silenced.[70]

Significantly, Justice Alito made clear that he was not prepared to further expand the range of permissible restrictions on student speech: "[T]he opinion does not hold that the special characteristics of the public schools necessarily justify any other speech restrictions." He premised his agreement with the majority on his "understanding" that Chief Justice Roberts's opinion "goes no further than to hold that a public school may restrict speech that a reasonable observer would interpret as advocating illegal drug use."[71]

Alito distinguished advocacy of one particular illegal act—using drugs—from political advocacy. He underscored his own view that Frederick's speech was not political. Frederick had described his banner as "meaningless and funny." He could not turn around and argue convincingly that it was political speech. Relying on those unique facts, Alito warned that he would not countenance incursions on political speech: The Roberts's opinion, he insisted, "provides no support for any restriction of speech that can plausibly be interpreted as commenting on any political or social issue."[72]

If Frederick had intended his banner to communicate a position on legalizing marijuana or reducing criminal penalties for using it, the banner would have been political speech. The potential for political speech about illegal drugs was especially clear in Alaska, where the electorate had already voted on several referenda about legalizing drugs.[73]

The division between encouraging people to use drugs and political advocacy about illegal substances has became even harder to maintain in the years since *Morse,* as nearly half the states (including Alaska by a ballot measure in 2014) have decriminalized the use of marijuana for medical or recreational purposes.[74] A student might well urge peers to try drugs in the context of supporting (or opposing) legalization or reduced penalties or protesting the imposition of mandatory minimum sentences on minors for drug use or trafficking. All of these would be examples of political speech that could not be suppressed under *Morse.* School censorship of such speech would need to be evaluated under *Tinker,* and the school would need to show a reasonable fear that the speech would cause material disruption.

Douglas Mertz emphasizes that Frederick's testimony convinced the district court judge that his speech had a clear political purpose: "to protest the state of free speech in the school system and the community at large." Frederick certainly succeeded in focusing attention on the status of student speech, though not with the result he presumably had in mind. Mertz advises students that if they want to use "humor and parody" to make a political point, "make it so clear that even a Supreme Court justice can't miss it."[75]

Despite Alito's anticipatory efforts to constrain *Morse*'s impact, a broader reading of *Morse* is already on display in some lower courts where judges have read the Court's anxiety about violence and subpar learning environments in the face of drug use to justify restricting civil liberties wherever schools are failing: "From *Morse* and *Fraser* we infer that if there is reason to think that a particular type of student speech will lead to a decline in students' test scores, an upsurge in truancy, or other symptoms of a sick school . . . the school can forbid the speech."[76] And although the majority in *Morse* made clear that the speech-free zone it was creating only applied to advocating the use of illicit substances, still other lower court judges have expanded its sway to other social messages delivered in school, as I shall show in subsequent chapters.

Although Chief Justice Roberts stopped short of ratifying the school's broad assertion that it could prohibit all speech that is "offensive," his opinion undermined *Tinker*'s vitality, initially by articulating what was already clear: *Tinker* is only one of a number of approaches to student speech.

One appellate court has noted the confusion this lack of resolution promotes: The *Morse* plurality states that still other "hitherto unrecognized grounds" for limiting student speech might arise.[77] The prospect of new, as yet unarticulated grounds could provide broad shelter to officials who claim immunity because they weren't sure what limitations the law imposed. But this reasoning violates the premise of the qualified immunity defense. "I thought it was legal" is not the same as "I have a new idea for what the law should permit."

Roberts's opinion emphasized that *Fraser*—whatever it stands for—had allowed content-based restrictions on speech without any evidence of disruption. Like *Hazelwood*, *Morse* built on *Fraser* by relieving schools of the obligation to show a threat of material disruption. The decision did not impose any substitute standard for evaluating whether school censorship of speech about drugs was constitutional.

Instead, *Morse* calls the state's interest "important—indeed, perhaps compelling." The almost casual collapsing of "important" and "compelling" led Schauer to sum up the Court's "ambiguous" position this way: In the school context the state has a "more or less compelling interest in dealing with the problem of juvenile drug use."[78] That murky framing is a far cry from either strict scrutiny or *Tinker*.

Finally, Chief Justice Roberts's rendering of the school speech precedents proposed to narrow the range of circumstances in which students could invoke *Tinker*'s protections. Continuing the pattern of retrospectively limiting *Tinker*'s meaning seen in *Fraser* and *Hazelwood*, the Chief Justice alluded to the "stark" facts in *Tinker* involving "political speech" at the heart of the First Amendment. Moreover, he called the armbands "passive" expression, implying they were less likely to prove disruptive than shouts or chants or perhaps even than Frederick's inaudible but bold banner. Roberts appears to suggest that *Tinker* should reach only speech with expressly political content that is banned because of its viewpoint.[79]

It is no easy matter to define what speech qualifies as "political." In the 1980s, few law professors or judges thought that advocacy of rights for gays and lesbians amounted to more than a search for personal autonomy. They failed to perceive the connection to slowly emerging assertions of political rights, including the right to marry. Transgender rights were not even on any non-transgendered person's radar, as far as the literature suggests. Would political speech, in Roberts's view, be limited to elections and wars, or would it include positions on the rights of homosexuals, same-sex marriage, or the current state of the auto industry as related to unemployment and globalization? Are there other government messages besides "just say no" that are so critically important to student health and safety that the state cannot tolerate contradiction?

Unlike the earlier Supreme Court cases, most of the opinions in *Morse* did not explicitly reveal the Justices' vision of education or its role in democracy. But a close parsing of the Chief Justice's use of terms like *safeguard* and the paternalistic tone of the opinion, Aaron Caplan proposes, suggests that "school staff do not teach or train; they safeguard and provide care." By emphasizing that Frederick's speech violated school policy, the opinion appears to elevate obedience to authority. Caplan, a law professor who worked on Frederick's appellate team, criticizes the *Morse* decision for implying that policy must be followed just "because it is the policy."[80]

Only Justice Thomas used the opportunity *Morse* presented to share his thoughts about education, and they were not encouraging to advocates for student rights. He wrote separately, and only for himself, to say that children have no rights in schools. Channeling Justice Black and adding his own originalist slant, Thomas compiled evidence to show that schools at the time of the American Revolution emphasized order and discipline, not "freewheeling debates or exploration of competing ideas." Since, in his view, constitutional rights are limited to those recognized by the Framers, Thomas forthrightly urged the Court to overturn *Tinker*.[81]

The school district triumphed before the Supreme Court in *Morse*, winning a new legal doctrine: The school would prevail after trial if the principal reasonably construed Frederick's banner to advocate using illegal drugs. The parties returned to the lower courts to determine the critical facts.

Six years had passed since Frederick had displayed his banner. He had long since left the high school without a degree, and at some point during the litigation the district had expunged his disciplinary record. The trial court dismissed Frederick's lawsuit as moot because the judge believed there were no current legal issues between the parties. That might have been the case in a landlord–tenant dispute, but constitutional claims cause a different sort of injury that is not so easily relegated to a file cabinet.

Meanwhile, an outsider successfully challenged the incumbent school board president in Juneau, running his campaign on, among other things, the impact of Frederick's lawsuit. Financially, he said, "I think it's a waste of resources." He also attacked the message the school board's position sent: "I have serious concerns [about] what we're trying to teach our children when we penalize . . . speech issues. Kids are generally aware of drugs and alcohol and should be able to express their views, not have them suppressed," he said. "Whether they are speaking in support of the war in Iraq or speaking out against racism, teenagers should be able to have their voices heard."[82]

After the trial court dismissed the case for the second time, Frederick again appealed to the Ninth Circuit to reinstate his claims. At oral argument in the Ninth Circuit before the same panel of three judges that had originally ruled in Frederick's favor, the board's attorney was "mauled," according to James Foster, a political scientist who was in the courtroom. Before the opinion was issued, the parties agreed to settle their dispute. The school district paid Frederick $45,000, agreed to host a forum on student speech rights featuring a "knowledgeable neutral person" hired at district expense, and abandoned its original position: Students would no longer be "subject to discipline for speech that is controversial or in disagreement with policies or positions" of the school board or schools.[83]

Applying the guidance the five foundational Supreme Court cases offer is not easy for principals, lawyers, or judges. The incoherence created by the proliferation of categories and standards has undermined the simpler regime of a single standard that sent a clear message of respect for the speech rights of students. Adding to the uncertainty, the Supreme Court sets out only the most general principles, leaving lower courts to fill in the details. The next two chapters examine how the court's rulings in *Fraser* and *Hazelwood* and the questions the Justices failed to resolve have played out in the corridors and classrooms of the nation's schools and in the lower courts.

PART II

Pushing Porous Boundaries

CHAPTER 3

Dissing and Discipline

Sans-Gêne Speech

> It is a myth to say that any person has a constitutional right to say
> what he pleases, where he pleases, and when he pleases.
>
> —Tinker v. Des Moines Independent Community School
> Disctrict (1969) (Black, J., dissenting)

Justice Alito, writing in 2000 from his seat on the Third Circuit, concisely summarized the new regime that ended *Tinker*'s dominion over student speech: "Under *Fraser,* a school may categorically prohibit lewd, vulgar, or profane language. Under *Hazelwood,* a school may regulate school-sponsored speech (that is, speech that a reasonable observer would view as the school's own speech) on the basis of any legitimate pedagogical concern. Speech falling outside these categories is subject to *Tinker*'s general rule: it may be regulated only if it would substantially disrupt school operations or interfere with the rights of others."[1] In 2015, he would have needed to update the list of rules with only one later exception to *Tinker:* Under *Morse,* schools may bar and punish all speech that appears to advocate the use of illegal substances unless the speech is political.

Unfortunately, the clarity with which Alito spelled out the distinctions will not always be apparent as we turn from the elevated level of Supreme Court deliberation to the often dramatic cases and controversies that regularly play out across the nation. This chapter, focusing on *Fraser,* and the next, focusing on *Hazelwood,* explore how schools and lower courts have adapted, interpreted, and applied the generalities gleaned from Supreme Court decisions. (I don't devote a separate chapter to the contemporary understanding of Morse v. Frederick because of its recent vintage and limited scope, though I will discuss its aftermath where relevant).

As we consider the reverberations of these decisions, an indisputable conclusion emerges: The incoherence created by the proliferation of categories and standards has undermined the simpler regime of a single standard that sent a clear message of respect for the speech rights of students. Both judges and educators are frequently confused or mistaken about where the speech they dislike falls within the taxonomy of censorship and, as a result, about what the law requires. The choice of legal standards often appears haphazard, and courts often let schools get away with censorship under the guise of deference. Because of this confusion, my discussion of contemporary applications of *Fraser* inevitably necessitates consideration of the alternative categories of student speech governed by *Tinker* and *Hazelwood*.

School systems are prone to misunderstand or disregard the narrow opening *Fraser* created to teach children to "keep a civil tongue in your head," as my great-grandmother used to say. Relying on vague definitions and shifting rationales, educators have punished students for "inappropriate," "off color," and "insubordinate" speech that bears little relationship to Fraser's nominating speech. One school got away with claiming that *Fraser* authorized it to suspend a kindergartener who used words to accompany the thumb and pointer finger he held up as a play "gun" just as children have presumably done since the advent of handguns.[2] Principals move decisively to discipline disrespectful speech directed at teachers, asserting that *Fraser* gives them the authority to punish such ideas no matter what kind of words students use. Officials have even silenced and punished students who used "incivil" expression while reciting published poetry that refers to "hell" or uttered barely audible curses not intended to be heard by anyone. None of these falls within the exception *Fraser* created when it withdrew lewd public speech from constitutional protection in schools.

In this chapter I seek to restore the boundaries that fall around the zone of civility *Fraser* empowers schools to enforce. To encourage restraint and help officials and judges understand what speech *Fraser* allows educators to punish, I will distinguish among four speech situations in which students utter disrespectful words that officials reprimand.

But first, I need to document how potentially serious the penalties for cursing and disrespectful speech at school can be. Second, I need to define the wide array of speech that educators strive to bring within *Fraser*'s parameters to help readers grasp the lines I'll draw later in the chapter.

"Bitch": Go Directly to Jail

It is impossible to fully grasp the importance of keeping discipline for student expression within constitutional limits without understanding what happens to many of the young people who break school rules about "inappropriate" speech. Rude or crude speech is unlikely to garner much sympathy from many adults. Just as I distinguished between the advice Matthew Fraser's parents might have given him if he had shown them the speech he planned to give and the penalties the school imposed, it is critical to separate positive efforts by educators to encourage polite discourse from exercising the state's coercive powers to punish children. The potential repercussions of violating school rules have not changed much since the Barnette sisters risked being sent to a reformatory for refusing to say the Pledge of Allegiance.

When schools are confronted with student speech that authorities believe they are allowed to punish, at least three modes of response are possible. The first is pedagogical, the second involves punishment confined to the campus, and the third excludes the student from the campus for a period ranging from the rest of the day to permanent expulsion.

The first option can be referred to as an instructional approach, or what might be called "constructive intervention." Such intervention involves seizing teaching moments to clarify and model more positive or socially acceptable approaches to expression that help students learn from their mistakes.[3] Constructive intervention doesn't raise any constitutional concerns because it doesn't involve penalties or restrict the student's privileges or activities at school. Nor does it create a permanent disciplinary record that parents might seek to expunge through litigation.

Constructive intervention demonstrates that a robust vision of First Amendment rights for students does not require educators to ignore incivility and impertinence that do not satisfy the demands of *Tinker* or fit within the manner of speech *Fraser* governs. Acknowledging that students may choose their mode of expression within the limits of school speech doctrine would not deprive educators of the opportunity to impress students with the need for proper deportment. No court decision prevents a teacher from sending a student to the principal's office for a lecture or calling in the parents of a recurrently disrespectful child to urge them to address the problem at home. The Constitution is no obstacle to teaching norms of civility, including the words not to be used in polite company that can get people fired from their jobs when directed at bosses, coworkers, or customers. It only prevents the school as an arm of the state from imposing a formal penalty with long-term repercussions on the wayward student for expression that the First Amendment places beyond the school's authority to regulate.

Sometimes, however, what appears to be constructive intervention is a just a preliminary step prior to punishment if the student does not back down. Alternatively, a meeting in the principal's office might not be intended as an intervention at all but is used instead to satisfy the initial due process requirements of notice and an opportunity to respond before the school punishes the speaker.

The second, more visible approach to student speech authorities view as problematic levies on-campus penalties of the sort imposed on Matthew Fraser. Discipline confined to the school takes many forms, all of which can affect a student's college admissions and some of which could affect military enlistment or employment prospects. They include permanent disciplinary records that need to be reported on applications, being barred from speaking at major events and from other honors, or becoming ineligible for elective office or varsity teams.

The third response to student speech violations involves suspension, expulsion, reassignment to schools for disturbed students, and even referral to the juvenile justice system.[4] These reactions may certainly be appropriate when students pose a risk to school safety. *Tinker* clearly allows schools to respond decisively to such dangers. All too often, however, schools respond disproportionately to speech for which adults could not be punished, for which young people could not be punished outside of school, and that poses no risk to safety or order. The consequences can be life changing.

While the Supreme Court has repeatedly been asked when and whether schools can discipline students for their expression without offending the Constitution, it has never considered the nature or proportionality of the penalties schools impose for speech violations. Lower courts too have been reluctant to scrutinize school disciplinary decisions, beyond the occasional passing comment that a more moderate approach might have been wiser but was not constitutionally required.

The Children's Defense Fund first demonstrated in 1975 that suspension and other exclusionary disciplinary measures diminish a student's prospects for academic success and increase the risk of juvenile delinquency and incarceration. Reliance on school exclusion as a disciplinary policy has persisted, even though repeated studies have shown that it starts students "on a trajectory from the classroom to the justice system," known as the "school-to-prison pipeline." A student who has been suspended once is more likely to be suspended again, to be left back, and to fail to graduate on time or at all. These pathways do not prove that only "bad" children are suspended. On the contrary, the studies show that suspension has a devastating impact on children's lives.[5]

And the risks of entering the school-to-prison pipeline are not evenly distributed. The U.S. Department of Education confirmed in 2014 what earlier studies have repeatedly shown: "Nationwide . . . youths of color and youths with disabilities" are far more likely than other students to be expelled or suspended. They are also much more likely to be "referred to law enforcement" by school authorities.[6]

These patterns are closely connected to the exercise of student speech rights. Studies in New York City, Texas, and elsewhere have revealed that the "overwhelming majority of suspensions were for minor [ ] offenses, such as insubordination." In New York, 81 percent of suspensions were based on infractions of the school code like "using profane language or lying." In Texas too, rude speech including the use of profanity contributed to a huge proportion of suspensions while only 3 percent of suspensions were attributable to violent or serious offences. Penalties for disrespectful speech range from suspensions lasting from one to one hundred days or more to expulsion or assignment to alternative schools for seriously disturbed children. The children who were disciplined for "minor misbehavior" violated school codes but did not threaten material disorder or violence and did not break any laws.[7] Cases discussed throughout this book offer multiple examples of students who were excluded from school because of what they said.

Responding to a growing body of research with similar findings, in 2014 the U.S. Department of Education urged schools to reserve exclusionary discipline for the "most serious offenses" and as a "last resort." It recounted, "Unfortunately, a significant number of students are removed from class each year—even for minor infractions of school rules," including rules governing speech. The department advised that law enforcement should never be asked to handle "non-violent conduct, such as . . . use of profanity, dress code violations [including controversial slogans on T-shirts], and disruptive or disrespectful behaviors."[8]

The path from school to detention can become a shortcut when schools refer students to the juvenile justice system for disrespectful speech. These offenses generally do not rise to a level of insubordination for which young people could be treated as defiant or uncontrollable outside of school. The students have not broken any laws—including the special-status offense laws that apply only to minors and for which they could be charged as delinquents. The risks of entering the pipeline to court have risen with the proliferation of armed police officers at schools; these officers frequently advise principals about the law and immediately arrest offenders who might have never come to the attention of law enforcement for minor infractions in the past.[9]

The enormous leeway schools have to punish students for violating internal disciplinary codes regularly blends into the state's power to charge minors as delinquents. The seriousness of the potential penalty raises the constitutional stakes.

Very few state appellate courts have considered whether delinquency adjudication (largely governed by state law) based solely on rude speech in school is constitutional. Some of the states that have ruled on the question have concluded that prosecution for offensive speech in school does not violate the Constitution if the criminal statute adopts the Court's language about the standards that apply to student speech. Courts in some states, for example, have upheld statutes that limit prosecution of offensive student speech to expression that was "disruptive" or "interfere[d]" with the educational process, signaling that *Tinker* would not protect the speech.[10]

In striking contrast, the Supreme Court of Arkansas ruled that a student could not be adjudicated a delinquent just for lobbing a curse word at a teacher. The eighth grader had been suspended and adjudicated a delinquent for referring to her science teacher as a "bitch" during class. The court overturned the state statute that made it a misdemeanor to "abuse or insult a public school teacher while that teacher is performing" his or her job, on the ground that the law violated the First Amendment.[11]

School discipline lies in the discretion of school officials, the court concluded, but adjudication as a delinquent (the equivalent of prosecution and conviction) based on a school infraction pushes far beyond even that considerable discretion. The Arkansas statute's elision of what should be a clear divide between school speech code violations and criminal prosecution resembles the watering down of Fourth Amendment protections against unreasonable search and seizure in the special environment of the schools that permits campus searches that would be unconstitutional outside of school to yield evidence introduced against juveniles in drug cases.[12]

The student who called her teacher a bitch in Arkansas was not alone in finding herself in juvenile court. Sound social policy should discourage schools and juvenile prosecutors from turning a student into a juvenile offender based on a moment of thoughtless or even intended offensive expression that violates the school code though it is constitutionally protected outside of school. Violating a student speech code, by itself, shouldn't turn a student into a dropout or a delinquent.

Manners of Speech

A lack of clarity about the kind of speech that was at issue in *Fraser* contributes to misunderstandings. Matthew Fraser was suspended for violating the school code—the school's equivalent of criminal law—which barred "the use of obscene, profane language or gestures," a common code provision today. The Court described Fraser's speech to his peers as "an elaborate, graphic and explicit sexual metaphor," "indecent," "vulgar," and "lewd."[13] No subsequent opinion has precisely defined the *manner* of speech schools may punish without depriving students of expressive rights.

Lacking a clear definition of the speech *Fraser* covers, courts have resorted to strings of adjectives, including the words and phrases quoted above, as well as broader concepts like "insubordinate" or inconsistent with "civility and sensitivity" to capture the disfavored manner of speech that exposes students to discipline. When he sat on the Third Circuit, Justice Alito explained that *Fraser* applies to "'lewd,' 'vulgar,' 'indecent,' and 'plainly offensive' speech in school." "Offensive speech" could cast a wide net, but Alito immediately narrowed it. *Fraser,* he continued, "permits a school to prohibit words that 'offend for the same reasons that obscenity offends'" but does not remove other kinds of potentially offensive speech from the protections of the Speech Clause.[14]

A Seventh Circuit judge similarly stated that *Fraser* allows schools to punish "student speech that is vulgar, lewd, indecent, or plainly offensive." He didn't stop there: In his view, educators may permissibly enforce "'civility (including manners) and traditional moral, social, and political norms.'" The last element—punishing speech that varies from "political norms"—is impossible to reconcile with the essence of First Amendment liberties. It pushes even beyond the most expansive view that *Fraser* requires deference to the school's interest in "teaching students the boundaries of socially appropriate behavior."[15]

There is no single English word, or even phrase, that captures the diverse kinds of utterances that school officials believe *Fraser* should reach. At the risk of preciousness, an antiquated French colloquialism—*sans-gêne*—may compactly capture the kind of language school officials (and some judges) apparently believe *Fraser* encompasses that goes far beyond the lewd.

Literally translated as "without shame," the term describes a person who has no respect for the feelings of others, who takes extreme liberties, or who acts too familiar (an elusive concept in the United States, where we have no formal mode of address comparable to the French *vous* and call each other by first names without preliminaries). The term also embraces insolence and excess *(désinvolte)*. The person labeled *sans-gêne* is audacious, impolite, cheeky, and generally bad-mannered. The characteristics of *sans-gêne* are summed up in French as *inconvenance,* which includes traits such as effrontery, impertinence, crudeness, grossness, and indecency. In short, the *sans-gêne* person either does not understand what is expected in civil society or disregards it entirely without embarrassment, both states of mind commonly seen in adolescents.

Outside of school, speakers over the age of eighteen (who have crossed the magic line to adulthood) have the legal right to express themselves in the crudest terms. In Cohen v. California, the Supreme Court in 1971 reversed nineteen-year-old Paul Robert Cohen's criminal conviction for wearing a jacket emblazoned with the words "Fuck the Draft" in a municipal courthouse at the height of the movement against the Vietnam War. Cohen may have chosen these "distasteful" and "crude" words, the Court reasoned, intentionally, "as much for their emotive as their cognitive force." He had every right to do so, the opinion explained, because "one man's vulgarity is another's lyric." Free speech in a "diverse" nation, the opinion continued, leads to a "verbal cacophony" that is a measure of our strength as a society. The Court rejected the state's argument that it could require civility in certain public spaces because that stance "seems inherently boundless." The Court held that "the Constitution leaves matters of taste and style [ ] largely to the individual." The state simply may not regulate such choices.[16]

Because students have diminished rights to crude expression, no one seriously maintains that a young protester must be allowed to wear Cohen's jacket in the classroom. Indeed, the *Fraser* opinion approvingly quoted Judge Jon Newman of the Second Circuit, who asserted that "the First Amendment gives a high school student the classroom right to wear Tinker's armband, but not Cohen's jacket."[17] Since the "lyric" Cohen chose has lewd connotations, after *Fraser* there can be no legal ground for asserting that Judge Newman was wrong.

Focusing on the manner of speech means that schools don't infringe constitutional rights when they discipline students who refer to a teacher as a "dick," "skank," or "tramp" (all of which have lewd, sexual overtones) even when not addressing the teacher directly. Cases involving students disciplined for using all of these words have reached federal courts, and the courts ruled against the students in all of them. Judges treat such plainly rude utterances in school as beyond the protection of the First Amendment—comparable to slander or obscenity. Such language is "widely considered to be lewd or vulgar" and "especially when used towards a person in authority, disrespectful."[18] How far the ban on certain words extends to language that may be *sans-gêne* but not lewd is less clear.

Fraser means that schools can enforce certain forms of what the Supreme Court called "socially appropriate" behavior as part of their educational mission so long as the school makes the student's *manner* of expression the basis for punishment and refrains from disciplining the *thought* that underlies the expression. The theoretical boundary between content and the manner in which ideas are expressed isn't well defined. Even lawyers and judges find the distinction difficult to preserve, as the incidents and cases discussed below reveal. Placing rude speech in the right typology would help schools to evaluate how much discretion the First Amendment gives them to punish it and may also help them think about when it makes sense to do so.

Sans-Gêne in Action

Looking beyond simple cases like calling a teacher a skank, I'll examine four distinct factual patterns apparent in cases involving restrictions on *sans-gêne* expression: (1) public speech in school-sponsored settings such as electioneering; (2) language used to express a general attitude of insubordination; (3) private speech addressed to the speaker herself; and (4) an offensive manner of expression used in classroom curricular discussion or in a writing assignment submitted to a teacher. These patterns are distinguished by the kind of language students used, where the student spoke and who heard the expression, and the relationship between the incident and the reasoning that led the Supreme Court to exempt lewd communications in school from First Amendment protection. The first two categories are generally legitimate targets for school discipline if certain conditions are satisfied. The latter two should trigger closer scrutiny for potential violations of student rights because, among other things, they don't generally affect other students or the educational order.

The Speech Clause has never meant that individuals can say whatever they want, wherever they want. Justice Holmes famously remarked that the

First Amendment does not create a right to falsely shout "fire" in a crowded theater. And, as Chapter 1 explained, some expression, like libel and obscenity, is not protected by the Speech Clause. Communication that furthers criminal acts, like fraud, blackmail, or collusion to avoid antitrust laws, cannot hide behind the Speech Clause. Similarly, the state may impose reasonable regulations regarding when and where speech occurs by, for example, limiting decibel levels late at night so long as it does not prefer some messages over others.

Tinker built on temporal and spatial distinctions within the domain of free speech when it announced that it would apply "First Amendment rights . . . in light of the special characteristics of the school environment." But, as *Tinker* recognized, the campus itself is composed of many distinct spaces with different functions, including classrooms, the cafeteria, and the playing field. Consistent with *Tinker*'s announcement that First Amendment protections extend to students in each of these spaces, Justice Brennan insisted that authorities would offend the Constitution if they punished Fraser for delivering the identical speech "to an ad hoc gathering on the playground."[19] But this is exactly what schools increasingly appear to be doing, as they discipline uncivil speech in every space and in every part of the daily schedule.

In part, this tendency reflects the incentives that make administrators highly susceptible to pressure to enforce broader community values and to respond to complaints from the most sensitive members of the community. Administrators want to avoid public controversy that might call their performance into question, and school board members presumably want to be reelected. When they receive complaints about speech that offends, it seems that too often no one stops to analyze whether the speech is lewd or offends in some other way or to sort out whether the discomfort stems from the manner of expression, which *Fraser* permits schools to regulate, or the message, which it doesn't.

"He Chose Mary . . . You Should Too": Giving Offense in School Elections

School-sponsored elections provided the context for *Fraser*. Student speech in this setting is intended to reach the student public and always resembles *Fraser* at least in that respect. Because elections are school sponsored, *Hazelwood* gave educators great discretion to control the manner of expression students use when seeking office, even if the speech isn't lewd. Students who offend the school's definition of propriety during a campaign are subject to discipline and will find judges extremely reluctant to intervene, no matter how much the judge believes that the school might have "overreacted."[20]

Lewdness and an overbroad reading of school sponsorship may overlap as they did in 1997 when Adam Henerey distributed eleven condoms bearing stickers that proclaimed "Adam Henerey, The Safe Candidate" to classmates. The school ended his candidacy and barred him from holding office. But Adam may have been engaged in political speech beyond the campus election, taking a position on safe sex or publicizing the Supreme Court's ruling that adolescents have contraceptive rights. Henerey's lawsuit hit a roadblock. The Eighth Circuit treated the condoms as school-sponsored speech, though it is hard to believe that any reasonable observer thought the condoms bore the school's imprimatur, a prerequisite for finding school sponsorship.[21]

Adam Henerey, like Matthew Fraser, exhibited poor judgment, which does not make either of them stand out among teenagers. Henerey's campaign condoms arguably fit within *Fraser*'s scope as lewd or sexually suggestive and therefore were subject to discipline.

Campaign speeches by other students whose punishments the courts have sustained lacked any sexual overtones. If the speech was not lewd, the unlimited discretion *Fraser* accorded educators to censor it should not apply. But if the imprimatur aspect of *Hazelwood* is satisfied, authorities will normally be able to control student electioneering.

School officials in Mississippi, for example, successfully defended their censorship of a campaign poster for a student named Mary, which featured a Madonna and Child with the slogan "He chose Mary . . . You should too." Rejecting Mary's free speech claim in 2003, the judge lamented that parents who variously complained that the poster established a preference for Christianity or demeaned it had undermined efforts to teach about democracy and tolerance. The judge wondered how students would learn to handle disagreements in such a sanitized environment. "It is likely that the children . . . would have handled these issues with admirable aplomb," he mused, "had not adults voiced their opinions." The judge upheld the school's decision to remove Mary's posters as "not irrational," which was all that the law required because the electoral speech was school sponsored.[22]

Dean Poling, an honors student and the son of a minister, campaigning for student council president in Erwin, Tennessee, targeted an assistant principal named Davidson. Speaking at a mandatory assembly, Poling made fun of Davidson for stuttering even though Davidson had no speech impediment, as Poling admitted while giving his campaign speech. He accused Davidson of trying to "play tricks with your mind." The speech "brought the house down." Informed that his talk was "in bad taste," Poling apologized but was punished anyway by losing his eligibility for the office he sought. In response, Poling's classmates elected him as their class president, just as Matthew Fraser's peers wrote his name in on the ballot after the school told them they could not chose him as commencement speaker. Students regularly elect candidates whom the school has barred from office as a penalty for campaign speech that elicits administrative ire.[23]

When the Sixth Circuit upheld the district court's ruling in favor of the school in 1989, it commented that the incident didn't involve either "heroes" or "villains." Poling was "probably no more anarchistic than many of his teachers [were] at his age." He just forgot that "assistant principals . . . are sentient beings also." The judges deferred to the school district.

Although judges opine on a plethora of subjects from antitrust to trademark to maritime law, when it came to speech rights in public schools and appropriate penalties, the panel members considered themselves "outsiders" who were "at a loss even to understand the full significance" of Poling's remarks. As a matter of law, both *Fraser* and *Hazelwood* instructed them that the determination of what "manner of speech" is "inappropriate" rests with the school board. Like many other judges presiding over student speech cases, the *Poling* panel observed that school officials may have overreacted, but they believed it was not up to the federal courts to determine whether the penalties a school imposed were proportional to the student's offense.[24]

The dissenter in *Poling*, however, perceived the political message in Dean Poling's campaign speech and thought that school officials had indeed crossed a line. The dissent presented Poling as a "populist" candidate, quoting his campaign speech:

> [Y]ou want to break the iron grip of this school, vote for me . . . I can try to bring back student rights that you have missed and maybe get things that you have always wanted. All you have to do is vote for me, Dean Poling.[25]

Poling's speech was neither vulgar like Fraser's nor invasive of the rights of other students, as *Hazelwood* suggested the censored articles might be. The essence of Poling's violation was disrespecting a faculty member, which may be the most serious offence within the genre of *sans-gêne* speech.

Lower courts often fail to consider the possibility that penalties flowed from the student speakers' viewpoints as much as from their choice of how to communicate their ideas. Judges are required to carefully and independently examine the facts when free speech claims are at stake. The responsibility is even more pronounced where school officials, sensitive to public opinion, function as both prosecutor and judge, as they do whenever they punish student speech.

Public speech in the quest for student elective office falls as close as possible to the facts of *Fraser,* though *Fraser* doesn't give schools discretion to punish electioneering speech unless it is lewd. When school elections provide the setting, courts will usually find that *Hazelwood* allows officials to enforce many kinds of civility and to target expression that is merely *sans-gêne:* rude or offensive in some inchoate way that isn't sexual.

"You Ain't Got Nobody Pregnant": Giving Offense by Insubordinate Attitude

It is often a challenge to separate insubordinate conduct from the words that are part of the behavior. Dissenting in *Cohen,* Justice Blackmun regarded the slogan "Fuck the Draft" as a form of acting out, not a protected utterance.[26] Small wonder that students and school officials may be confused about how far student speech rights extend, particularly when the student is behaving disrespectfully to school authorities.

Judges instruct that "under contemporary constitutional concepts," the question of whether "admittedly 'discourteous' and 'rude' remarks" have constitutional protection in school is "a serious one." The question of where the boundary falls is part of the larger puzzle of how to distinguish between what Justice Stevens called the enforceable "permissible rule" impinging on speech and an impermissible rule whose enforcement always violates the Speech Clause.[27] Even permissible rules may be administered in a way that infringes constitutional rights—for example, when enforced only against disfavored viewpoints.

The lines between conduct, verbal insubordination, and protected speech can be difficult to discern, especially in the heat of the moment. Common sense sometimes seems to evaporate, as in the controversy over high school student Crystal Kicklighter's rebellious minutes.

Crystal Kicklighter did not use expletives, addressed her rude comment to a fellow student rather than a teacher, and then refused to speak as instructed; she was suspended for what amounted to *sans-gêne* speech and a hostile attitude. Her story is fairly typical of many school suspensions that follow defiant words and posturing, except that the students involved are disproportionately males of color.[28]

Kicklighter, a white girl in Georgia, became pregnant by her black boyfriend in 1994. As her eleventh-grade class was being called to order during the first week of school in the 1994–1995 school year, a male classmate rudely exhorted Kicklighter to "sit [her] pregnant ass down." Kicklighter retorted, "'You just mad because you ain't got nobody pregnant.'" Instead of chastising both participants for "an inappropriate exchange," the teacher warned Kicklighter not to make "off-color" remarks in her classroom. To my mind, "your pregnant ass" seems more off-color than Kicklighter's retort. Regardless, Kicklighter refused to sit. She challenged her teacher to "check the 'Declaration of Independence' with respect to free speech rights."[29] (The Declaration says nothing about speech rights.)

The principal suspended Kicklighter for five days and demanded that she apologize to the entire class. Kicklighter stayed home for nearly two weeks. Believing that she "had done [her] time," Kicklighter finally returned to class without offering the apology that was a condition of her return, only to be arrested in the classroom. As the police removed her from the building, Kicklighter accused the principal of evicting her "'because I am pregnant by a black boy.'"[30]

Kicklighter remained home for the entire academic year. Like many students who receive disproportionate punishments, having missed almost a full year of school and perhaps sensing that school officials who repeatedly urged her to consider an alternative school would be happy to get rid of her, Kicklighter officially dropped out early in the following academic year.[31]

Kicklighter sued, alleging among other things that the school district had violated her speech rights by conditioning her return to school on compelled expression (an apology) in violation of *Barnette*'s holding that the Constitution bars compelled speech. Kicklighter's attorney made what the court rightly labeled "the sweepingly broad pronouncement" that the "'First Amendment shields the student's mind and thought from intrusion by the school master.'" The judge quipped back: "[A]n educator's usual objective is to penetrate a student's mind."[32]

At base, this simple case centered on Kicklighter's demonstrable lack of respect for her teacher, her classmates, and the very enterprise in which the school was engaged. The principal zeroed in instead on her words and her refusal to mouth a coerced apology. If the school was right to suspend her, as a pedagogical matter the behavior that delayed the beginning of the lesson, not her words or her refusal to speak, should have been designated as the reason for disciplining her. Although the school's legal argument did not rely on Kicklighter's disruptive behavior in class, the school probably could have disciplined her under a generous interpretation of *Tinker* because she prevented the class from starting. The court upheld the suspension, despite its unanticipated effect of cutting Kicklighter's education short.

The court may, however, have treated her claim about compelled speech too cavalierly. The Supreme Court reiterated in 1977 that "the right to speak and the right to refrain from speaking are complementary components of the broader concept of 'individual freedom of mind,'" which supports freedom from compelled expression. Kicklighter's objection to a compelled apology deserves consideration.[33]

From an administrator's perspective, the sincerity of an apology from an obstreperous student may be less important than the formality. In some instances, it matters a great deal whether the recipient of an apology believes it is sincere—for example, a spouse expressing remorse for infidelity or a convicted criminal seeking leniency in sentencing. In others, what may matter most is the very act of apologizing, as when a parent lets a child resume normal activities after saying, "I'm sorry."

While the Constitution does not require it, a sounder social policy would have led the school to help Kicklighter find a face-saving way to continue her education. Why not reduce the penalty to "time served"?

Differences of opinion about how to balance free speech and respect have a long pedigree and are exacerbated when the issue becomes how much unruliness society should tolerate in schools. Back in the days of the early republic, it did not take long for disrespect and freedom of speech to come to loggerheads. In 1798, the town drunk of Newark, New Jersey, was arrested for disrespectful, threatening speech about President John Adams when he referred to "John Adams' ass" as the president exited the town and voiced the desire that officials aim their ceremonial cannons at said body part.[34] The ensuing controversy pitted Adams's dedication to freedom against the need to respect the chief executive. So too, in most instances, disrespectful behavior and student speech become entangled, making analysis of the school's action much more complicated.

Disparate narratives, composed by judges considering a single controversy in 1969 just after *Tinker* was decided, exemplify the obstacles to separating insubordination from protected expression. The judges read contradictory stories into identical facts: one supporting free speech, the other stressing

insubordination. Paul Kitchen ignored his Houston high school's requirement that students obtain permission to hand out written materials on or
adjacent to campus. Kitchen was suspended for selling an alternative community newspaper after the principal found a letter to the editor in it titled
"High Skool is Fucked." The letter made a serious point, though not in
elegant prose: Students are bored, no one is learning, and rules are emphasized to the exclusion of ideas. The district court judge concluded that the
principal intended to suppress the ideas in the newspaper. He blocked the
suspension.[35]

When the school appealed the ruling, the three judges on the appellate
panel read the situation very differently. They emphasized Kitchen's disregard of the school's procedures, including the requirement that school officials review materials students planned to hand out, violation of the rule
against selling materials, and disrespect for the principal. If the school had
disciplined Kitchen for ignoring a "permissible rule" respecting distribution
of written materials near the campus, without examining the content of
those materials, it would have undercut any First Amendment challenge.
The appellate court treated the case as if it had little or nothing to do with
the content of the newspaper Paul Kitchen distributed. In fact, the school
had additional grounds for disciplining Kitchen: He had directed expletives
toward the principal, first on learning that he had been suspended and again
during his suspension. These continued offenses led the school to suspend
Kitchen for the rest of the semester.

Unlike the district court judge, who had heard a series of legal actions
in his courtroom about the short shrift these particular school officials
gave to free speech, the Court of Appeals concluded that Paul's defiance
"outweigh[ed]" the protection of the First Amendment.[36]

When insubordination takes the form of vulgarities addressed directly to
school authorities, schools always have the discretion to punish the student.
Fraser allows officials to punish students who tell the principal to "fuck off,"
as Paul Kitchen apparently did, regardless of how irrational or objectionable
the official action that triggered the *sans-gêne* speech may seem. Students
must find polite ways to protest instead of descending to vulgarity. No
matter how frustrated students are, schools may inculcate civility by insisting
that students find acceptable ways of expressing themselves to get their
point across.

In another instance, Ryan Posthumus, an honors student in Norton
Shores, Michigan, commented to a friend that the dean of students was a

"dick." The dean had confiscated Posthumus's graham crackers as the students stood in line for the senior honors assembly. Posthumus was suspended, as much for "insubordination" as for vulgar and disrespectful language, both of which the court held unprotected by the First Amendment. The court sustained the school's decision to suspend him through commencement for "severe inappropriate" behavior, even though it was unclear whether Posthumus had intended anyone but the friend standing next to him to hear his comment.[37]

It seems likely that some of the student's contemporaries would counter that the word *dick*, like the phrase *it sucks*, has been severed from its original sexual connotation and is in such wide circulation among teenagers as to be nothing more than a term of disapproval or frustration. The use of such terms looks very different depending on the observer's age and immersion in popular culture. At a court hearing about the penalty imposed on a student who called a school employee a "douchebag," her classmates testified that the term means nothing more than "stupid, moron, idiot," or "jerk." Expert witnesses have offered similar analyses of other impolite terms in trials stemming from on-campus student *sans-gêne* transgressions.[38]

As Justice Brennan explained in *Fraser*, the school in that case did not, and could not, reasonably assert a need to protect students from language with which they are likely familiar: "[T]o my mind, [Fraser's] speech was no more 'obscene,' 'lewd,' or 'sexually explicit,' than the bulk of programs currently appearing on prime time television." He wrote in 1986, before the advent of cable television released prime time from the restraints imposed on indecency. In the first ten months of 2009, according to one study, the words *douche* and *douchebag* "surfaced at least 76 times" on network television, signaling "an expansion of the boundaries of taste" as "once unspeakable slurs become passé from overuse." Similarly, network television use of the word *bitch*, which led to one student's adjudication as a delinquent in 2001, tripled between 1998 and 2007, when characters on 685 separate episodes uttered it a total of 1,277 times.[39]

In light of these cultural transformations, citizens and school boards may debate what words amount to such serious transgressions that serious penalties should flow whenever they are used. The Constitution, more than two centuries old, provides no guidelines.

Judges are prone to uphold discipline designed to enforce civility toward authority figures even when the expression is not lewd, when *sans-gêne* speech is not communicated to the target's face, and when expression is contained in broader commentary that deserves First Amendment protection. One court held, for example, that a school could remove a basketball player from the team for circulating a letter to her teammates urging them to stand up to the coach: "It is time to give him back some of the bullshit that he has given us" (apparently applying *Fraser* to what the court termed the "profane" word *bullshit* in a letter sent privately to selected recipients). But, as slang goes, *bullshit* is mild and cannot be viewed as profane in contemporary usage.[40]

Schools go too far when they bar all criticism of faculty members as insubordinate. Student complaints that do not use *sans-gêne* terms are constitutionally protected from penalties and from retribution unless the school can show a reasonable apprehension of material disruption. The Ninth Circuit provided lucid instructions to school officials and district court judges in Pinard v. Clatskanie School District, a case that led to four published federal court opinions. The dispute began when a high school's varsity basketball coach told the players that if they wanted him to quit, all they had to do was tell him. They did. All the members of the team (except for the coach's son) signed a petition seeking his resignation. The petition explained, "[W]e no longer feel comfortable playing for him."[41]

They had good reason for discomfort. During the season, the coach had verbally abused, intimidated, and slapped players. He used language and symbols that would surely have led to discipline if used by students, such as making a triangle shape with his fingers as he called one player "a fucking pussy" in front of the team. Telling players they could not report anything that happened in the locker room to other authorities, the coach threatened to "fuck with [their] minds" and "make [their] lives a living hell." Instead of chastising the coach for his own offensive language and behavior or for the negative role model he presented, the school cut most of the players from the team. Eight of them sought vindication in federal court.[42]

The trial judge granted summary judgment to the school under the misapprehension that *Tinker* only protected speech about matters of concern to the general public. The Court of Appeals took the students' speech claim seriously, reversed the district court, and emphasized that the players' petition and subsequent oral communications about the coach were constitutionally protected. The Ninth Circuit clarified that even in school a constitutional distinction exists between criticisms, no matter how harsh, as long as they are couched in polite terms, and insubordination subject to penalty.[43]

Some judges disagree. They posit that disrespect for school authority itself gives rise to disorder. One court ruled in 2008 that a challenging "tone of voice and argumentative stature . . . certainly disrupts the educational process." As the judge considering the case in which a student called a school official a "dick" opined in 2004, "Insubordinate speech always interrupts the educational process." Failing to punish "such conduct," the judge continued, fosters "an attitude of disrespect toward teachers and staff."[44]

Note that the second judge reframed the student's rude utterance from expression to "conduct" because of the student's wording. This is a critical transformation because it is often said that the noncommunicative aspects of speech merged with conduct are not protected by the Speech Clause. Constitutional scholar Eugene Volokh has argued that this is too simple a dichotomy when words are involved: "[D]ecisions should not turn on the characterization of speech as 'conduct,' at least when the speech is being restricted precisely because of what it communicates, and because of the harms that may flow from that communication."[45]

The harm genuinely insubordinate speech can cause is clear. The problem is how to define and confine the scope of the speech educators can legitimately punish as insubordinate, especially when they point to intangibles such as "tone of voice" or facial expression that students will never be able to rebut. Speech that authorities can construe as insubordinate is as "boundless" as the state's asserted grounds for banning Cohen's "Fuck the Draft" jacket. There is a real risk that too much protected criticism or voicing of differences could be penalized. As the Sixth Circuit summed it up in ruling that a student has a constitutional right to criticize a coach, "[W]hile public schools are not run as democracies, neither are they run as Stalinist regimes."[46]

Another way to think about the intersection of speech and conduct is that words can be part of a course of conduct involving insubordination. Volokh applies the concept of "speech acts" to speech with negative consequences and proposes that conduct associated with speech acts can be regulated "more heavily" than the ideas contained in the expression. Kent Greenawalt has called similar speech "situation-altering utterances," by which he means words that alter obligations, usually in settings involving contracts or threats. He argues that situation-altering speech should be treated solely as conduct. The constructs Greenawalt and Volokh offer, while differing in some details, could help educators (or their attorneys) sort out the distinctions between students who have an insubordinate attitude and those who engage in insubordinate conduct.[47]

When students refuse to follow instructions given by educators, they are engaged in insubordinate conduct that can be separated from the words the student uses. One simple example involves a student who refuses to follow the teacher's instructions to take something to the other side of the room or hand in an exam. The conduct in not undertaking or completing the act is subject to discipline. If accompanied by insubordinate words, the ideas in the words could be treated as integral to the conduct under either construct. But if the student mouths insubordinate ideas while following the teacher's instructions, the ideas he expresses should not be punished unless the words he uses implicate *Fraser* or the speech threatens material disruption under *Tinker.*

Morse wouldn't put down his banner, and Kicklighter wouldn't sit down when told to do so. Despite their accompanying use of protected expression, the conduct itself—refusing to obey a command from an educator—opens them to discipline. Disciplining conduct relies on a less subjective evaluation, based on behavior instead of tone of voice, underlying attitude, or the content of speech. The key is for educators to be clear about what they are allowed to punish and to avoid clamping down on protected speech when they cannot identify proscribable conduct.

A slightly altered set of facts helps clarify the distinction between speech and conduct. Imagine a student who uses a deferential, even obsequious, tone and language—"no ma'am"—when refusing to comply with instructions to sit down, hand over a snack, or take an exam. It is the student's noncompliance that challenges the educational structure, not the words the student uses to convey resistance. If taken up by groups of students, the conduct signaled by Herman Melville's Bartleby the Scrivener's polite mantra "I would prefer not to" when asked to perform any task could bring learning to a halt.

A gray zone remains in which students do what they are told while voicing disagreement in *sans-gêne* terms. This is Posthumus, the student who relinquished his snack to the dean of students and then referred to the official as a dick. What if Posthumus had instead muttered "what a jerk" or "what a dumb rule"?

"Shit": Stranded at School—Offensive Private Speech

Some speech is barely audible, uttered in transitional spaces such as school corridors, and should be considered private because the student never intended it for public consumption. For example, A. Anderson, a good student who uttered "shit" when she learned, after the school bus had left, that her mother would not be not be able to drive her home, clearly was speaking to herself. The only people who heard her barely audible expletive were two adults working in the principal's office as she passed by. Unbending application of rules against "profane or inappropriate language on school property" (known more generally as "zero tolerance," which many schools extend to cursing on school grounds) led to an academic penalty that lowered her grades. The judge thought the suspension a disproportionate response to Anderson's crime but, like many other judges, deferred to the education professionals.

The rules of legal evidence have a way of describing Anderson's comment: When people make "excited utterances" in response to external events, they lack the opportunity for the "deliberative reflection" that facilitates lies or, in this instance, self-censorship.[48]

Even though the Court's general speech jurisprudence doesn't apply in schools, it can provide useful guidance. Here, Justice Stevens's discussion of "the customs of speech" might have helped to defuse the reaction to Anderson's instinctive response to bad news. "There is a critical distinction," Justice Stevens wrote in the context of broadcast indecency, "between the use of an expletive to describe a sexual or excretory function and the use of such a word . . . to express emotion. One rests at the core of indecency; the other stands miles apart." The former "may be illegal under some conditions, . . . the latter merely 'impolite.'" Stevens found a perfect illustration of the "merely impolite" in the ubiquitous "four-letter word uttered on the golf course" after a bad shot.[49]

It doesn't serve any societal goal to punish a student for indecent speech her peers never heard. She knows the vulgar word before she uses it. Anderson did not expose vulnerable students to inappropriate language because they did not hear her; she didn't undermine the educational atmosphere of the school for the same reason. She didn't disrespect the adults who heard her only by inadvertence, and she had no way of knowing they would prove hypersensitive. Nothing supported the school's decision to punish her, except for legal doctrine interpreted to give schools unlimited discretion to squelch impolite words, even if they have no discernible impact.

On the other hand, uniformity matters. When school officials impose harsh penalties on *sans-gêne* expression, they should be careful to treat similar language similarly. Students pay close attention to uneven enforcement of rules. A student at a different school, who signed himself "Disgusted," complained: "'How come a student is suspended for saying "asshole," yet this kid gets [it] printed in a *school* magazine?'"[50] No student at Anderson's school would have been able to point to her expletive if she had escaped discipline.

Courts allow school officials to punish barely audible *sans-gêne* speech just as they are allowed to punish a lewd presentation to a school assembly. There appears to be a general consensus that learning decorum—like learning how to restrain expressions of disrespect for faculty—falls within the parameters of a sound education.

Whether or not this is a constitutionally permissible approach, it would be simpler and better policy for schools to ignore private outbursts unaccompanied by other offenses, leaving decisions about disciplining private language to parents. Introducing the concept of "private though barely audible" *sans-gêne* excited utterances might help school disciplinarians to consider context and intent before imposing penalties.

Unfortunately, school officials and courts are likely to reject the argument that some *sans-gêne* speech is "private" in the sense that the speaker never intended anyone else to hear her words. To determine whether the speaker intended that the *sans-gêne* expression reach the ears of listeners, a court would have to examine motive, a state of mind remarkably resistant to evidentiary proofs. Yet judges are certainly capable of distinguishing speech intended to be heard from barely audible speech that has not caused any of the sorts of harm that justify deference to penalties imposed by school officials.

Fuck: *"Words We Do Not Use in Class, at Home, or in School"*

Fraser speaks to the manner of expression in a public space; Bethel High School specifically cited the embarrassment Fraser's words caused younger students, much as the FCC argues censorship of indecent words protects children. *Hazelwood* too bases the school's authority on the accessibility of the speech to others, subsumed in the imprimatur requirement. But, as I have shown, some speech is not intended for public consumption.

Similarly, some *sans-gêne* speech is not directed *at* a teacher. Like self-directed, virtually inaudible speech, English essays, creative writing exercises, and other assignments may not be intended for public consumption. *Sans-gêne* language may appear in a creative writing assignment by a student who does not know better or, more rarely, may be responsive to the teacher's lesson plan. For example, it may pop up in dialogue designed to show how real people talk or in a lesson about what polite people don't say.

Officials are more likely to punish the teacher than the student who uses *sans-gêne* language in curricular work. So my analysis of student expression in the classroom starts with the pressures that teachers experience and the penalties they may incur when they fail to vanquish *sans-gêne* language. These pressures on teachers surely impede some constitutionally protected if disfavored student expression.

The Supreme Court has never discussed the extent to which the First Amendment protects teachers' speech. Every Circuit that has considered the issue agrees teachers have no constitutional protection from professional discipline when they tolerate students' use of vulgar language in classroom discussion or written assignments, but they disagree about what legal tests apply.[51]

Teachers even lack legal protection if they turn students' vulgarity into a "teaching moment." Schools permissibly punish teachers who allow students to write and perform plays containing realistic dialogue showing how some people talk that includes "an unusual amount of profanity"; permit a student to read aloud a poem she had not reviewed that turned out to describe oral sex; or use an HIV/AIDS curriculum that asks students to share vocabulary about sexual parts and activities, resulting in the voicing of vulgarisms.[52]

Controversial teaching techniques can be used to promote sound educational goals, but pedagogical success does not necessarily create legal rights. Cecilia Lacks had tenure in the Missouri school district where she had taught English for more than twenty years. She was a highly regarded teacher who used a nationally recognized "student-centered" approach that invited students to use their own voices before teaching them how to express themselves in more refined tones. She encouraged students to read their work aloud to each other, in some instances before she had seen it. She also asked the students to perform plays they had written that contained extensive profanity intended to capture how people really talk.[53]

The school district fired Lacks after a single student complained about vulgar words that other students wrote and read aloud. Her dismissal and her unsuccessful battle for reinstatement garnered international attention. Lacks lost her job and her pension, but she received the PEN/Newman's Own Award, given to one person in the United States each year who defended First Amendment rights at personal risk.[54]

The district's rules banning student profanity treated words uttered in the hallway and the classroom identically. As the district interpreted the school code *after* it fired Lacks, verbalizing curse words was forbidden even if a student was reading aloud from a published work—including Chaucer, many of the court opinions quoted in this chapter, and presumably this chapter itself. The school board held Lacks responsible for her students' vulgar expression. To reach that result, the courts accepted the district's claim that *Fraser* or *Hazelwood* applied to teachers too, a proposition that draws no support from the Supreme Court decisions.

One of the charges against Lacks stemmed from poems written by an African American ninth grader named Reginald McNeary. McNeary had been "totally disengaged" for most of the school year. When Lacks's class began a unit on poetry, he sat in the back with his head down, initially refusing to join the circle of chairs from which students shared their work. After a few sessions, he joined the group, and for the first time all year, he spoke. He read his poem "Hard Core Gangsta Rap" aloud. Lacks had not yet seen the work, which she later described as "full of anger." It contained "a great deal of street language."[55]

Under Lacks's guidance, McNeary soon turned to more constructive topics, couched in more acceptable language, starting with a poem called "Hate":

> We are so busy hating we don't even pray.
> Some whites hate blacks and some Germans hate Jews.
> But they are wrong because no one can choose.
> How dark or bright or light people are to be.

At the end of the three-week poetry unit McNeary presented "Alone," which went on to win the district-wide poetry prize despite the lines "I don't give a damn" and "I never gave a damn about any other." McNeary's success didn't save Lacks's job.[56]

When Lacks sued, the federal district court reinstated her, gave her back pay, and ordered the district to pay her attorneys' fees. A jury then awarded her $750,000 in damages, including $500,000 for violation of her expressive rights. The Court of Appeals, however, threw the decision and the award out, holding among other things that Lacks had "willfully violated" district policy about inappropriate language.[57]

In exceptional cases, judges have supported teachers who defy convention in the hopes of reaching their charges. The highest court in Massachusetts, for instance, held that a school district had wrongfully fired a special education teacher who used a thirteen-year-old's profanity during a discussion of "words with multiple meanings" as a teaching moment. Joyce Hosford responded to a student's mutterings about "the f-word and the words we do not use in class." Another student offered the word *shit* and used it in a sentence, invoking "its literal meaning." Hosford commented, "'Grammatically, that is correct,'" but instructed, "'I suggest you not use it in school or at home.'" School authorities objected to the stream of words the students offered in the closing minutes of class: *bitch, slut, blow job,* and *prick.* After giving a "literal definition" of each term, Hosford cut off discussion, directed students to the dictionary, and ended the class.[58]

The judges, scoffing at the notion that the very same boys who used these words would have been offended or harmed by hearing them, commended Hosford for seizing an opportunity to convey a lesson about why and where some language is "inappropriate." The court reversed the trial court's ruling upholding the termination, ordered Hosford reinstated (as an untenured teacher), and remanded for determination of the amount of damages.[59]

Recognizing that calm adult guidance may well be the best response to student *sans-gêne* expression, the court applied *Tinker*'s material disruption standard in *Hosford* and found that no disorder flowed from the lesson. Indeed, one might argue that the lesson would tend to diminish disorder and disrespect going forward, at least if the students remembered to avoid the words the teacher labeled unacceptable. Applying *Tinker* to *sans-gêne* expression in this instance made sense despite the vulgar language because *Fraser* involved a large school assembly, not a small setting.[60] The opinion reflected a nuanced approach to education, one that trusted a teacher to take advantage of a teaching opportunity with a small class she had known for a long time.

The words students used in these classrooms are the same words that lead some parents to pressure schools to remove books from the library or the curriculum. Outside of schools, the Speech Clause protects otherwise obscene works if the work "taken as a whole" offers some "serious literary, artistic, political, or scientific value." When schools censor library or teaching materials that contain *sans-gêne* language, however, their decisions are generally upheld unless based on an improper motive such as viewpoint discrimination.[61] Schools are allowed to censor based on offensive language without reference to the overall value of the work or the literary context in which the words appear.

Judges routinely voice regret that as long as school officials enunciate clear rules and apply their policies fairly, the Constitution does not protect a student's ability to use *sans-gêne* expression in creative writing or access it in written materials, and it doesn't safeguard the teacher who fails to squelch her students' uncivil expression even when it has some value within the curriculum. Many judges recognize that students themselves already use the contested language. As one judge commented, "Even extremely sheltered adolescents, exposed only to the most sanitized media, cannot completely avoid contact with terms and concepts" that many parents "consider objectionable." These words abound on television, in music, on the Internet, on streets, and on public transportation.[62]

Schools and courts appear even more perplexed about what legal standard governs the use of forbidden words written by published authors and read aloud by students. In 2006, a Nevada school reprimanded a ninth grader who had won a district-wide Poetry Out Loud competition by reciting "The More Loving One," written in 1957 by W. H. Auden. The school barred him from repeating the poem at the statewide competition because it contained the words *hell* and *damn*. Although the poem was included in the national competition's anthology of approved poems, the school claimed that the text undermined its goal of confining the students' vocabulary to what it called "pristine language":[63]

> Looking up at the stars, I know quite well
> That, for all they care, I can go to hell . . .

Auden's use of the word *hell* in this verse is no more inappropriate than in Milton or even biblical commentary. It was not used as a swear word but in its pristine meaning.

The poem continues:

> How should we like it were stars to burn
> With a passion for us we could not return?
> If equal affection cannot be,
> Let the more loving one be me.

Because Auden's intimate life was shared with other male poets, including Christopher Isherwood, and his "passion" presumably homosexual, it is fair to wonder about the school's actual motives for censoring the poem.

The student obtained a court order that stopped the school from interfering with his participation in the statewide finals. The court correctly rejected the school district's argument that it was entitled to deference under either *Fraser* or *Hazelwood*. It held that *Fraser* was inapplicable because the poem was not "vulgar, lewd or obscene." *Hazelwood* was irrelevant; the competition was not part of the curriculum, and the reading could not be construed as school sponsored. Finally, the court concluded that reciting the poem at a contest could not plausibly substantially disrupt the school's educational mission. This was clearly the right result.

And yet even this sensible opinion was flawed because it did not steer clear of the rampant confusion about the law in this field. Though it may sound like the court was using *Tinker*'s material disruption test, things were not so simple. The judge adapted an amalgam of *Fraser* and *Tinker* created in passing in *Morse:* Schools are allowed to prevent only "the sort of vulgar, obscene, lewd or sexual speech that, especially with adolescents, 'readily promotes disruption and diversion from the educational curriculum.'"[64]

Although the student won his personal court battle, the rule the judge crafted waters down the substantial disruption requirement. It suggests that the risk of disruption exists whenever *sans-gêne* words (and perhaps even insubordinate ideas) are voiced. But the Supreme Court has directed otherwise. If a student's speech does not cross the threshold of the language a school may bar under *Fraser* and is not "school sponsored," it should be fully protected under *Tinker*.

Reflective exercise of common sense in the first instance instead of severe penalties for teachers or students would help to defuse most of these controversies. Creative teaching may be stifled to the disadvantage of students when schools take an absolutist stance in enforcing rules against *sans-gêne* expression. And where teachers know that they are at risk if they tolerate such speech, they are likely to clamp down on it. The resulting chill is at odds with First Amendment principles and basic educational goals such as fostering familiarity with respected literature and encouraging intellectual inquiry and creativity.

Lewdness, Rudeness, and Insubordination under the Constitution

Hazelwood defined *Fraser* as reaching "speech that was 'sexually explicit' but not obscene" and stated that schools could distance themselves from "vulgarity," which is at odds with "the shared values of a civilized social order." The Supreme Court left the precise "determination of what manner of speech . . . is inappropriate" to local school boards, giving them wide-ranging discretion to discipline *sans-gêne* expression.[65]

School officials who punish broadly defined incivility and insubordination often believe that they act with impunity under *Fraser* or *Hazelwood* if they make "reasonable" decisions. They assert that *Hazelwood* can be stretched to address inappropriate words or manner of expression whether or not it is lewd or even school sponsored. Some courts accept that claim even where the speech lacks the essential characteristic of lewdness required to trigger *Fraser* or the appearance of school sponsorship needed to invoke *Hazelwood*. Other judges ask whether the insubordinate language threatened to cause substantial disruption (applying the *Tinker* standard).

Very few judges have expressly applied *Fraser* in the past decade. *Fraser* has atrophied as a judicial standard in part because most judges correctly understand its reach to be limited to cases involving "sexually suggestive," "racy," or "lewd" speech.[66] Of course, Matthew Fraser did not use any objectionable words. He counted on his peers to understand what the court termed his "elaborate metaphor." The boundaries of the case would have been narrower if Fraser had said, "Vote for my friend because he has the largest dick in the school." But what if he had used the more polite "penis" or more medical "reproductive organ" instead? If the courts held that those terms too could be censored in school electioneering (as I suspect they would be tempted to do), we'd have a rule about content and ideas, not mode of communication, which would be even more in tension with the general principles animating the Speech Clause.

The judge in Posthumus v. Board of Education, the case involving the snack-eating student who told his friend the assistant principal was a "dick," initially focused on the speaker's choice wording and had no doubt that this was the manner of expression for which *Fraser* "provides the appropriate framework." But he fell into an easy trap. Instead of focusing exclusively on the manner of the student's speech—that is, his choice of word or choice wording—as *Fraser* requires, the judge also considered the content of the speech, which he labeled "insubordinate speech directed at a school official." By delving into the student's message, the judge implied that the school could have punished Posthumus even if he had chosen his words more carefully. The judge unnecessarily reached beyond the mode of expression to allow the school to punish a student for disrespectful ideas.[67]

Posthumus claimed he was "only giving 'his opinion regarding [the assistant principal's] confiscation of his unopened food."[68] What if he had said, "That man has a far too rigid view of the rules"? More polite, but still insubordinate. And yet it seems unlikely that a student would receive more than a rebuke for using the expurgated language I have put in his mouth. That would be the correct outcome.

There is no reason to fear that students will be free to disrespect and undermine teachers and principals if I am right that the First Amendment extends to much of the rude but not lewd speech discussed in this chapter. Freedom of expression does not provide cover for genuinely insubordinate behavior. In many instances, constitutional claims might have been avoided if schools and judges had not conflated conduct with protected expression. As Justice Breyer has pointed out, if the principal in Anchorage, Alaska, had punished Joseph Frederick for refusing to roll up his "Bong Hits 4 Jesus" banner and his belligerent attitude instead of focusing on the banner's content, no constitutional rights would have been implicated.[69]

Similarly, if Posthumus had engaged in insubordinate conduct by refusing to hand over his snack or snatching it back from the assistant principal's hands, the school could have punished his behavior without implicating any First Amendment rights, even if the act had been accompanied by rude words. The school would merely have had to emphasize that it was punishing the behavior, not the expression.

Fraser's deference to officials is limited to lewd *language* or a lewd manner of expression. Because the opinion did not address "disrespectful" *language*, it surely doesn't extend to disrespectful *ideas,* which *Tinker* expressly contemplates and protects.[70] There is no legal justification for permitting school authorities to invoke *Fraser* when they punish all sorts of speech that is rude or insubordinate but lacks the essential element of lewdness.

Educators have not just pressed to apply *Fraser* to disrespectful utterances; they have continually worked to expand the definition of the disrespectful speech governed by *Fraser* and the realm of school-sponsored speech governed by *Hazelwood* so that between the two doctrines they can contain purely verbal rebelliousness.[71]

Using *Hazelwood* to reach disrespectful speech raises separate concerns. When students criticize their school or its personnel as Posthumus did while standing on line for an assembly (removed from any school-sponsored platform), the speech cannot reasonably be construed as bearing the school's imprimatur. What reasonable observer would conclude that a school gave its imprimatur to a speech accusing the administration of not giving a damn about students or, for example, of releasing carcinogenic materials near the campus? Ultimately, if the court is choosing between the rule of *Fraser* or *Hazelwood,* it makes very little difference to the outcome because both are extremely deferential to school authority and both tacitly instruct that the school usually wins.

Courts that apply *Tinker* to *sans-gêne* speech outside the context of student elections or where the speech is rude but not lewd are right to do so. *Fraser* carved out an exception to *Tinker* and left *Tinker* in place for all student speech that did not resemble Fraser's lewd talk in an assembly devoted to student elections.

However, even courts that apply *Tinker*'s exacting material disruption test in cases about *sans-gêne* speech that is neither lewd nor public do not always respect *Tinker*'s demands. Consider *Anderson*, the case involving the girl who muttered "shit" in frustration as she passed through the principal's office. The judge initially characterized the matter as being about "profane or inappropriate language." He did not, however, apply *Fraser* because it reaches only "sexually suggestive language." He ruled out *Hazelwood* because the speech was not school sponsored but was, in *Hazelwood*'s terms, purely individual expression that happened to occur at school. He then abruptly announced that *Tinker*'s material disruption requirement does not apply to "indecent language" and—in a decision peppered with disapproval for what he viewed as the school's overreaction—concluded that the law supported deference to a school's disciplinary choices. The opinion does not offer any guidelines about how to limit a school's definition of or response to "inappropriate" language.[72]

The proper choice of legal standards is not a technicality or a game for logicians. It matters enormously. Since the Supreme Court erected its taxonomy of censorship for student speech, placing the speech in the right category determines the level of constitutional protection the speech receives. Put most concretely, the choice of standard generally signals which party will win.

Accomplishing the delicate balance between order and freedom always poses a difficult challenge. It requires both a school code of conduct that satisfies constitutional concerns and thoughtful application of that code. One possibility might be to generate a speech code that gives sufficient notice of types of language that are forbidden (beyond the lewd) and then treats *sans-gêne* expression as a type of "noise" that is inappropriate on school grounds without focusing on the attitude behind the choice of words. The imposition of discipline would then focus on student conduct instead of the content of student expression.

Many readers may be shaking their heads in wonder at some of the language quoted in this chapter or at the severe penalties that can derail children's lives after they use lewd or rude language at school—or both.

Some may worry that schools ignore cultural and class differences about acceptable language or ask if mainstream middle-class morality should dominate school codes. It is certainly true that parents don't all have the same approach to language, rules, and discipline in their homes. An emphasis on cultural difference with respect to cursing, however, would undermine the many parents within every racial and socioeconomic group who are strict about the words their children use at home.

No court appears to have ruled that schools may not prohibit and punish the use of traditionally forbidden words. The parents who sue over school penalties for speech that legitimately falls under *Fraser*'s umbrella dispute the penalty, not the school's authority to regulate the vocabulary used on campus.

Debates over the manner of speech are deeply entwined with deeper cultural conflicts about the proper balance of discipline and autonomy in training the young. Disputes over *sans-gêne* speech go to the heart of Justice Black's disagreement with the *Tinker* majority. In schools, as one judge put it, constitutional imperatives favor balancing the important task of teaching civility with the equally crucial mission to nurture the "independence of thought and frankness of expression" that "occupy a high place on our scale of values."[73]

CHAPTER 4

School-Sponsored Speech

Hazelwood's "Imprimatur" Conundrum

[S]tudents may not be regarded as closed-circuit recipients of only
that which the State chooses to communicate.

—Tinker v. Des Moines Independent Community School
District (1969)

In the wake of Hazelwood v. Kuhlmeier, the construct of
"school sponsorship" threatened the doctrine that "educating the young for
citizenship is reason for scrupulous protection" of students' individual rights.[1]
Observers of every political and philosophical stripe agree that *Hazelwood*
tipped the balance between order and freedom in favor of authority. It exponentially extended the realm of permissible censorship and intruded radically on student speech rights. Commentators differ only on whether they
regard the change as a triumph for order or a tragedy for freedom.

Those who laud *Hazelwood*'s revamping of school speech doctrine fail to
recognize that some schools claim even more discretion than the Court's
opinion afforded them. Officials exploit the construct of school sponsorship
to roll students' rights further back than the Supreme Court had envisioned.
Just as schools wrongly assert that *Fraser* allows them to punish students for
an array of impertinent, *sans-gêne* speech that isn't lewd, schools have pushed
relentlessly to bring virtually every sort of speech on campus within the
definition of *school sponsored,* including the spontaneous speech of students
in their classrooms.

School administrators have invoked *Hazelwood* in contexts that bear no
resemblance to articles in a school's official newspaper prepared under close
supervision in a class for academic credit. They have called speech school
sponsored that is so critical of the school no sentient observer could think
the ideas were the school's own. Principal Morse invoked *Hazelwood* in
defense of her decision to censor the "Bong Hits 4 Jesus" banner although,

if it meant what she thought it did, the pro-drug sentiments could not have reasonably been attributed to the school.[2] In case after case, school officials simply ignore the threshold requirement for invoking *Hazelwood*'s deferential treatment: The speech must appear to bear the school's imprimatur.

This chapter explores how far some school districts go in using the school-sponsorship doctrine to colonize a large proportion of student speech. After a brief review of the elements of the *Hazelwood* test, I analyze two arenas in which illegitimate encroachments abound. First, I examine censorship of expression outside the core curriculum in venues that usually (though not always) qualify as school sponsored, where the school does not present any legitimate pedagogical rationale for censorship. Second, I consider the nascent effort to extend the doctrine to student speech within the classroom, constricting student's ability to question curricular messages or exercise autonomous critical thought.

The (Not Utterly Permissive) *Hazelwood* Test

In order to fully grasp the troubling way schools have misconstrued, misapplied, or ignored *Hazelwood*, it is necessary to return briefly to the test set out in the Supreme Court opinion. In theory, censorship does not qualify for *Hazelwood*'s deferential treatment unless the school satisfies two prerequisites: The speech must be supervised within an activity that serves a curricular purpose and it must appear to bear the school's imprimatur. If the school meets those threshold requirements for showing that the contested speech should be categorized as school sponsored, the court must then ask whether the censorship was "reasonably related to a legitimate pedagogical concern."[3] If the school can't point to a legitimate pedagogical rationale for silencing school-sponsored speech, educators overstepped their authority. This may be a standard with few teeth, but it is not as toothless as some school administrators and lower court judges appear to believe.

The first step in the analysis requires a sound understanding of what amounts to school sponsorship. Justice Alito's simple summary while he was an appellate court judge captures the gist of the most defensible account of school-sponsored speech: *Hazelwood* allows regulation only of "what is in essence the school's own speech, that is, articles that appear in a publication that is an official school organ."[4] Even if Alito's tenet errs on the side of narrowness by emphasizing the circumstances that most closely resemble the facts in *Hazelwood*, the yardstick of the "school's own speech" captures the decision's key requirements. Had more judges shared Alito's understanding, *Hazelwood*'s impact would likely have been diminished.

Schools must show they sponsor student speech before the Constitution allows them to control it at their discretion. The process begins with showing a link to curricular learning "whether or not . . . in a traditional classroom setting, so long as [students] are supervised by faculty members and [the activities are] designed to impart particular knowledge or skills." The Supreme Court counted all "curricular activities," including those that do not involve "credit, grades, or formal instruction," as school sponsored if they impart knowledge or skills.[5] It obliterated any meaningful legal distinction between a newspaper produced by a class and one issued by an extracurricular club. As a result, almost all of the incidents discussed in this chapter satisfy the curricular component of school sponsorship.

But that is just the beginning of the analysis. The Supreme Court also required schools to demonstrate that the expression appears to bear the school's imprimatur. To do so, a school must show that "students, parents and members of the public might reasonably perceive [the expression] to bear the imprimatur of the school."[6] In other words, there must be a credible risk that observers will attribute the speech to the school or believe that the school approved or endorsed the content of student expression.

The confusion of school administrators and school board members who aren't attorneys is understandable. The Supreme Court suggested the imprimatur requirement might be loosely construed because even a mistaken public perception might satisfy it. The Court did not try to contain the scope of school-sponsored speech by, for example, disentangling utterances in distinct zones within the school, as I try to do by differentiating among official school publications, other speech that is available to the entire student body or community, a student's responsive comment in a classroom, or speech in settings sheltered from the public.

Establishing that student expression is curricular and bears the school's imprimatur only brings student speech within the *Hazelwood* framework. Officials have to overcome one more hurdle to justify censorship of school-sponsored student speech: The trial judge is required to ask whether the school's regulation of the expression was "reasonably related to legitimate pedagogical concerns." Here again, the Supreme Court did not provide any guidance about how lower courts should evaluate the school's pedagogical rationale, but lower courts have fleshed out an approach that imposes only modest demands. Judges are not required to assess actual motives when evaluating reasonableness under *Hazelwood*. A reasonable explanation based on pedagogy suffices.

The legal standard "does not require that the guidelines be the *most* reasonable or the *only* reasonable limitations, only that they be reasonable." On its face, the test gives schools great leeway—they can almost always convince the court that they satisfied this minimal requirement.[7] But the test is not entirely without substance. The school must offer some rational pedagogical rationale for censorship. A formulaic "for educational reasons" will not suffice.

Lenient as it is, *Hazelwood* did not give carte blanche to school authorities. When they pay too little attention to its modest constraints, officials risk failing to satisfy the imprimatur requirement or to convince a court that they had a legitimate rationale for censoring student expression.

"Legitimate Pedagogical Goals": School-Sponsored Speech outside the Classroom

School sponsorship extends beyond the printed word to performances in which the school selected the material (a play, music, or the antics of the marching band at a football game). Expanded further, it might reach the expression of a student who represents the school in an official capacity. The student government president, for example, might be asked to explain the school's policy on a particular subject—like the honor code or who can participate in varsity sports—to her peers or to a group of parents. If her role is summarizing, not critiquing, she may be required to stick to it.

In this section, I explore decisions to silence expression that no one disputes generally meets the definition of school sponsorship: school plays and school newspapers. Educators repeatedly censor protected speech in these settings without any valid pedagogical justification. They have done so to preserve their own reputations, to avoid controversy, and to silence academic debate—all of which violate the First Amendment even under *Hazelwood*.

School Plays: "Preventive Maintenance"

School plays are normally governed by *Hazelwood* because faculty members select the script (that is, the content) and supervise the performance. The main legal question is whether censoring or canceling a play the school has already selected is "reasonably related to legitimate pedagogical concerns."

The selection of plays and other materials for student performances has long generated disputes among adults that create disappointments for hard-working student theater troupes. Even before *Hazelwood,* judges regarded school plays as part of the curriculum and therefore the state's own speech.[8] Censorship of performances reveals some of the crassest and most ill-considered decisions—decisions that reflect short-sighted incentives for administrators to appease the most conservative and disputatious community members and to give short shrift to reasonableness requirements.

Cancellations occur regularly. Performances are called off at the last minute, commonly under circumstances that smack of a desire to avoid confrontations with offended citizens. Too often school authorities cancel a performance to placate one parent or citizen activist who objects to the content. This is an unvarnished form of the heckler's veto in which those who object to speech are allowed to silence it instead of being advised to absent themselves. When school officials censor based on a single complaint or even a handful of alarms, they often provoke a different sort of upheaval than the disagreement they hoped to avoid.

Recurrent undermining of teachers' judgment in selecting scripts leads them to conclude dejectedly that "parents rule."[9] To be more precise, the parent who complains rules. Parents who don't object to the play that was chosen have no reason to share their views until after the principal has announced the cancellation, when it is too late to reverse course without embarrassment.

School principals commonly appear to be so averse to public disputes, or so unsure of what the law permits or requires, that they respond to a single parent's concerns by telling the teacher to bowdlerize the script or scuttle the performance. Such censorship is rarely challenged in court—probably because *Hazelwood* is so heavily weighted in the school's favor. But disputes over cancellations are reported regularly in the press and on websites.[10]

A close examination of the patterns in these disputes suggests that school district victories should not always be a slam dunk. Under the circumstances I've described, the school may not be able to establish a good pedagogical reason for the censorship. If a principal reviews a script before the teacher announces the choice, any reason for rejecting the script will do. But there is a palpable difference between a principal's decision not to approve a project in the ordinary course of curricular review and a subsequent decision to cancel or expurgate a production in response to outside pressure after rehearsals have begun. The former is routine. It involves entrenched, common exercise of curricular authority. The latter should sound a constitutional alarm because it is an unusual, irregular intervention after the principal has signed off on the project and turned it over to the teacher to bring to fruition. An extraordinary intervention should trigger a closer look at the motives and rationale for expunging speech, as it does in other settings.

An analogy to the school library is useful. Schools may decline to order books for the library for any reason at all, including a decision that the content is not suitable. But a plurality of the Supreme Court advised in Island Trees Board of Education v. Pico in 1982 that unusual procedures that cause materials to be removed from a school library based on controversial content raise warning flags of potential constitutional violations.[11]

When school censorship follows social and political threats, it smacks of impermissible motivation whether in the library or on the auditorium stage. The incentives to avoid controversy or worries about the next school board election can entice officials to silence speech that offends the most sensitive ears rather than to stand up for potentially contentious topics, language, and viewpoints. In these circumstances courts have the authority to probe the school's account of its decision.

Even conformity to national norms does not guarantee safe passage from community pressure. In 2007, when *Grease* and *The Crucible* were among the top choices for school performances nationwide, a brouhaha still developed in Fulton, Missouri, over the high school's choice of *Grease* as the school play.[12]

The Fulton incident is striking in its transparency. Sensitive to the small community's conservative bent, the teacher directing *Grease* expurgated the script, slashing profanity and references to drugs. That didn't stop several members of the Callaway Christian Church who had not seen the play from complaining after the performance that the play glorified "immoral behavior veiled behind the excuse of acting out a play." One complainant said he was upset because he had heard rumors that Rizzo, the "bad girl," wore only a top in a pajama party scene.[13]

It was too late to stop *Grease,* so the principal moved against the next production, a performance of *The Crucible*. Arthur Miller's canonical play, written during Senator Joseph McCarthy's infamous hearings on alleged communist conspiracies, is often interpreted as an attack on political conformity. It was required reading for Fulton's eleventh graders. Instead of reading the script himself, the principal based his decision to cancel the performance in part on a website plot summary: "Salem woman accuses an ex-lover's wife of witchery . . ."[14]

Apparently oblivious to the play's message, the principal explained that he wanted to avoid any risk of renewed controversy. He described his decision to cancel *The Crucible* as "entirely a preventive maintenance issue."[15]

Students and teachers were perplexed. When they couldn't figure out what the principal objected to, they came up with a number of theories, including "people get hung; there's death in it" and it "makes Christians look bad."[16] Clearly, the cancellation had not transmitted any educational message to Fulton's students.

When a local reporter asked if the school would allow a production of *Romeo and Juliet*, the school superintendent was unable to answer with a simple "yes." Instead, he "hesitated. . . . 'Given the historical context of the play,' he equivocated, 'it would be difficult to say that's something we would not perform.'"[17]

If the cancellation of *The Crucible* had reached a courtroom, it should have been a simple case. Under *Hazelwood*, the case would have turned on the legitimacy of the school's rationale. From a lawyer's perspective, the principal was too candid for his own good. He admitted that he was motivated by administrative convenience and a desire to avoid complaints. He failed to offer a single pedagogical reason for cancelling the play.

And yet a student lawsuit against the Fulton Schools might have backfired in the longer run. The school system might have learned to be more sophisticated the next time around—"sophisticated" in the sense that administrators would learn to attribute their censorship decisions to educational motives.

It's almost always possible to identify an educational motive. The school could have argued that it wanted to use performances as an opportunity to introduce new materials not read in English classes or that students weren't mature enough to understand *The Crucible* without the aid of supervised class discussion, which only the eleventh graders received.

From a constitutional perspective, it is troubling that some districts have prevailed in lawsuits about similar disputes by claiming that they wanted to avoid controversy. *Tinker* expressly disavowed that rationale, and *Hazelwood* never hinted that avoiding controversy was a legitimate pedagogical consideration. Teaching students how to experience differences of opinion and respond to controversy is part of education's civilizing function. Worries about "controversy" are nothing more than the "mere desire to avoid the discomfort and unpleasantness that always accompany an unpopular viewpoint" that *Tinker* cautioned cannot "justify" suppressing speech. As *Tinker* made clear, "[I]n our system, undifferentiated fear or apprehension of disturbance is not enough to overcome the right to freedom of expression. . . . Our Constitution says we must take this risk." A handful of lower court rulings to the contrary threaten to make schools the very "bastions of orthodoxy" decried by the Supreme Court and to subvert the central values enshrined in the Speech Clause, applicable even in schools.[18]

Censorship of School Newspapers after Hazelwood

School newspapers—the subject of the controversy in *Hazelwood*—are usually, though not always, school-sponsored speech. As school officials exert their power to censor student journalists, they often assert school sponsorship in circumstances where no one would mistake an article for the school's own speech. Even if schools satisfy the imprimatur requirement, however, they must still show that the decision to suppress speech was "reasonably related to legitimate pedagogical concerns."

School newspapers serve a number of important functions beyond providing a vehicle for student expression. They encourage civic engagement among readers, generate the habit of following the news, and provide an opportunity for debating local and national policies. The best even gain regional or national visibility. As community newspapers fold under economic pressure, student journalists increasingly provide the only source of local news.[19]

The Student Press Law Center (SPLC), an advocacy group that promotes student First Amendment rights and participation in "meaningful civic life," receives about 2,500 requests for help each year from students and teachers who believe they are the victims of school censorship. That translates to roughly ten alleged incidents of censorship every day of the school year reported to just one public interest organization, and it's fair to assume that many acts of censorship are never reported, perhaps the majority. The complaints, from every state and the District of Columbia, increased by 350 percent between the Supreme Court's 1988 decision in *Hazelwood* and 2003, and they continue to pour in.[20] The ACLU and its state affiliates, as well as other groups, also receive inquiries from student journalists and their faculty advisors.

Very few of these complaints end up in court, in large part because of the many obstacles facing a family thinking about suing its school district. It takes a great deal of courage for children and their parents to confront the school that they and perhaps their younger siblings still attend. If students wait until they graduate to sue, courts may not allow the case to proceed. The disincentives mount in light of the trial court's discretionary power to order the student to pay the district's costs, including reasonable attorneys' fees, if the school district prevails.[21]

And schools resort to methods of intimidating or silencing student writers that cannot be challenged in court. One former school board member from Iowa warns that school districts increasingly reassign or fire faculty advisors, cut funding for publications, or shut them down when students fight to preserve their voices. The threats don't need to be explicit to be effective. Savvy student editors need only to read *The Huffington Post* or any number of other websites to know, for example, that the principal in Fond du Lac, Wisconsin, seized control of the high school newspaper in 2014 after it published a serious story about rape culture. School districts have discretion to make these administrative decisions, though community or political action can sometimes convince officials to back down.[22]

So it should not surprise anyone that lawsuits about the rights of student journalists have become very rare. According to the SPLC, "only a handful of . . . high school journalism cases have gone to court [since *Hazelwood*]."[23] Student journalists and their advisors think they will lose in court given the holding in *Hazelwood*.

Intriguingly, however, school districts disproportionately lose in the recent reported cases involving newspaper censorship. While this seems counterintuitive—*Hazelwood* indicates schools should win—it seems plausible that only students with extraordinarily strong cases decide to pursue their claims.

The fact that a school funds or publishes a paper doesn't necessarily make it school sponsored. In Draudt v. Wooster City School District Board of Education, decided in 2003, a federal judge in Ohio denied student journalists the preliminary injunction they sought when officials threw out the entire run of the paper containing an article about students who drank at a party in someone's home. But after reviewing pertinent factors, including whether the paper is part of the curriculum, whether a faculty member supervises and grades the students, how much control the school and advisor actually exercise, and the school's policy and practice, the same judge concluded the newspaper did not qualify as school sponsored. The school would have to offer more than a reasonable rationale for censorship because the school had opened the paper to student expression.[24]

Even where school newspapers qualify as school sponsored, which they usually do, school officials may no more censor publications than cancel performances without a legitimate pedagogical reason. This is where school districts are most prone to stumble.

Both before and after *Hazelwood*, the motives underlying school newspaper censorship have a predictable, even quotidian quality. Authorities take umbrage at criticism. They worry that a story will harm the school's reputation. Perhaps they fear roiling community sensitivities. Back in 1965, a vice principal in Des Moines justified the suppression of black armbands by telling one of the *Tinker* protesters that a demonstration would "bring bad publicity to the school." At about the same time in New York City, a principal refused to publish an editorial that blamed the faculty for student apathy.[25]

Many school districts still stifle criticism and fend off articles they fear may generate scrutiny of the campus. Schools censor student journalists who expose violations or weaknesses connected to the school and its occupants: accurate accounts of a teacher's arrest, an unnamed student caught shoplifting while on a school trip, or a student who brought a gun to a well-regarded suburban high school.[26] None of these motivations has much to do with educational purposes.

Such concerns on the part of administrators may be timeless, but *Hazelwood* encouraged school districts to expand on the new powers the case granted them to adopt more stringent rules and to impose a heavier hand in overseeing the content of school publications. As the SPLC assessed the situation, *Hazelwood* made censorship "standard operating procedure at some schools" and "an ever-present threat" at every school.[27]

The threat of unbridled censorship was on full display in a lawsuit that reached New Jersey's highest court in 1994. The state had given school officials power to censor student publications that posed "a danger to student health." A middle school principal relied on that regulation when he blocked publication of reviews of two R-rated films, *Rain Man* and *Mississippi Burning*. He admitted he feared that parents would complain about the articles.[28]

When the young film reviewers sued, the trial and appellate courts scoffed at the principal's concerns. Students were already well aware of both films, which many of them had seen. A poll showed that *Rain Man*, a film about an autistic savant and his brother, was one of the most popular films among the students at the school. During a unit on the civil rights movement, a history teacher had recommended students watch *Mississippi Burning,* in which FBI agents investigate the suspicious disappearance of three civil rights workers.

The state supreme court held that the school didn't have any legitimate reason for the censorship. "Substantial deference to educational decisions does not require a wholesale abandonment of First Amendment principles," the state's highest court underscored. School funding of publications does not purchase freedom from the demands of the First Amendment. The court shouldered its responsibility for enforcing the law, announcing that for school officials "to say that censorship here was justified by pedagogical concerns does not make it so." The educational policy must be well defined, the court declared, and have a clear relationship to the censorship. The rationales the school offered—ranging from following the movie industry's informational rating code to helping parents—were not even "reasonable."[29]

If the true motive for censorship in the New Jersey case remains obscure, it was utterly transparent in the case of the Utica, Michigan, school that in 2002 excised a story from the school paper: Officials thought it made the school look bad. The young journalists had been investigating a pending lawsuit against the school district. Residents of a home located next to the garage that housed the school buses, one of whom was dying of lung cancer, had sued the district. They claimed that diesel fumes from the idling buses had made them sick. The controversy was no secret. The local paper had written about the dispute, and the school board had discussed it at a public meeting.[30]

The student paper followed up with its own investigation. Katy Dean and another reporter interviewed the plaintiffs and watched a tape of the school board discussing the lawsuit at a public meeting. Dean also investigated the effects of diesel exhaust on health. No representative of the school system was willing to talk with the reporters. The principal approved the idea for the story and went further: Since students parked near the same garage, he suggested the paper might also explore whether students should be parking near the fumes.

After the principal reviewed the draft article, he forwarded it to the superintendent. She responded that the draft contained some "inaccuracies." The primary inaccuracy, she said, was a conflict between the article's findings and the opinion of the expert witness the school district had retained to testify on its behalf. The district's expert witness said just what the district had retained him to say: Exposure to idling diesel buses would not have affected the dying man's health. Since the school district had rebuffed the opportunity to tell its side of the story, it was impossible for the students to cover the disagreement. After conferring with the school district's lawyer, the superintendent ordered the principal to delete the article from the paper on the ground that it was "'inappropriate for the school newspaper to comment'" about ongoing litigation.[31]

The superintendent also complained that Dean had cited *USA Today* for scientific data. She didn't give Dean a chance to improve the article by, for instance, looking at and citing the underlying sources of scientific information on which *USA Today* had relied. Dean might have learned a valuable lesson about research and sources. Instead, she received a lesson about authoritarianism and fighting back. The students filled the empty space in the newspaper with an editorial about censorship. As with *Hazelwood*'s teen pregnancy article, the local newspaper published Dean's story.[32]

When Dean sued the school for violating her speech rights, the court fully vindicated her claims. In Dean v. Utica Community Schools, Judge Arthur J. Tarnow ruled in 2004 that neither the newspaper as a whole nor the censored article met the definition of school sponsorship. Applying the standards from *Draudt*, he concluded that the paper was produced under very different conditions from Spectrum at Hazelwood East High School. Utica had accorded the students enormous independence; they had written about many potentially controversial topics; and the school had failed to treat the publication as a class.[33]

Finally, Tarnow found that the article "clearly did not bear" the school's imprimatur because "no reasonable reader" could think the authors' viewpoint belonged to the school. The article disclosed that the district had resisted the students' efforts to get to the bottom of the story and that every official refused to talk to the reporters whose potent criticisms of the school were the very impetus for the censorship.[34]

Just as critically, the school would have lost even if the court had found the publication to be school sponsored because the judge went on to hold that the censorship did not serve *any* legitimate pedagogical purpose. The school system refused to publish the article solely because of its viewpoint: that the idling buses had likely affected the plaintiffs' health.

The judge grasped the broader stakes for American civic life. He demanded the school district live up to the promise on the paper's masthead to "train the students in the function of the press in a democratic society." Journalists, even those who are students, he emphasized, must "question authority, rather than side with authority . . . if the role of the press in a democratic society is to have any value." Quoting Presidents Harry S. Truman and Dwight D. Eisenhower, the judge warned, "'Once a government is committed to the principle of silencing the voice of opposition, it has only one way to go, and that is down the path of increasingly repressive measures, until it becomes a source of terror to all its citizens and creates a country where everyone lives in fear.'"[35]

Just as some judges have been more skeptical than others when evaluating educators' rationales for newspaper censorship, some states offer students legal protections that exceed what the federal Constitution requires. As of 2014 at least nine states and the District of Columbia have enacted laws that go beyond the First Amendment in limiting the ability of school officials to censor student expression.[36]

Illinois almost made it into that circle following an incident at Naperville North High School outside Chicago that never reached the courts. Naperville North has long been proud to be included among the top high schools in *U.S. News and World Report*. Its student paper has garnered many prizes over the years.

In 1997, student reporters learned that some of the district's administrators had taken costly junkets in the midst of budgetary cuts. They found expense vouchers in public documents, including one hotel bill for five nights of reimbursement for a conference that lasted only two days. The principal refused to publish the article unless the students removed the names of the employees who were implicated. The student reporters were incensed. They wanted "their voice back."[37]

The students acted decisively. Stymied at school, they brought their article to the *Chicago Tribune*, which vetted the story and published it—naming names. Ironically, as often happens, the entire episode received far more regional and national attention than it would have attracted if the article had appeared in the school paper. The *Tribune*'s decision to publish the full story confirms that no legitimate lesson about journalism inspired the principal's edits. Responding to this sorry episode, the Illinois state legislature voted by an overwhelming margin to protect the rights of student journalists—to no avail. The governor vetoed the bill.[38]

The California legislature has deprived educators of the "broad power to censor expression in school sponsored publications for pedagogical purposes" recognized in *Hazelwood*. The state had adopted a student speech rights statute even before the *Hazelwood* decision and has continually updated it since in response to emerging legal issues. The current statute authorizes students to control the content of school publications and prevents school officials from engaging in "prior restraint of such publications" unless the material would expose the school to prosecution (e.g., for violating the obscenity statutes) or the risk of civil lawsuits (e.g., for libel).[39] Schools in California that want to regulate student speech—no matter where it falls in the Supreme Court's taxonomy—must satisfy the *Tinker* standard or show a "clear and present danger of unlawful acts" before they can censor or discipline student expression.[40]

Courts in the state have stringently enforced the statute's protections for student journalists. California, courts have repeatedly held, "confers editorial control of official student publications on the student editors alone, with very limited exceptions. . . . The broad power to censor expression in school sponsored publications [recognized in *Hazelwood*] is *not available to this state's educators*."[41]

The California law would have ensured publication of another article that received national attention in 2014 when the *New York Times* published an op-ed by the editors of a school paper in Ann Arbor, Michigan, after the principal quashed a special edition on clinical depression among adolescents. The articles included personal stories from local teenagers, all identified and all with signed parental consent forms. The courageous editors—who are both receiving treatment for depression—hoped to attack the stigma attached to mental health diagnoses, to encourage communication, and to help other students find support.[42]

Whether to publish this series was a closer call than other disputes examined in this chapter, as the editors themselves conceded with remarkable maturity. "From an administrative perspective," they wrote, the principal's decision "made some sense. It is her job to protect the students to the best of her ability. She believed that . . . those who shared their experiences—and most important, their names—would be put at risk because of potential bullying" and that reading the articles could trigger relapses. But, the girls pushed back, "by telling us that students could not talk openly about their struggles, they reinforced the very stigma we were trying to eliminate."[43] The principal's rationale satisfied *Hazelwood*'s criteria, but in California the decision about publication would have rested with the editors.

Core Curricular Speech: Marketplace
of Ideas or State-Owned Monopoly?

The censorship of student expression discussed in this chapter would be troubling enough even if it were limited to the realm of school plays and newspapers where claims of sponsorship are ordinarily at least plausible. But the same overreach has been evident on an even more unsettling front: inside the classroom. Essentially this second arena builds on the argument that *Hazelwood* extends the aura of school sponsorship to all student speech within the core curriculum, even if the expression is never made public and could not reasonably be construed as bearing the school's imprimatur. The student expression targeted by this expansive reading takes place in classroom discussions, written assignments, and tests. The claim would extend authority over a much broader terrain than the *sans-gêne* speech in classroom assignments discussed in the last chapter. If this interpretation spreads and courts fail to constrain it (as several have already done), classrooms are at risk of being converted into the "'enclaves of totalitarianism'" Justice Brennan warned against in his *Hazelwood* dissent.[44]

The *Hazelwood* majority was not entirely blameless in encouraging this line of thinking. At one point, it offered a passing comment that hinted at an alternative way of understanding school sponsorship wrapped in its reinterpretation of *Tinker*'s shield against government intrusion. Recall that the *Hazelwood* majority confined *Tinker*'s scope to "personal expression that happens to occur on the school premises."[45] This kind of observation does not bind anyone, including the lower courts. But it has supported arguments that all classroom student speech is school sponsored because the student didn't *initiate* conversation about curricular matters and the speech didn't *just happen* to be voiced at school. Combined with the accepted doctrine that most extracurricular speech is school sponsored, this interpretation leaves virtually no space or time for pure personal expression other than the cafeteria, hallway, or playground. Understood in this way, *Hazelwood* would, as school law expert Mary McCarthy presciently predicted in 1993, eviscerate "the free exchange of ideas in public education."[46]

To fully appreciate the threats posed by the argument that core curricular expression is school sponsored, we first need to consider the provenance of classroom speech and disaggregate its components. Ideas stream into what children learn in schools from three primary sources: texts and materials the school district selects, what teachers say and provide in class, and what students themselves share in class discussions or create in response to assignments. The status and legal treatment of each of these sources of information and ideas depends on who is "speaking" as well as on the context in which the expression takes place. As I shall show, the degrees of sponsorship and of First Amendment protection vary greatly across these streams of content and viewpoint.

The Curriculum and Required Texts

The state in one of its guises—the local board, the state legislature, or federal guidelines—generally chooses core curricular materials. From the earliest Supreme Court decisions about public schooling in the 1920s to the present, no one has seriously challenged "the State's power to prescribe a curriculum for institutions it supports."[47] The state has virtually free rein to decide what subject matter public schools will cover, how the subjects will be defined and treated, and what textbooks teachers will use.

The curriculum is, to repeat once again Justice Alito's apt words, the school's own speech in its purest form, unmediated through "sponsorship." The state can include or omit virtually any topics or materials it wants, immune from the strictures of the Speech Clause. When the government speaks, it chooses the subject and viewpoint. It need not present opposing interpretations. Some states choose textbooks with pronounced ideological viewpoints. If they have large populations, like Texas, their ideology may determine what books are available in other parts of the country because publishers adjust content and viewpoint to attract sales in major markets.

Textbooks may be biased. They may present the happy holiday story of Native Americans sharing food with the Pilgrims without mentioning the seizure of Indian lands, an opinionated account of undocumented immigrants, or demeaning images of girls, African Americans, or Africans. Even more likely today, in many parts of the country, literary selections and historical accounts eschew any potentially controversial language, plot, or narrative. Educators go so far as to promote what Diane Ravitch calls "cultural equivalence" in which no civilizations are seen as more advanced than others in any respect.[48]

In history and the social sciences, such concerns might lead a school district that teaches about the Holocaust to steer clear of more recent episodes of genocide in Rwanda, Bosnia, or Cambodia to avoid offending local constituents who hail from those places. When the curriculum imposes such judgments or designates one viewpoint about a contested historical event, there is no constitutional right to be exposed to the story told by the other side, as a federal court held in rejecting a challenge to a course that included the Armenian genocide in a unit about human rights without covering the Turkish government's denial of historical events.[49] And if the curriculum presented only the Turkish account, which denies that Armenians were slaughtered and driven out, teachers would not be able to present the other side of the story without the school district's consent.

Such politically charged curricular choices do not normally implicate constitutional concerns. The Supreme Court has instructed that if citizens are unhappy with the message the government advances—whether on public television, through a federal agency, or in the local schools—they should hold the government accountable at election time.[50]

Limits on Speech by Teachers

Questioning and evaluating the materials the state provides are at the crux of learning to think critically, which is one of the announced goals of our educational system. Critical thinking is deemed essential to both the developmental goal of autonomy and the exercise of democratic rights such as informed voting.

Since the state doesn't have an obligation to present a range of viewpoints, the salient legal question is whether anyone in the classroom has a constitutional right to offer alternative views for the students' contemplation. Teachers can't serve that function.

Pervasive regulation limits teachers' ability to introduce facts and narratives that differ from the curricular message. As a matter of federal constitutional law, teachers have no legal protection when they expose students to competing interpretations of curricular messages or to controversial materials outside the official readings. School districts vary in the extent to which they exercise their discretion to restrain or cultivate classroom expression; state laws or union contracts may also create regimes that are more solicitous of teachers' speech rights within the curriculum.

None of the opinions in the Supreme Court's school speech quintet addressed teachers' speech rights despite *Tinker*'s famous observation that neither "students [nor] teachers shed their constitutional rights to freedom of speech . . . at the schoolhouse gate." A series of cases have diminished the speech rights of public employees since then, though the Supreme Court has reserved judgment on whether the same rules apply to teachers' classroom expression.[51]

Public schoolteachers have never had leeway to talk about whatever they want while on duty because their instructional speech is part of the government-mandated curriculum. Schools have disciplined and even fired teachers who discarded the prescribed curriculum, discussed student gossip, posted their personal religious speech in the classroom, or failed to submit "controversial materials" for administrative review, all without violating the teacher's speech rights. They may also prevent teachers from wearing political buttons to work.[52]

Those forms of speech are not all equivalent. Teachers' religious speech may violate the Establishment Clause by appearing to proselytize. A school district can reasonably conclude that political paraphernalia worn by authority figures may have disproportionate influence, but it can also permissibly ignore campaign buttons on teachers' clothing. Discussing gossip and its impact is different from gossiping *about* students. The former may involve questions about how gossip affects people or how to respond to gossip; the latter can hurt individual students.

Schools also have the authority to prevent teachers from offering alternatives to the official interpretations in textbooks in subjects like biology, where the state may endorse evolution or creationism. Biology teachers must obey the law in their district about teaching evolution, intelligent design, or creationism regardless of their personal beliefs or whether the district's guidelines comport with the Establishment Clause, at least until the courts rule.[53]

When teachers aren't free to offer "controversial" materials to supplement the content the state has endorsed without fear of repercussions, students experience a diminished range of ideas. It is impossible to reconcile this treatment of curricular speech with *Tinker*, which treated classrooms as the quintessential marketplaces for ideas. One reason for exposing students to material some people regard as controversial is to stimulate a cornucopia of images and arguments. Another is to let students practice the art of evaluating competing views and forming their own opinions. As one judge observed about controversial books, the reactions they elicit are "what makes them worth teaching."[54]

Constraints on teacher expression can send perverse messages to students about how our society really treats the constitutional values we claim to hold dear, as one case that reached the Seventh Circuit illustrates. If widely known, the result in Mayer v. Monroe County Community School Board, decided in 2007, would squelch student curiosity, restrain honest exchange in the classroom, and, disregarding *Barnette*'s warning, send a message that "important principles of our government" are nothing more than "mere platitudes."[55]

Like most teachers, Deborah Mayer made spontaneous decisions every day about how to respond to unanticipated questions from students. Her school district failed to differentiate among a teacher's forthright answer to a student's legitimate question about the subject under discussion, a prepared lecture, and a teacher's promotion of her own convictions.

In 2003, students in Mayer's combined fourth-, fifth-, and sixth-grade class read about antiwar demonstrations as part of Indiana's mandated current events syllabus. During the discussion, a student asked Mayer whether she had ever "participated in political demonstrations." Mayer responded that "when she passes a demonstration against this nation's military operations in Iraq," she honked her car horn to show support. The school declined to renew her contract after some parents complained that she had shared antiwar views with the class.[56]

The child's earnest question put Mayer in a difficult spot. Mayer answered truthfully, confining the discussion to a few brief moments. She testified that she had reminded the children that "it was important for people to seek out peaceful solutions to problems," as they are taught "on the playground so that they can seek out peaceful solutions to their own problems and so that they won't fight and hurt each other."[57]

After this incident, the school clarified that teachers could not "promote any particular view on foreign policy." It isn't accurate to say that Mayer "promoted" a view. She merely answered a child's question. She made it clear that she was describing what she had done, not what everyone does or should do. Experts on child development agree that most elementary school children could understand that a teacher's response to that question concerned only what she herself had done or believed.[58] Mayer never suggested that students should share her views or that her position represented a community consensus about the war in Iraq.

What if Mayer had anticipated the student's precise question and asked an attorney for advice about how to handle it, saying that above all she wants to teach her students well? It isn't at all clear what the lawyer should tell her because her only legally protected option is silence and all alternatives open to her are bad as a matter of pedagogy.

Mayer could have lied to her students and simply told them that she never participated, although doing so would have been dishonest. Saying "no" would also have conveyed a point of view—either that she supported the war or that the right of assembly is disfavored and respectable people don't exercise it.

Another option might have been to tell her students truthfully that she wasn't allowed to answer the question. That response would have undermined the whole notion of inquiring minds by placing some serious questions off limits. Students wouldn't know what other questions might be forbidden. Declining to answer (or suggesting that this question would be more appropriate in private after class) would have amounted to saying there was something shameful in either participating or not participating, depending on what Mayer was hiding. Even worse, it would have conveyed that citizens might have the right to express their opinions but they should be wary about disclosing their views. Students would learn to fear the consequences if others condemn their beliefs.

The trial court and the Seventh Circuit both found that the First Amendment did not protect Mayer's classroom speech. They ruled that the school could fire her even if it did so in response to one comment she made in class. The appellate panel held that in the Seventh Circuit schools may discipline or fire teachers for what they say in their classrooms.

Writing for a unanimous appellate court, eminent conservative judge Frank Easterbrook took a very narrow view of the teacher as a person who merely transmits the state's message: "[T]he school system does not 'regulate' teachers' speech as much as it 'hires' that speech. Expression," he explained, "is a teacher's stock in trade, the commodity she sells to her employer in exchange for a salary." At its starkest, this suggests that teachers are like taxis—the driver must follow the route the patron designates. Teachers, the argument goes, understood the bargain when they accepted the job.[59]

Judge Easterbrook conceded that a risk of indoctrination to majority viewpoints exists in closely controlled classrooms. But he urged that power to indoctrinate "should be reposed" in the elected school board whose members can be voted out of office, not left to "teachers' idiosyncratic perspectives."[60]

Some other judges agree. One court expressly stated that schools need "enhanced control" over what teachers say in the classroom. Another went further, contemplating that the potential to "influenc[e] young minds" argues against entrusting teachers with even minor curricular choices.[61]

If the Speech Clause protected what teachers say in class, teachers' unauthorized classroom speech admittedly could prove problematic to parents of every stripe. Approaching a more permissive regime for teacher expression through what legal scholars refer to as a Rawlsian "veil of ignorance" in which we don't know in advance what a teacher's values or views will be helps clarify some of the potential issues. Would each parent take the risk-avoiding strategy of constraining teachers on the hunch that teachers may have different ideological slants than the parent? Or would parents opt for robust debate, despite the risk that a teacher might deliver a political diatribe in class, evincing distain for other viewpoints?

One can think of some wise and perhaps less charged boundaries as well. Teachers shouldn't share too much about their personal lives (as one did when she read sixth graders a poem she wrote about sex with her husband) or avoid the curriculum in favor of their personal interests (like my high school history teacher who preferred to tell us about opera).

At a minimum, I propose that students would benefit if school districts allowed teachers to bring in scholarship representing a range of views about matters the curriculum covers, an approach entirely in keeping with the vision in *Barnette* and *Tinker.*

Student Contributions to Classroom Inquiry

Taking a closer look at whether the First Amendment requires the state to allow individuals—this time students, not teachers—to propose (or even allude to) narratives that challenge its lessons illuminates the risk to pluralist democracy when schools assert authority over classroom dialogue. As I shall demonstrate, no sustainable interpretation of *Hazelwood* supports the expansive claim that student speech in response to classroom lessons is school sponsored, not least of all because no reasonable person could attribute the students' ideas to the school.

Keep in mind that *Tinker*'s fundamental constitutional guarantees have never been repudiated, including the affirmation that students "may not be regarded as closed-circuit recipients of only that which the state chooses to communicate" in class.[62] Given the severe constraints under which teachers operate, the marketplace of ideas in classrooms may depend on whether students have a constitutional right to share what they have learned from any number of sources, including their families, subcultures, and every sort of media. The hard-fought disagreements over curricular decisions about topics like sex education, evolution, and ethnic studies that have received so much attention form the backdrop for disputes over students' expressive rights in many communities.

Tinker took student speech rights within the classroom as a given. The classroom cacophony of viewpoints was the starting point for *Tinker's* analysis. Speech rights, the Supreme Court made clear, "do not embrace *merely the classroom hours,*" and are *"not confine[d] . . . to* supervised and ordained discussion in *a classroom setting.*"[63] The initial question was how far speech rights extended beyond the classroom.

Morse implies that the state must tolerate competing views on most topics. Otherwise the Supreme Court would not have had to invent a new rule directed at speech that undermined one particular message: Don't use illegal substances. One could infer that the narrowness of *Morse* means the "marketplace of ideas" requires schools to endure a student's comments on the decimation of Native American people and culture during a class on the happy Thanksgiving celebration even though the comments undermine the school district's message.

Justice Stevens, however, dissenting in *Morse,* read the Chief Justice's opinion with alarm. He accused the majority of being "deaf to the constitutional imperative to permit unfettered debate, even among high school students." A "rule," Justice Stevens continued, "that permits only one point of view to be expressed is less likely to produce correct answers than the open discussion of countervailing views." And, quoting *Tinker,* he reminded us, "'our Constitution says we must take that risk.'"[64]

Justice Brennan had anticipated exactly this deafness when he dissented in *Hazelwood.* He warned that "free student expression undoubtedly sometimes interferes" with the school's pedagogical message, pointing to the subversive retort in social science class that "socialism is good" and to the scamp who trumpets his "sexual escapade[s]," who today could be seen as undermining a school's abstinence-only curriculum. "If," Justice Brennan admonished, "mere incompatibility with the school's pedagogical message were a constitutionally sufficient justification for the suppression of student speech, school officials could . . . convert[] our public schools into 'enclaves of totalitarianism.'"[65]

Some readers may harbor concerns about the risk that classrooms will devolve into chaos. Recognizing that students are entitled to challenge official interpretations does not mean that they may turn a classroom's "marketplace of ideas" into a Tower of Babel. Nothing in the Supreme Court's student speech doctrine overturns the educational norm that teachers set the agenda in class (pursuant to the state's instructions) and evaluate student expression.[66] There is no First Amendment right to "spout off," ignore the question, or give the wrong answer.

A school's claim that *Hazelwood* applies to student speech in class merges several disparate kinds of expression. Student speech within the core curriculum arises in a number of contexts, including submissions in response to assignments or exams, a student's voluntary contribution to class discussion, and asking a question.

Responses to assignments can be held to rigid demands. For example, the Sixth Circuit ruled in Settle v. Dickson County School Board that a student had no basis for challenging a grade after she failed to comply with the terms of an assignment. The teacher had told students to choose a topic they were unfamiliar with, submit the topic for advance approval, and use at least four sources; Settle didn't fulfill any of those requirements when she submitted a biography of Jesus. "The bottom line," Judge Batchelder explained, "is that when a teacher makes an assignment . . . the student has no constitutional right to do something other than that assignment" if she expects credit for it.[67]

Students are free to share their views in papers and exams as long as they remain responsive to the lesson plan and demonstrate that they have learned what the lesson was designed to teach. A student who rejects the concept of evolution may, for instance, be required to master the lessons taught in biology class. Students might salve their consciences by careful phrasing, although this has not been tested in court. A student could protect her integrity by prefacing her answers with phrases like "the authors of our textbook state . . ."

Courses vary in how much room they offer for students to express their individuality. Two plus two will always be four—at least in traditional math. Subjects and verbs must agree. In other areas of study, such as literature or social studies, a range of perspectives is almost inevitable.

Students' responses to the teacher's verbal questions and their voluntary offerings in class discussion can be confined to the topic at hand, but free expression is undermined when students are corralled into one authorized approach to a topic. A student in social studies class should be able to challenge the assertion that "real democracies never have disputed elections" (if the student cites the long-contested 2000 presidential race resolved by the Supreme Court in Gore v. Bush or the eight-month battle to determine the winner in the 2008 U.S. Senate race in Minnesota between Al Franken and Norm Coleman) or even to argue that, if the assertion is correct, the United States is a failed democracy.

All of these examples occur within "school itself." When students challenge restrictions on their own core curricular speech, *Tinker*—not *Hazelwood*—should be the standard. The school will likely prevail under *Tinker* if the student has not fulfilled educational requirements. The First Amendment, as the *Hazelwood* majority observed, does not stand in the way of educators ensuring "that participants learn whatever lessons the activity is designed to teach." Justice Brennan's riposte, "[that is] the essence of the *Tinker* test, not an excuse to abandon it," remains true today.[68] It should be far easier for a school to show that a student's comments in class disrupted learning than to demonstrate that student expression in the cafeteria did so.

At first glance, the assertion some schools make that all classroom speech is school sponsored seems to fit because *Hazelwood* concerned curricular expression. It seems a simple proposition that what goes on in class is curricular. But that is just the beginning of the inquiry into school sponsorship.

Students' classroom expression doesn't fit within the definition of school-sponsored speech for a number of reasons. For a start, imagine if the school had punished the little girl who asked Mayer about antiwar demonstrations on the ground that the student's speech was "school sponsored." It is hard to credit the idea that any observer would conclude that the school had reviewed and approved the girl's question. If the school disciplined the student who asked the question, a parent would likely respond, "Really? You punished my daughter for being engaged in the material and asking a serious question?"

Faced with this hypothetical, a judge would need to ask whether the girl's speech fit the definition of "school sponsored" and, if so, whether the school's reprimand was "reasonably related to a legitimate pedagogical goal."

This leads to a related hypothetical courts have yet to confront. What if the students in Mayer's class had been prevented from addressing the same question to one another? "Has anyone here been to a demonstration?" And what if third grader Paul Tinker were silenced or punished when he attempted to reply, "Sure, my family goes to antiwar demonstrations all the time"?

As these musings suggest, the most significant—almost insurmountable—hurdle to finding students' classroom expression is school sponsored is that it fails to meet the imprimatur requirement. Even very young students aren't likely to assume that a peer's speech represents the official ideas of the school. No one knows in advance what will come out of a student's mouth, as I pointed out when discussing the irrationality of holding teachers responsible for their students' profanity. Students learn quickly that their peers do not always give correct or even appropriate responses in class.[69]

The school cannot be said to "sponsor" such speech in the sense of approving it unless the teacher adopts the point of view as her own. When common sense fails, it is relatively easy for a teacher to remind students that controversial speech by their peers expresses the speaker's own views or, if accurate, that the student's belief has no evidentiary basis, as in "no scientist agrees that the moon is made of cheese."

Classroom speech by students fails to satisfy *Hazelwood*'s imprimatur requirement for another reason: Classroom comments rarely go beyond the four walls of the site. Students may repeat what their peers say in class, but that hardly amounts to publication or endorsement by the school. As with lewd speech, student curricular writings usually occur in private exchanges between the student and teacher. There is no reason to anticipate that the broader community will ever hear the views. Student speech in the core curriculum doesn't reach a larger audience that might mistake the student's ideas for expression bearing the school's imprimatur.[70]

Despite the mismatch between the imprimatur requirement and classroom expression, some courts have accepted school officials' assertions that *Hazelwood* governs classroom speech—allowing censorship of student speech at the heart of the educational mission. The Sixth Circuit, for example, concluded that a student's submission in response to an assignment was "part of the class curriculum and was, therefore, school-sponsored expression."[71]

This position authorizes schools to control everyone's contributions to educational discussions, whether among peers or between the teacher and individual students. It allows schools to assert not only that they control the curriculum but also that they control responses to the curriculum. In this vein, schools have claimed that school sponsorship is triggered when a student performs material of her own choosing at a talent show and when students present at show-and-tell—an exercise even the youngest children understand from their own experience allows students to choose topics they find personally compelling.[72]

The argument that peers could attribute extemporaneous student speech to the school itself is not limited to any particular subject matter, even though the cases so far have largely involved student expression about or rooted in religion. The justifications schools offer in these cases are not limited to concerns that students might believe the district endorsed private religious beliefs.

Even if a school satisfied the imprimatur requirement as applied to student speech in the core curriculum, it would have great difficulty establishing a legitimate pedagogical reason for cutting off inquiring minds, diverse views, and robust debate in classrooms. Martin H. Redish and Kevin Finnerty make the provocative argument that compulsory education in public schools in the United States does not differ significantly from indoctrination in totalitarian societies. Students, they say, "are exposed for the bulk of the day only to the viewpoints of authoritarian governmental agents in school classrooms." Because of this closed and hierarchical environment "schools present a uniquely dangerous form of government speech of the type traditionally utilized by totalitarian societies as a means for destroying citizen mental autonomy."[73] Unlike totalitarian societies, however, our educational system rests on an assumption that autonomy is essential to seeking a meaningful life and to exercising citizenship rights.

School districts or states that want to preserve unfettered debate in classrooms in order to encourage critical thinking could adopt a simple rule to clarify their intent to avoid indoctrination: Students have the right to offer opinions backed by age-appropriate evidence in the classroom unless their expression threatens material disruption or invades the rights of others. Such a rule would make explicit what an accurate reading of school speech doctrine already requires.

Room for Difference: Viewpoint Discrimination in School-Sponsored Speech

If more judges were ultimately to construe student classroom speech as school sponsored, the risk of indoctrination would turn on whether the courts also decide that viewpoint discrimination is permitted when schools regulate what is in essence their own speech. In *Dean,* the case involving the news story about the idling school buses, the judge ruled that disagreement with a student's point of view could never be a legitimate pedagogical ground for censorship. That's the law in some parts of the country, but in others it remains an open question whether the normal First Amendment categorical bar on viewpoint discrimination applies within school-sponsored expression.

In contrast to *Barnette* and *Tinker,* both of which reiterated the fundamental importance of a free exchange of ideas and a right to disagree with prevailing wisdom, *Hazelwood* didn't address whether students could dispute the school's messages in school-sponsored venues. The Supreme Court didn't need to consider whether a desire to repress a student's opinion could ever be a "legitimate" pedagogical goal because Hazelwood East High School conceded that viewpoint discrimination would have violated the student journalists' First Amendment rights. If *Hazelwood* had announced that schools could not discriminate among viewpoints when regulating school-sponsored speech, the assertion that students' classroom expression is like the school's own would be less troubling.

Once again, Justice Brennan's *Hazelwood* dissent called the majority to task, implying that his brethren were wearing blinders. He believed that the principal had in fact censored the article on birth control precisely because it encouraged students to learn about and exercise their options. The "case before us," Justice Brennan wrote, "aptly illustrates how readily school officials (and courts) can camouflage viewpoint discrimination as the 'mere' protection of students from sensitive topics. . . . The mere fact of school sponsorship does not, as the Court suggests, license such thought control."[74]

Although the Supreme Court has never decided whether viewpoint discrimination in regulating student school-sponsored expression violates the Speech Clause, Chief Justice Roberts offered his own take on this question in *Morse*. After ruling that Frederick's banner didn't appear to be approved by the school, he opined that a school "doesn't have to tolerate at school events" viewpoints that undermine its own message. Dissenting, Justice Stevens fired back (correctly in my view) that this trivialization of cardinal principles "invites stark viewpoint discrimination."[75]

As an appellate judge in 2000, Justice Alito rejected the position the Chief Justice would espouse in 2007.[76] Alito argued that viewpoint discrimination offends the Constitution regardless of where the speech falls within the taxonomy of student speech. He urged that where a judge finds viewpoint discrimination against student speech—even in the classroom—the judge should set aside the special doctrine that governs school speech and apply strict scrutiny.[77]

But some school officials are oblivious to constitutional norms. One principal in Connecticut, for example, freely admitted that he canceled a drama workshop about the experiences of Iraq War veterans because of his discomfort with its antiwar "point of view."[78] If Chief Justice Roberts were correct that schools can censor viewpoints that conflict with their preferred messages, a student could be prevented from arguing that Bradley (now Chelsea)

Manning or Edward Snowden, each of whom leaked classified government documents, served the public interest or, alternatively, depending on the school district's message, is a traitor.

Viewpoint discrimination in classrooms is hardly new. My editor at Harvard University Press recalls his own experience at the outbreak of the Korean War, around the same time as Ethel and Julius Rosenberg were charged with being Soviet spies, when he brought what he had learned at the family dinner table to share with classmates during show-and-tell. He suggested that the South Korean government had provoked North Korea, and he doubted that the Rosenbergs were guilty. Classmates understood the teacher's response—"Whose side are you on?"—as an invitation to pummel the young dissident after school. He didn't find himself in a haven for nonconformists.

Schools sometimes prohibit student speech with a religious "point of view" in and outside of the classroom. C.H. v. Oliva, the case that prompted Justice Alito's comments on viewpoint discrimination, arose when a school temporarily removed a kindergartener's poster from the display of all the posters the class produced on the Thanksgiving theme "what I am thankful for." Zachary was "thankful for Jesus," a choice the school deemed inappropriate. His teacher later restored the poster but in a much less prominent position. While the public display of a poster might lead some observers to assume it bore the school's imprimatur, the context and the assignment itself made clear to all observers that the views it contained were Zachary's alone (or Zachary's and his mother's, as the facts suggested).

The Third Circuit, reviewing the case en banc, could not determine whether the removal and relocation amounted to viewpoint discrimination or, if it did, whether viewpoint discrimination in a school display violated the Constitution. The judges left the question unresolved.[79]

Analogizing schools to other institutions highlights the radicalism of the claim that schools can regulate viewpoints in school-sponsored speech. The adjective *reasonable* attached to viewpoint discrimination is a constitutional non sequitur, impossible to imagine in any context other than a total institution such as the military or a prison, although, as several scholars have pointed out, "students, soldiers and prisoners" are often lumped together as the occupants of total institutions in which civil liberties may be severely compromised to serve strong competing government interests.[80]

It is difficult or impossible to create a total institution in a public school. Unlike prisoners, students leave at the end of every day. Schools compete with family, peer culture, and media influences for the student's identity and values, a reality that is often reflected when students themselves speak in class.

The analogy is not as far-fetched as it may appear, however, because the Rehnquist Court expressly analogized minors to prisoners. Chief Justice Rehnquist proposed that children have diminished expectations of liberty because "juveniles, unlike adults, are always in some form of custody"—their parents' or the state's.[81] His characterization of the relationship between the young and the Constitution conflicts starkly with the view that prevailed in *Barnette* and *Tinker:* Children too are persons entitled to liberty.

An asserted parallel between students and prisoners, and schools and prisons, is deeply disturbing and deeply flawed. Unlike prisoners or soldiers, students are neither lawbreakers nor volunteers. They are not in school because they broke the law or because they enlisted or because of any trait in their control. Students attend school because the law requires them to submit to educational authority based on the number of years since their birth. Schools also differ from prisons and armies because they are tasked with teaching, among other things, a capacity for analytic thinking—a form of inquiry that requires the thinker to examine and question the basis of assertions made by authority figures. Unlike prisons, schools are also expected to teach constitutional rights, respect for rights, and how to exercise rights, all of which are best accomplished by "honoring rights."[82]

The appellate courts display the same division as the Justices over whether *Hazelwood* permits "reasonable" viewpoint discrimination. Most courts that have directly ruled on the question have refused to take *Hazelwood*'s silence as a green light for schools to censor student speech based on its viewpoint.[83]

The Second Circuit announced its own demanding standard: "[A] manifestly viewpoint discriminatory restriction on school-sponsored speech is, prima facie, unconstitutional, *even if* reasonably related to legitimate pedagogical interests."[84] This means that in New York and Connecticut, censorship violates the Constitution if disapproval of the student's viewpoint played *any* role in the decision, no matter how reasonable other pedagogical reasons for barring a student's school-sponsored speech might be.

While educators and trial courts in judicial circuits that have not yet spoken await clarification, they might find guidance about how to tell a "legitimate" pedagogical concern from an "illegitimate" one in Justice Brennan's 1982 plurality opinion in Island Trees Board of Education v. Pico. *Island Trees* raised the question what constitutional limits if any apply to a school's decision to remove books from the library collection because of their content. Justice Brennan offered this standard: It is constitutionally permissible to remove books based on the "educational suitability" of the content, but it violates the Speech Clause to remove books in order to suppress disfavored ideas.

Fleshing out that test, Justice Brennan suggested that "educational suitability" includes criteria such as "'good taste,' 'relevance' and 'appropriateness to age and grade level.'" Removing materials because they include "unpopular" ideas or for "narrowly partisan or political" reasons is classic viewpoint discrimination that requires closer scrutiny.[85]

This approach could be usefully adapted to *Hazelwood*'s reasonableness standard to help school administrators and courts evaluate whether a proffered pedagogical ground for censorship is "legitimate" or violates the First Amendment. In the process, the test could help to constrain stark viewpoint discrimination in classrooms, publications, and performances.

It could also help to avert the potential danger manifested in current trends. If the Supreme Court were to adopt Chief Justice Roberts's stance on viewpoint discrimination at school, officials would be unleashed to openly censor students based on politics, values, or criticism of the school's message and personnel. If more schools assert that speech in classrooms is school sponsored and convince more courts that there is no room for questioning or deviating "from the official viewpoints of state authorities," as the judge in *Dean* put it, classrooms could become precisely the closed-circuit environments the First Amendment forbids.[86] The resulting indoctrination, immune from challenge, would surely subvert critical thinking, democratic values, and the skills needed for citizenship.

PART III

Tinker Redux

CHAPTER 5

Unsettled Waters

Attacks on Pure Student Speech

> [We] sail into the unsettled waters of free speech rights in public
> schools, waters rife with rocky shoals and uncertain currents.
>
> —Guiles v. Marineau (2d Cir. 2006)

In 2003, an Indiana high school unlawfully prevented David
Griggs from wearing a T-shirt that recited the text of the "Creed of the
Marines," an ode to the Marines' M-16 rifle, and displayed a picture of the
gun. Griggs had donned the shirt to show his support for U.S. troops
overseas.[1]

At about the same time in Vermont, a middle school trampled on First
Amendment rights when it disciplined Zachary Guiles for wearing a T-shirt
critical of President George W. Bush, his leadership, and his history of substance abuse. The shirt called Bush "a chicken-hawk president and . . . a
former alcohol and cocaine abuser." It showed "three lines of cocaine and a
razor blade" as well as a portrait of Bush holding a martini glass. Phrases
including "AWOL: Draft Dodger" and "Lying Drunk Driver" were peppered about the shirt.[2]

These two incidents had much in common. Both shirts bore silent political speech, clearly protected under *Tinker*. Both schools had rules barring
the subject matter of the shirts, which the schools construed variously as
reaching images of guns and drugs. Both schools censored the shirts and
sent the boys home. And both boys successfully sued to vindicate their
speech rights in federal courts, as I will explain later in this chapter.[3]

At a minimum, *Tinker*'s demanding constitutional standard applies (in
Hazelwood's words) to all of a "student's personal expression that happens
to occur on school premises." In this severely shrunken territory of what
I call "pure" student speech—speech that isn't school sponsored, lewd, or

129

pro-drug—school officials continue to attack student expression. Rampant doctrinal confusion allows some of them to get away with it.

Teachers, administrators, and boards of education often display complete ignorance of what the Constitution requires. One might think that West Virginia v. Barnette settled once and for all that children don't have to say the Pledge of Allegiance in school, but students are labeled defiant when they assert their right not to participate. Remarkably, the son of one of the Barnette sisters was sent to the principal's office for doing exactly what his mother had done. She recalled, "[M]y older son was sent to the office for not saluting the flag. The principal came back and said your teacher obviously doesn't remember the Supreme Court decision."[4]

So too, when a Dearborn, Michigan, high school principal told yet another high school student he couldn't wear a shirt that called President George W. Bush an "International Terrorist," she claimed the shirt promoted terrorism. Worse, she relied on Justice Black's dissent in *Tinker*, declaring that the decision gave schools "the right to control speech."[5]

In this chapter, I consider four contemporary threats to *Tinker*'s expansive ruling. First, school officials fail to recognize expression, including symbols and communicative conduct, as speech that the First Amendment protects. Second, schools remain confused about how to categorize each speech event in order to identify the appropriate constitutional standard and urge courts to use any test other than *Tinker*. Third, administrators too quickly label as "threatening" speech that has no credible link to a risk of violence. Fourth, school officials endeavor to stretch the meaning of material disruption to cover the most minor inconvenience or distraction. In each instance it is hard to tell whether actions that undermine *Tinker* stem primarily from confusion, willful ignorance, or manipulation.

A final danger runs throughout in the form of befuddled and reluctant judges. Justice Breyer has lamented that the lower courts find the law governing student speech "complex and often difficult to apply."[6] Sometimes judges completely miss the mark, getting the law wrong or applying it incorrectly to the facts. When they err in either way, they send confusing messages to school officials. In other instances, judges seem disinclined to balance rights against the specter of school shootings, however remote the risks in any given case.

The Threat to an Expansive Definition of Protected Expression

The first threat to *Tinker*'s vibrancy today stems from educators' failure to recognize the universe of expression that the Supreme Court acknowledged as protected speech in 1969. Even after the Court rounded out the quintet of decisions that govern student speech today, *Hazelwood*'s own framing of *Tinker* preserves personal student expression as immune from school censorship absent a reasonable apprehension of material disruption or a showing that the speech collides with the rights of others.

But some schools deny that symbols and conduct constitute expression. Other schools and even some judges (including Chief Justice Roberts) would limit the speech *Tinker* protects to expression officials acknowledge offers a political viewpoint.

When students challenge a school's suppression of their speech, the first question that courts must resolve is whether the students were "speaking" within the meaning of the First Amendment. Words, whether spoken, written, or set to music, are always speech. *Tinker* itself involved symbolic speech—a black armband, widely understood as a symbol of protest against the war in Vietnam. The Court had long recognized the value of "symbolism" such as the Christian cross as a "short cut from mind to mind," as *Barnette* had put it. So too *Tinker* described black armbands as "the type of symbolic act that is within the Free Speech Clause" and treated them as "closely akin to 'pure speech.'"[7]

In 1969, when the Court decided *Tinker*, it had not yet expressly addressed the conditions under which symbols or conduct amount to expression protected by the First Amendment. A few years later, in 1974, the Supreme Court defined symbolic speech in Spence v. Washington, and it elaborated on the treatment of symbolic speech in its 1989 decision in Texas v. Johnson. Symbolic speech and expressive conduct have constitutional protection if the person engaging in the expression intends to communicate a particular message and if it is likely that those who view the conduct will understand the idea it conveys.[8]

Students sometimes fail to convince authorities that they are engaging in protected speech at school even when they use words. For example, if the school is located in a judicial circuit that limits *Tinker*'s reach to overtly political speech, officials may dismiss students' views about school governance, refusing to accept that the expression has political implications and may not be silenced. Students may be unable to persuade the principal or, later, a judge that this local politics resembles the antiwar speech at issue in *Tinker.* Some judges have held that schools did not violate student rights when officials banned T-shirts that challenged school dress codes or boasted about being in a gifted students program.[9]

Tinker differentiated passive communicative expression from what it rather dismissively referred to as "regulation of the length of skirts or the type of clothing, [or] hair style." Those were hotly contested issues during the boisterous 1960s when girls first wore miniskirts and pants to school and boys showed up in ponytails or with facial hair. Courts upholding administrative decisions about how students present themselves regularly cite *Tinker*'s offhand comment that the armbands at issue in that case were far more important than controversies over the length of boys' hair and girls' miniskirts.[10]

However dismissive the Supreme Court was, historian Jo Paoletti has shown that disputes over student appearance had at their core serious disagreements about culture, politics, and nonconformity, including challenges to expectations about gender. Schools expected girls to dress "modestly," which remains a theme in disputes seen today in photoshopped cover-ups of girl's décolleté and shoulders in yearbook pictures. Boys were expected not only to look like boys but to comply with rules in preparation for their roles in the adult world. Roughly eighty lawsuits have been filed over these issues since 1965, and the Supreme Court has repeatedly declined to review the decisions.[11]

There is no constitutional right to an exemption from a school dress code in order to express one's individuality—to say "I have rights" without a more particularized message. Students do not engage in protected speech when they refuse to obey a school dress code as a matter of principle, wear pajama bottoms to school, or violate rules by showing up with numerous body piercings. A girl who violated a school code barring hats by wearing an African headdress to school in 1998, for example, failed to convince a court that others would understand her cultural message. The court arguably should have entertained the possibility that many of her peers would have understood the position she was staking out about her Afro-Caribbean heritage.[12]

In each of these instances, courts found that the conduct conveyed an insufficiently clear message to warrant First Amendment protection. Where conduct fails to communicate, schools may regulate it for any reason that doesn't violate constitutional or statutory bans on discrimination.

Building on the concept of conduct as speech, courts have more recently recognized the potentially expressive aspects of clothing choices related to identity and identity politics. So, for example, a teenage boy who wanted to wear female clothing to a school dance was engaging in protected expression of "a particularized message, namely her [*sic*] identification with the female gender." In contrast, an adult woman who wanted to wear a skirt to work rather than the pants that were part of her uniform was not engaging in protected expression because her choice of attire did not send a particularized message that anyone would understand.[13]

Students engage in protected symbolic speech when they display widely understood symbols of culture or ethnicity. For Native Americans, protected symbolic speech includes wearing traditional tribal dress or long braided hair; Southerners so inclined engage in protected speech when they display the Confederate flag, as do African American students who display a picture of Malcolm X.[14]

Outside of school, expressive conduct receives slightly less protection than expression that takes the form of words. In 1968, ruling on the case of United States v. O'Brien, an appeal of a conviction for burning a draft card, the Supreme Court articulated its approach to regulations aimed at conduct that cause an "incidental restriction on alleged First Amendment freedoms." Most important, if the regulation that impinges on expression actually addresses conduct rather than speech (littering as opposed to pamphleteering), it need only further a "substantial government interest" (not a "compelling" one). Admittedly, it can be difficult or nigh impossible to sort out the communication from the conduct.[15]

But school officials don't need to worry about the *O'Brien* approach to expressive conduct. *Tinker* did not consider whether educators' restrictions on conduct that incidentally diminishes expression should be evaluated under a distinct standard. It didn't need to because students' verbal expression already receives diminished constitutional protections compared with speech by adults in the world at large.

In school, rules that apply to everyone and do not clearly target any particular expression may legitimately restrict expression that qualifies as symbolic speech. For example, a school dress code may ban all words and symbols on clothing and require shirts with collars if the regulation is not designed to constrict debate, even though it suppresses potential communication. The government's asserted interest may be order, discouraging competition and distraction, or fostering a respectful attitude through more formal attire. Indeed, 19 percent of schools required students to wear uniforms in 2009–2010, up from 12 percent a decade earlier.[16]

Schools may also ban all head coverings, including hats, baseball caps, and scarves, but may not single out scarves worn by Muslim girls or skullcaps and kippahs worn by religious Muslim and Jewish boys—at least under federal law, though state law may provide greater protections for religious expression. Whether insisting that those who wish to express their religious beliefs obey rules that were designed for everyone without reference to religious exercise amounts to wise social policy in a diverse nation is a separate question from what the Speech Clause permits or forbids.

Schools may also expressly target selected communicative conduct such as gang colors or symbols to control organized antisocial behavior without offending the Constitution. In schools with histories of gang involvement, such paraphernalia always threatens material disruption. No court to my knowledge has overturned a dress code aimed at controlling gang symbols.

Too often, schools punish potentially expressive conduct that doesn't pose any threat of disruption, such as thirty seconds or so of doing the Harlem Shake, a suggestive dance that took off as an Internet meme in 2013. According to the National Coalition Against Censorship, more than one hundred students around the country have been suspended for making videos of themselves doing the Harlem Shake during free time. Is the Shake just teenage high jinks or protected expression? Some adult Harlem Shakers have used the meme as political speech. These include "Team Mitch," campaign volunteers for Republican House Majority Leader Mitch McConnell, who posted a Harlem Shake video outside the Kentucky Derby site on March 6, 2013, and many Egyptians who performed the Shake that same year at demonstrations calling for President Morsi's resignation while chanting, "Leave, leave."[17] Unaccompanied by words, dancing students' messages may not be transparent—other than (perhaps) "We are young, and we want to be free."

And yet, the powerful expressive component of such displays was unmistakable in 2014 when the Iranian government briefly jailed six young people for posting a video of their take on Pharrell Williams's international sensation "Happy," this time "Happy in Teheran," which received more than 150,000 views before authorities acted and well over a million views after the government arrested the filmmakers. Equally revealing was the outpouring of outrage in the United States and elsewhere over this censorship. Were the performers seeking or abusing looser government scrutiny? Was there a political subtext? No matter how imprecise the message, residents of the free world rallied to support the right to express it. Absent a threat of material disruption, freedom of expression requires that schools tolerate similar joyous outbursts.

Schools permissibly regulate other forms of conduct that has an expressive component, such as "inappropriate public displays of affection," as long as the school enforces its rules evenhandedly and allows other means of communicating the same sentiment. Readers who are not lawyers may be wondering why this even merits discussion, but challenges to such rules have reached federal courts.

Displays of affection such as French kissing, groping, or entwined bodies certainly convey easily understood messages. A school may control such communicative conduct if it enforces the policy against both heterosexual and same-sex couples. A comparable message may be sent, as one judge pointed out, by "holding hands, quick kisses, short hugs, and putting arms around each other." If same-sex couples claim to be making a political statement about equal rights by displaying greater ardor, they will have to find another means for spreading their message. The judge cogently concluded that general rules barring physical displays of affection did not violate the First Amendment rights of two romantically involved girls because explicit sexual behavior at school is inherently disruptive. It is, the judge underscored, "inconsistent with the focus of a school: to learn."[18]

Default or Last Resort? Threats to *Tinker* as the Governing Standard

Chapters 3 and 4 showed that disputes over the standards that govern judicial review of school censorship are fiercely contested, largely because the choice of standard generally determines the substantive outcome. The second threat to *Tinker*'s vitality comes from challenges to its position as the default rule—the rule that applies unless a school can persuade a judge that one of the exceptions has been triggered.

After students have convinced a court that the First Amendment protects their expression, the court must classify the speech within the school speech taxonomy of *Tinker, Fraser, Hazelwood,* and *Morse* in order to determine the correct legal standard. Most lower courts agree with Justice Alito that *Tinker* provides the legal standard under which courts should review allegations that schools have violated students' speech rights unless one of the exceptions specified in the three subsequent Supreme Court cases applies.[19]

The Third Circuit, for example, presumes that *Tinker* governs all school speech cases unless an exception proves otherwise. The stringent limits on school authority set out in *Tinker* apply after the court eliminates each of the carve-outs (*Fraser, Hazelwood,* and *Morse*) in turn.[20] Under this approach, *Tinker*'s doctrine provides a standing safety net for student speakers.

As with *sans-gêne* expression and sentiments officials wish to control under the guise they might be seen as the school's own, officials sometimes fail to identify the right legal standard before they respond to pure student speech. And, after the fact, schools regularly argue that their actions should be judged under any standard other than *Tinker* because it is the hardest standard for the school to satisfy and the one most likely to result in the court ruling against the school. In one incomprehensible episode, a school claimed authority under *Morse* to prevent a student from handing out invitations to a church Christmas party, though no one suggested a link to illegal substances. It's hardly surprising that judges did not find the school's argument credible.[21]

Despite the dominant regime under which *Tinker* remains the lodestar, some judicial circuits take a constricted view of *Tinker*'s scope. Those courts ask whether *Tinker* can be ruled out as the standard for the controversy before them rather than using *Tinker* as the default position. Judges accept schools' invitations to squeeze the case into other frameworks—*Fraser, Hazelwood,* or *Morse*—even when the facts don't fit the rubric. One court accepted the expansive claim that *Morse* allowed officials to punish any speech that raises the specter of "mass school-shootings," and others have applied similar reasoning.[22]

Sometimes courts scrunch parts of different tests into unrecognizable doctrines. This tendency led one appellate court to chastise a trial judge for accepting a school's rationale that "conflate[d] the rule of *Hazelwood* with *Fraser,* and, in doing so, eviscerates *Tinker.*"[23]

As a result, some lower courts punt their obligation to scrutinize deprivations of student speech. Even worse, as constitutional scholar Erwin Chemerinksy has charged, the lower courts have shown a growing tendency to ignore all of the Supreme Court's school speech doctrines. Certain judges defer to any reasonable decision made by school officials. On more than one occasion, judges have discarded legal doctrine altogether and analyzed student speech claims under the standard most forgiving to government officials: rational basis review. Rational basis, or reasonableness, is the standard school officials in Des Moines urged the Court to apply in *Tinker,* and the

Court expressly rejected the proposal. Rational basis review lacks even the modest controls inherent in *Hazelwood, Fraser,* and *Morse.* For example, under *Hazelwood,* the rational basis must be grounded in pedagogy. Under *Fraser,* the speech must be lewd.[24]

To circumvent school speech doctrine, a judge might treat a school rule inhibiting speech as permissible under standards drawn from the Speech Clause, which allows content-neutral regulation of the time, place, or manner of speech. First Amendment doctrine also permits the state to limit speech on government-owned property under a public forum analysis that centers on the purpose to which the property is dedicated and whether the state has opened it up for individual expression.

However, the time and place of the school day are simply too broad to permit suppression of all unauthorized speech by young people who are required by law to attend school. Any effort to do so would be likely to resemble what a unanimous Supreme Court condemned in 1987 as a "'First Amendment Free Zone'" when overturning the Los Angeles airport's ban on all "First Amendment activities." The Court rejected the argument that the airport had merely imposed a time, place, and manner restriction, noting that the rule would bar reading and conversation as well as the proselytizing and begging the airport was trying to vanquish.[25] Exactly which parts of student communication would a school's time, place, and manner regulation control?

Although the Court entertained public forum analysis in *Hazelwood,* judicial inquiry into whether a school created a forum for student speech in a particular part of the school conflicts with *Tinker*'s recognition that conversation in the cafeteria and locker room as well as debate in the classroom plays an important role in students' lives. In a handwritten draft, Justice Fortas included a footnote that was omitted from the final opinion in *Tinker,* anticipating the argument that all or part of the campus could be off-limits for student speech: A school, he wrote, "is a public place, and its dedication to specific uses does not imply that the constitutional rights of persons entitled to be there are to be gauged as if the premises were purely private property to which the public has, with some exceptions, only such rights as are specifically granted by the owner, which rights need not include the right to assemble, to demonstrate or to express opinions." To Fortas, a school campus was more like a public park than a private shopping mall (whose landlord may bar leafleting and demonstrations without violating the Constitution), with the distinction that speech at school may not materially disrupt the core function of education.[26]

Morse sowed further confusion about the school speech taxonomy. Chief Justice Roberts complicated an already opaque set of rules by reminding us that the "mode of analysis set forth in *Tinker* is not absolute." His observation that "the rule of *Tinker* is not the only basis for restricting student speech" made a greater impression on certain judges than did the reaffirmation of the *Tinker* line of cases.[27]

Even before *Morse* appeared to open the door, the Sixth Circuit ignored *Tinker's* clear instructions when it opined that schools have broad authority to curtail speech that is "inconsistent with its basic educational mission." This view makes *Tinker* the outlier, not the lodestar. As one Sixth Circuit judge formulated the issue after *Morse*, "[T]he general rule is that school administrators can limit speech in a reasonable fashion to further important policies at the heart of public education. *Tinker* provides the exception— schools cannot go so far as to limit nondisruptive discussion of political or social issues that the administration finds distasteful or wrong."[28] This approach supports school censors who cite educational concerns ranging from preventing bullying to eradicating intolerance. While not always incompatible with the material disruption test, it would go a long way toward obliterating speech rights where no threat of material disruption exists.

If judges have on occasion exhibited confusion or recalcitrance when asked to enforce constitutional protections for student speech, school administrators sometimes seem completely at a loss about what rules govern and when they apply. Let's begin by considering the very simplest cases that resemble the facts in *Tinker* in every respect. Assume this exceedingly narrow definition of the principle enshrined in *Tinker,* drawn from Chief Justice Roberts's opinion in *Morse:* Students who engage in political speech at school through silent symbols and words worn on their bodies or clothing in a manner that neither materially disrupts education nor collides with the rights of others may not be barred from speaking based on their viewpoint. The rule seems pretty clear.

The law seems unambiguous enough that student speech rights should be assured in episodes that fit this description. Not so.

Schools all over the country have prevented and penalized students' symbolic, nondisruptive political expression. I offer five examples, all of which involve black armbands or their analytical equivalent—silent messages about politics on clothing.

First, in 2006, a high school in Arkansas punished students for wearing black armbands to protest a new student dress code. When the students sought injunctive relief, the federal courts viewed the resulting litigation in Lowry v. Watson Chapel School District as identical to *Tinker* in all respects. It made no difference, the Eighth Circuit held, that the protest was directed at a local school board policy instead of "national foreign policy." Upholding the injunction the trial court had issued, the appellate court reiterated that the Constitution does not permit school districts to punish students for a "non-disruptive protest of a government policy." The district paid for trampling on students' rights: The courts ordered the school district to reimburse the students for attorneys' fees and expenses in excess of $55,000 because the "free speech right vindicated" served "all of the students in the school district."[29]

In a second incident, a school in Lynn, Massachusetts, reprimanded a girl in 2012 for wearing a shirt that said, "All the Cool Girls are Lesbians." The school inexplicably reasoned first that the shirt was "political" and then that it could be censored because it was "offensive to some people." The district reportedly backed down after the girl convinced the mayor to look at the law.[30]

Third, a year later, a Connecticut school district forced a boy to remove a T-shirt with an antigay message: a rainbow with a slash through it. After the ACLU threatened legal action, that district also relented.[31]

Fourth, an incident in Des Moines itself, forty years after the events that gave rise to *Tinker*, proves that the Barnettes are not the only ones having Groundhog Day experiences. In 2005, Roosevelt High School—the same school *Tinker* plaintiff Christopher Eckhart attended—told students to cover up antiabortion T-shirts. The principal feared that students who disliked the message that abortion kills babies would become disruptive. The principal quickly rescinded the ban after being reminded of the governing legal principles. Making the most of the coincidence under the headline "History repeats," the Des Moines Register commented: "If other students react in a disruptive way, deal with them."[32]

And, in a final example, a high school in Connecticut censored T-shirts proclaiming "Team Avery" that supported a candidate for a student government office. The school had barred Avery Doninger from running for office as a penalty for an alleged violation of the speech code. Administrators regarded the shirts as a challenge to their authority to bar Avery's candidacy. Remarkably, the Second Circuit ultimately concluded that although the school violated the speech rights of every student who wanted to wear a Team Avery shirt, the administrators were immune from suit because the legal doctrine had not been clear enough in 2010 (forty years after the *Tinker* decision) that educators should have known they were trampling on constitutional rights.[33]

None of the school districts in these controversies pointed to any tangible risk of incipient disruption, much less established a well-founded risk of material disruption. Faced with facts so closely tracking those in *Tinker* and no legal ground that would justify suppressing ideas, either the districts reversed course when confronted with the law or federal courts easily found that the censorship violated the clear doctrine set forth in *Tinker*.[34]

In First Amendment parlance, restrictions and penalties "chill" speech. Speech is chilled when potential speakers just give up—they don't even try to express their ideas because they are afraid of the likely consequences. The chill remains even if the school ultimately reverses course or a court overturns the policy or penalty. This is exactly the wrong lesson for schools—our laboratories for democracy—to teach.

"The Constitution Is Not a Suicide Pact": True Threats and Fears of Violence

Exaggerated fears of links between speech and campus violence pose the third challenge to *Tinker*'s vibrancy. The adults to whom students' safety is entrusted certainly deserve compassion and empathy as they struggle to balance legitimate fears about school violence with individual rights. As Justice Jackson famously observed, the Constitution is not a "suicide pact."[35]

Nothing in even the most liberal interpretation of student speech rights prevents schools from responding vigorously to speech that will likely lead to violence or make reasonable listeners fear for their safety. The recurrent problem is how to tell when threats are concrete enough to justify restrictions on speech. When the risk of violence is real, nothing in the student speech jurisprudence holds school officials back from acting immediately to protect children and teachers.

Speech that raises reasonable fears of violence falls into two categories. The first, known in constitutional law as the "true threat," lies outside the scope of First Amendment protections. It is akin to libel, obscenity, or incitement. The state may ban true threats and prosecute the speaker no matter where the expression takes place.[36] The second lies within the speech at the heart of *Tinker* that appears to threaten material disruption.

I begin with true threats. I then turn to intimations of violence that may threaten material disruption and the interaction between the two categories.

A true threat is not just any threat that meets the dictionary definition; it is "a constitutional term of art." The Supreme Court has defined a true threat as words used "to communicate a serious expression of an intent to commit an act of unlawful violence to a particular individual or groups of individuals."[37]

True threat doctrine is very narrow. It is not intended to deprive jokesters, no matter how ghoulish, of First Amendment protection or to impose penalties for pranks, misunderstandings, or impossibilities. A crude bit of "political hyperbole" to one's buddies (an eighteen-year-old, called for military duty, saying to a small group at a political demonstration, "If they ever make me carry a rifle the first man I want to set my sights on is L.B.J.") isn't a true threat.[38]

Courts have found true threats where adults repeatedly hurled epithets at an abortion clinic doctor and in direct statements such as "I will kill you."[39]

Similarly, the Delaware Supreme Court upheld the delinquency adjudication of a high school student for making true threats to an African American teacher, including, "I have an uncle in the mob and cousins in the KKK and they will string you up in the woods."[40] Few students are so direct.

In 2015, the Supreme Court held that prosecutors must show that the speaker knew "the threatening nature of his communication." If the speaker intended to intimidate, it doesn't matter whether the speaker plans to follow through on the threat; it is nonetheless a "true" one.[41]

When school officials fear that a student has issued a true threat, they can immediately isolate the student, alert law enforcement authorities, and conduct any necessary searches without fear of reprisal even if they turn out to have been mistaken. The doctrine provides a defensive perimeter against school shootings and other violent incidents. Schools can—and must—respond forcefully to protect students and staff whenever students articulate true threats directed at the school, no matter where they are when they issue the threats.

Temporary removal pending investigation is not punishment, courts have ruled, because schools cannot function without "fair latitude" to make inquiries that will enable them to protect other students and the speakers themselves as well as the adults who work in the building.[42]

Schools have virtually unlimited discretion, which one appellate court labeled "unusual deference," to remove a student from contact with others while officials investigate whether a statement that scared listeners amounted to a true threat. A bomb threat always violates the law—no special context is required to punish the speaker. Schools appropriately weigh what they know about the speaker and his or her past conduct when they craft a response to speech that seems dangerous. A student with a poor disciplinary record who has brought alcohol and fireworks to school, engaged in fights on campus, and vandalized school property should be taken seriously when he communicates threats, including threats to kill himself.[43]

Schools may suspend and even expel students who sound true threats without worrying about speech rights, as illustrated by the paradigmatic case of D.J.M. v. Hannibal Public School District. High school student Dylan Mardis confided to a classmate his frustration that a girl he liked had rejected him. Mardis told his friend that he could get a .357 magnum, which he would use to shoot specific students he described as "'midgets'" and "'fags.'" He then planned to turn the gun on himself. The classmate told an adult that Mardis's statements scared her and then shared the conversation with school authorities. Specific details like these, including the listener's fearful reaction, help to establish that a threat is a true one.[44]

The school correctly treated Mardis's statements as true threats, the courts held, even though there was no evidence that Mardis ever set his plan in motion or was doing more than sharing a fantasy. Judges have similarly upheld the responses of schools to threats to shoot a high school guidance counselor and threats contained in a rap song targeting a fellow student's life.[45] A threat delivered directly to its target is even more likely to generate fear than one communicated to a third party, such as a mutual friend.

True threats affecting schools lead to two parallel sets of proceedings: The school may discipline the student and even expel him from the school system, and the state may prosecute the student, resulting in a period of confinement. Dylan Mardis, who threatened to massacre schoolmates with a .357 magnum and then shoot himself, was (1) arrested and sent to a psychiatric facility; (2) sent to a juvenile detention facility after being released from the hospital; and (3) suspended from school—initially for ten days and then for the remainder of the school year.[46]

Mardis, however, presented an unusual set of facts.

Courts commonly reject the true threat label after schools have relied on it to punish and eject students because most school threats don't look anything like what courts have recognized as true threats. Judges take note that police investigators and prosecutors have not pressed charges after concluding that far from being a "true threat," a student's words never contained any realistic threat at all. When it comes to true threats, schools don't get a break—they must show that student speech meets the legal test.[47]

Schools have treated student expression as a true threat where they could not even meet the much lower requirements for showing a risk of material disruption. As a result, courts have had many occasions to consider true threat doctrine and the material disruption standard in tandem.

Sometimes judges find that a school was justified in suppressing expression that it mistakenly treated as a true threat because the speech threatened material disruption. Drawings and writings hinting at attacks on teachers or fellow students or suicidal gestures are generally subject to suppression under this standard.[48]

In countless other cases, however, school administrators overreact to speech that is not threatening, or their initial fears turn out to be unfounded. Here it is helpful to examine three distinct aspects of threats, whether "true" or materially disruptive. The first involves the degree of risk: How realistic and imminent does the threat seem? The second considers the potential severity of the risk: If the threat is carried out, how much damage will occur? Finally, we need to separate quick actions to protect the school population pending a full investigation from penalties imposed on the speaker after any intimation of danger has passed. The Constitution allows officials to protect people based on what they know before the facts have been fully investigated but may prohibit penalties imposed on the speaker in the event further information reveals that no threat of violence ever existed. Officials too often dig in their heels and insist on continuing to isolate or punish a student speaker long after any threat has been shown to be illusory.

An apparent lack of a sense of humor among adults can exacerbate the distance between adolescents and officialdom. After one school characterized a cartoon as containing "threatening statements," the judge took a very different view. The drawing, which showed a staff member "shooting two students," he explained, "does not suggest that this speaker intends to shoot anyone. It merely conveys [the author's] apparent belief that school is deathly dull and that the administration does not want it any other way."[49]

These incidents also reveal several disturbing factual patterns. In some cases—which I call "private expression"—the student never communicated his ideas to anyone. In a second set of cases I label "recipient projection"—in which observers construe the actions they fear as being the speaker's intention—it would never have been reasonable to treat the expression as suggesting a risk of violence or disruption. In a third group I call "stale expression," the communication was held privately for such a long time that it doesn't make sense to treat the speaker's ruminations as likely to lead to action. Staleness also describes situations in which the school continues to treat speech as threatening even after officials learn that it isn't.

The constitutionality of a school's response to expression that arguably augers a violent outburst turns on whether officials reasonably interpreted the threat or the risk of substantial disruption based on what they knew at the time. The speaker's subjective intent (e.g., humor, fiction), disciplinary record, and ability to carry out the threat are valid subjects of inquiry when a court subsequently evaluates the constitutionality of the school's actions. But after an investigation demonstrates that the perceived emergency was illusory, disciplinarians are required to base any continuing penalties on the facts the investigation revealed.[50]

Perhaps the most perplexing cases involve private expression, speech no one besides the speaker ever accessed—at least until it became stale. If the speaker shares his threatening words with others, a school can and should consider whether other students are likely to feel threatened or to panic. But private expression resembles the barely audible, self-directed *sans-gêne* speech discussed in Chapter 3. Like that insolent speech, alleged threats can't have any impact at school unless someone knows about them.

Expression takes on elevated significance when it causes listeners to react fearfully, and schools should weight the impact frightening words have on others. But if the speaker never shared his thoughts with anyone, a school's concerns about incipient panic would normally be hard to justify.

In one example of private expression unmasked, an Arkansas teacher discovered a "hit list, to shoot list" with the names of nineteen students in a seventh grader's notebook. After the school turned the boy over to law enforcement, he was adjudicated a delinquent based on the "terroristic threats" in his notebook. An appellate court reversed, holding that the essential element of the state's "terroristic threatening" statute was "communication, not utterance." There was no evidence that the boy communicated his threats or had the "'purpose of terrorizing another.'" People can't be frightened by expression they never learn about. The court held that the First Amendment protected the speech even in school.[51]

Similarly, a federal court held that a school violated the speech rights of a teenager who drew a violent picture in a notebook he never showed to anyone else. He had stored the notebook in a closet in his room for two years until his younger brother, looking for writing paper, took the book to school. A teacher discovered the drawing, which the school labeled a true threat. It expelled the artist, who challenged the penalty in court. The court found that the artist had never "communicated in some knowing and intentional manner"; in fact, he considered the drawing as private as a diary. The passage of two years rendered any potential threat so stale that no reasonable person would fear that the speaker would act on his words. The court ruled that the school was within its rights to act quickly to safeguard the student body but should have rescinded the penalty it imposed on the artist as soon as it learned that the drawing was ancient.[52]

Despite these two examples, cogent competing arguments can be offered about whether students must communicate their threatening ideas before a school may anticipate that the speech will cause material disruption. If the speaker makes threats that are fresh rather than stale and that raise realistic concerns for school safety, it should not matter how the threats were discovered. Where threatening language was never shared with others and is of recent vintage, it seems especially important to consider the likelihood that the speaker would act on his threat before a more thorough inquiry can be conducted and the severity of the threat if the speaker carried through on his words. Does he plan to cause a flood by stopping up a toilet or to plant a bomb? Courts allow schools to act preemptively to protect the school in either case. However, judges almost never insist that the level of segregation and penalty reflect the severity of the risk to the school community.

Both penalties for stale speech and recipient projection were evident in the fate of Sarah Boman, who publicly displayed her creative work without permission. Boman, an accomplished art student, used a technique in which the visual artist fashions words into a shape, such as repeated words arranged to portray an obsessive or deranged mind. One day she made a poster containing a fictional narrative set forth in a spiral that read in part, "Please tell me who killed my dog. I miss him very much. He was my best friend . . . Did you do it? Do you know who did it? I'll kill you if you don't tell me who killed my dog. . . . Tell me. Tell me. Tell me. . . . I'll kill you if you don't tell me."[53]

Boman hung the unsigned poster on a classroom door. Before any students saw the poster, the school janitor removed it and brought it to the principal. Within fifteen minutes the principal learned that Boman had created the poster as a work of art. Concerned that the words seemed threatening, the principal suspended Boman for five days. He also recommended that the district consider further penalties. After an investigation, the school district suspended Boman for 81.5 school days, roughly four months, the rest of the school year.

When Boman pursued an administrative appeal to a hearing officer, her art teacher and art professors from a local college convinced the officer that there was no reason to fear her. The poster was art, and the "madman" was fictional, not self-referential. Authorities had no basis for anticipating that her return to school would create any disruption. Boman had not even violated a school rule. The hearing officer recommended that the school board allow her to return to school.

The school board rejected the hearing officer's findings. Instead, the board conditioned Boman's return to school on her agreeing to undergo a psychological evaluation to establish that she "is not a threat to students and staff."[54]

Boman sued the school district in federal court for violating her speech rights. The court agreed with her that as soon as the school district investigated the poster it became clear that "there simply was no longer any factual basis for believing that the poster constituted any sort of threat. The lines in the poster were essentially a work of fiction like the lines of a play—and when understood as such they represented no threat at all."[55] The court granted Boman a preliminary injunction restraining the school's disciplinary actions and ordered the district to reinstate her.

The school continued to insist that the poster had not only created a reasonable risk of disruption but that it "in fact caused a substantial disruption" in the school, a proposition the court roundly rejected. While the principal's initial fears on seeing the poster were reasonable, once Boman explained herself (just fifteen minutes later) it became clear that she posed "no threat to anyone." As in other cases, the court distinguished a school's permissible initial actions, designed to safeguard against danger, from punitive measures imposed after officials learned that the speaker had never posed any risk at all.[56]

Disagreements among adults in the community did prove disruptive, but they weren't Boman's fault. Some thought that the school had treated Boman too harshly. Others were angry that Boman had sued the school district, and they blamed the victim for causing the district to incur legal expenses. These divisions, the court correctly noted, "undoubtedly make operation of the school more difficult" but could not be attributed to Boman's "conduct in putting up her poster."[57]

If other students had seen Boman's poster, the incident would have briefly appeared to present a sound basis for reasonably anticipating disruption, or at least a close call. But once authorities learned who the artist was and Boman explained her creative intent, officials could have easily assuaged students' fears by sharing information. In reality, of course, Boman's speech was silent; no one saw it except for the janitor who took it down and the principal. When the facts quickly became known, there was no reason to send Boman home for the rest of the school day, let alone suspend her.

Once Boman explained her project, her expression could only be deemed hostile through viewers' projections. After the poster was removed (even before the principal learned about it), there was no risk that it would disrupt the campus by frightening other students. But the school punished Boman severely after any risk of disruption had dissipated and refused to modify the penalty even after its fears should have been assuaged.

Judges, like school officials, are not immune to recipient projection, and they often read their own awareness of societal ills into the facts of individual cases even though the rules of evidence tell them not to. Since the 1999 Columbine rampage in which two high school seniors sprayed automatic weapon fire, killing twelve students and one teacher and seriously wounding twenty-four others, and the 2007 Virginia Tech shooting in which thirty-three people died, more than 160 reported opinions have taken judicial notice of the serious risks that haunt school officials charged with protecting students and teachers.[58] Sometimes courts devote so much attention to famous school shootings while proclaiming they are applying the material disruption standard that it is hard to disentangle whether they are discussing disruption or true threats or even assessing the conditions at the particular school that is being sued for violating a student's expressive rights.

For example, in a lawsuit involving school discipline based on an allegedly fictional work in a student notebook that contained "a dream" about shooting an identifiable teacher, the appellate court devoted nearly three pages of its opinion to "well-known student-perpetrated shootings." Citing Wikipedia (whose standards do not satisfy the norms for evidence in courtrooms) and unverified news reports to document "this climate of increasing school violence," the court ruled that the school's anticipation of disruption was more than "mere speculation or paranoia" and justified suspending the student. The court focused much more on general societal ills than on evidence about a particular student.[59]

This sensibility leads some judges to identify with school officials, even those who, as one judge put it, "overreact to normal teenage angst." Montwood High School in El Paso, Texas, clamped down on a promising high school sophomore named E.P. (later disclosed as Ponce) because of a fictional diary he wrote, modeled on a writing course his mother had taken.

Ponce's creative writing project described plans for a neo-Nazi group, arson, and killing a dog. After reading the notebook and meeting with Ponce and his mother, the principal allowed Ponce to return to classes. Later, the school turned Ponce over to the police, who held him briefly and then released him when the prosecutor declined to press charges. The school transferred Ponce to an alternative education program and placed a permanent notation in his record that he posed a "'terroristic threat' to the safety and security of the students and the campus."[60]

The case typifies the panicky responses to artistic works that form a recurrent theme in school speech cases. The school never investigated whether the incidents described in the notebook bore any relation to reality. Had Ponce, for example, ever hurt an animal? Did he know any neo-Nazis?

When Ponce sued the school for violating his speech rights by punishing him for a work of fiction, the trial judge repudiated the school's justifications. He concluded that the school had not shown any "facts which might reasonably have led school authorities to forecast substantial disruption." The judge read the state's failure to press charges as undermining the school's stance that Ponce's words amounted to a "terroristic threat" and rejected the school's insistence that Ponce's continued banishment was necessary.[61]

Indeed, the judge found that the principal obliterated his own argument that he thought Ponce posed an imminent threat by sending Ponce back to class after their initial meeting. An imminent threat, the judge noted, would require "*immediate* action to segregate" the "potentially dangerous student[]."[62]

When the Fifth Circuit reviewed the case, however, it reframed the entire episode in light of mass shootings, found in favor of the school, and vacated the lower court's opinion. The very first sentence of the appellate opinion reads, "The appeal presents the question of whether student speech that threatens a Columbine-style attack on a school is protected by the First Amendment." To ask this question is to signal the answer.

It is "untenable in the wake of Columbine and Jonesboro," the appellate opinion states, "that any reasonable official who came into possession of [E.P.'s] [*sic*] diary would not have taken some action based on its violent and disturbing content." Because threats of violence directed at a school "are as much beyond the constitutional pale as yelling 'fire' in a crowded theater," the court accepted the school's characterization of Ponce's speech at face value. Although it did not need to, the panel relied on *Morse*, which it interpreted as giving schools the power to respond to any "direct threat."[63]

The court never asked whether the school ever had a basis for reading Ponce's words as realistic threats. Swept up in the narrative of school violence, the court neglected its obligations to analyze the school's evidence and collapsed its analysis of the school's initial decision to isolate Ponce and its continued refusal to allow him to return to school after officials' fears had been shown to be unfounded.

Like the school officials who never scrutinized Ponce's background, the appellate judges brought unsupported presumptions about the general dangers of school shootings into their deliberations about a specific individual. Despite all the merited anger about a wave of mass shootings in schools, government data collected since the 1992–1993 school year reveal that schools are as safe now as they have ever been. In 2010–2011, the last year for which national data are available, eleven students died in school-related incidents, still too many, but the lowest number since 1993 when there were thirty-four student deaths by homicide at school.[64] And even if the judges' dire expectations were supported by evidence, generalizations would not relieve school officials of the obligation to provide support for their specific fears about Ponce or any other student.

Ultimately, it doesn't really matter whether speech that school officials fear threatens violence at the hands of the speaker amounts to a true threat or could cause material disruption as long as it satisfies one of the legal requirements that justify suppressing expression. That was the thinking of the Second Circuit when it declined to make its way through the morass of true threat analysis in student speech cases. It reasoned that *Tinker* provides "significantly broader authority [than true threat doctrine] to discipline a student's expression reasonably understood as urging violent conduct."[65] This makes a great deal of sense. The approach promotes the flexibility schools require while preserving the court's limited resources.

The Second Circuit's approach relieves school officials and school board members who aren't attorneys of the harrowing task of what the court regards as "complex true threat analysis" when facing a potential crisis. Judges, in contrast, who are accomplished lawyers, also have the benefit of legal briefs about the law and its application to the facts from both sides and the luxury of analyzing controversies calmly at their leisure.[66] Since a school defending against a student's challenge to school discipline on the basis that the student's words amounted to a true threat is likely to also offer the alternative defense that the speech was materially disruptive, it is far more efficient for the court to begin with the more easily satisfied standard.[67]

"Material Disruption" Untethered

Material disruption constitutes the primary justification schools use when they constrain student speech under *Tinker.* Schools assert a fear that speech will lead to material disruption far more often than they allege that student expression threatens the serious violence that casts a shadow over the decisions I have been discussing.

The fourth, and most significant, challenge to *Tinker* arises from the efforts of some school officials to push the boundaries of "material disruption" beyond recognition, just as they have stretched the concepts of lewdness and school sponsorship. As the Eleventh Circuit explained, "some slight, easily overlooked disruption, including but not limited to 'a showing of mild curiosity' by other students, discussion and comment . . . , or even some 'hostile remarks' or 'discussion outside of the classrooms by other students'" does not suffice to show a risk of material disruption.[68] The elusive zone falls somewhere between such minimal and routine flurries of activity and the possibly serious threats of violence discussed above.

It is indisputably the judge's job to assess the constitutional legitimacy of the school's claim that "'undifferentiated fear or apprehension of disturbance' transform[ed] into a reasonable forecast that a substantial disruption . . . will occur." Lawyers and judges draw lines of this sort every day. And yet some commentators fear that the question of when speech "may be fairly characterized as 'disruptive'" is just too difficult. One federal judge posited in 2010 that the notion of "disruptive" student speech "'crosses into a constitutional gray area.'" "While simple in theory," another judge observed sympathetically, "this standard is difficult to apply across the myriad possible disruptions faced by school administrators."[69]

School officials must decide rapidly how to respond to political hyperbole, racially offensive speech, and speech supporting or condemning homosexuality, among other hot-button topics. Material disruption includes many situations that fall far short of danger to life and limb, and schools also sweep in many minor inconveniences that they regard as material interference with education. The courts have encouraged that tendency by failing to articulate the boundaries of material disruption more precisely.

Over the years, a few principles have emerged that help officials to respond quickly when safety is at stake without worrying that they will be held legally accountable if their fears turn out to be unfounded. These principles, placed alongside judicial decisions about facts that fall on either side of the material disruption line, help to clarify what the first prong of *Tinker* means.

The most salient feature of the standard is that it was not designed to be easily satisfied. *Tinker* pointedly instructed school officials that "undifferentiated fear or apprehension of disturbance" never justifies restrictions on student speech. Such speculative fears are "not enough to overcome the right to freedom of expression." School officials, the Court explained, must be able to show "facts which might reasonably have led school authorities to forecast substantial disruption or material interference," amounting to "something more than a mere desire to avoid the discomfort and unpleasantness that always accompany an unpopular viewpoint." If the school can't do that, prohibition or punishment of speech violates the student's rights.[70]

The general borders of "material disruption" are clear from the *Tinker* opinion itself and from the two Fifth Circuit decisions on which the *Tinker* test was modeled.

The Supreme Court provided guidance by listing some potentially proscribable acts the *Tinker* protesters did *not* engage in. They weren't "aggressive." They did not lead "group demonstrations." They "neither interrupted school activities nor sought to intrude in the school affairs or the lives of others" and caused "no interference with work and no disorder."[71]

The two Fifth Circuit cases on which the Supreme Court relied and which lower courts continue to consult neatly separate material disruption from inconvenience or minor disorder. Both cases involved student speech in pursuit of racial equality in Mississipi in 1964. Each involved students suspended from school for wearing "freedom buttons" about one inch in diameter proclaiming the wearer's support for the principle of "one man, one vote." The buttons were serious—one could even say "high stakes"—political speech. Students had been at the forefront of the civil rights movement in the South, at least since the battle to integrate Little Rock, Arkansas's Central High School under the protection of federal troops in 1957.[72]

In Birmingham just one year before the freedom button controversy in Mississippi, black youths had marched out of school to confront Sheriff Bull Connor's fire hoses and dogs and to welcome arrest as part of the boycott led by Martin Luther King Jr. Preparing for the launch of the Children's Crusade, King's young colleagues stirred up a crowded church gathering. "Tomorrow," William "Meatball" Dothard told the audience, "students are gonna show you old folks what you should have done forty years ago. They're gonna make you ashamed to see that they have to go through what you should have gone through earlier for them, to make their life better."[73]

Reminding the crowd of the gospel song they all sang, with its ringing phrase "if you don't go, don't you hinder me," Meatball exhorted the anxious adults: "Parents, don't hinder the kids in the morning, . . . teachers, don't take your roll books in the morning." The next day, Ambassador Andrew Young recalls, high school students marched right over the fence that surrounded their segregated campus.[74]

The deep South was in turmoil as the events surrounding the decisions of two high schools to bar freedom buttons unfolded. The summer of 1964, known as Freedom Summer, witnessed the signing of the first federal Civil Rights Act since Reconstruction, accompanied by a huge drive to register African American voters in southern states that brought hundreds of volunteers south. Three volunteers in their early twenties disappeared from Philadelphia, Mississippi, in June and were found six weeks later; they had been shot to death and mutilated.[75]

The freedom button cases arose during the following school year. In Blackwell v. Issaquena County Board of Education and Burnside v. Byars, the Fifth Circuit recognized the expressive rights of high school students and then adopted a standard under which courts could assess whether abridgments of those rights violated the First Amendment.[76]

The circuit court applied the same fact-specific test in both cases. In each, students wore and distributed "'freedom buttons' depicting clasped black and white hands," which their schools had banned. The court reached what at first glance appear to be antithetical results in the two cases, which raised the same legal question.[77]

In *Blackwell,* the court found substantial disruption of class instruction, indeed "a complete breakdown in school discipline." About thirty students at the segregated African American high school in Rolling Fork, Mississippi, showed up wearing freedom buttons in January 1965. Some of them were sent to the principal's office for interfering with classes by talking noisily in the hallway. The next school day about 150 students wore buttons to school. They distributed buttons, in some instances accosting peers "by pinning the buttons on them even though they did not ask for one." A young student began to cry. A "state of confusion" resulted, and classwork was disrupted. The principal called students together to ask them to "'remove [the buttons] so that order could be restored.'"[78]

Students became hostile. One called the African American principal an "Uncle Tom," a phrase that some might regard as the kind of "fighting words" that can be prohibited in any setting consistent with the First Amendment. On day three, as the number of students wearing buttons continued to grow, the principal warned that he would suspend any student who wore a freedom button in the future.

The next day, the button-wearing students ignored the principal's order that they leave the school and continued to invite other students to join them. A school bus driver handed buttons out to students in classrooms. Some students who had left reentered the building and tried to pin buttons on their peers, while other demonstrators threw buttons into the school through open windows. Classroom instruction came to a halt. After several weeks of continued turmoil, the school system suspended about three hundred African American students for the duration of the school year.

The court confidently resolved that the suspended students had gone far beyond disrespect for authority: They had created "much disturbance" that interfered with "the orderly progression of classroom instruction," the essence of what would become the legal test under *Tinker*.[79]

In contrast, in *Burnside*, the same judges on the same day held that the school violated the rights of button-wearers by suspending them from their segregated school—the Booker T. Washington High School in Philadelphia, Mississippi. In Philadelphia, the student demonstrators had donned "the 'freedom buttons' as a means of silently . . . encourag[ing] the members of their community to exercise their civil rights." The school had alleged that the buttons caused a "commotion" because other students wanted to see them or asked about them, but the educational process proceeded. The court concluded that "wearing buttons is certainly not in the class of those activities which inherently distract students and break down the regimentation of the classroom such as carrying banners, scattering leaflets, and speech making, all of which are protected methods of expressions, but all of which have no place in an orderly classroom." In short, schools may not punish students for expressive activity that does not involve "some student misconduct" by the speakers themselves.[80]

Anticipating the concerns about order Justice Black would later voice in his *Tinker* dissent, the Fifth Circuit summed up the balance it envisioned. "[R]espect for those in authority must be instilled in our young people," it stated starkly. But, it continued, "we must also emphasize that school officials cannot ignore expressions of feelings with which they do not wish to contend. They cannot infringe on their students' right to free and unrestricted expression as guaranteed to them under the First Amendment to the Constitution, where the exercise of such rights in the school building and school rooms do not materially and substantially interfere with the requirements of appropriate discipline in the operation of the school."[81]

Burnside and *Blackwell* taken together suggest that students can be punished for speech only when their own accompanying conduct threatens material disruption. Interrupting a class by unfurling banners or making speeches, as happened in *Burnside,* resulting in "a total breakdown of good order and discipline," is materially disruptive. When the speaker's conduct interferes with the school's educational functions, the school may discipline the speaker without violating the student's constitutional rights.[82] A student's claim that his or her conduct is expressive does not immunize disruptive behavior from penalty.

Burnside, Blackwell, and *Tinker* show that communication by itself should rarely if ever be treated as substantially disruptive. In addition, they instruct that students cannot be punished for expression solely because a school rule (such as no black armbands, no buttons) bars their speech.

The Fifth Circuit opinions that framed *Tinker*'s adoption of the material disruption test underscore that courts must scrutinize the details, including the context, when they evaluate competing claims that schools have violated speech rights and that student expression threatened material disruption. Whether a school has more than an undifferentiated fear and "more than a mere desire to avoid the discomfort and unpleasantness that always accompany an unpleasant viewpoint" as *Tinker* requires may turn on the individual student's history as well as the history of the school.

But as the paradigmatic cases receded in time and the Supreme Court signaled that *Tinker* no longer reigned as the only school speech doctrine, some school officials apparently abandoned any effort to explore what counts as disruption under the law. Schools tend to view demonstrations as inherently disruptive, especially when other students are in classes, and courts have quickly accepted the schools' characterizations of protests as "near riots."[83] They seem to have lost sight of the school as a training ground for active citizenship, which may include fighting to make the law more just.

In a departure impossible to reconcile with First Amendment principles, schools have also argued that some speech is inherently disruptive based on its content: The information it contains is too explosive for young minds. This stance violates the core premise that students have speech rights, which include the right to receive information. One school asserted that the mere distribution of information about birth control and abortion could lead to disruption among middle school students based on their immaturity, and the Eleventh Circuit deferred to that decision. In doing so, the court ignored Supreme Court's rulings that minors have constitutionally protected rights to both contraception and abortion that the literature could help them pursue.[84]

Sometimes the responses of the school officials themselves disrupt education. For example, a principal in Florida who not only suspended a girl who wore a T-shirt promoting respect for gays but also lambasted her for her non-Christian beliefs and outed her lesbian cousin to her family created widespread support for both girls. He then accused the girls of fomenting disruptive controversy. The court found that "Principal Davis, not the innocuous symbols and phrases at issue, bears sole responsibility for any unrest that occurred . . . [He] catalyzed the 'Gay Pride' movement because of his animosity toward students who were homosexual and his relentless crusade to extinguish the speech supporting them." Where teachers or administrators cause disruption, they cannot use the resulting unrest to justify limitations on student speech.[85]

Schools offer some bizarre rationales for anticipating substantial disruption. Some are so lacking in substance that it is hard to believe school officials acted in good faith. Examples offered to courts include one phone call from a parent to an administrator, modest rearrangement of administrative schedules, a few students missing part or all of one class, "general rumblings" among students, and a few minutes of talking during class. One school pointed to "divisiveness" among the girls on the volleyball team. That, a judge responded, is an "extremely weak" claim that "does not come close to meeting the *Tinker* standard."[86]

As another judge cogently explained, at a typical high school, students "frequently argue about sports, social relationships, and topics of interest to teenagers, circulate petitions, and are loud. . . . .Classes are disrupted every day by students' conversations. Students pass notes and whisper to their classmates. Students write on themselves and draw sketches unrelated to their classwork." The court scoffed at the incidents the school had offered to show disruption as "indistinguishable from the typical background noise of high school."[87]

But too many school administrators either are unaware that the apprehension of disorder must be pinned to some "specific and significant fear" supported by details or don't take that legal requirement seriously. In 2011 and 2012, for example, a number of schools in different parts of the United States banned breast cancer awareness bracelets carrying the slogan "I [heart] boobies! (KEEP A BREAST)." Three cases reached the federal courts after schools punished students who refused to remove the bracelets. In each school, students had worn the bracelets without incident for weeks, months, and even an entire semester before authorities confronted them. None of the schools offered plausible evidence that officials reasonably feared disruption, even where they argued that *Tinker* permitted them to ban the bracelets. Recognizing the weakness of their position under *Tinker*, some of the schools convinced judges that the bands were "arguably lewd" and could be banned under *Fraser*.[88]

Applying *Tinker* in a case about the boobies bracelets arising from a Pennsylvania middle school, the trial judge condemned the school for censorship based on "at most a general fear of disruption." The school had pointed to two "isolated incidents," both of which followed the ban (and thus did not justify the ban at its origin). In the first, a student told a teacher that she thought some boys had "made remarks to girls about their 'boobies'" in response to the bracelets.[89]

In the second post-censorship episode at the same middle school, a boy made spherical gestures and told girls who were discussing the bracelets that he "want[ed] boobies," which led the school to discipline him. Discipline for the boy who "wanted boobies" may be regarded as a success for the bracelets, which, among other things, aimed to teach people how to talk maturely about breasts and breast health. Message sent and received at this middle school, at least by one boy who presumably learned from his mistake. "Such isolated incidents," the judge concluded, "are well within a school's ability to maintain discipline and order" and fell far short of creating a substantial disruption or a reasonable fear of one.[90]

In an unusual move reserved for important and difficult cases, the Third Circuit agreed to review the preliminary injunction sitting en banc. The full appellate court affirmed the preliminary injunction by a vote of nine to five. It termed the "record of disruption even skimpier" than the one the Supreme Court found insufficient to support censorship in *Tinker*.[91]

The court left unanswered the question of whether disruption arising *after* a school restricted speech could ever satisfy *Tinker*. Analytically, while an event after the school censored speech would provide support for a school's assertion that its anticipation of material disruption had been reasonable, it is hard to see how a later development could retroactively support an anticipation of material disruption that officials had not articulated when they suppressed student expression. At most it would show that *had* the school anticipated disruption, the worries would have been justified.

Even after the Supreme Court diluted the material disruption test by creating three exceptions, its borders remain clearer than they may appear or than is widely understood. The normal background noise of schools—chatter, texting, inconvenience, fleeting distractions, unpleasantness and controversy or responses to administrative reactions to student speech—does not amount to material disruption. Nor can student speakers permissibly be held accountable for disruption that amounts to school officials doing their jobs—including the job of keeping the educational process intact. *Tinker* itself makes this clear. The administrators at the schools the Tinker children attended devoted time to dealing with the armband controversy. No one suggested that doing so disrupted the educational process. Minor burdens on the time and attention of school officials are no more sufficient to show material disruption today than they were in 1969.

The sharp lines that should divide material disruption from an undifferentiated fear of controversy bring into relief the legal errors in the way schools responded to the T-shirts described at the beginning of this chapter. We are now prepared to analyze David Griggs's shirt bearing a picture of the M-16 rifle and quoting the creed of the Marines and Zachary Guiles's impolite montage of words and pictures critiquing President George W. Bush.

In each case, the only legal question was whether the school could show "facts which might reasonably have led [it] to forecast substantial disruption." In *Griggs,* a trial court starkly concluded that "no such facts exist." Griggs had already worn the shirt to school without provoking any comment or causing any disruption before authorities accosted him. Officials admitted that they had never considered whether Griggs's shirt was likely to cause disorder before telling him to remove it. In fact, the shirt did not garner any reactions from other students until after the school censored it. At that point, some students asked questions "along the lines of 'why won't they let you wear that shirt?'" This, the court concluded, "is not close at all."[92]

Zachary Guiles wore his shirt critiquing the second President Bush off and on for two months in 2004 without causing any disruption. The shirt prompted political discussions with other students, as Guiles had hoped it would. The school did not take any action against the shirt until one mother who saw the shirt complained. At that point, officials pointed to a school rule that barred all "images displaying drugs and alcohol" and told Guiles to remove his shirt. He refused. The school sent Guiles home and noted his disobedience on his permanent record. Later, in an effort at compromise, the school agreed that Guiles could wear the shirt but only if he taped over the images of the President with drugs and alcohol. The pictures were protected expression and political commentary at that. The school also insisted that Guiles cover the word *cocaine*, which he did, adding the word *censored* over the tape.

Guiles sued, seeking injunctive relief and asking to have his disciplinary record expunged. As in *Griggs*, school officials conceded that Guiles's shirt had not caused any disruption. They never even argued that they had a reasonable belief the shirt *would* cause disruption in the future. Guiles won in district court. The school district appealed the ruling.

On appeal, the Second Circuit panel (which included then-Judge Sotomayor) seemed to sigh audibly as it opened its opinion: We "sail into the unsettled waters of free speech rights in public schools, waters rife with rocky shoals and uncertain currents." The court acknowledged "some lack of clarity in the Supreme Court's student-speech cases" and in the definition of "what constitutes 'substantial disorder'." Ultimately, however, the court underscored, *Tinker*, the "generally applicable rule," "established a protective standard for student speech," one that means "schools must tolerate a great deal of student speech that is not lewd or vulgar." There was no excuse for the school's confusion over what standard applied—a confusion shared by the trial judge who applied *Fraser* to speech that may have been offensive but was not remotely lewd. Joining a majority of eight other judicial circuits, the court held that *Tinker* always governs a student's personal shirt and the messages it communicates.[93]

Had *Guiles* been decided after *Morse*, the emerging doctrine would not have improved the school's legal position. *Morse* allows schools to censor advocacy of illegal drugs such as cocaine. But Guiles didn't applaud Bush's reputed drug use; he condemned it.

The Constitution, the court underscored in *Guiles*, protects the whole message as well as the student's chosen manner of expression. Pictures of a martini glass, a man drinking from a bottle, and lines of cocaine with a razor "are an important part of the political message . . . accentuating the anti-drug (and anti-Bush) message." By covering the images, the school "diluted Guiles's message, blunting its force and impact."[94]

The same could be said—though it wasn't—of alternative breast cancer awareness bracelets offered by one middle school to replace the banned "I [heart] boobies" slogan, which stated prosaically "Sauk Prairie Eagles support breast cancer awareness."[95]

Once the proper law was applied and the facts were properly understood, *Guiles,* like so many other school speech controversies, turned out to be a very simple case, one in which the school was completely unprepared to offer a credible defense of its censorship. Officials had apparently made little or no effort to acquaint themselves with the law, much less obey it.[96]

The turbulent waters of student speech rights are no destructive Siren call that should cause us to "stop our ears with beeswax" like Ulysses as the Second Circuit intimated in *Guiles. Tinker's* material disruption test set a safe course. For those who have trouble following the path, one federal judge offered a simpler formulation, consistent with *Tinker's* essence. His concise maxim: "'When in doubt, do not censor.'"[97]

CHAPTER 6

Words that Harm
The Rights of Others

[There is] little basis for the . . . sweeping assertion that "harassment . . . has never been considered to be protected activity under the First Amendment." Such a categorical rule . . . belies the very real tension between anti-harassment laws and the Constitution's guarantee of freedom of speech.

—Saxe v. State College Area School District (3rd Cir. 2001) (Alito, J.)

"Homosexuality is a sin! Islam is a lie!" declares one boy's T-shirt. Other students sport the Confederate flag, taunt classmates with vicious racial slurs, or call a girl "a cum-guzzling slut." One school suspended a six-year-old for addressing a classmate as a "poo poo head," while a middle school student was told she could not share her view that a classmate was headed to hell. These sentiments are beyond educators' authority to discipline unless the school meets *Tinker*'s demands.

This chapter tackles the problem of hurtful speech, encompassing interwoven issues of group disparagement and hate speech, insults hurled at individual targets, and bullying that is confined to words. Each of these speech forms may implicate the second prong of the two-part test promulgated in *Tinker*, which intimates that schools can regulate speech that collides with the rights of others. Without expressly relying on the test, schools frequently claim that they are entitled to silence speech out of respect for the sensitivities of listeners. In its zest to quash bullying and similar offenses, even the federal government has given short shrift to speech rights and shirked its responsibility to explain constitutional constraints.

Lower courts have mainly ignored the "rights of others" language in school speech cases in part because the Supreme Court has never applied it or fleshed out what *Tinker*'s second prong means. In 2005, one court commented that it was "not aware of a single decision that has focused on

160

[*Tinker*'s 'invasion of the rights of others'] language as the sole basis for upholding a school regulation of student speech."[1] No court has done so since, and for good reason.

As I will demonstrate, the rights of others rubric alone never provides a sufficient rationale for censoring student speech, no matter how unpleasant. *Tinker*'s second prong has been found to justify censorship only when accompanied by a reasonable apprehension of material disorder.

The hostile words that students direct at schoolmates and the codes many schools adopt to control hate speech, harassment, and verbal bullying form the most common backdrop for considering *Tinker*'s rights of others language. I begin by exploring what the legal rights of others consist of in the context of speech by peers. I then scrutinize examples of group disparagement based on race, ethnicity, and sexual orientation to probe the limitations and potential of *Tinker*'s second prong before turning to hurtful speech directed at a specific individual and the related problem of repeated hurtful speech that rises to the level of bullying.

Finally, I shall suggest ways of responding to the problem of hurtful speech. First, I propose an infringement matrix that schools and judges could use to ascertain if the speech has interfered substantially with a single student's access to education; the infringement matrix is related to but distinguishable from speech that materially disrupts a whole class or the entire school. Second, I offer examples of successful teaching moments in which schools respond to hurtful words hurled from one child to another with the classic First Amendment prescription of more and better words. The chapter closes with a warning about the importance of not forcing students to parrot educators' views.

What Are the "Rights" of Others?

Throughout this book, I have been talking about *rights* as the term is used in constitutional law. The Bill of Rights protects individuals against government actions that impinge on liberty. The First Amendment restricts the state's authority to abridge certain individual freedoms, including freedom of expression. When used in reference to speech by a student, "colliding with the rights of others" cannot mean rights in the constitutional sense of rights against the state because the state is a mere bystander when a peer causes the harm.

One of the definitions *Black's Law Dictionary* offers for a right is "a legally enforceable claim of one person against another, that the other shall . . . not do a given act." While normally seen in property law, as applied to students who seek to be free from speech that collides with their rights, this might mean that the listener or target of the speech may expect the school to prevent the speaker from impinging on the listener to the extent the Speech Clause permits. This definition cannot by itself create new substantive rights to be protected from offensive sentiments. But once we identify the kinds of hurtful speech that listeners have a legal right to be protected from, schools can certainly demand that students stay within the boundaries of speech that is legal outside of school.

Justice Brennan anticipated just this question: What "rights" does *Tinker's* second prong have in mind? "If that term is to have any content," he urged, "it must be limited to rights that are protected by law." *Law*, as he used it, includes constitutional rights, rights to be protected from speech that violates the criminal code, and protection from civil torts that have speech at their core, such as defamation or intentional infliction of emotional distress.[2]

Under this approach, schools must allow hurtful student speech that does not violate any civil or criminal laws unless school speech doctrine allows a school to silence the speaker. If the speech violates the laws that apply outside of school, the school may silence and discipline the speaker, who remains at risk of civil lawsuits by the victims or prosecution by the state. A number of lower courts have adopted Brennan's very narrow interpretation of *Tinker's* "rights of others" language.[3] I am not aware of any judges who have expressly rejected his proposed interpretation.

If hurtful student speech directed at groups or individuals is to be prohibited, the legal concept of harassment offers the best means for making such speech off-limits under *Tinker's* second prong. Unfortunately, state laws barring harassment can be notoriously vague and broad and, when used to constrain speech, raise a myriad of constitutional questions that neither courts nor scholars have sufficiently probed.[4]

State definitions of illegal harassment vary, but laws in at least twenty-two states share the following common elements: (1) a course of conduct, not a single event; (2) directed at a specific victim; (3) the conduct actually causes the victim emotional distress or could cause emotional distress to a reasonable person; and (4) the conduct (including expression) lacks any legitimate purpose. Many states require that the harasser have an intent to harass or knowingly engage in harassment. Some provide non-exhaustive examples of harassment, such as repeated phone calls in the middle of the night.[5]

Harassment codes are designed to be notoriously vague. The elasticity of harassment laws, as Aaron H. Caplan points out, reflects the impossibility of anticipating every noxious act and the "value judgment—that it is better to enact a broader, vaguer law than to allow unforeseen bad actions to go unremedied." This impulse to protect is seen in criminal harassment statutes barring conduct that merely "annoy[s]" and can go too far. In 2014, for example, a criminal court in New York City found a performer guilty of harassment for using "foul language" in front of two young children in Times Square, though there was no pattern of behavior.[6]

Although no reported cases use *Tinker*'s second prong as a shorthand for speech proscribed by the criminal or civil codes, such as harassment or defamation, illegal speech that victimizes someone would also infringe on "the rights of others" even under Justice Brennan's narrow construction of rights.

And yet, schools that model their behavioral codes on civil or criminal harassment statutes inevitably run into problems when the codes are applied to student speech and challenged in court. Part of the problem is that statutes regulating harassing speech don't always comply with the strictures of the Speech Clause, and they often go unchallenged because defendants in civil cases involving harassment commonly lack lawyers. In contrast, students who sue their schools for inhibiting freedom of expression often have skilled representation from pro bono attorneys under the auspices of civil rights groups like the ACLU. As a consequence, the First Amendment implications of harassment codes may have received closer scrutiny in cases about student speech than in cases involving adults in the world at large.

Harassment sometimes involves abusive expression about group characteristics. The harasser may focus on the target's gender, appearance, race, ethnicity, sexuality, or religion, transforming a "simple" case of harassment into "hate speech" aimed at a group the law specially protects from denigration. Hate speech may be part of a pattern of harassment that targets an individual or may disparage a group without being directed at a specific person.

The lines that divide harassment, bullying, and hate speech have legal significance but may not be clear to educators. As we will see, like hate speech, verbal bullying may be immune to penalty, but harassment can be punished at school and elsewhere. The labels matter. Some incidents meet the legal definitions of harassment, bullying, or hate speech, as a few examples from the school yard illustrate. In the first, two African American brothers ages eight and ten were repeatedly called "niggers" or "blackie" by classmates, were blocked from using playground equipment, and were told to "shut up" when they spoke on the playground or school bus. Other incidents involve allegations that girls are sexually promiscuous, popularly known as slut shaming. In one episode, over a period lasting several months, peers falsely accused a twelve-year-old girl of being a prostitute and repeatedly asked when she was going on the stroll.[7] Understandably, responsible adults may want to silence all of these vile utterances and stifle the views they express. If the speech amounts to harassment, then a school can silence and discipline it.

Many advanced democracies, from Canada to Great Britain and Germany, have criminalized speech that degrades groups of people. They have acted out of concern about the harms hate speech causes, whether issued to all who can hear it or directed to a targeted individual. Historically disempowered groups—including racial and religious minorities, women, and LGBTs—have also applied pressure to pass and enforce such laws. Indisputably, noxious sentiments about groups assault human dignity, as proponents of bans on hate speech assert.

Political theorist Jeremy Waldron adds what he identifies as a more concrete harm—the risk, substantiated by history, that when taken seriously vicious speech will lead to violent persecution.[8] Schools may be viewed as microcosms in which group disparagement that is linked to a history of violence supports administrators' claims that they anticipate material disruption.

In the United States, however, the Speech Clause stands in the way of outlawing disparaging speech about groups as a general matter. When antiharassment codes—whether criminal or civil statutes or school rules—are too specific (in an effort to avoid vagueness), they risk violating the Constitution if they regulate some kinds of hostility (such as racial or ethnic bias) but not others (like bias against short people). This is the lesson of the Supreme Court's ruling in R.A.V. v. St. Paul, when it overturned St. Paul, Minnesota's Bias Motivated Crime Ordinance in 1992.[9]

Commentators have pointed out the conflict between efforts to instill civility and free expression. Columnist Nat Hentoff, a leading authority on the First Amendment and student rights, thought hate speech codes so patently unconstitutional that he accused educators of enfolding the rules "in student codes of conduct in the hope that judges won't find them there." Similarly, when Justice Kagan was still a law professor, she mused that an "exceedingly narrow speech code" aimed at discriminatory harassment, including racist hate speech, at a university might satisfy what she called "a reasonable system of First Amendment law." But, she made clear, it cannot survive constitutional analysis in the United States. And, in fact, courts have overturned numerous well-intentioned statutes and regulations designed to eliminate insults—including every university hate speech code that has been challenged in court and some public school speech codes too.[10]

Justice Alito's 2001 opinion for a Third Circuit panel in Saxe v. State College Area School District (an opinion I have quoted several times without explaining the questions before the court) overturned a high school "anti-harassment" code that was not distinguishable from a classic hate speech code. The school adopted its code to "'provid[e] all students with a safe, secure, and nurturing school environment.'" The rules outlawed "verbal or physical conduct based on . . . actual or perceived race, religion, color, national origin, gender, sexual orientation, disability, or other personal characteristics, . . . which has the purpose or effect of substantially interfering with a student's educational performance or creating an intimidating, hostile or offensive environment." Nicknames based on stereotypes, mimicry, and bullying were among the enumerated violations that could lead to penalties including expulsion. The school thought its code addressed "harassment," but it didn't limit forbidden speech and conduct to acts that fit the legal definition of harassment. For instance, in contrast to statutes criminalizing harassment that satisfy the First Amendment, the code did not require that the speech be aimed at a specific individual and could be used to punish a single statement rather than an ongoing pattern of behavior.[11]

The Saxe children identified themselves as Christians who believed, as "their religion teaches, that homosexuality is a sin" and that they needed to speak out against it. They feared that their school's code barred them from expressing their views and sought both to clarify whether it applied to the speech they wanted to engage in and to overturn the entire code.[12]

The district court ruled for the school, accepting its assertion that the harassing speech it aimed to control was not protected anywhere. The Third Circuit disagreed. The *Saxe* opinion clarifies that even if student speech seems to harass, it is protected unless it meets the criminal code's definition of harassment or falls within a legitimate exercise of the school's powers under school speech doctrine.

Justice Alito's opinion emphatically rejected the trial court's basic premise that all harassing speech can be silenced. He stressed that there was no support for the district court's assertion that "'harassment'—at least when it consists of speech that is banned solely on the basis of its expressive content—'has never been considered to be protected'" speech under the First Amendment. There is, Justice Alito emphasized, "no categorical 'harassment exception' to the First Amendment's free speech clause." Because the school district's disciplinary code "prohibits a substantial amount of speech that would not constitute actionable harassment under either federal or state law," its broad reach aimed at content proved fatal. "'Harassing' or discriminatory speech, although evil and offensive," Justice Alito wrote, "may be used to communicate ideas or emotions that nevertheless implicate First Amendment protections."[13]

Alito warned there is a "very real tension between anti-harassment laws and the Constitution's guarantee of freedom of speech." Applying *Tinker*, the Third Circuit held that the code prohibited too much protected speech (including the Saxes') that did not "rise[] to the level of a substantial disruption."[14]

Briefly addressing *Tinker*'s second prong, Alito stated that the "precise scope of *Tinker*'s 'interference with the rights of others' language is unclear." Whatever the phrase meant, it would not save the district's hate speech code because the code failed to "require any threshold showing of severity or pervasiveness" and "could conceivably be applied to cover any speech about some enumerated characteristics the content of which offends someone."[15] "Severity" and "pervasiveness" will prove important as we consider what if anything can be done to stop "offensive" speech.

Despite the seemingly bright line rule that the Speech Clause is not an easy fit with efforts to outlaw hate speech, the impulse to protect people from group disparagement and directed harassment has led some constitutional law scholars to minimize the conflict between certain speech codes and the First Amendment. Professor Jack Balkin argues that the real goal of such rules in the workplace is not to stifle speech but to "dismantle unjust forms of social stratification" and achieve "civil equality" throughout society no less than on the job. He posits that federal rules permissibly encourage private employers to control what their workers say to each other ("women should stay home and have children" or "women are taking men's jobs") by holding the companies responsible for hostile work environments.[16]

In a parallel effort to quell group insults, many school districts in the United States have adopted "hate speech" codes like the one overturned in *Saxe* that forbid "'derogatory comments,' oral or written, 'that refer to race,

ethnicity, religion, gender, sexual orientation, or disability.'"[17] Those categories, like the rules many private employers impose in workplaces, largely
overlap with federal laws that bar harassment based on certain group characteristics. Some schools go further, adding other "characteristics," such as
personal appearance, height, lack of athletic prowess, and even "values" to
the categories that are off-limits for teasing or hostile comments.[18]

In the private workplace, hate speech rules extend to all audible statements disparaging enumerated groups, including those not addressed to a
particular individual. In schools, however, as in the legal definition of
harassment, it may make a difference whether an individual is targeted.

No matter how well intentioned, regulatory efforts to control group disparagement confront constitutional barriers. School speech codes suppress
the viewpoint of the speaker in direct contravention of every First Amendment
principle. Disparaging words repudiated by right-minded people as beyond
the pale often implicate political disagreements at the heart of the Speech
Clause, raising the same concerns that require us to tolerate protests like flag
burning no matter how much such acts offend observers.[19]

As a matter of constitutional law, it's a good deal simpler for private
employers to enforce the workplace codes that Balkin celebrates than it is
for the state to apply anti-disparagement rules in schools. The government
mandates that employers protect workers from a hostile work environment,
but it relies on private parties to enforce that mandate, if need be by silencing
expression. In school, the government itself enforces the rules without an
intermediary. That is state action, which triggers constitutional protections.
Unlike the government, private employers in the United States have a good
deal of discretion to impose conditions on workers and may fire them for
noncompliance. Workers in turn may quit or express their opinions outside
the workplace, but students are compelled to spend their days in school.

Schools face another complexity: The goal of fostering a tolerant citizenry
may collide with the constitutionally protected interest that parents have in
imparting their own values to their children. As the Supreme Court construed the issue as far back as 1925, our "fundamental theory of liberty . . .
excludes any general power of the State to standardize its children."[20]
Students who violate norms of tolerance, just like students who support
voting rights or oppose a war, are often expressing the values they learned
at home.

Sometimes what one judge called "difficult parents" actively join in
mocking or vicious behavior toward members of the school community

and undermine the school's ability to teach their charges to behave more empathetically. These adults are largely beyond the school's control unless their statements and actions amount to harassment under the state code. But if a child displays at school the "foul language and prejudicial views" picked up "from his parents at home," the same judge continued, the school should discipline the child to the extent the law permits. His caveat: "Administrators have to tiptoe on a narrow path when dealing with a child's unwarranted prejudices as opposed to his sincerely held religious beliefs."[21] Parental values and religious beliefs commonly give rise to speech with political implications about controversial topics such as abortion and sexual orientation.

Group Disparagement

That schools should protect students from wounding words permitted elsewhere sounds attractive. The heightened vulnerability of young people—a longstanding consideration in the jurisprudence that governs minors—seems to justify such paternalism. The custodial nature of the school's relationship to children would seem to oblige educators to protect their vulnerable charges from emotional as well as physical harm. Students aren't free to leave, the argument goes, and should not be forcibly exposed to inflammatory comments from their peers. When words that harm individuals or groups are used in school, educators have an opportunity, indeed a duty, to use the occasion to advance lessons about social cohesiveness.

The problem is real. Schools today, like those of earlier generations, have witnessed the same racial, ethnic, and cultural upheavals that have shaken the larger society. Evangelicals and nonbelievers, proud descendants of white Southerners and "Black and proud" African Americans, conservatives, recent immigrants, and LGBTs are all on the front lines in clashes over what can be said (or worn on a T-shirt) and what should never be said.

Lower courts generally agree that *Tinker* governs disputes about whether schools may permissibly discipline students for disparaging speech.[22] All too often, however, efforts to censor and punish hurtful words defy the stringent requirements of *Barnette* and *Tinker*.

Three different circumstances affect the legal treatment of group disparagement. First, each school's specific context and history affect the likelihood of material disruption. Second, some schools abdicate by ceding control to hecklers, a problem I analyze in the context of disputes surrounding attitudes toward immigrants. And third, free expression may be undermined when educators worry so much about the sensitivities of listeners that they overlook the political value and significance of the speaker's ideas.

Gauging the Impact of Offensive Speech in This School: Racial Sensitivities

The nation's original sin of slavery, the compromises that preserved slavery when the Constitution was drafted, and the painful legacy it left set the stage for racial strife among students that realistically threatens material disruption. One might surmise that bans on racially charged symbols and words in school would easily pass constitutional muster even if bans on other kinds of hate speech can't. After all, bans on racist speech serve the underlying goal of the Fourteenth Amendment "to do away with all governmentally imposed discrimination based on race."[23] The key word here is *governmentally*. There is no government action when students hurl insults at each other.

One particular symbol—the Confederate flag—has generated its own subset of jurisprudence within school speech doctrine. In the 1970s, a special line of cases began to emerge featuring disputes about displaying that highly charged emblem—an act the First Amendment protects for students along with adults. Initially emerging in school districts with a long history of racial animosity undergoing court-supervised desegregation, the early cases centered on schools that officially displayed Confederate symbols or permitted students to sport such emblems. When the flaunting of Confederate symbols was first challenged in court, the rulings tended to allow schools to bar racially divisive symbols that were likely to exacerbate existing racial tension or ordered them to adopt and enforce such rules.[24]

The courts likened these symbols when used by students to "fighting words" or incitement, neither of which is sheltered by the Speech Clause. In classical First Amendment jurisprudence, a speaker whose words would cause the average listener to slug him isn't engaging in protected speech. Neither is a speaker who aims to incite listeners who agree with him to violence. In the right circumstances, an African American might perceive the Confederate flag as an invitation to engage in fisticuffs, or the flag might incite segregationists to resist a school integration order or to attack African

American students. Under these conditions, both forms of speech could be silenced even outside of school, and on campus they would surely raise a threat of material disruption.

After a hiatus, litigation over bans on the Confederate flag including images on hats, shirts, and notebooks has proliferated since the late 1990s in response to school codes that forbid "racial or ethnic slurs/symbols" and other material that "is racially divisive or creates ill will or hatred." Ill will and hatred toward the twenty blacks who attended a Missouri high school with 1,100 white peers were on full display in B.W.A. v. Farmington High School, which reached a federal appeals court in 2009.[25]

The school banned racist speech including Confederate symbols following a series of ugly, racially charged incidents involving students on- and off-campus in 2005–2006. A white elementary school student had urinated on a black student, allegedly saying, "This is what black people deserve." A group of white students, one of whom carried an aluminum bat, assembled outside a black student's home, where they shouted racist comments. When the black student's mother intervened, a white student hit her in the eye, leading to a "melee." Later, whites returned to the house, hurling epithets and threatening to burn the house. A few days afterward, a group of white students confronted the same African American student at school, bringing the matter squarely within the school's disciplinary authority. By the end of the school year, both victims' families had moved out of the district, a common pattern.[26]

All these events preceded high school student B.W.A.'s decision to wear Confederate emblems on his hat, belt buckle, and T-shirt during the 2006–2007 school year. When officials ordered him to remove them, he withdrew from school. A crowd protested across the street from the campus; some displayed the Confederate flag. Students complained that the external protests were exacerbating the existing racial tension within the school. The school suspended two additional students who donned the same emblems. "[R]acial vandalism and property damage" to the school followed.[27]

B.W.A. and his two supporters sued, alleging the school had violated their speech rights by discriminating against their viewpoint and had failed to show "a concrete and substantial fear of disruption." The trial court ruled for the school, and the Eighth Circuit affirmed the decision.[28]

The appellate court focused exclusively on the school's reasonable forecast of material disorder. Consistent with other judicial circuits, the court upheld the constitutionality of the ban on the grounds of "the substantial race-related events occurring both in the school and in the community, some of which involved the Confederate flag." Moreover, the court held, "viewpoint discrimination" does not violate "the First Amendment if the *Tinker* standard requiring a reasonable forecast of substantial disruption . . . is met." Under these conditions, the school is not merely suppressing "unpopular viewpoints."[29]

In other words, the risk of material disruption trumps constitutional concerns about viewpoint discrimination. This posture proves extremely significant because in most disputes over disparaging speech only one side of the argument is accused of violating the rules. It is conceivable that members of a group targeted as minorities might shout back, "You honky pigs, descendants of slave owners and rapists," but in most instances they control themselves. The facts in *Farmington* hint at the likely reason: It is just too dangerous to engage in that kind of exchange.

The Farmington case epitomized a pattern in which the history of racial relations in a community enters judicial consideration of the risk of disruption at school. In 2013, a different appellate court noted that a school was in a "small Southern town in which whites and African Americans were segregated, including in school, for more than a century" following the abolition of slavery. Racial tension accompanied forced integration of the schools in the 1970s. "Over the past four decades," the court continued, "this tension has diminished, but it has not completely disappeared." Given the town's history, officials appropriately weighed incidents outside of school, including the recent "burning of an African-American church by two high school students," when barring racist expression on campus.[30]

An uncomfortable issue of equity lies just under the surface in these decisions. When courts divide schools into two classes based on past racial turmoil, students who are already disadvantaged by attending a school plagued by racial strife are also subjected to diminished First Amendment rights compared with peers in more peaceful, arguably "better" schools.

As I showed in the last chapter, it isn't always as easy to define what amounts to a realistic fear of material disruption, but Farmington surely had strong grounds for anticipating disorder. In contrast, an appellate court held that a single fistfight limited to two combatants is insufficient to support silencing symbols perceived as being racist.[31] Between those two extremes, there is no clear way to calculate how many incidents, their level of seriousness, or how many students must be involved to create an environment that justifies bans on racially divisive symbols. In each instance, school officials (and perhaps, later, judges) must gauge such imprecise boundaries as how closely a history of disruption at the school must be tied to racial hostilities or whether it will be enough to show that the school has police patrolling the halls and entrances regardless of the reason for their presence.

There are even trickier questions. What happens if parents keep their children home from school to protest the speaker's view or in fear that disruption will occur? What if the Ku Klux Klan shows up to protest the school's discipline of a student for displaying Confederate symbols? In these circumstances, censorship would impute to the speaker the disruption listeners created. That might well be the easiest route to surface tranquility but at the impermissible cost of constitutional rights.

These are not far-fetched hypotheticals. In recent decades, schools have punished speakers after listeners "caused a near riot" in the cafeteria; after listeners threatened the speaker; and after parents kept their children home from school because they feared that disorder might follow controversial speech. Families have even felt compelled to flee school districts after fighting for their children's speech rights. So too provocative speakers have been evicted from school "for their own good" and forced to stay home because they might not be safe on campus, the problem I turn to next.[32]

Paternalism and the Heckler's Veto Ascendant

In discussing harassment laws, I alluded to a question I can't avoid when examining educators' efforts to protect students from group disparagement: Does the Constitution permit benignly motivated proscriptions on hurtful speech that neither meets the legal definition of harassment nor threatens material disruption in a school? The short answer is no. When educators silence speech out of well-intentioned paternalism, they strip *Tinker* of all meaning and run the risk of capitulating to hecklers.

Consider this easy case, involving a T-shirt war between Anglo and Hispanic students. The controversy was highly political—it involved illegal immigration, one of the most contentious political and policy issues of our time. In 2007, a judge held that the risk of disruption at a Texas high school evenly divided among Caucasian, black, and Hispanic students was sufficient to justify a ban on both the provocative "We Are Not Criminals" T-shirts many Hispanic students were wearing and the "Border Patrol" shirts many non-Hispanics reportedly planned to wear in response. The judge endorsed the Mexican American principal's paternalism: "Principal Garcia made the proper decision to ban the T-shirts in order to *protect* the

Hispanic students from the animosity of the other students, not to harm them by precluding their speech."[33] This sacrifice of speakers' rights based on the state's beneficent motive turns free speech doctrine on its head.

Protective censorship flies in the face of heckler's veto jurisprudence. The Supreme Court explained in 1949 that when a "surging, howling mob" gathers to protest vicious verbal attacks on political and racial groups, law enforcement officers must protect the speaker and remove those protesting his speech. A "function of free speech under our system of government is to invite dispute," the Supreme Court exhorted in overturning a statute that defined disturbing the peace as speech that "invites dispute." Using the language that Justice Fortas would later echo in *Tinker,* the Court emphasized that speech "may indeed best serve its high purpose when it induces a condition of unrest, creates dissatisfaction with conditions as they are, or even stirs people to anger."[34]

I don't minimize the difficulty of striking the right balance between order and rights in the school context. The complexity goes beyond the normal balancing that judges engage in all the time. School administrators must make quick decisions without the benefit of hindsight, as I have noted before. And the Court in *Tinker* didn't clarify whether the threat of material disorder could ever be read as an exception to the principle that a heckler should never be allowed to silence a speaker. It didn't need to in that case because the deceased soldier's friends did not in fact show any signs of responding violently to the armbands.

The threats student speakers sometimes face from their peers again highlight a special characteristic of the school environment: Neither the speakers nor the hecklers who threaten them can simply walk away and go home. They are a captive audience. Students may find themselves seated next to each other in class or a school bus, unlike the anonymous strangers usually depicted in discussions of the heckler's veto. Given compulsory school laws and restricted mobility on campus, schools have at least an implicit legal obligation to protect students from measurable harm at one another's hands. As Justice Alito observed in *Morse,* because schools can be dangerous places, "[S]chool officials must have greater authority to intervene before speech leads to violence."[35] Would the heckler's veto principle require authorities to turn a campus into an armed camp to keep a provocative speaker safe? At what cost to the community's resources and culture?

All of this sheds light on why conservative jurist and law professor Richard Posner, a Reagan appointee who is one of our most thoughtful appellate judges, considers the heckler's veto construct impractical in public schools when authorities fear "extreme disorder." In 2011, he observed, a "city can protect an unpopular speaker from the violence of an angry audience by deploying police, but that is hardly an apt response to students enraged by a T-shirt. A school has legitimate responsibilities, albeit paternalistic in character, toward the immature captive audience that consists of its students, including the responsibility of protecting them from being seriously distracted from their studies by offensive speech during school hours."[36] Distraction, however, is hardly the equivalent of material disruption. Students are easily distracted by all sorts of things beyond the school's power to control, from gossip to daydreams.

Discussing *Farmington,* I agreed that schools with violent histories need significant discretion to control expression that is likely to enflame and materially disrupt while also arguing that student speakers should not be punished for disorder that others cause. But it's not always easy to distinguish speech that smacks of "fighting words" from the heckler's veto. Some people in the crowd may hear the speaker's words as incitement (if they agree with his comments about a disliked group) while others (members of the group being disparaged) may hear the same words as a challenge to a fight. Both possibilities were in play at Farmington High School.

These complexities should not diminish the dramatic plight of a Long Island student subjected to prior restraint and ejected from his campus. His story demonstrates the dangers implicit in shifting responsibility to speakers when listeners materially disrupt the campus.

The surreal chain of events that reached the courts in DeFabio v. East Hampton Unified School District began with the accidental death of a Hispanic student in a motorcycle accident. Daniel DeFabio whispered to a friend between classes that he had just heard someone say "one down, forty thousand to go." As rumors spread that DeFabio originated the offensive comment (rather than just reporting what someone else had said), other students confronted him until he was whisked to safety in the nurse's office. Police officers escorted DeFabio out of the school building.[37]

After students threatened to bomb DeFabio's house and kill him ("true threats," which the school apparently ignored), officials suggested that he stay home for the foreseeable future. A few days later, still confined to his home, DeFabio asked the principal for permission to declare his innocence by addressing his peers over the loudspeaker, talking at an assembly, or distributing an open letter. The principal denied DeFabio's request, saying, "[I]t would make the students angrier and would cause more problems in the school." Officials repeatedly asserted they could not keep him safe on campus; they provided him with a part-time home tutor.[38]

The school district suspended DeFabio for the rest of the school year, depriving him of the opportunity to defend himself and fueling perceptions that he was guilty. When the school finally allowed him to meet with twelve representatives of the school's Latino community, the Latino students showed a naïve faith in American justice: They were sure the school wouldn't have suspended DeFabio unless he had originated the inflammatory statement. A state administrative inquiry later concluded that DeFabio's version of events was accurate and expunged his disciplinary record. That report was not completed in time to help DeFabio.[39]

Threats continued throughout the summer, while he was driving, by phone, and at his job, which he had to quit. Unable to obtain assurances that the school would protect Daniel the next year, his family sent him to the West Coast "for his own safety."[40]

When DeFabio's family sued the school district, alleging violations of his First Amendment right to defend himself to his peers, the trial judge ruled for the school. The judge surmised that distribution of DeFabio's statement might only have exacerbated the school's reasonable apprehension of "violence or other disruptions by angry and emotional students who may not believe Daniel's statement and are outraged by his false exculpatory statement."[41]

Affirming the lower court's ruling and granting school officials qualified immunity, the Second Circuit said the school had satisfied *Tinker*'s material disruption requirement by pointing to a risk that "administrators and teachers would be further diverted from their core educational responsibilities" if they had to respond to angry questions about DeFabio's explanation of his comment.[42] Another way of looking at these facts is that teachers and staff would have been doing their jobs and helping students learn how to listen and respond to thoughts with which they vehemently disagree.

Bizarrely, the appellate court went on to speculate that the school had not, in fact, censored DeFabio's speech. It reasoned that he could "have stood outside the school gates communicating his message to students as they left."[43] This stance is worse than disingenuous. If DeFabio could have done so without risking his life, the school's fear of disorder was baseless or greatly exaggerated.

Assuming the threats were real, as DeFabio's family thought they were, it is difficult to attribute to DeFabio rather than to other students the risk of disorder that might have flowed if he had been allowed to explain himself. DeFabio's repetition of "one down" and the defense he never had the opportunity to articulate were protected speech. Whispered to one friend, they couldn't possibly have been equated to fighting words likely to provoke a violent response. Nor did his proposed statement intend to incite a group of listeners to violence against a third party or against the speaker himself. DeFabio's explanation is distinct from the racially inflammatory waving of a Confederate flag at a school with a history of racial acrimony. DeFabio wanted to placate—not provoke—his audience.

The story of Daniel DeFabio realizes Justice Black's worst nightmares but with a twist: The inmates in charge of the asylum at East Hampton High School stifled speech instead of promoting it. The school allowed the mob to dictate its policy. School administrators abdicated responsibility for one student's safety and well-being. It seems likely that other schools would do the same thing if faced with similar facts because it is easier and costs much less money than doing what the Constitution (and, arguably, ethical precepts) requires.

Judge O'Scannlain, outraged by a similar case of what he regarded as mob rule sustained by a Ninth Circuit panel, explained in 2014 that "far from abandoning the heckler's veto doctrine in public schools, *Tinker* stands as a dramatic reaffirmation of it. Given the central importance of the doctrine to First Amendment jurisprudence, that should come as no surprise." By allowing the risk that "other students might have reacted violently" to T-shirts depicting the American flag on Cinco de Mayo in 2010 to justify suppressing the flag-wearers' expression, O'Scannlain charged, the court had broken with other circuits and overlooked "the bedrock principle" that the government may not "suppress speech simply because it is unpopular."[44]

He warned that "any viewpoint opposed by a vocal and violent band of students" could be suppressed if schools are exempted from the heckler's veto principle: "The next case might be a student wearing an image of Che Guevara, or Martin Luther King, Jr., or Pope Francis. It might be a student wearing a President Obama 'Hope' shirt, or a shirt proclaiming 'Stand with Rand!' It might be a shirt proclaiming the *shahada* [an Islamic statement of belief in the oneness of God], or a shirt announcing 'Christ is risen!' It might be any viewpoint imaginable, but whatever it is, it will be vulnerable to the rule of the mob. The demands of bullies will become school policy."[45]

A number of alternative, though more costly, approaches were available to East Hampton High School when a mob threatened DeFabio. The school could have hired a bodyguard to escort DeFabio to classes or paid for him to attend school in a neighboring district. Instead of suspending DeFabio, it could have barred the students who threatened him from campus.

Most important, officials squandered a rich pedagogical opportunity: to teach about nonviolent ways to resolve disputes; to herald the importance of reliable information and fact gathering; and above all to affirm the sacred values of due process and the rule of law.

Faced with a similar situation, a school in Marin County north of San Francisco did just that and did it so well that the appellate court (while ruling the school had violated a student's right to express anti-immigrant sentiments) commended the school for "model[ing] the civil discourse education should foster." What happened to DeFabio would be impermissible under California's expansive protections for student speech. The court in Smith v. Novato Unified School District reminded officials that, at least in California, disorder must be attributable to the speaker before the speaker can be penalized. Schools may not restrict expression unless the speech itself "incites disruption, either because it specifically calls for a disturbance or because the manner of expression (as opposed to the content of the ideas) is so inflammatory that the speech itself provokes the disturbance."[46]

Andrew Smith wrote a column titled "Immigration" for his school paper. One of roughly sixty African Americans who attended a school with about one thousand students, of whom about one-quarter identified as Hispanic or Latino, Smith argued that "a significant proportion of undocumented immigrants are criminals, and that any person who cannot speak English should be suspected of being an undocumented immigrant." This was clearly political speech, bearing on what the court termed "an emotionally debated contemporary issue."[47]

The day after "Immigration" appeared, a number of students walked out of class in protest. When several Latino parents arrived at school, the principal spent an hour talking with them. On the advice of the guidance counselor, the principal then met with the students who were boycotting classes and the parents who had joined them on campus. The school invited students to express their feelings, both verbally and on large sheets of paper provided by guidance counselors. Students expressed "anger," some "were crying." By lunchtime 100 to 150 students had joined the group. The principal apologized to the students but also warned them that she would not "tolerate any violence or threats of violence against the author." She urged Smith to let her know if he was threatened or assaulted. In contrast to DeFabio's situation, only one student confronted Smith, who escaped with a chipped tooth.[48]

The school sent a letter to all families on the first day some students boycotted class. The letter set in motion a productive community dialogue that helped diffuse the situation, but it also contained constitutional missteps.

The principal apologized for and disavowed Smith's column. We can think of the disavowal as a permissible disclaimer—it made clear that the school neither endorsed nor was responsible for the ideas in "Immigration," although it singled out one article for disapproval. But the school went further. It announced that "'the article should never have been printed . . .'" and indicated that "future speech similar to *Immigration* would not be tolerated."[49]

The school also erred by engaging in post-publication censorship when it sequestered all copies of the paper that had not yet been distributed. Although the school didn't discipline Smith, it violated his speech rights. The court correctly held that the school's actions after the column appeared were likely to chill Smith's speech in the future and to chill the speech of every student who agreed with him. Moreover, it emphasized that Smith's speech was "constitutionally protected from 'censorship by hostile reaction'" (the heckler's veto) under California law.[50] While the school hadn't gone as far as East Hampton High School did in bowing to hecklers, it still went further than the law allows in its efforts to salve wounded feelings.

But the school got other things right. It directed faculty to review the policies governing speech and tolerance with their students. The principal's letter to families invited parents and students to another meeting to be held the next day. About two hundred people attended the second assembly, where they vented their "dismay" in a safe, supervised setting. About two weeks later the District Board of Trustees devoted a public session to the column and its aftermath. Many people spoke, including Smith and his father. All of these actions were not only permissible but commendable.

The judges rejected Smith's claim that these meetings had infringed on his rights by disfavoring his viewpoint. The court explained that "by enabling the protestors to respond to offensive speech with their viewpoint," the school promoted "'the marketplace of ideas'" consistent with the "'vigilant protection of constitutional freedoms" that "is no where more vital than in the community of American schools" and serves "our nation's traditions of open debate."[51]

The disparaging speech I have been exploring involved plausible outbreaks of violence. No matter how the schools and the courts should have defined the boundary between order and expression, the outrage of listeners and the rights of speakers, fighting words or the veto of hecklers, an incontrovertible risk of material disruption existed in Farmington and East Hampton and could easily have emerged in Novato, California.

But officials have also banned the Confederate flag and other expression they view as insensitive in districts that have no history of racial strife, where there is little reason to anticipate disruption, and even in schools where "people of both races mix freely together and form good relationships." At other times, administrators just show poor judgment, as when a school punished a student who showed a few friends a four-inch-square Confederate flag while explaining the Civil War enactment he had participated in.[52]

Three kinds of mistakes are apparent in the episodes where schools impermissibly bar speech they perceive as disparaging groups of people.

First, educators and some judges have improperly invoked *Fraser*'s deference to educators in disputes involving racially provocative speech, alleging they can silence it under the umbrella of teaching civility. They point to the Supreme Court's observation that "it is a highly appropriate function of public school education to prohibit the use of vulgar and offensive terms in public discourse" and that the fundamental values of democracy "disfavor the use of terms of debate highly offensive . . . to others." One judge traced the school's authority over racist symbols to the "cultivation of the 'habits and manners of civility' that *Fraser* held 'essential to a democratic society,'" coupled with "a level of parent-like guidance."[53]

Any school would be able to satisfy this highly deferential standard under almost any set of facts; applying *Fraser*'s malleable deference beyond the sexually suggestive speech would eliminate any boundaries at all around school censorship as long as the school asserted concern for "civility." *Morse* appears to resolve the question because, as we have seen, the Supreme Court declined to invoke *Fraser* where the speech wasn't lewd. Most courts reject the argument that the "vulgar and offensive terms" *Fraser* covers can be stretched to include Confederate symbols or other racially insensitive speech.[54]

Second, school officials who have censored such expression and the judges who sometimes support them have invoked the most diffuse and ambiguous explanations of the "rights of others." They articulate worthy goals including avoiding hurt feelings, averting wounds to self-esteem, and making sure students "feel" safe. These beneficent motives don't overcome the transparent viewpoint discrimination that results where there is no risk of material disruption.

The legal reasoning underlying such episodes too often reveals a tendency to conflate *Tinker*'s two prongs, using the most underspecified threat to "the rights of others" as proof that an equally vague intimation of disruption exists. Concerns about the sensitivities of immature students have led some school officials to conclude that any time "you have hurt feelings" or "people that are offended," the educational process is inherently disrupted.[55]

The Eleventh Circuit merged and failed to fully develop both prongs of *Tinker* when it asserted that the Confederate flag evokes "real feelings—strong *feelings*." The court proclaimed it "is not only constitutionally allowable for school officials to closely contour the range of expression children are permitted regarding such volatile issues, *it is their duty to do so*."[56]

The chairman of the school board that oversaw Anderson County High School in Clinton, Tennessee, testified that he did not "know the constitutional limits on the Board's power to restrain student speech," but he thought that the district banned the Confederate flag "to avoid offending some students." He seemed unaware of the constitutional doctrines that govern school speech rights and didn't understand that the black armband worn during the Vietnam War had also elicited "real" and "strong" feelings on both sides of the issue. In the absence of disorder, a trial judge not only held that school district accountable, he allowed the student who had wrongly been disciplined to seek punitive damages because his school had paid so little attention to First Amendment rights.[57]

Schools must establish a link between the offense speech gives and the risk of substantial disorder. It isn't enough to speculate about a link or ask the court to impute one.

I'm not suggesting that educators should remain indifferent to the risk of emotional wounds, but they must limit themselves to constitutionally permissible responses, whether to prevent the initial outbursts or to salve wounds in the wake of hurtful words. A school will satisfy *Tinker*'s demands if it can demonstrate a sound basis for fearing material disruption, even if a desire to protect listeners from emotional distress initially prompted officials to focus on the potentially disturbing expression.

In 2008, the Sixth Circuit acknowledged the interaction among the injury a symbol like the Confederate flag can cause, the rights of others, and the potential for disruption. It concluded that a principal's belief that the flag offends—while not enough to justify censorship—did not undermine the school's well-founded fear of material disruption. Where a school had experienced "race-related altercations," the daily offense occasioned by seeing Confederate symbols could "disrupt the school's educational process." The court explained: "That the principal believed the flag to be *offensive* to African-American and other students . . . does not negate [the administration's] reasonable belief that the flag was also *disruptive*." In "a context of high racial tensions, race-related altercations, and threats of violence," the court found, "the flag would disrupt the school's educational process." The court acknowledged it was "evince[ing] greater sensitivity to the effect" of offensive speech "on the student audience" than is generally permissible under First Amendment doctrine but noted that schools need to attend to "all students' psychological and developmental" needs in addition to their physical safety. Where a risk of substantial disruption existed, the court held, the Confederate flag interfered "with the rights of other students to be secure and let alone."[58]

The third and final systemic error seen in the group disparagement cases consists of unwarranted confidence that officials and other listeners have correctly interpreted the speaker's message, a problem that may overlap with heightened sensitivity to the emotions of those who feel disparaged.

Members of the audience may hear offensive messages that the speaker did not intend or understand. If waving a Confederate flag is always equivalent to a matador with a red cape provoking a bull's performance, the speaker could be held responsible for any resulting disruption. But he might be unaware of the impact he has on others or have very different intentions, which may affect the calculus.

The three Sypniewski brothers were stymied by an increasingly elastic emphasis on the feelings of listeners when they wore Jeff Foxworthy T-shirts purchased at Walmart to school in Warren Hills, Pennsylvania. The brothers' story illustrates the third endemic analytic flaw in the bans on Confederate flags and other racially volatile symbols: The enforcers lack a rigorous way of interpreting what those displays mean. Such controversies require nuanced analysis on a case-by-case basis.

The Foxworthy shirts celebrated a popular comedian known for his self-deprecating "You may be a redneck if" act. The shirts listed the "Top 10 reasons you might be a redneck" including: "6. You know the Hooter's [*sic*] menu by heart. 5. Your mama is banned from the front row at wrestling matches . . . 2. You wear a baseball cap to bed. 1. You've ever told your bookie 'I was just kidding.'" The school district—equating redneck culture with white supremacy—told the Sypniewskis that the shirts violated the school's antiharassment code. This was political correctness run amok.

The school had witnessed some racial hostility, including offensive jokes and symbols. In response, it had adopted a new code barring racial intimidation "by name calling, using racial or derogatory slurs, wearing or possession of items depicting or implying racial hatred or prejudice . . . [material] that is racially divisive or creates ill will or hatred. (Examples: clothing . . . or any item that denotes Ku Klux Klan, Arayan [*sic*] Nation–White Supremacy, Black Power, Confederate flags or articles, Neo-Nazi or any other 'hate' group." The school system told the boys their shirts violated the code.

When the Sypniewskis sought a preliminary injunction, the school district said it had banned their shirts to enforce "mutual respect" on campus. After the district court ruled against them, the brothers appealed to the Third Circuit.

The appellate court ruled in Sypniewski v. Warren Hills Regional Board of Education in 2002 that the school could not suppress student expression just because it "causes hurt feelings" or "ill will" based "entirely on the reaction of listeners." The code impermissibly reached "relatively benign" terms and political speech. In the process, the school had ignored the balance that *Tinker* had struck by demanding respect "for both constitutional rights and effective education." The "mere association" of the term *redneck* with racism, the court ruled, was not enough to satisfy the First Amendment as framed by *Tinker's* two tests. Suppression of the Sypniewskis' pride in country culture had caused them "an injury that cannot be undone" by silencing their expression.[59]

The Third Circuit also observed that the school district had not shown that the expression had amounted to "abuse" of other students but didn't explain the significance of the term *abuse*. Cohen v. California, the 1971 Supreme Court decision that safeguarded the right to wear a "Fuck the Draft" jacket, included a cautionary note that sheds light on what abusing listeners means. It is unconstitutional for the government, *Cohen* tells us, "to shut off discourse solely to protect others from hearing it." If the government is primarily concerned with the impact the speech will have on others, it must show "that substantial privacy interests are being invaded in an essentially intolerable manner."[60] Abusive speech may be intolerable, and speech may be intolerable because it is abusive. Whatever the scope of abusive or intolerable speech, the Sypniewskis' shirts did not approach the line.

Warren Hills in Pennsylvania is hardly the only school district to have sacrificed the rights of speakers to the sensibilities of listeners. The risks to expression mount steeply as courts move beyond the rationale of "material disruption" and realistic forecasts of upheaval to consider the rights of others. As the Fourth Circuit underlined while upholding a narrowly tailored ban on the Confederate flag, "prohibiting students from having the Confederate flag at school is not automatically constitutional" despite "the emotions that it may cause." Each incident "is, at its core, a student-speech case governed by *Tinker* and its progeny."[61]

This brings me to the problem at the heart of the third analytical flaw in many of these disputes: How do we assess what the speaker or the symbol means? In the context of the desegregation cases of the 1970s and earlier, the virulence of the repugnant epithets targeted at specific blacks supported the equation of the Confederate flag with unambiguous racism. Some political extremists, epitomized as recently as 1996 by the New Albany Declaration of white supremacy and states' rights, clearly intended to communicate precisely the message most African Americans perceived when they saw crowds waving the symbol of the Confederacy.

But those perceptions don't tell us what other speakers at other times in other school districts intended such symbols to communicate. What the Confederate flag meant to those who waved it in the late 1960s might not be what it means to individuals who display it half a century later. (Obviously, when a government displays such symbols on state property, different issues arise.) Judges, like teachers, bring their own experience to bear when they rule that the Confederate flag is "racially divisive in nature" regardless of what the people displaying it intend to communicate.[62]

It may be easier for many of us to see the breakdown in rigorous thinking when we look at the Sypniewski brothers' Foxworthy shirt than when we look at the Confederate flag, to which most people bring presumptions that are difficult to modify. In *Sypniewski*, the school district didn't present any evidence that the word *redneck* had the disruptive potential of an established inflammatory symbol like the Confederate flag but relied instead on a "mere association" of terms like *redneck* or *country music* with racism. The very equation of working-class Southern culture with racism reflected a kind of reverse bigotry that disparaged Jeff Foxworthy fans, the same working-class population that took such offense at candidate Barack Obama's leaked remarks about "bitter" people who "cling to guns and God" in 2008.

Scrutiny of terms like *nigger* and *niggah* and *faggot* and *queer* reminds us that the significance of names and symbols continues to evolve. It is widely understood today that *Redskins* is an insensitive name for a sports team. On the other hand, law professor Randall Kennedy has unearthed the many meanings of *nigger*, beyond insult and animus, depending on who is speaking and the point the speaker wants to make. The most distressful of epithets, often linked to violence, it can also be used affectionately as in *my niggah*, but only under the right circumstances.[63]

So too with the Confederate flag. As one historian warned in 2005, the complex meanings of the emblem have changed over time. "For many people today," he observed, "the Confederacy and the flag are part of their personal and familial heritage, devoid of ideological content." For some, it means nothing more than "honoring their ancestors."[64] Some people who wear symbols of what they regard as "Southern pride" really mean just that and don't intend to declare racial superiority, even if history makes it hard for many observers to separate the two concepts. Who among us really knows what the hip-hop artist Kanye West means by donning the Confederate symbol? Presumably he doesn't mean he hates black people.

A potential censor would need a weighted scale that gives certain groups in a pluralistic society the license to use hurtful words, which would conflict with our image of Themis, the blindfolded goddess of Justice. If we came to terms with the weighted scale, the potential censor would still need to determine whose understanding of the symbol or statement should receive the greatest weight—the speaker's or the offended observer's? What about irony or humor? Should license be given to the white fan of hip-hop who wants to show his affinity by using the term *niggah*? Or to two African Americans who call each other *my niggah* or all manner of politically incorrect joking about one's own race, religion, and ethnicity, let alone that of others? Who would decide, and on what basis?

Competing views of the Confederate flag—as an enduring racist emblem or a neutral symbol of Southern heritage—clearly mark it as political speech. It is a catalyst for eliciting divergent views of both historical and contemporary conflicts. Even in schools, one judge cautioned, "repressing" exchanges of views elicited by the Confederate flag "would be as unreasonable, and hopefully unthinkable, as a rule that forbids students to discuss the Constitution of the United States on the basis that it recognized slavery or forbids the display of the American flag because it has been carried by hate groups."[65]

These were the interpretive conundrums that one appeals court judge had in mind when he took his colleagues to task for overlooking the difficulties of making factual determinations about whether a symbol like the Confederate flag is "racially hostile and contemptuous." Judge Danny Boggs, a Reagan appointee, jabbed, "[P]erhaps . . . semioticians could reveal its abstract meaning." Context should also matter, he observed, because "a Confederate flag on a book cover might be thought of as different in meaning than a Confederate flag accompanied by 'forget, Hell' text, as in some cartoons."[66]

Judge Boggs identified several quandaries, starting with core definitions. Even if the Constitution allowed schools to bar inflammatory speech involving race, the term *racially hostile* is itself "both undefined and unlimited." Is race a scientific category or a social construct? Other groups may be harder to categorize. If schools bar anti-Semitic speech under a rule reaching racially hostile expression, courts might have to delve into a centuries-long debate about whether Jews are a race or are those who participate in a religion, a debate heavily burdened by historical events.[67] Are "Anglos" a race that can object to symbols of Mexican pride they see as derisive? Can a student's political views be suppressed if they seem hostile to others as, for example, when a student agitates for deportation of undocumented immigrants?

If the reasoning that racially offensive speech is so damaging that students should not have to confront it were accepted, schools could censor a large swath of personal identity expression and even literary and historical inquiry within the curriculum. Concerns about racial and cultural expression that hurts others have led parents to challenge assigning Mark Twain's *Huckleberry Finn* as "racist" as well as to protest their children's exposure to Shakespeare's avaricious Jew Shylock and his angry black protagonist Othello or John Steinbeck's *Of Mice and Men* for its depiction of persons with disabilities.

Many parents learned growing up and convey to their children that the "N-word" and similar slurs addressed to any number of races, religions, and ethnicities should never be used; others didn't and don't. The Constitution permits individual students to say hateful things (or what others deem hateful) and use hateful symbols, as long as they do not materially disrupt education. Racists and segregationists are entitled to express their views as much as proud Southerners, integrationists, and post-racialists. Whether they intend to communicate hostility or believe they are only demonstrating pride in their own culture, silenced students may be prone to conclude—as *Barnette* warned—that authorities treat *their* freedom of speech as a "mere platitude."

Recognition that the Speech Clause extends to racist expression or speech that causes racial affront does not render educators powerless to react to speech that offends many students and citizens. Schools can transform offensive speech into teachable moments. In the real world children will grow up to live in, they will likely have to learn how to respond to speech they find objectionable and even unbearable without sinking to the offensive speaker's level or slugging him. It may be best to learn how to respond, whether by walking away or questioning, as a student under the watchful guidance of teachers rather than as an adult at a bar. Under the Speech Clause, the best remedy for nasty speech is more and better-quality speech that offers alternative visions and models civil responses.

"No . . . Hurt Feelings Defense": Sensitivity, LGBT Students, and Politics

Targets for belittlement, and perceived belittlement, have proliferated in recent decades, in direct response to mounting demands for recognition and rights from a variety of groups. "Homosexuality is a sin," declared the T-shirt James Nixon purchased at a church meeting and wore to school. "Islam is a lie!" the shirt continued. "Abortion is murder!" Nixon's school told him he could not wear the shirt because it might offend students and staff members who were Muslims or homosexuals or had had abortions. The school was wrong, as a federal court ruled in 2005.[68]

Since 2005 several federal appellate courts have invoked *Tinker*'s second prong in analyzing the impact of disparagement on LGBT students. Almost a third of states expressly barred disparagement based on sexual orientation in schools as of 2012, and in April 2014 the federal government reinterpreted the federal statute that bars gender discrimination as extending to sexual orientation.[69]

Discussion of LGBT rights in the twenty-first century indisputably involves political speech. Complaints against schools, however, suggest that educators lie at two extremes: solicitous concern for the feelings of LGBT students at the cost of free expression and assertions that schools lack any legal duty to control harassment and violence aimed at LGBTs and may be powerless to control similar conduct that falls short of harassment. All of these concerns bring us back to the central question Justice Alito addressed in *Saxe:* Does the Constitution permit a school to impose benignly motivated limits on hurtful speech that does not meet the legal definition of harassment or threaten material disruption?

In 2006, the Ninth Circuit looked to *Tinker*'s second prong in analyzing whether a student had the right to wear a T-shirt that called homosexuality "shameful." The majority in Harper v. Poway Unified School District concluded that students have a right to be protected from "cruel, inhuman, and prejudiced treatment by others." Verbal assaults based on "core identifying characteristic[s]," the court found, "cause young people to question their self-worth and rightful place in society." Harassment "injure[s] and intimidate[s] them . . . and interfere[s] with their opportunity to learn." The court assumed that the shirt's slogan proclaiming "Be Ashamed" was directed to LGBTs, not to the school as a whole, and found that LGBTs were targeted and harmed.[70]

Nuxoll v. Indian Prairie School District, the leading case from the Seventh Circuit, neatly unveiled the danger of viewpoint repression in school speech codes. Alexander Nuxoll, an evangelical Christian in the ninth grade, wore a shirt bearing a number of slogans, including one he had devised: "Be Happy, Not Gay." The rules at his school barred "derogatory comments" about "sexual orientation" among other characteristics. Nuxoll read the school code through the lens of *Tinker* as giving him the right to express his opinions as long as he did not use inflammatory terms. He believed that the gay students themselves had opened a conversation by participating in the Day of Silence, a national demonstration designed to promote tolerance toward LGBTs. In response, the next day, Nuxoll joined students who opposed homosexuality in a "Day of Truth." His co-plaintiff, Heidi Zamecnik, had worn a T-shirt that riffed, "*My* Day of Silence."[71]

School officials told Nuxoll he couldn't wear his shirt unless he blocked out the phrase "Be Happy, Not Gay." Nuxoll and Zamecnik sought injunctive relief that would protect their rights to wear the slogan in the future and challenged the constitutionality of the school's anti-disparagement code. As the appellate court summarized it, the code appeared "to cover the full spectrum of highly sensitive personal-identity characteristics," banning all "derogatory comments . . . that refer to race, ethnicity, religion, gender, sexual orientation, or disability."[72] Although this rule strikes me as transparently aimed at hate speech that is immune from regulation even in schools, the courts allowed the code to stand.

The district court denied Nuxoll's motion for a preliminary injunction because the judge thought that in "a high school setting" the educational interest in protecting gay students from psychological harm permits officials "to restrict speech that expresses" a "negative" view "toward a group of students."[73]

Nuxoll appealed to the Seventh Circuit, which in 2008 ordered a preliminary injunction protecting Nuxoll's right to display the "Be Happy, Not Gay" sentiment pending the trial court's resolution of whether the shirt violated the school code. The appellate panel sent the case back to the trial court and reviewed the district court's subsequent decision in 2011.[74]

Judge Posner authored both of the Seventh Circuit's opinions, which offer a glimpse of rapid legal and social change affecting how judges understand the law.

At the outset, in 2008 Judge Posner downplayed the value of student speech for public discourse: "[T]he contribution that kids can make to the marketplace in ideas and opinions is modest." That diminished respect was surprising because in an earlier opinion overturning regulations on violent video games Judge Posner had credited teenagers with being close to bearing adult responsibilities including voting and joining the armed forces. Channeling Justice Black's *Tinker* dissent, in *Nuxoll* Judge Posner observed, "[C]hildren are in school to be taught by adults rather than to practice attacking each other with wounding words."[75]

Posner weighed what he considered insignificant speech rights against the school's important goal of protecting the psychological health of students by controlling insults that aim at "unalterable or otherwise deeply rooted characteristics," such as race, gender, and sexual orientation. These are traits, he wrote, "about which most people . . . especially including [] adolescent schoolchildren, are highly sensitive [and] easily upset . . . because for most people these are major components of their personal identity."[76]

In conflict with the Third Circuit in *Saxe,* Posner interpreted the school's regulations as an acceptable means of preventing the disruption insults could cause in light of the heightened sensitivity and distractibility of high school students. Posner inferred broad authority from *Morse* for schools to inhibit speech that might "lead to a decline in students' test scores, an upsurge in truancy, or other symptoms of a sick school" by upsetting members of the disparaged group. This approach hugely expands the kinds of speech that a court could find creates a reasonable fear of disruption under *Tinker*'s first prong and could bring many categories of content under *Tinker*'s second prong based on the *reactions* of others whether or not the speech invaded the *rights* of others.[77]

The court then turned to the second issue: whether Nuxoll's shirt transgressed the school's rules and, if it did, whether the school could show that the phrase it censored threatened substantial disruption. Recognizing that applying anti-disparagement regulations presents a host of problems like the ones I discussed with respect to racially charged speech and not one to shy from complexity, Judge Posner took on the postmodernist issues: What is "disparagement," and who decides whether speech is disparaging? What did Nuxoll's shirt really mean? We could also wonder whether it is possible to "disparage" a majority group ("honkies go home" or "straights are sick").

Judge Posner examined whether the slogan was likely to injure LGBT students. As is his custom, he drew on numerous social science studies that suggest negative comments about sexual orientation can undermine academic performance and could have profound psychological effects. The impact, he ventured, is no different from proclaiming, "'[B]lacks have lower IQs than whites'" or "'[A] woman's place is in the home.'" Judge Posner did not develop his hypothetical further but leaves us to wonder on what ground, if any, a school could forbid those sentiments pasted on a student's notebook cover consistent with the First Amendment.[78]

Because the judges on the panel entertained several possible readings of "Be Happy, Not Gay" the court sent the case back to the trial judge to determine whether the school had properly construed the slogan as violating its anti-disparagement rule. Whether the school reasonably anticipated that disruption would flow from allowing the slogan would depend on what the slogan meant and the conditions facing LGBT students at the particular school, not on the national studies Judge Posner had examined. The appellate court directed that school officials could not prevail unless they established a reasonable apprehension of disruption to "a minimally decorous atmosphere for learning."[79]

Despite the court's solicitude for the well-being of LGBT students, in the end it held that the second prong of *Tinker* does not provide an independent rationale for regulating speech. The school's argument that it could bar the slogan to "protect the 'rights' of the students against whom the derogatory comments are directed," Judge Posner explained, would not stand on its own to justify censorship in the Seventh Circuit. He emphasized that "people do not have a legal right to prevent criticisms of their beliefs or for that matter their way of life." The school, he wrote, agreeing with Justice

Brennan, can only "protect students from invasion of their legal rights by other students," not their feelings.[80]

The exchanges between Judge Posner and Judge Ilana Rovner, who authored a separate concurring opinion when the panel first considered *Nuxoll,* offer a lively dialogue about derogatory speech in general and speech about sexual identity in particular. Judge Rovner took Judge Posner to task on several fronts.

Judge Posner, she charged, had unnecessarily complicated a straightforward case: "We are bound by the rule of *Tinker,* a case that the majority portrays in such a convoluted fashion that the discussion folds in on itself like a Mobius strip."[81] In Judge Rovner's view, *Tinker* clearly governed, and there was no need to refer to *Morse,* much less explore the rights of others. Nuxoll intended to express derogatory views, but the school never had any basis for fearing his shirt would cause disruption.

Judge Rovner appreciated the innate significance of Nuxoll's speech: For "the last decade or two, state and national legislatures have been awash with debates over the limits placed on the rights of LGBT persons," including the right to benefits, the right to parent, and the right to marry, reaching even presidential politics. Nuxoll wanted to participate in this national political dialogue as it was pursued at his high school in discussions among young people who are already or are only "a few short years away from being eligible to vote, to contract, to marry, to serve in the military, and to be tried as adults in criminal prosecutions. To treat them as children in need of protection from controversy," Judge Rovner insisted, "to blithely dismiss their views as less valuable than those of adults . . . is contrary to the values of the First Amendment."[82]

Nuxoll's play on words echoed the abundant use of the term *gay* in the halls of his own school, Judge Rovner emphasized, and in "virtually every high school in the United States." Students use it daily in belittling comments like "'that sweater is so gay,'" she observed, "without causing any substantial interruption to the educational process."[83]

Finally, Judge Rovner feared that Judge Posner had given too much ground to school officials and misunderstood the task of public schools. "'Free speech and ordered learning,'" she said, are not "competing interests," as Judge Posner had framed them. Rather, she maintained "these values are compatible. . . . The First Amendment as interpreted by *Tinker* is consistent with the school's mission to teach by encouraging debate on controversial topics while also allowing the school to limit the debate when it becomes substantially disruptive. Nuxoll's slogan-adorned T-shirt comes nowhere near that standard."[84]

Back in district court after remand the school failed to produce evidence that a "Be Happy, Not Gay" shirt would provoke antigay harassment or "poison the educational atmosphere." The trial court granted an injunction that allowed Nuxoll to display the slogan (including at his graduation ceremony) and awarded Nuxoll and his co-plaintiff a symbolic twenty-five dollars each in damages. This time, the school appealed and the case returned to the same panel of Seventh Circuit judges near the end of Nuxoll's senior year.[85]

The Seventh Circuit affirmed the district court's decision. *Tinker's* rights of others language, Judge Posner repeated in 2011, does not provide an independent ground for limiting student speech. There is, he wrote, no "generalized 'hurt feelings' defense to a high school's violation of the First Amendment rights of its students." Intriguingly, after acknowledging the earlier debate with Judge Rovner, Judge Posner's 2011 opinion quoted at length from Rovner's 2008 concurrence about LGBTs' political quest for rights. A legal realist, Posner noted that attempts to apply *Tinker* can stumble on "out of date" judicial "intuition" about the world.[86]

By 2011 developments outside of that school and that courtroom had crystallized the significance of the debate at Nuxoll's high school, as more states legalized same-sex marriage and more Americans expressed the view that people should not be discriminated against because of their sexual orientation. And in 2014, as laws prohibiting the marriage of same-sex couples fell in state after state, Judge Posner authored the Seventh Circuit's decision on the issue. The court overturned laws in Indiana and Wisconsin banning the performance or recognition of same-sex marriages on the ground that such bans discriminate against a class of people "along suspect lines" forbidden by principles of equal protection, and lack even a rational relationship to any of the states' asserted interests.[87]

"You Can't Talk to People Like That": Disparagement Directed at Individuals

Throughout the litigation Alexander Nuxoll had conceded that he could not have adorned his shirt with the message "homosexuals go to hell" instead of "Be Happy, Not Gay" because those would have been "fighting words."[88] "You're going to hell" is exactly what Rachel Zimmer told two of her classmates.

Ensconced in a school bus during a daily commute, the eighth grader rendered her judgment to a fellow passenger because his brother was a homosexual. She also proclaimed in the hearing of one of the school's few Jewish students, "[I]f you do not believe in Jesus Christ, you are going to burn in hell." A federal judge construed these statements as fighting words in 2012 when Zimmer's parents sued the Carmel Clay school system in suburban Indianapolis after the school bus driver chastised Rachel for her comments.[89]

When employed by the state, bus drivers, "lunch ladies" who staff the cafeteria, and many others are the state's agents, bound by the Constitution; for legal purposes in a student speech case, there is no significant difference between a teacher and a bus driver like Betty Campbell who drove Zimmer to school.

M.E., the boy with the gay brother, sought Campbell's help after about five conversations in which Zimmer told him he was going to hell. He was proud of his brother, he said, and he felt Zimmer was harassing him.

To avoid singling Zimmer out, Campbell addressed all the students on her bus collectively shortly after Barack Obama was elected president in in 2008. The students had been arguing about the election with particular emphasis on Obama's support for gay rights. As the bus pulled up at school, Campbell flashed the lights to get everyone's attention. She began by noting, "This week we had a very historic election." She then launched into a colloquy on pluralism: "'It's called diversity in this country . . . we've got kids on this bus who are Jewish, Catholic, I've had Muslims, I've had Buddhists, Sikhs, fine . . . I don't care if you're gay . . . All those diverse things are what make this country what it is. I don't care if you are evangelical. What I will not tolerate is your own personal views being espoused on this bus that you are going to hell if you don't do it the way I do it.'"[90]

Campbell concluded, "'I don't want to hear one more word about anybody going to hell if they are gay or if they're Buddhist or whatever, 'cause it is none of your damn business.'"[91]

Campbell's heartfelt words in some ways represent the best of grassroots American pluralism: All groups, all religions, all kinds of people deserve respect. Personally offended by what she saw as Zimmer's intolerance and incivility, Campbell demanded that students on her bus behave respectfully toward each other. She wanted to prevent aggressive students from hectoring others, wounding them, or disparaging their values. She did not demand that Zimmer change her views, nor could she have without violating *Barnette*'s precepts.

That afternoon, after dropping everyone off, Campbell parked her bus in front of the Zimmer house. She asked Zimmer and her older sister, who she knew, to join her on the bus (which was equipped with recording devices) for a conversation. Campbell first confronted Zimmer for keeping her headphones on while Campbell addressed the students that morning and then turned to Zimmer's statements. "She is throwing religion in people's faces. You can't do that. This is a public school. . . . You can't go off and tell other people you are going to hell, or you gotta do it my way. They don't have to do it your way." But Campbell's tolerance had limits. She suggested that if Zimmer couldn't act more in keeping with the civic ethos, the family might consider sending her to a parochial school.[92]

When Rachel's mother Sherri arrived home and joined the conversation, Campbell explained, "I didn't want to take it to the office." But Rachel's mother shot back. "Rachel told them 'they might go to hell'? I don't think there's anything wrong with that." Sherri added, "[L]et's take it to the school."[93]

The Zimmers pulled Rachel from the bus for the rest of the school year and demanded the district fire Campbell. The school district did not fire Campbell, and it didn't punish Rachel. That didn't stop the Zimmers from filing a lawsuit in which they asserted that Campbell had violated Rachel's rights to free speech and religious exercise. A federal judge treated Rachel's utterances as fighting words, outside the protection of the Speech Clause, and granted summary judgment to the school.

The judge went on to explore whether the school could permissibly have silenced Rachel's expression if he had not treated her statements as fighting words. He determined that the school could still have restricted her speech under *Tinker*.

The *Zimmer* court saw a risk to order in Rachel's provocative words. The judge agreed with Campbell that there is a crucial difference between "Be Happy, Not Gay" and the finger-pointing inherent in the declaration that you personally "are going to burn in hell" because of your relatives, your religion, or your sexual orientation. The former arguably, but minimally, intrudes on the feelings of others, while the latter is literally in their faces—assaulting, invading, colliding with other students and their core identities. This more aggressive verbal stance, directed at identifiable peers, seems closest to what the *Tinker* Court meant by its alternative test.

No reasonable jury would conclude, the judge in *Zimmer* reasoned, that Campbell had dissuaded students from exercising First Amendment rights when she articulated the school's policy "that one may not 'throw' or 'push' her views in another's face." Betty Campbell summed it up better than many judges: "[Y]ou can't talk to people like that," at least not while they are confined on a school bus.[94]

This works as a matter of etiquette, but it is not obvious that such an approach will stand up as a matter of law because the rights of others do not stand alone as a permissible ground for silencing speech. In 2013, a judge in a different part of the country aptly summarized the relationship between *Tinker*'s two prongs: "*Tinker* implies that some sort of threat or direct confrontation is a necessary predicate" to a finding that speech invaded the rights of others.[95]

If the "rights of others" means only the right to pursue their education without interruption or distraction, the standard would be redundant and totally subsidiary to the material disruption test. The first prong of *Tinker* relieves school officials of any obligation to allow student speech that disrupts the school's essential educational function.

Returning to the Fifth Circuit cases from which the *Tinker* Court drew its solution once again clarifies *Tinker*'s meaning. In Blackwell v. Issaquena County, the court ruled that the school's suspension of demonstrators was justified because they accosted fellow students, pinned buttons on them *"whether they wanted them or not,"* and caused a younger student to break down in tears.[96] This sounds like a violation of personal space, of the right not to speak, and of the right to be protected in a controlled environment. It is also, however, inseparable from disruption, the first prong of the *Tinker* test.

To be legally enforceable, the "rights of others" must mean more than a conflict with the sensibilities or preferences of those who hear the offensive speech. In the world at large (outside the schoolhouse gates), there is no right to be sheltered from the content of speech that the Constitution protects.[97]

The contrast between Nuxoll's slogan, broadcast to all who read it, and Zimmer's face-to-face jeremiad seems to offer a neat solution to the problem of "the rights of others." And yet the court's marginally justified classification of Zimmer's statement as "fighting words" doesn't resolve all the ambiguities the case presents. As stirring as Campbell's defense of tolerance may be, she was still silencing and condemning Zimmer's heartfelt theological and political speech.

The distinction between aggressive and passive speech only begins the process of fashioning the more nuanced criteria needed to define "the rights of others." In *Nuxoll*, the appeals court deemed it significant that Nuxoll's T-shirt was only "tepidly" negative; and, as I will show shortly, a few nasty words are not the same thing as the systematic harassment seen in bullying.

Manipulating the details of the Zimmer incident points the way to other important distinctions. Would it matter if Zimmer said calmly, "I'm worried about you, that you might go to hell?" Or if she volunteered her innermost beliefs two or three times rather than five but backed off once rebuffed? Perhaps the age of the children involved might also matter. What if Zimmer's comments so upset the targets of her speech that they developed somatic symptoms or avoided the school bus? All of these considerations—of intent, of concert, of repetition, and of interference in educational opportunities—would contribute to a subtler understanding of the degrees and forms of infringement on the rights of others that might give independent meaning to *Tinker*'s second prong.

To this end, I propose an "infringement matrix" for school officials to examine before invoking the rights of others and for judges to use in evaluating censorship under *Tinker*'s second prong. To measure how aggressive words are, in conjunction with linking them to disruptiveness, the infringement matrix would direct decision makers to look at a variety of factors drawn from the decisions discussed in this chapter. The factors should include whether the asserted infringement resembled harassment by virtue of being directed to one or more targeted individuals and whether it was aggressive and "in your face," pervasive, severe, objectively offensive, threatening, or, in *Cohen*'s terms, "intolerable." None of these factors is quantifiable, but they can all be measured by assessing, among other things, the level of hostility, volume, and incursion into physical space, whether the speech continued after the target requested the speaker to back off and desist, the specific language used, the numbers and ages of the speakers and targets, and the demonstrated impact on the targets and their ability to participate in educational activities. No single factor would be dispositive; I would urge consideration of the totality of the circumstances, including the presence, frequency, and degree of each factor.

Applying the infringement matrix with a nuanced hand and a preference for protecting student expression that respects the intent of *Barnette* and *Tinker* would have safeguarded the shirts worn by Nuxoll and the Sypniewskis, as the current doctrine did, but it would also have supported the conclusion that hecklers impermissibly disrupted Daniel DeFabio's education. The infringement matrix would likely have resulted in Rachel Zimmer's insensitivity being treated as a much closer question, depending on how intrusive fact finders concluded her approaches to M.E. really were and whether the school could show the required link to material disruption.

The Speech Rights of Bullies: "Simple Acts of Teasing and Name-Calling"

Many of the group disparagement episodes discussed earlier in this chapter can easily be reconceptualized as involving bullies and individual victims: the African American boy whose schoolmate urinated on him; the threats that drove Daniel DeFabio from East Hampton High School; gay children relentlessly hounded in the school corridors. Imagine if eighth grader Rachel Zimmer had not spoken just for herself but had roused a group of peers to encircle and then persecute M.E., the boy with the gay brother, and done so relentlessly, throughout the day, throughout the week, throughout the campus.

All of these scenarios fit within the stringent definition provided by Norwegian researcher Dan Olweus, an internationally recognized expert on bullying. According to Olweus, bullying occurs only when a person "is exposed, repeatedly and over time, to negative ['mean or hurtful'] actions on the part of one or more other persons, and he or she has difficulty defending himself or herself." Like harassment, it requires a repetitive pattern. And to fit the definition, there must be an imbalance of power between the bully and the victim. Bullying may or may not involve physical contact.[98]

The social desirability of suppressing the malevolent acts of bullies may seem so self-evidently uncontroversial that only a contrarian could raise questions about it. But I can't escape the necessity of asking whether campus bullies too have speech rights and, if they do, when anti-bullying efforts cross the boundary to impermissible restraint of speech. I have not found any courts that have considered either question.

In approaching these questions, once again we need to be careful not to conflate distinct issues. Most importantly, bullying conduct and bullying words are not comparable. As then Judge Alito put it in in *Saxe*, "There is of course no question that non-expressive, physically harassing *conduct* is entirely outside the ambit of the free speech clause."[99] My discussion of bullying is limited to words that are not accompanied by conduct. This sometimes requires me to draw on analyses developed in cases that present both speech and conduct, treating the speech for purposes of my analysis as if the conduct had never happened. These modifications and hypotheticals facilitate exploration of questions courts have not yet confronted.

But I should warn that excising violent conduct transforms the most widely publicized bullying episodes, all of which included physical acts, from tripping and throwing things at victims where girls were the tormenters, to spitting, hitting, shoving, kicking, beating up, performing mock rapes, and causing injuries so serious they require hospitalization and surgery. The 2010 documentary *Bullied* captures the egregious torture Jamie Nabozny endured that included all the attacks I've just listed and more as well as words—*faggot* and worse. Jamie ran away and attempted suicide more than once, as school authorities shrugged off his complaints that he was being tortured because of his sexual orientation: "[B]oys will be boys," they said. They thought he shouldn't flaunt his proclivities.[100]

Bullying usually relies more heavily on words than on brute force. It often includes "name calling, teasing or taunting, spreading rumors. . . ." In a 2011 study of college students, 88 percent of respondents who reported being victims of bullying characterized the abuse they experienced as psychological rather than physical. The U.S. Department of Education confirms these self-reports. It found that less than one-third of bullying incidents result in physical injuries such as bruises, cuts, or bloody noses.[101]

Two distinct legal issues tend to get tangled up when people try to sort out how schools respond to this kind of ugly verbal barrage: a school's *obligation* and a school's *authority* to protect children from bullies.

It may surprise some readers that when courts are asked whether schools have an obligation to protect children from bullying peers, the answer is, "Almost never." Even when students suffer physical assaults, no judicial circuit has found that schools generally have a responsibility to protect students from harm at the hands of their schoolmates.

Lacking a legal duty, schools often fail the victims in several ways, as Emily Bazelon has pointed out in her incisive analysis of bullying. They fail to intervene, to punish the bully, or to protect the victim even in the face of violent conduct. Not least of these failures is schools' inability or unwillingness to foster a culture in which bullying is viewed as abhorrent.[102]

Judicial reluctance to force schools to protect the targets of bullying stems in part from the legal principle that people who have suffered injuries at the hands of private persons can only sue the individuals who injured them. Where the government does not directly cause the harm, it normally cannot be held accountable. The Supreme Court drew on this principle when it held that the state had no enforceable obligation to protect "poor Joshua" DeShaney, a very young boy whose father beat him so badly he suffered irreversible brain injuries and had to be institutionalized for the rest of his life. Even though the assault happened while child welfare officials were monitoring his care, the Court held that only the father in whose custody he remained could be held legally responsible for Joshua's incapacitating injuries.[103]

Schools may, however, be held accountable for extreme peer-on-peer harassment that involves discrimination based on certain attributes covered by federal statutes: gender under Title IX of the federal Education Amendments of 1972 ("Title IX"), race under Title VI of the 1964 Civil Rights Act, and disability under the Individuals with Disabilities Education Act (IDEA). Some courts have relied on Title IX to protect students from egregious harassment based on sexual orientation where the school treated assaults differently depending on the victim's gender, even before the federal government clarified in 2014 that Title IX covers sexual orientation.[104]

In 1996, the Lambda Legal Rights project made new law representing Jamie Nabozny when it convinced the Seventh Circuit that he should be permitted to sue his school district because it violated both Title IX and the Equal Protection Clause by ignoring the attacks he endured. Nabozny persuaded a jury that the school would have protected him from the mock rape and other assaults had he been a girl, and the school district quickly settled before the jury could decide the amount of damages—giving Nabozny nearly $1 million.[105] Although some similar results have followed, it remains difficult to hold schools to account when peers bully students.

Judicial reluctance to intervene is traceable to the very case that offers the most fertile ground for legal arguments that schools should be responsible for protecting students from debilitating attacks by peers: Davis v. Monroe County Board of Education, in which the Supreme Court in 1999 interpreted schools' responsibility for harassment by peers under Title IX.[106]

In *Davis*, a girl in fifth grade alleged that a sexual bully harassed her at school over several months, rubbing his body against hers and peppering her with vulgar and unvarnished statements as "I want to get in bed with you" and "I want to feel your boobs" (which he also attempted to do). The school failed to protect the victim or to punish the perpetrator, who was later convicted of sexual battery based on the very same conduct that led the Davis family to sue the school. The Supreme Court ruled that Title IX allowed a student's family to sue a school that responded with "deliberate indifference to known acts" of "student-on-student harassment that is so severe, pervasive, and objectively offensive that it effectively bars the victim's access to an educational opportunity."[107]

Justice O'Connor's opinion for a five-person majority posited that words alone would not normally be enough to show the requisite "severe, pervasive, and objectively offensive" behavior: "[I]n the school setting, students often engage in insults, banter, teasing, shoving, pushing, and gender-specific conduct that is upsetting to the students subjected to it. Damages are not available," the Court underscored, "for simple acts of teasing and name-calling among school children . . . even where these comments target differences in gender." In *Davis*, the bully's physical conduct was critical to the decision to allow the lawsuit to proceed.[108]

O'Connor's language erects significant barriers to lawsuits that seek to hold schools accountable for what children say to each other. Schools have no legally enforceable obligation to protect students from classic bullying unrelated to the victim's gender or race. And even when gender or race is involved, the school will only rarely be held accountable.[109]

That high bar was not high enough for the dissenters in *Davis*. In direct contravention of *Hazelwood*'s concern that student words will be attributed to the school itself, Justice Kennedy wrote: "I am aware of no basis in law or fact . . . for attributing the acts of a student to a school" and brushed off the essence of Davis's claim. Almost every child is teased at some point, he postured dismissively, whether for being a "four-eyes" or overweight or "the school bully calls him a 'scaredy-cat at recess.'"[110]

To say that schools rarely have a legally enforceable obligation to protect students from bullying conduct does not mean that schools lack authority to punish or isolate the bully who uses physical force. Recall Justice Alito's bright line: Assaultive conduct is "entirely outside the ambit of the speech clause," meaning it is entirely *within* the reach of the school's discipline.

Many schools and school districts have enacted codes that expressly bar all verbal bullying regardless of whether it is accompanied by physical acts or whether the target belongs to a group with statutory protection. And, too often, regardless of whether the hurtful speech really amounts to bullying. Educators (and parents) mislabel a great deal of behavior as bullying that does not satisfy accepted definitions; in Bazelon's words they "overdiagnose."[111]

Efforts to stop or punish purely verbal jabs raise constitutional questions that remain largely unexplored. School codes encompass acts that put students "in emotional unrest by spreading rumors, manipulating social relationships . . . engaging in social exclusion, extortion, intimidation and ridicule . . . creating verbal statements or written remarks that are taunting, malicious, threatening or sexual."[112] The good intentions behind such efforts in no way diminish the risks and dilemmas involved in expanding either the obligation or the authority of schools to respond to purely verbal or emotional "bullying." Among other practical questions, how would a school enforce such a code? For example, how would students and parents know what separates a reasonable and permissible choice about which children will be invited to a birthday party from impermissible "social exclusion"?

Other high school codes simply state, "Do not bully anyone" or "[B]ullying [is] not permitted." The message, "If it might be construed as bullying, students may not do it," raises familiar issues about definitions and fair notice to miscreants. The first quoted code, which undoubtedly sweeps in protected speech, warns that violations may lead to discipline ranging from mandatory counseling and parent conferences to exclusion from extracurricular activities and suspension or expulsion.[113] A better rule, related to my infringement matrix, might steer clear of content by requiring students to respect another child's clearly stated request to be left alone: "Don't speak to me again. I don't want to hear what you have to say." Then again, the bullies might tell their victims to shut up and stay away, undermining the school's message that we should respect and learn to listen to each other. Further details would need to be fleshed out as cases are decided.

The legal reasoning behind many school codes aimed at bullying expression is extremely murky. The rules often fail to stipulate whether the school presumes that malicious speech about other students is inherently likely to disrupt a large swath of the school, whether officials assume bullying expression collides with the victim's rights, or whether the authors considered the speaker's rights at all. This ambiguity is intensified by judicial failure to instruct schools on whether a looser standard than *Tinker* may apply to hostile student speech directed to particular peers.

Educators who aren't attorneys should not be expected to have internalized the norms of free speech, but it is inexplicable that the federal government, including the Justice Department, manifests the same cavalier attitude when it comes to the treatment of anti-bullying efforts under the First Amendment. As the federal government moves full speed ahead to make schools responsible for controlling bullying sentiments and behavior, it has pointedly disregarded student speech rights. The Department of Education, the Department of Justice, and the United States Commission on Civil Rights, along with other agencies that collaborate to ensure that schools combat peer-to-peer bullying, have given school districts shallow and in many respects misleading advice.

The Department of Education transmits the federal government's view of the legal duties and powers of school officials through "Dear Colleague Letters" on specific topics. A 2010 Dear Colleague Letter about bullying merged discussion of bullying "conduct" with "verbal acts and name-calling" and "teasing" that might be protected speech without acknowledging any distinction. The letter mentioned the First Amendment only in a footnote containing one substantive sentence, which indicated that some "harassment may implicate First Amendment rights to free speech or expression." It referred readers to a 2003 Dear Colleague Letter about the First Amendment for explanation.[114]

The 2003 First Amendment Letter in turn offers no concrete help. It was issued in response to questions from colleges about hate speech codes: Did the government intend universities to intrude on First Amendment rights in order to comply with civil rights regulations? The answer boiled down to "of course not." The letter doesn't refer to First Amendment standards generally, much less to *Tinker* or student speech doctrine, neither of which should apply to universities. In short, the letter offers no guidance that would help schools navigate the complex intersection of some students' right to speak with authorities' desire to keep other students feeling safe while trying to comport with federal laws. No publication helps educators separate what *Davis* called "simple acts of teasing and name-calling" from grave verbal attacks permitting or requiring a disciplinary response.[115]

Lacking usable guidance from the attorney general's office, educators may respond reflexively instead of contextually to words that seem like bullying. One school, for example, suspended a six-year-old for half a day and created a permanent disciplinary record after he called a classmate a "poo poo head," an incident unlikely to have prompted substantial disruption on the playground. Those officials missed a perfect opportunity for the whole class to discuss the ways we should talk to each other. Sadly, the offender's mother also seemed to miss the point of the Speech Clause. She mounted a campaign to remove from reading lists the children's book from which her son had learned the term "poo poo head."[116]

Calling someone a poo poo head, a weakling, or a bigot arguably fits most judges' definition of "tepid"; calling a girl a "cum-guzzling slut" may merit the label *scalding* and likely crosses the line *Cohen* drew to the "intolerable" insult that can be silenced after just one occurrence. Most parents would probably hope schools could silence the latter. But the question remains, on what legal ground can schools stop tepid or scalding disparagement of a fellow student?

Some states have demonstrated a better understanding than the federal government of the importance of taking First Amendment rights into account when requiring schools to control bullying. The anti-bullying law New Jersey enacted in 2010 obliges schools to respond appropriately to "harassment, intimidation, or bullying" if it "substantially disrupts or interferes with the orderly operation of the school or the rights of other students," incorporating both prongs of the *Tinker* standard.[117] The language implicitly acknowledges that *Tinker* protects bullying speech unless the school has legal grounds to restrain it.

Deprivation of educational opportunity may offer a concrete standard for defining bullying speech that collides with the target's rights. A single student may suffer when a peer's verbal harassment materially disrupts his or her personal educational experience, as distinct from material disruption so substantial that it interferes with an entire class or school day. Laws in every state give children the right to receive an education that meets a minimum standard the state has designated. Meaningful access to education was at the heart of the Supreme Court's ruling in *Davis:* The victim was able to hold a school accountable when it failed to respond to harassment "so severe, pervasive and objectively offensive" that it effectively barred her "access to educational opportunity."[118] Justice O'Connor used the example of a student who might be excluded from a science lab, but total exclusion is not required to satisfy the standard set out in *Davis.*

In 2011, Jack Weinstein, a district court judge renowned for tackling challenging legal problems, crafted a similar standard to govern schools' responsibility for peer-on-peer bullying of students with disabilities, whom IDEA promises the right to an "appropriate" education. The test he promulgated circumvents the necessity for a school to predict widespread disruption. It allows students with disabilities who have been targeted by bullies to demand that their schools protect them from a hostile educational environment if they show "only that [the bullying] is likely to affect the opportunity of the student for an appropriate education."[119]

The Department of Education apparently agreed with this reasoning. In 2014 it issued new guidance on preventing the bullying of students with disabilities that indicated "a change in academic performance or behavior," including "a sudden decline in grades," should trigger a meeting of the educational planning team to determine if the student's academic needs are still being met in accordance with federal law. Students, it urges, should not be expected "to avoid or handle the bullying."[120]

Weinstein's standard—substantial restriction of one individual's learning opportunities—could well be applied beyond the students with disabilities protected by federal law. In the spirit of the infringement matrix I have described, Weinstein seeks to differentiate tepid from scalding bullying that is limited to words, adding precision to the phrase "collides with the rights of others." I offer one more caveat. If this approach is adopted, judges should reserve it for egregious circumstances to avoid silencing too much expression.

Constricted educational opportunity also drove the outcome in Zeno v. Pine Plains Central School District, which imposed a million-dollar penalty on a 95 percent white school district that failed to protect an African American boy from savage bullying that lasted more than three years. The torment included brutal taunts: graffiti saying "Zeno will die," racial slurs, references to lynchings, and other intimidation—including a threat "to rape his younger sister." Anthony Zeno suffered "frustration, loneliness and emotional anguish" that unsurprisingly resulted in "'substantially adverse educational consequences.'" Zeno dropped out of high school instead of staying to complete the math credits he needed to acquire a New York State Regents diploma. He accepted a less valuable form of diploma designed for students with learning disabilities, which is not accepted by most four-year colleges or the military.[121]

Upholding both the verdict and the million-dollar award in 2013, an appellate court concluded that the jury "reasonably could have found that the harassment would have a profound and long-term impact on Anthony's life and his ability to earn a living." Building on *Davis,* however, the court significantly restricted the decision's impact on future lawsuits by emphasizing that physical attacks were required for a successful claim against a school district. Zeno could not have won if he had not "endured threats and physical attacks" as well as what it termed "mere verbal harassment."[122]

In case after case, victims of bullying seek one common remedy. It isn't money. Zeno, like many other victims, asked the school to implement "proactive solutions" including universal sensitivity training for students and staff. Long before Zeno commenced litigation, his school declined an offer from the county's branch of the NAACP to provide Zeno with a safety escort at school and to offer a Human Rights Commission racial sensitivity course at the school, at no cost to the school district. Instead, the school offered the bullies an optional one-day course on bullying that didn't mention race. The court ruled that the jury was entitled to find that this response, together with the modest penalties the school imposed on the bullies, amounted to the "deliberate indifference" *Davis* envisioned in the parallel gender cases. A school's responses, the court held, must be "reasonably calculated to end harassment," even if they don't succeed.[123]

As events surrounding Smith's "Immigration" column demonstrated, schools can constitutionally educate their charges, creating school cultures that frown on or isolate intolerance and harassment so long as they are meticulous in respecting speech rights. Schools can try to stimulate empathy, drawing on easily available sample curricula developed by nonprofit organizations or creating their own. Peer groups that aim to combat harassment and seeking assistance from experts have also generated success stories in combatting bullying.[124] If these interventions succeed, educators would be spared the need to figure out when harassing speech is constitutionally protected and when they can punish it.

Efforts to teach empathy, respect, and civility must, however, heed *Barnette*'s invocation against compelled expression and *Tinker*'s commands about classrooms as marketplaces for conflicting ideas. Free speech imposes a more demanding standard than *parens patriae* when forcibly silencing bullies or requiring conformity to norms of toleration.

Some observers have charged that demanding conformity to tolerance may cross the line to "thought control." Decisions about which opinions are so beyond the pale that we should not condone them, those commentators say, could be considered a form of viewpoint discrimination that "turn[s] on what we think about the thing being tolerated."[125] It belittles the values of the disrespectful, which may run deeper than "I don't like you" or "you're a weakling." Does being a student mean you have no right to express your view that homosexuality is sinful? Do LGBT students in turn waive the right to call those who condemn homosexuality "bigots"?

Crossing the Line from Teaching Tolerance to Homogeneity

The seeming paradox of enforcing tolerance perfectly symbolizes an array of ironies stemming from the tension between free expression and the rights of others that has run through this chapter. Never was that tension more sharply joined than in a Michigan high school on Anti-Bullying Day in 2010. The day is also known as "Spirit Day," in recognition of LGBT teenagers who have committed suicide. The Gay/Straight Alliance of Howell High School had received permission to post fliers about the event, but the school did not officially sponsor it. Teacher Jay McDowell donned a purple T-shirt with anti-bullying slogans on the designated day and devoted his economics class to a discussion of bullying. He showed a video about a student who had committed suicide after being bullied about his sexual orientation. McDowell asked a girl who was wearing a Confederate flag on her belt buckle to remove it. She did.[126]

Daniel Glowacki, a student in the class, voiced his concern that McDowell's shirt and message discriminated against him and other Roman Catholics. Glowacki announced, "I don't accept gays."[127]

McDowell called Glowacki's comment inappropriate. When Glowacki refused to modify his stance, McDowell told him to leave the classroom. Another student said he agreed with Glowacki, asked to be excused, and left.

When Glowacki complained, the school exonerated him and reprimanded his teacher. The school concluded that Glowacki had not caused any disruption and that McDowell had "'modeled oppression and intolerance of student opinion.'" Students, the district correctly reminded McDowell, could not be disciplined for their beliefs. It gave McDowell "First Amendment training."[128]

Despite this resolution of the dispute, the Glowacki family sued, alleging that Daniel's rights had been violated and that his younger brother's potential speech had been chilled. Applying *Tinker*, the court found that McDowell had discriminated against Glowacki's viewpoint, interfering with the "'robust political debate'" to which the nation is committed. It rejected the school's argument that Glowacki's statement interfered with the rights of a gay student in the class because "it was not a bullying remark" addressed to a specific individual. There was, the court explained, "no indication" that Glowacki "threatened, named or targeted a particular individual."[129]

Teaching tolerance, the court directed, is best achieved in an atmosphere that shows how divergent views can be expressed "'in a civilized and respectful manner'" and "'includes the tolerance of even the most intolerant or disagreeable viewpoints.'"[130] Tolerance can—and should—be taught, but those who teach it must personify their own lesson, staying within the limits the First Amendment imposes.

Ultimately, the students who remained in the classroom after Glowacki left may have framed the issue most eloquently: Against the teacher's insistence that "'a student cannot voice an opinion that creates an uncomfortable learning environment for another student,'" the class pressed, "Why didn't" the two students who left the room "have free speech?"[131]

CHAPTER 7

Off-Campus Taunts and
Online *Sans-Gêne* Speech

It would be an unseemly and dangerous precedent to allow the state, in the guise of school authorities, to reach into a child's home and control his/her actions there to the same extent it can control the child when he/she participates in school-sponsored activities.

—Layshock v. Hermitage School District (3d Cir. 2011) (en banc)

State legislatures, teachers, some parents, and even agencies of the federal government increasingly look to school disciplinarians to rein in student speech that takes place off campus, outside of school hours, and online. In many ways, the spreading tentacles of school authority outside the schoolhouse gate mirror the expansive interpretation some schools use to censor speech on campus. The assertion of authority over off-campus speech is a breach of remarkable proportions, amounting to an abuse of power. The federal government has encouraged this invasion of liberty by requiring schools to control bullying wherever it occurs and threatening to strip districts of federal funds if they don't meet this demand. These radical departures conflict with longstanding jurisprudence and *Tinker*'s vision of one regime inside the schoolhouse gate and another outside.

Educators have punished students for online postings that a hall monitor is "mean" and that a teacher is the "worst," sarcastic tweets referring to teachers, off-campus performances, uncoerced sexts, and online riffs poking fun at school personnel or attacking fellow students that reflect poor judgment and are disturbing and hurtful but not illegal.

In the unsettled and rapidly emerging arena of online speech, the law requires schools to show a connection between off-campus speech and events at school before schools can punish student expression, just as the law requires when speech is verbal or written. This chapter analyzes the legal standards that apply when schools discipline students for off-campus speech, much of which takes place online. I argue for even stronger restraints on schools' power to regulate student expression outside the school day and off campus, both as a matter of constitutional law and to remain consistent with the vision behind *Tinker's* acceptance of a relaxed First Amendment standard during the school day.

I'm not suggesting that society is powerless to control vicious speech outside of school whether posted online, shouted from rooftops, or in pamphlets distributed at rush hour. As with much of the speech discussed in the last chapter, legal remedies exist for speech that the law doesn't protect. The state can pursue the speaker whose off-campus speech violates the law through the juvenile justice system, and private parties who have been defamed or otherwise damaged can bring civil lawsuits. More important, schools can always instruct. They may intervene constructively by teaching students about the norms and expectations that govern communications outside of school. They should tell students that online trails have repercussions and that employers are within their rights to fire adults who post rants on Facebook.[1] Educators just can't punish students for protected expression outside of school.

Controversies over school discipline for off-campus speech have accelerated dramatically since the turn of the twenty-first century. In the seventeen years between Tinker v. Des Moines and Bethel School District v. Fraser, only eight reported cases involved off-campus speech. For more than a decade after that, not a single judicial opinion concerned the efforts of educators to discipline young people for what they said outside of school because the law was so clear that off-campus speech was off-limits to school officials.

But with the advent of online communication, schools stepped up their efforts to restrict off-campus expression. In the fifteen years between the first case involving school discipline for cyber-speech in 1998 and 2014 more than twenty-five cases centered on such episodes, generating far more than twenty-five reported opinions. This dramatic spike may reflect the more aggressive stance of school officials, the evidentiary trail left by digital speech, a growing awareness of civil liberties among students and their families, or a combination of the three.

Adults have often panicked at new formats for speech, and today they express alarm at what seems to be unrestrained or increasingly pervasive rude, crude, and brutal content reaching wide audiences by going viral. Unease prompted by these developments has lent support to educators who seek new powers over the young. Schools have seized on new modes of communication to justify expanding their jurisdiction to punish protected speech by people who happen to be students wherever and whenever it occurs. One law professor argues that adult distress over imprudent or hostile online expression has reinforced "the policing function of public schools" in response to social problems. As if to prove her point, a PTA president urged schools to ban cyberbullying and sexting because "these kids are just lawless."[2]

Organizations representing school administrators urge courts to empower them. The National School Boards Association argues that the legal distinctions between on- and off-campus speech are "anachronistic" because online communications have obliterated all boundaries, and some federal judges agree.[3]

Others on the front lines resist statutory changes that require them to monitor off-campus expression. "Now we have to police the community 24 hours a day, where are the resources?" worried an official of the New Jersey Association of Schools Administrators in 2011 when the state gave schools power to discipline bullying wherever it occurred.[4]

Schools offer strong rationales for asserting control over off-campus expression, especially online speech. When off-campus expression targets school staff, administrators argue, a disruption on campus inevitably follows. If schools can't punish spiteful and even revolting speech about teachers, they reason, word will spread, undermining respect for authority. They fear that malicious online speech has the potential to destroy educators' careers.

When they turn to student postings about peers, officials worry that social networking sites hidden from adults encourage vicious bullying and that schools can protect children on campus only by rooting out student-on-student bullying everywhere.[5] Online speech encourages anonymity while discouraging empathy because the speakers and the targets of nasty expression are hidden from each other and from the audience. Speech on social media sites pursues victims into private spaces, spreads quickly, and can't be fully eradicated.

They have a point. Contemporary modes of communication are certainly more difficult to control than older, more "conventional" means of sharing ideas. Online communication has created some new problems and exacerbated others.

But bear in mind that censors have leveraged anxieties about children's well-being to impose new regulations on speech with the introduction of every advance in technology or entertainment. From the dime novels and stereoscopes of the late nineteenth century through movies, television, and comic books, rock music, and, most recently, the Internet and violent video games, commentators predicted the downfall of morals and the ruin of youth. Each time the Supreme Court was asked, it reaffirmed that the First Amendment applies to *all* modes of communication and applies to children as well as to adults. As a federal judge stated in 2012, "The movement of student speech to the internet poses some new challenges, but that transition has not abrogated the clearly established general principles which have governed schools for decades."[6]

Once again, we confront a problem the Supreme Court has never addressed: whether schools can extend their scrutiny of student speech into public spaces or the privacy of the home. The Court skirted the edges of the problem in *Morse* by bringing Joseph Frederick's "Bong Hits 4 Jesus" banner under the umbrella of a school activity. Recall Chief Justice Roberts's classic understatement: "There is some uncertainty at the outer boundaries as to when courts should apply school speech precedents." In *Morse*, however, Chief Justice Roberts also expressly reiterated that had "Fraser delivered the same speech in a public forum outside the school context, it would have been protected."[7] Beyond this, the tenor of the Court's decisions about school speech and the doctrine that parental rights have a constitutional dimension point clearly in one direction: The school's authority generally ends at the campus perimeter.

I begin by examining a theme that has run throughout this volume just under the surface of my focus on the individual rights of students: the respective zones of power over children that the Constitution accords to educators and parents. I revisit some topics discussed in earlier chapters, including *sans-gêne* expression and verbal bullying as it plays out off campus. The chapter also takes up sexting, an entirely new genre of speech, which should be immune to government regulation unless the state's intervention survives strict scrutiny.

The Division of Authority between Parents and Schools

The Supreme Court has only once allowed a limitation on speech rights outside of school based on age—when it upheld a separate definition of material that is obscene for minors but not for adults in Ginsberg v. New York (a case I discussed in Chapter 1). Outside obscenity, from Barnette v. West Virginia to its 2011 ruling that California could not restrict minors'

access to violent video games, the Supreme Court has repeatedly emphasized that minors too have speech rights. The statute the Court upheld in
Ginsberg, however, left it to parents to determine whether their offspring
could access these titillating materials. The Court considered it significant
that the state did "not bar parents who so desire from purchasing the maga-
zines for their children" and implied that a similar statute that overrode
parental decisions might not prove constitutional.[8]

The state generally argues that two interests justify regulating the flow
of speech and entertainment to children outside of school. First, the state
relies on its *parens patriae* interest in the well-being of children, which the
Supreme Court has long treated as self-evident: "The well-being of its
children is of course a subject within the State's constitutional power to
regulate."[9] Second, the state proclaims that it limits children's access to
potentially harmful communications in order to help parents exert their
own authority.

The second rationale denies the wide range of values and childrearing
choices found among American parents. Presumably parents don't want the
government to substitute its judgment for their own. In the United States,
parental decisions about how to raise their own children have constitutional
dimensions. As *Ginsberg* summarized it, "[C]onstitutional interpretation
has consistently recognized that the parents' claim to authority in their own
household to direct the rearing of their children is basic in the structure of
our society. 'It is cardinal with us that the custody, care and nurture of the
child reside first in the parents, whose primary function and freedom include
preparation for obligations the state can neither supply nor hinder.'" The
Supreme Court reiterated this principle in 2000: The "liberty interest . . . of
parents in the care, custody and control of their children . . . [is] the oldest
of the fundamental liberty interests."[10]

Applied to the balance of power between public school officials and parents, these doctrines mean that the state may require parents to educate
their children and that parents may satisfy compulsory education laws by
choosing among public or independent schools or home schooling.[11] Once
parents choose public schools, however, they generally have no constitutional right to micromanage curricular requirements or to control the values
the state communicates to their children. With few exceptions, courts have
ruled in the state's favor when parents challenged curricular choices, campus
discipline, or searches.

Similarly, as the recurrent lawsuits parents file alleging that a school has
overstepped its powers in silencing or punishing their child's speech make

clear, on campus the school's powers trump the parents' unless and until a court decides a school has violated the law. The state isn't required to consult parents about discipline during the school's custodial shift, whether the offense involves weapons, headphones, or words.[12]

Parents and authorities representing the state (from law enforcement officials to nongovernmental agencies such as the Society for the Prevention of Cruelty to Children, which was authorized to remove children from their homes) have long competed for dominance over children. The judges who are called on to resolve the resulting conflicts bring to the bench their own views of how to parent and of whether children are best served by the sure and steady exercise of adult authority that protects them from bad influences (including speech that reveals there is no Santa Claus) or by nurturing children as "civic learners" who must practice and perfect the habits of citizenship.[13]

In public schools and elsewhere, an implicit agreement underlies the enormous power citizens cede to government: Citizens give the state's agents day-to-day powers in exchange for constitutional assurances that the government will respect individual rights. When school officials extend their disciplinary reach to punish off-campus speech that uses bad language or pokes fun at school officials (no matter how tastelessly), they breach that social compact. As the chief judge of the Second Circuit explained in 1979, "Our willingness to defer to the schoolmaster's expertise in administering school discipline rests, in large measure, upon the supposition that the arm of authority does not reach beyond the schoolhouse gate."[14]

Substantial deference to school authority rests on the premise that officials rule over children only during the school day.[15] When schools claim jurisdiction over children in public spaces and even at home, officials undermine the very basis for the discretion they have to control children during school.

As early as 1859, long before our modern understanding of privacy rights developed, Vermont's highest court held that a student's off-campus contemptuous language to a teacher could be punished at school only if it had "a direct and immediate tendency to injure the school, to subvert the master's authority, and to beget disorder and insubordination." Otherwise, after children return home, the court ruled, "the parents, and they alone, have the power of punishment."[16] That remains true today.

Parents agree. Those who challenge the penalties imposed by schools often punish their child at home for the very same behavior that got the child into trouble at school. But parents bring to the task of child rearing an incalculable variety of values and sensibilities to questions of taste and morality. They don't all punish or reward the same expression or impose the same penalties.

Whatever behavior and language they tolerate or punish, most parents don't want school officials intruding into their homes and substituting their authority for parental control. Survey data from 2012 indicate that a decisive majority of Americans (57 percent) reject the proposition that "public schools should be allowed to discipline students who use their own personal computers from home to post material that school officials say is offensive." Only 34 percent support public school intervention.[17]

And yet, some school officials blame parents for their parenting styles, for letting their children listen to rap music, or for standing by helplessly as their offspring surpass them in mastering technology. A 2013 study revealed that three-quarters of parents say they "don't have the time or energy to monitor their kids' Internet use."[18] The study did not ask an even more important question: Would you make time to monitor your children's Internet use if you thought it was really important to know what they were doing online?

A small group of legal scholars who criticize parental permissiveness link the problem to the *Tinker* regime which, in their view, ceded too much independence to the young. Bruce Hafen, a family law expert who occupies a very high leadership position in the Church of the Latter-Day Saints, placed what he calls the "excesses of our flirtation with children's liberation" in the context of "a general erosion of institutional authority, the erosion of marriage, [and] the sexual revolution" in 1987. Writing just before the Supreme Court announced new legal doctrine in *Hazelwood*, he lamented what he saw as a tendency (reflected in *Tinker*) to value freedom for its own sake over the discipline that is a prerequisite to learning. Hafen called for a better balance between "too much direction and not enough."[19]

Most critically, Hafen rejected the notion that schools were simply agents of the state, bound strictly by constitutional restraints. Instead, he proposed that schools "are not merely state agents, but are mediating institutions whose authority is derived both from parents and from the delegation of state power."[20] Even if that were the correct view of the regime under which schools operate—a proposition that has been untenable since *Barnette* was decided—it would hardly give schools authority to overrule parents in their own homes. Those very parents, in Hafen's interpretation, are a crucial source of educators' authority. The delegation of power over children is not a reciprocal proposition.

Similarly, Anne Proffitt Dupre, a former teacher turned lawyer and law professor, in 2009 condemned *Tinker,* first for ignoring what she saw as the social reality that children aren't yet prepared to exercise freedom responsibly and then because she believed that *Tinker* had "strayed from its moorings." *Tinker*, she charged, serves as an excuse "to support all kinds of student speech" as parents abandoned their disciplinary role and backed their children's challenges to school authority, in her view undermining teachers' confidence and control and forcing school districts to squander resources on litigation expenses. Dupre argued that *Hazelwood* and subsequent decisions began to restore the proper balance between freedom and authority, although she did not take a position on how far off campus the "'long arm of *Tinker*'" could permissibly reach.[21]

Allowing schools to punish constitutionally protected off-campus expression would directly challenge parental authority. In our legal system, parents may discipline their own children according to their own values (as long as parents do not impose penalties so severe that they cross the line to child abuse). They always retain the discretion to decide whether and how to punish their children for behavior they view as uncouth or deplorable, wherever it occurs—in school, on the streets, at home, or online.[22]

When schools report offensive off-campus speech to parents, the families are free to ignore the speech or even to commend it if they choose (e.g., "You always hated that teacher, he flunked you, I am glad you gave him the finger!"). Another possibility, of course, would be for a parent to use the episode as an opportunity for a dialogue about why offensive and thoughtless outbursts are both wrong and ineffective.

"An Unconstitutional Usurpation"

Courts have long repudiated the proposition that educators' authority over children extends wherever school officials find them. When it came to freedom of speech, a clear line separated the school day and the school campus from the rest of universe, where a robust, undiminished Speech Clause protects expression.

The lower court judges who tackled the problem of off-campus speech while *Tinker* still governed the entire universe of student speech unanimously rebuffed school officials' efforts to discipline students for what they said outside of school. In Shanley v. Northeast Independent School District, one of two seminal appellate court opinions on off-campus speech, the Fifth Circuit in 1972 overturned a suspension a Texas school district imposed on students who distributed what the judges regarded as "probably one of the most vanilla-flavored" underground papers "ever to reach a federal court."[23]

Suspending the underground journalists was just one piece of a more general attack on students' expressive rights in a district where the school code told students they would be punished at school if they participated "'in a boycott, sit-in, stand-in, walk-out or other related activity,'" wherever it occurred and whatever its goals.[24] The court condemned that rule and held the off-campus newspaper lay outside the school's reach, even though other students brought the papers onto the campus: Off-campus speech was immune from school discipline.[25]

The *Shanley* court lambasted school authorities for failing "to recognize even the bare existence of the First Amendment" and for a "quaint approach" to freedom that had been laid to rest in *Barnette*. It excoriated the school district for claiming that it could impose "whatever conditions the state wished" on students as if they were prisoners and for intruding on parental rights: "It should have come as a shock to the parents of five high school seniors . . . that their elected school board had assumed suzerainty over their children before and after school, off school grounds, and with regard to their children's rights of expressing their thoughts. We trust it will come as no shock whatsoever to the school board that their assumption of authority is an unconstitutional usurpation of the First Amendment."[26]

The judges in *Shanley* anticipated and addressed worries about lawless youth: Outside of school students "are subject to the civil and criminal laws of the community, state and nation." The court pinned down some of the ways young people can be held accountable for speech-related offenses: "A student acting entirely outside school property is potentially subject to the laws of disturbing the peace, inciting to riot, littering and so forth."[27] Similarly, if off-campus expression meets the legal definition of defamation or harassment, it is unprotected.

A few years later, a second seminal case—Thomas v. Granville Central School District—arose after Donna Thomas and her friends were disciplined for producing an admittedly vulgar underground newspaper modeled on the National Lampoon, known for its "sexual satire." The students prepared and sold the paper off campus, though while working on it they had used a class-room storage closet, consulted a teacher, and discussed their plans on campus. As in *Shanley* and many other cases, another student brought the paper to school. After the school punished the journalists, Thomas challenged the penalty in court. The school conceded that it lacked authority over off-campus speech but argued that the students' passing engagement with the project at school and the paper's appearance on campus had transformed the publication into school speech. The trial court agreed with the school and denied the students the relief they sought. But when Thomas appealed, the Second Circuit reversed in 1979.

Thomas announced a simple rule: "[S]chool authorities are powerless to impose sanctions for expression beyond school property." It reasoned that the school could not obtain jurisdiction over the speech just because a peer brought the paper to campus, where "all but an insignificant amount" of the activity "was deliberately designed" to take place outside of school. Chief Judge Kaufman, writing for the court, continued: Where "school officials have ventured out of the school yard and into the general community where the freedom accorded expression is at its zenith," the students' "actions must be evaluated by the principles that bind government officials in the public arena."[28]

Parents "still have their role to play in bringing up their children," Judge Kaufman underscored in *Thomas,* "and school officials, in such instances, are not empowered to assume the role of *parens patriae.*" If the underground newspaper was vulgar, he continued, that—along with acts like watching an X-rated film on the family television—would be "proper subjects of parental discipline," but it was none of the government's business.[29]

Both *Shanley* and *Thomas* involved press freedoms at the First Amendment's core, but the barriers they erected to encroachments on student expression outside of school extend to speech that lacks the higher calling of a paper—even an underground paper. When Jason Klein, a student, drove across the parking lot of a Maine restaurant in 1986 outside of school hours and gave "the finger" to the driver of another car who was a teacher at his school, he probably had no elevated social message in mind. The school suspended Klein for ten days because he had violated a school rule barring "vulgar . . . conduct toward a staff member." Klein sued. A federal judge overturned the suspension because any connection between the off-campus incident and the school was "far too attenuated to support discipline" of this "ruffian" for whom "parental discipline [was] roundly deserved" (and had in fact been administered).[30]

The opinion is notable for the judge's cogent analysis in the face of behavior some might think unworthy of a court's attention. He succinctly disposed of the school's disingenuous arguments. He rejected the specious claim that the gesture was not "speech": The "finger" was "commonly understood to mean 'fuck you.'" If not for that common understanding, the finger would not be a vulgarity. Because no one else witnessed the interaction, the judge also rejected the argument that if disrespect went unpunished it would spill over onto the campus. Finally, he scoffed at the claim that the disrespectful act could have prompted imminent violence. "'The finger,' at least when used against a universe of teachers," the judge observed with a verbal wink, "is not likely to provoke a violent response."[31]

Taking rights seriously, he observed that schools may "'seek to inculcate'" taste but may not "'in the effort to do so, transgress upon'" what he termed "political freedom." In the same vein as the concerns explored in the last chapter about securing freedom of thought and expression while teaching tolerance, the judge observed that a student's "freedom of expression may not be made a casualty of the effort to force-feed good manners to the ruffians among us."[32]

When students use traditional means of communication, from armbands to pamphlets to vulgar gestures, it's usually easy to draw lines between the school day and the rest of the week. We can ask where the speech was created, where it was distributed, and whether the speech occurred on the school's watch, that is, during the school day, on the school bus, or during extracurricular activities and school trips. In the world of *Thomas*'s underground paper, which looks so simple in retrospect, an unambiguous geographical boundary separated school from the rest of the world.

And yet, in 1979 the *Thomas* court entertained a hypothetical at the outer margins "in which a group of students incites substantial disruption within the school from a remote locale."[33] It left unresolved the parameters of the exception it might be willing to carve out to permit schools to discipline speech likely to incite campus chaos—perhaps comparable to the potential for racial conflagration seen in B.W.A. v. Farmington.

Let's consider the circumstances under which an off-campus speaker could permissibly be held accountable for subsequent disturbance on campus by imagining two scenarios involving conventional off-campus speech.

The first involves an off-campus rally protesting the town's decision to stop monitoring the quality of its water supply. The rally is not aimed at the school or its policies in any way. At the rally, attended by more than one hundred students, many of their parents, and hundreds of other adults, a student gives an impassioned speech about environmental concerns and local governance. The speaker does not promote the theme in school the day after the rally, except to discuss it with friends in the cafeteria (a form of communication *Tinker* expressly protects). Other students who heard the speech, however, spread the word about it among the student body. If students become distracted and disorderly as a result, can the school hold the original orator responsible? Under *Tinker*, it can't. The protected speech took place off campus, outside school hours. Even if a court applied *Tinker* to the off-campus expression, the orator did not create any link between the rally and the school.

Modest changes in the facts paint a very different legal picture. In my second hypothetical, a student at the same rally urges schoolmates to "strike on Monday; don't hand in homework, don't raise your hands or answer the teachers' questions." These facts illustrate the risks the *Thomas* court apparently contemplated: student speech from outside that aims to interfere with the school's orderly functioning. If the students follow the speaker's lead, the school could fairly attribute the resulting disruption to her. The outcome would not be any different if the remark emanated from the mimeographed pamphlets of the 1960s, the photocopied broadsides of the 1980s, or the student's Twitter account. Speech calculated to disrupt a school can be thought of as an arrow aimed directly toward the campus, not one like Longfellow's shot "into the air" which "fell to earth, I know not where."

While online communication presents new complexities involving speed, scope, and permanence, fundamental questions about who is responsible when off-campus speech spreads are not unprecedented. The first generation of off-campus speech cases epitomized by *Shanley* and *Thomas* told the schools off-campus expression was none of their business. These cases contemplated at most a very narrow exception that turns the general principle that off-campus expression is beyond the school's power into a rebuttable presumption. Framed in the way most favorable to claims of authority by school officials, the rule would read as follows: Off-campus speech is immune to school discipline unless the school can show that the speaker intends to substantially disrupt the campus and his or her words are likely to have the impact the student hopes for.

Speech "from a Remote Locale"

Online speech, social media sites, Twitter, texting, and the like have given new meaning to the concept of speech "from a remote locale" that the *Thomas* court imagined as a peripheral possibility. School officials, viewing technological changes as propelling school discipline toward an apocalypse if they could not control criticism of administrators and teachers wherever it took place, have claimed pervasive authority over what students say and how they say it even from the privacy of their homes. The National School Boards Association and other groups representing school officials have argued that online speech is so threatening that the courts should release them from *Tinker*'s strictures to trust their own discretion.[34] Panic over the crudeness and disrespect often seen in digital speech has led some educators and even judges to disregard the most basic legal principles about the First Amendment in and out of school.

Disrespectful student speech about school employees provides the primary source of emerging law that threatens to blur the distinction between on-campus expression and off-campus speech by people who happen to be public school students. Without waiting for legal clarification, schools have plunged in to punish students for all sorts of online speech about school personnel. Students are especially likely to face repercussions on campus if they use crude terminology online, like *douchebag* or *fat ass*. In many ways educators' concerns about off-campus expression merely reprise the effort to stamp out *sans-gêne* attitudes, now on a larger battleground.[35]

School authorities appear to take online speech targeting teachers much more seriously than they do insensitive speech about fellow students. Administrators slap down all manner of criticism and complaint no matter how mild, even when it originates, and largely stays, off campus. A Minnesota school issued a detention to a twelve-year-old girl who posted a message on her closed Facebook page that she hated an adult hall monitor who was "mean to me." A school in Florida suspended a girl and removed her from advanced placement courses after she set up a website for complaints about "Ms. Phelps," "the worst teacher I've ever met," even though the student disabled the site before the school learned about it. No one threatened Ms. Phelps, but the school considered the site an instance of "cyber bullying . . . towards a staff member."[36]

In 2014, national attention briefly focused on an honors student and athlete expelled from his high school for sarcastically answering a tweet that asked if he had kissed a certain teacher: "[A]ctually, yes," he responded. The school interpreted his joke as violating the rule against "threatening" or "intimidating" staff members. All over the country students are being suspended for off-campus tweets about teachers they passed along with less than a second's thought or simply flagged as a "favorite."[37]

Beyond the geographical limits to school authority, it is irrational to accuse students of bullying teachers. The most widely accepted definitions of bullying emphasize that the aggressor must have more power and status than the victim. The definition also requires that the abuse be repeated, not a one-off as it is in many instances that schools read as bullying of staff.[38] A pattern of behavior is also required to meet most legal definitions of harassment. If student attacks on teachers amount to harassment or cross some other legal line, the expression is not protected by the First Amendment and can be reported to the appropriate authorities outside of school. Most of the statements schools treat as student bullying of teachers and staff, however, do not cross those lines and are entitled to First Amendment protection.

The ability to comment, whether seriously or humorously, about the people who hold power is a central component of freedom. Ruling that a school had violated the rights of the girl who invited friends to join her on a website about the "worst teacher," the court was impressed by the authoritarian implications of allowing schools to silence all negative comments about their instructors. The judge warned that "students everywhere would be prohibited from the slightest criticism of their teachers, whether inside or outside the classroom," a constitutionally repugnant prospect.[39]

Educators are not alone in succumbing to the temptation to disregard the law when it doesn't lead to the results they want. Judges often empathize with teachers who feel attacked and understandably worry about diminishing respect for authority. Some judges have expressed concern that online attacks on teachers have rendered them unable to work and subjected them to extreme stress, sleeplessness, and depression. They feared that schools could have difficulty recruiting and retaining teachers if demoralizing postings from off campus went unpunished.[40] These concerns might affect the weight of the government's interest in regulating the speech but fail to take account of the countervailing First Amendment values.

Emphasis on the mode of speech ignores the reality that earlier generations of teachers suffered from demoralizing communication in the form of face-to-fact taunts, typed letters, and handwritten petitions. In 2002, an appellate court held that a school had no obligation to protect a homosexual teacher who was hounded by students and their parents until he collapsed emotionally and ultimately lost his job.[41] However, the question here is not whether schools must protect teachers who are the unhappy subjects of students' expression on social media sites but whether the Constitution permits schools to intervene.

Many judges, like others of a certain age, seem to stumble when forced to apply established doctrine to a new world of communication in which, as one judge wrote, off-campus "speech can become on-campus speech within the click of a mouse" and has the potential to reach hundreds of students. (The youngest sitting federal judges are in their early forties; none of them grew up with the Internet.) We are not, those judges insist, "living in the same world" as *Thomas*.[42]

The view that technology makes it too hard to define where speech originates or to contain speech within a physical space leads decision makers to ignore the role of geographical boundaries throughout our civil and criminal justice systems. Geography determines which laws apply and who can enforce them. The elementary principle that an "offense against one authority . . . perpetrated within the jurisdiction of another authority is usually punishable only by the authority in whose jurisdiction the offense took place"[43] applies as well to the division between school authority and civil or criminal authority.

Instead of placing responsibility for unprotected off-campus speech by students outside of school where it belongs, some contemporary courts transmute off-campus speech into on-campus expression based on minimal contact with the campus—and increasingly do so when the speaker had no role in creating that connection. In contrast to the *Thomas* court's forgiving approach to fleeting intersections of the paper and the campus, by 2002 one court found sufficient justification for officials to treat speech as taking place in school when a student who sought to expose the author opened the offending website from a school computer.[44]

Other courts since then have also allowed schools to penalize off-campus expression carried onto school property by third parties, including complaining parents and teachers who Googled themselves. One judge treated a YouTube video created and posted off campus as school speech based on the fact that a school official accessed it from her own office while looking into a parent's complaint. If the disciplinarian's own actions bring the speaker within the school's zone of authority, schools would always be able to punish off-campus speech, upending the presumption that off-campus speech is beyond the school's reach.[45]

These judges resemble modern-day alchemists. Instead of turning worthless substances into gold, they empower authoritarian school districts by demolishing the barriers that distinguish the campus and the school day—and the special legal regime that rules there—from civil society. In the process they expand school authority beyond any recognizable limits.

Perhaps the most bizarre exaggeration of school authority occurred when a California school district chastised a father who used a parent e-mail chain to ask whether other people thought the kids had too much math homework. Many did, but a parent who disagreed with him forwarded the chain to the math teacher. So far this sounds just like what happens with student Facebook postings. The pattern continues. The vice principal summoned the father to his office, where he accused the grown man of "cyber-bullying." The teacher felt threatened, the official reported, and the school expected parents to live up to demands of the school code.[46]

This father's story creates the impression that some school officials have no idea what they mean when they talk about bullying and are impervious to limitations on their power to control other people's speech. The standard the school seems to be applying to parents as well as students looks a great deal like a general right for teachers to be protected from hurt feelings, the very argument the Seventh Circuit disavowed with reference to LGBT students in *Nuxoll.*

In another perverse vignette, in 2007 a high school principal in Wilton, Connecticut, told students they could never perform *Voices in Conflict,* a play the students had written about the experience of Iraq War veterans using the soldiers' own words. He canceled a scheduled class workshop after one mother insisted it would offend friends of a recent graduate who had died in Iraq. The sensibility of friends of deceased soldiers was the very justification the Supreme Court had rejected in *Tinker.* Granted, the authors and performers of *Voices in Conflict* were taking a drama class, which made the speech school sponsored if the play took place under the school's auspices.

But the principal didn't stop there. He told the drama students they could not perform the play privately for their families and friends. Their teacher, Bonnie Dickinson, recounted the principal's declaration: "You may not perform this play ANYWHERE." When a parent of one of the students in the class alerted the *New York Times* to the story, one student told a reporter, "Our school is all about censorship."[47]

Of course the school had no authority to stop the students from continuing their work off campus or from performing the play in any off-campus location they could find, as long as they did not claim that the school sponsored the play. But Dickinson told me she didn't know that because none of the training she received when working on her master's degree in education touched on the First Amendment rights of teachers or students.

This episode had a happy ending. The *New York Times* story led to an influx of legal advice and support from writers and theater professionals. The students performed the play to full houses in their community, in an off-Broadway venue in New York, and on Martha's Vineyard and won national awards for standing up for their rights.[48]

Other school administrators have also lost sight of both general Speech Clause doctrine and the rules imposed by the quintet of student speech decisions from *Barnette* through *Morse* when they confront offensive, uncomfortable speech, especially online speech created by students outside of school. They sometimes corral judges into supporting them.

In one of the more egregious examples, the Second Circuit had a hard time finding a rationale for sustaining a Connecticut school's punishment of Avery Doninger, who posted from her home computer that the high school's administrative staff were "douchebags." It wasn't clear that the doctrine governing school speech rules fit the expression the school and the judges found distasteful and disrespectful.[49]

So the court transmuted the school speech standards in Twister-like fashion. Because the school had no discretion under *Fraser* to punish off-campus vulgarity, the court struggled to bring crude speech under *Tinker*'s umbrella, proclaiming that calling school officials douchebags was not only vulgar but "potentially *incendiary*." In *Fraser,* however, the Supreme Court had expressly rejected the school's argument that vulgar speech was *always* disruptive. The judges in Doninger v. Niehoff found some minimal disruption in phone calls and e-mails to the school office, several administrative meetings, and the assertion that "the students were all riled up," not quite enough to show material disruption. They then turned to Doninger's position as a student leader who should set a good example for others in order to bring in a bit of *Hazelwood*'s approach. Instead of choosing a school speech standard and finding the school satisfied it, the court announced that the "cumulative effect" of all of its findings permitted it to rule for the school.[50]

As legal doctrine, this looks a lot like the Red Queen's "Sentence first—verdict afterwards" in Wonderland.

In fairness, the legal doctrine defining whether schools have any role in disciplining online speech students create off campus is undeveloped. Less than half of the appellate jurisdictions have considered the issue, and they have taken varying approaches. As a result, students' rights to off-campus digital expression can vary wildly depending on where they live.

Nonetheless, the seemingly unique legal issues posed by the online speech of off-duty students once again demonstrate the resiliency and capacity of the student speech quintet. The foundational cases I have been discussing throughout this book suggest both the right questions to ask about digital student expression and the answers to those questions.

Appellate judges have given three types of answers to the question of what connection, if any, a school show must between off-campus online speech emanating from the students' own devices and the school campus in order to have authority to punish the speaker. The answers include conditional acceptance of school authority where the speech is intended to reach the school, allowing schools to discipline off-campus speech that seriously threatens danger on campus, and an unwavering rule that off-campus speech is immune to penalties at school.

Under the first and dominant approach, schools can discipline students for off-campus speech only if threshold conditions are met. Almost universally, courts require the school to show a "nexus," or close connection, between the speech and the school or that it was "reasonably foreseeable" that the speech would reach the school community. Foreseeability requires the school to show that the student speaker intended the speech to reach the school or that the speaker should have anticipated that someone would share the speech on campus. Given the central role schools play in the lives of most students—it is their workplace and largely defines their social lives—a reasonable student would frequently write about people and events that touch on the campus and would understand too that the contents would be likely to reach the school. The example I used earlier in the chapter about speech at a rally that encouraged students to disrupt school the next day is easily translated into a Twitter stream or a Facebook post that the school could regulate to prevent substantial disruption of education. Only one appellate court has upheld school discipline for off-campus speech that reached the school without deciding that the school's authority was contingent on foreseeability.[51]

Two other appellate circuits agree that the school must show a nexus between the speech and the campus but add an additional stringent requirement: A school may discipline off-campus speech only if it communicates a serious, identifiable threat directed toward the campus.[52] This is a higher hurdle than *Tinker*'s reasonable apprehension of material disruption. Adopting this position in 2013, the Ninth Circuit emphasized that it is easier for a school to satisfy *Tinker*'s demanding material disruption requirement than to demonstrate the risk of dangers that would justify a school's assertion of authority over off-campus expression. The court held that only the most concrete threats trigger the power to punish off-campus speech.

More specifically, the Ninth Circuit allows schools to respond to online threats but not to puerile satires of the sort that have reached other appellate courts: "A student's profanity-laced parody of a principal is hardly the same as a threat of a school shooting." Schools may regulate the latter but not the former. This pragmatic approach allows schools to reach off-campus speech when there is a pressing need to do so but not in the normal course of events.[53] This approach is consistent with the treatment of threatening speech discussed in Chapter 5.

Finally, in the third school of thought, a majority of the judges in the Third Circuit sitting en banc "reject[ed] out of hand any suggestion that schools can police students' out-of-school speech." In companion cases that reached it in in 2012—Blue Mountain v. J.S. [Snyder] and Layshock v. Hermitage School District—the Third Circuit considered two profanity-laced parodies of principals of the sort the Ninth Circuit had brushed off. In each case, honors students with clean disciplinary records working from family computers created mock MySpace profiles for school officials that they thought were hilarious. One centered on the principal's physical bulk, "on a theme of 'big,' because Trosch is apparently a large man"; the other, labeled a "joke," portrayed the principal as a bisexual "sex addict and pedophile."[54]

Decades after *Shanley* raised the specter of a school district acting as if it had the powers of a feudal lord over its subjects (the students over whom it wanted to exercise "suzerainty"), the Third Circuit was compelled to restate a fundamental proposition: "It would be an unseemly and dangerous precedent to allow the state, in the guise of school authorities, to reach into a child's home and control his/her actions there to the same extent it can control the child when he/she participates in school sponsored activities."[55]

"Reaching into a child's home" may be more than a metaphor. Some schools have begun to surreptitiously monitor students' use of social media, allegedly to uncover threats against other students in time to intervene, even hiring private contractors to engage in surveillance. This development presents a host of legal questions about privacy and Fourth Amendment rights in addition to concerns about the chilling impact on speech once students realize they are being watched. Parents objected so strenuously to one principal who monitored their children's Facebook accounts under a false identity that she had to resign.[56]

If schools are located in judicial circuits that permit officials to discipline students for off-campus speech under the right conditions, a second question remains: Which First Amendment standard determines if the penalty violates the student's speech rights?

Most of the lower court judges who have considered the issue agree that *Tinker*, the most protective school speech standard, should govern. This means that after school officials demonstrate a nexus between off-campus speech and the school, they must at minimum still demonstrate that *Tinker* would have allowed them to restrict or punish the speech had it occurred on campus.

We have already seen that some courts require more. They would impose a stricter version of the material disruption test where off-campus speech is concerned that a school could satisfy only by showing an apprehension of a specific, identifiable threat to the campus population such as bringing a gun or bomb to school.

Strikingly, school authorities resist these requirements, seeking yet another unprecedented expansion of power. They assert discretion to discipline student speakers *without* showing disruption, and for off-campus speech at that. In J.S. v. Blue Mountain, the school argued it could "punish any speech by a student that takes place anywhere, at any time, as long as it is about the school or a school official, is brought to the attention of a school official, and is deemed 'offensive' by the prevailing authority." The en banc Third Circuit scoffed at this claim: "Under this standard, two students can be punished for using a vulgar remark to speak about their teacher at a private party, if another student overhears the remark, reports it . . . and the school authorities find the remark 'offensive.'"[57]

Even some of the judges most attentive to the mandates of the school speech quintet seem to have lost sight of the warning in *Thomas* that First Amendment protections are "at their zenith" outside of school. In the Third Circuit, the *Layshock* majority entertained the possibility that under some future facts *Tinker* might allow a school to punish off-campus speech that would be legally protected if uttered by an adult, but that when voiced by a student threatened to materially disrupt the school.

Five of the seventeen judges on the *Layshock* bench, concurring, signed a separate opinion to stake out their position that even if schools could discipline off-campus expression without trampling individual rights, courts should be required to apply the most demanding standard of review—strict scrutiny—to the student's expression: "[T]he First Amendment protects students engaging in off-campus speech to the same extent it protects speech by citizens in the community at large." They insisted on jurisprudential consistency: A school cannot invoke *Tinker*'s relaxed First Amendment standards outside the special environment for which it was created.[58]

Those concurring judges got it right. To simply ignore the distinction between student speech on the school campus during the school day and the speech students engage in elsewhere flies in the face of the very conditions under which the Supreme Court originally relaxed protections for student speakers inside the schoolhouse gate. Outside of school Tinker's armband is always protected. So are contemporary dissident comments whether on web pages, on Twitter, or perhaps delivered by drone at some not too distant time.

It would be exceedingly difficult for a school to show a compelling interest in restraining off-campus student expression that doesn't contain a specific threat. Among other things, online lies and parodies of the sort the Third Circuit had before it may be immune from regulation unless they involve fraud or similar offenses. In 2013, a federal court dismissed a lawsuit aimed at a fake social media profile in which the adult defendant had used another person's name and likeness. Ruling that the federal statute on abuse of the Internet did not reach fake profiles, the court viewed Internet deception as business as usual: "'[L]ying on social media websites is common: People shave years off their age, add inches to their height and drop pounds from their weight.'" Creating fake profiles for others is just the next step.[59]

Some offensive juvenile humor may also be immune from civil lawsuits because a defamation claim requires the plaintiff to prove that the speaker presented falsehoods as facts. No one would think the absurd claims some students find amusing were true. A New York court considered a defamation action that looked a lot like *Layshock* and *Snyder*, except the target was a classmate, not an authority figure. A girl created a private Facebook site on which she announced that a classmate had contracted AIDS in Africa where "she was seen fucking a horse, . . . sharing needles with heroin addicts . . .

screw[ing] a baboon [and later] hired a male prostitute who came dressed as a sexy fireman." This description, the court found, was so hyperbolic that no one could read it as "a statement of fact." While "display[ing] an utter lack of taste and propriety," the judge tut-tutted, "the statements can only be read as puerile attempts by adolescents to outdo each other."[60]

Peer-on-Peer Cyber-Harassment

It is difficult to justify the disproportionate solicitousness that some schools show to teachers as compared to students who are victims of digital harassment. As the Seventh Circuit explained in 2002, if schools lack the resources to support both faculty members and students who experience harassment, any discrepancies must favor safeguarding the students, "even if that harassment [of staff] is offensive and cruel." In "a school setting," the court emphasized, "the well-being of students, not teachers, must be the primary concern of school administrators. Not only are schools primarily for the benefit of students," it continued, "but . . . children between the ages 6 to 14 are much more vulnerable to intimidation and mockery than teachers with advanced degrees and 20 years of experience."[61]

But schools too often ignore or minimize vicious speech directed at peers that might be actionable. In one example of shocking under-responsiveness to harassing speech aimed at a student, a prestigious Los Angeles private school (not bound by First Amendment or jurisdictional constraints) disregarded repeated death threats students posted on a classmate's website, including "I'm going to pound your head in with an ice pick," "Faggot, I'm going to kill you," "Go [to] the 405 [Freeway] and jump," and "I want to rip out your fucking heart and feed it to you." These statements terrified the target. They were either true threats, tangible specific threats, or harassment to which schools may always respond. Unable to get help from either the school or law enforcement agencies, the victim and his family moved to another part of the state.[62]

It is unclear why responding to the serious threats, which violated several criminal laws, was relegated to the school rather than to law enforcement and the justice system. Unfortunately, law enforcement personnel, including both police and prosecutors, commonly belittle the importance of online bullying, harassment, and stalking, as they did in this case once they discovered that threats came from schoolmates, replicating a pattern familiar to advocates for victims of domestic violence. As online privacy expert Danielle

Citron has shown, law enforcement officers and prosecutors too often fail to follow up on reports of online harassment, even when it includes threats of violence, regardless of whether the victims and the harassers are minors or adults.[63]

It makes intuitive sense that schools have better claims to authority over off-campus speech when they seek to protect students from peers than when they act to protect the sensibilities of teachers and other adults. But much as we might hope some responsible adult could intervene to protect young people from one another when parents fail to control what their children do online, schools don't have unlimited authority to restrain hurtful speech off campus any more than they have complete discretion to control wounding speech in school. They have less authority off campus and may not have a legal rationale for intervening even in response to illegal speech acts that take place outside of school.

Although they may proceed with the best of intentions, schools often assert powers they may not have. The same suburban school code provision that stated simply, "Do not bully anyone" goes on to deal with "cyber-bullying": "If you bully someone, not only will there be school consequences, we must submit your name to a State . . . database. Bullying includes negative use of Facebook. Practice Cyber Civility!"[64]

Whether schools can turn that slogan from a hortatory invocation or an acceptable lesson plan into an enforceable rule reaching off-campus speech is quite another matter. Once again, it may depend on the state in which the student lives, whether the speaker addresses the cyber-comments to the school community, how many people can access the material, and whether the expression disrupts the campus. If a course of bullying conduct includes face-to-face expression and graffiti at school as well as online speech, perhaps schools could consider the off-campus expression in the same way that schools look to a community's history of racial strife in assessing the risk of material disruption. The resulting discipline would not be based on communications outside of school but on the risk of material disruption at school.

Despite their lack of legal authority, schools do reach out to punish single speech events outside of school, including some that would not be susceptible to discipline under *Tinker* had the expression taken place in the cafeteria, as a case from Beverly Hills illustrates.

J.C., a Beverly Hills High School student, videotaped a group of her girl-friends gossiping in a restaurant about a classmate in classic mean-girl mode:

She is "'the ugliest piece of shit I've ever seen,'" "'spoiled,'" a "'slut.'" That evening, J.C. posted the video on YouTube from her home computer, contacted about a dozen other students from school to tell them it was there, and then (for reasons that are unclear) told the subject of the conversation about it as well and left the video online at the victim's request. The victim brought her mother to school the next day, where they showed the video to authorities, who suspended J.C. for two days. Lucky to have an attorney for a father, J.C. sued, seeking to overturn the suspension.[65]

The district court applied *Tinker* to the off-campus expression because it was foreseeable the video would reach the school where it could cause disruption but held the suspension violated J.C.'s First Amendment rights because no disorder resulted. No reasonable jury, the court held, could conclude that minor inconveniences—including a victim crying for twenty minutes, a speaker who missed an afternoon of school, and meetings between administrators and the girls on the video—satisfied *Tinker*'s material disruption test. (Several appellate court rulings narrowing school officials' power over off-campus expression were issued after the ruling in *J.C.*, including the Ninth Circuit's clarification that a school's authority over off-campus expression was limited to cases that involve "identifiable" violent threats.)[66] In the future *Tinker* will not apply to a case like *J.C.* in California and other states within the Ninth Circuit.

J.C. was more fortunate than another insensitive speaker who created an even more vile web page about a fellow student. She accused her target of having herpes and enlisted roughly one hundred fellow students to join her in ridiculing the girl on the site. Building on the theme, another student quickly added a photo of the target, with an arrow pointing toward her "pelvic region," and the caption "'Warning: Enter at your own risk.'" The group's name included the term "students," most of the participants attended the same school, and the "warning" was posted from a school computer. The school suspended the website's creator and barred her from various extracurricular activities on her return to school. When she challenged the penalties, the district court ruled for the school.[67]

The Fourth Circuit affirmed, rejecting the student's argument that all off-campus speech was immune from school discipline. The speech implicated "the high school's legitimate interest in maintaining order . . . and protecting the well-being and educational rights of its students." Applying *Tinker*, the court agreed with the school that it was foreseeable the website would reach the school and "create a substantial disruption there." It found the nexus between the site and the school especially strong, given that "every aspect of the webpage's design and implementation was school-related." The court held the school's authority to respond to the "targeted, defamatory," and concerted "attack" on a classmate as within—but at the "outer boundaries" of—a school's power. The posting threatened the school's ability "to provide a safe school environment conducive to learning."[68]

The court carefully sought to bring the case within *Tinker*'s parameters, and largely succeeded, but wandered onto less defensible ground when it emphasized that the callousness displayed on the website was "not the conduct and speech that our educational system is required to tolerate."[69] This is the kind of subjective, fluid marker aimed at content—not conduct—that offends the Speech Clause, an offense all the more extreme when a school goes after off-campus expression, no matter how unpleasant and uncivil. If the speech amounted to harassment under state law, the victim and her parents could have reported it to the police or filed a lawsuit against the authors. But a lot of very troubling expression doesn't amount to harassment under the law.

Other responses by the school would not intrude on First Amendment rights: lessons in empathy and on appropriate use of networking sites, and conferences with the offending students and their parents. Such measures, reliant on compliance by families and students, won't always succeed. The Fourth Circuit noted that the girl who had created the "particularly mean-spirited and hateful" site alleging a classmate had herpes later resisted "the school's efforts to bring order and provide a lesson following the incident." There was nothing the school could do about her resistance either.[70] As the judge said in *Klein,* the case about the student who made an obscene gesture at his teacher in a parking lot, the Constitution limits our ability to force-feed the "ruffians among us."

Schools have even intruded on private talks conducted online by willing participants. In one case, school officials intervened after two young people had an online conversation from their homes that had something to with sex. In their zeal to suppress speech they regarded as disreputable, school officials harangued and abused a girl for protected speech in a private dialogue.

When school officials in rural Minnewaska, Minnesota learned that twelve-year-old R.S. and a male schoolmate had engaged in a "sex-related conversation" on "the internet, off school grounds, and outside school hours," they pulled R.S. out of class. They interrogated her in the presence of police officers without contacting her mother. The boy had initiated the exchange, but R.S. readily admitted she had voluntarily taken part. Despite her confession, school officials demanded her usernames and passwords. Crying and threatened with detention, R.S. turned over the keys to her accounts, which the officials searched. They "expressed surprise" that she used profanity in private sites, read her personal correspondence, and commented negatively on her answers to what she called "'fun and funny'" Facebook sex quizzes. Although she wasn't punished, R.S. felt so humiliated that she stayed home for two days. She said she no longer felt "secure" or "safe" at school. Her mother sued, alleging that the school had violated her daughter's First and Fourth Amendment rights.[71]

In 2012, a federal court rejected the school district's argument that it hadn't violated R.S.'s rights and allowed a suit the ACLU had filed against the district to proceed. R.S. would win if she could prove at trial that her story was true. In March 2014, the school district settled; it agreed to pay $70,000 in damages and to revise its policies on student privacy.[72]

A few months after R.S. and her school settled, the Supreme Court addressed the significance of cell phone privacy for the first time in Riley v. California. *Riley* held police could not search cell phones without a warrant when arresting adults. Speaking for a unanimous Court, Chief Justice Roberts began the discussion by observing that "modern cell phones . . . are now such a pervasive and insistent part of daily life that the proverbial visitor from Mars might conclude they were an important feature of human anatomy."[73]

Cell phones and laptops have several things in common. Both contain, as Roberts noted with respect to cell phones (a label he called a "misleading shorthand" for a "minicomputer" on which one may place phone calls), "vast quantities of personal information." These devices collect "in one place many distinct kinds of information—an address, a note, a prescription, a bank statement, a video—that reveal much more in combination than any isolated record. . . . The sum of an individual's private life can be reconstructed through a thousand photographs labeled with dates, locations and descriptions." In short, digital records offer a "cache of sensitive personal information" in proportions previously unavailable even in a thorough search of a home.[74] This treasure trove was opened when R.S.'s school demanded and obtained her passwords.

There was no victim in Minnewaska before the school made R.S. into one. Her exchange with her schoolmate was voluntary. If the school were concerned about the children's well-being, it could have told R.S.'s mother about the conversations it had learned about from the boy's family and left the matter in her hands. The court correctly considered R.S.'s private postings "a far cry" from student statements that have led courts to approve intervention after off-campus threats of violence or tangible disruption.[75]

R.S. demonstrates that the erosion of boundaries between home and school is not entirely attributable to the state. Some parents who discover troubling material on their children's devices or learn that their child has been bullied rush straight to school officials seeking help, demanding that administrators intervene in other parents' child rearing. The guardian of the boy who initiated online discussions about "naughty things" asked the school to intervene without even attempting to talk to R.S.'s mother. The school could have explained the limits of its authority and suggested that the families work together to solve the problem before (or instead of) illegally invading R.S.'s privacy and usurping her mother's role in discussing sensitive matters of values and judgment.[76]

My inquiry into online communication has so far been limited to expression on devices that belong to the student, used on networks to which their families subscribe privately. With few exceptions, the reported incidents to date have arisen in that posture. But other possibilities exist.

Schools have a pronounced interest in supervising speech on social media sites they set up for teams and extracurricular groups, Twitter accounts used to announce snow days and the like, and platforms such as Blackboard that teachers establish and require students to use for interactive projects or tracking assignments. Such sites may properly be thought of as part of school itself even though students post to them and open them from outside school. Students shouldn't expect privacy on such sites because they know that faculty members will also be accessing them.

The transition to digital devices raises important questions about rights and socioeconomic status that have yet to be addressed. A closer question about oversight of digital communications might be presented if a school district allows students to use the school's network at any time of day for personal as well as educational purposes to access any sites they desire in order to reduce the socioeconomic gap in access to information. If some students can afford to subscribe to a supplemental private service, I wonder whether students who only have access to the school's network will be at risk of receiving less protection for their personal expression. Will we see a new digital divide between wealthier students who buy their own equipment—

or who possess privately owned laptops or tablets in addition to the equipment the school provides—and their less materially privileged peers who rely exclusively on devices and networks provided by their schools?

Similarly, initiatives to eliminate printed textbooks in favor of digital learning require school districts to provide students with tablets or computers (especially in low-income school districts). More than six hundred school districts have already begun this process. Laudable as it is, it is not without risks to civil liberties. One Philadelphia suburb that provided laptops to every high school student installed remote controls that activated webcams. Employees used these to capture material on the screens and to spy on roughly forty students in their homes and bedrooms. Discovery prompted concerns over privacy, Fourth Amendment rights, and violations of state and federal laws governing wiretaps as well as a lawsuit that the district settled at a cost of roughly $2 million in legal expenses for both sides and damages. The suit didn't raise First Amendment issues, but with slightly different facts it could have, if a student had been disciplined at school for what he said rather than for what the school thought he did (eating candy the school mistook for illegal drugs).[77]

If communications on school-owned equipment and networks the school provides are treated as in-school speech governed by the school speech cases, then students from families with more modest incomes would not have the same expressive rights off campus as their wealthier peers. They could not use lewd expressions under *Fraser*, urge peers to "get wasted" under *Morse*, or engage in some more valuable controversial speech that *Hazelwood* allows schools to block. Surely this would be a socially unacceptable outcome even if it didn't violate the Constitution.

Under this scenario schools should not try to extend their imprimatur by imposing a tagline that reads, "sent from an iPad owned by the Anytown School District." Students should be allowed to express themselves outside of school regardless of who owns the equipment they use.

Cyberbullying from Off Campus

Educators' assertions of almost limitless authority over student expression wherever and whenever it occurs are reinforced by legislative responses to bullying that empower schools to address off-campus bullying speech and often require them to do so. Emerging anti-bullying statutes rest on the unique circumstances created by compulsory education, which brings bullies and the bullied together, and the imperative that schools provide a safe environment for learning. Every state except Montana requires schools to adopt policies addressing bullying, and by 2013 forty-four states required schools to punish bullies. As of January 2015, twenty-one states had passed statutes banning what they called "cyberbullying," which many failed to define, and most of the remaining states prohibit electronic harassment. At least fifteen states assign schools responsibility for controlling off-campus behaviors, including hostile expression.[78]

When New Jersey amended its strict anti-bullying law in 2011, it made schools responsible for off-campus bullying, including bullying "by electronic devices": "[E]ach school's policy shall include . . . appropriate responses to harassment, intimidation, or bullying . . . that occurs off school grounds" if the incidents are reported to any "school employee." In the first year after the statute became effective, the state's schools reported more than twelve thousand bullying incidents to a central authority. A newspaper's review of public documents revealed that many of those reports involved off-campus speech.[79]

In one instance a twelve-year-old boy called a girl classmate "a horse." Another tweeted that a girl was a "grenade," which, according to urbandictionary.com, means "the solitary ugly girl always found with a group of hotties." This surely is mean, but it wouldn't meet the *Tinker* standard if uttered in the cafeteria. None of these matters has yet reached the courts.[80] If the facts as reported are borne out, some of the discipline schools imposed seems unlikely to survive legal challenges.

California, citing what it called "the inalienable right to attend classes on school campuses that are safe, secure, and peaceful," in 2012 made "bullying committed . . . by means of an electronic act" a ground for expulsion. The statute explicitly built on *Tinker*'s second prong by including in the definition of bullying "communications" that are likely to cause "a reasonable pupil to experience substantial interference with his or her academic performance" or bring that pupil "in fear of harm" to "person or property."[81]

California's lawmakers recognized that school officials do not wield unlimited authority over young people. To their credit, when they directed school districts to protect students from off-campus bullying, including aggressive online communications, they tried to confine schools' power over off-campus speech within the outer contours of educators' legitimate authority.

The statute restricts a school district's disciplinary power to violations "related to school activity or attendance that occur at any time," including on school grounds, going to or from school grounds, off campus during lunch period, and during or en route to or from "a school-sponsored activity." Despite limitations, the "at any time" language and the apparent extension of authority over conduct during unsupervised travel to and from school have the potential to undermine the apparent intent to restrict schools' disciplinary reach to speech that has a nexus with the campus.[82]

All of the recently enacted state statutes depend on lawyers and courts to provide more detailed guidelines for educators. Justin Patchin, codirector of the Cyberbullying Research Center, criticizes states for "passing laws saying effectively 'schools have to deal with this'" without specific definitions, instructions, or funding. It will take years before we learn which approaches are most effective and whether they stand up to judicial scrutiny.[83]

In the first reported decision bearing on cyberbullying statutes, in 2014, New York's highest court overturned a criminal cyberbullying statute challenged by a high school student who had been prosecuted for an unattributed Facebook page on which he posted photos and malicious comments about his classmates' alleged sexual preferences and practices. The court held that the statute as written could not "coexist comfortably with the right to free speech" because it reached too much annoying, embarrassing speech that is nonetheless protected.[84]

Meanwhile, the federal government's full-speed-ahead approach to making schools responsible for controlling bullying sentiments extends to off-campus expression. In 2011, the U.S. Commission on Civil Rights urged increased federal engagement in efforts to stop bullying wherever it occurs, delegating a central role to schools. It did not distinguish between face-to-face expression on campus and online communications from off campus. So far, the Commission's publicly available documents do not help schools recognize the difference between protected speech and harassment as defined by state law.

The Commission admitted that the Speech Clause might pose obstacles to the anti-bullying policies the federal government wants schools to pursue. Much like the Justice Department's approach to bullying sentiments expressed in person, the Commission dismissed constitutional concerns with the tepid observation that "[w]hile reasonable minds differ on the precise limits of the First Amendment, detailed guidance could indeed be useful to schools as they develop their anti-bullying policies."[85]

Three dissenting Commissioners—all Republican appointees—sounded alarms that the Commission's call for the federal government and schools to combat bullying everywhere threatens constitutionally protected student speech. When federal agencies minimize serious First Amendment issues, the dissenters pointed out, the resulting policies "will quite predictably lead school districts to overreact and trample students' freedom of expression by adopting various zero-tolerance approaches to curb 'offensive' speech in an effort to avoid lawsuits" by students who assert they were harassed by peers.

The Commission's minority report details how federal agencies encourage schools to unearth and punish "non-threatening student speech," including electronic communications that emanate from off campus. "Cyber-bullying," they charge, "seems nothing more than a derogatory label for electronic speech that someone else doesn't like." Testimony revealed that the online bullying schools might try to "stamp out" includes "'spreading rumors,' 'interfering with relationships,' and disparaging the target[] . . . in an attempt to make them feel badly about themselves."[86] None of these standing alone would satisfy *Tinker*'s requirements on campus or off.

The Department of Justice, too, gives inadequate legal advice to school districts about digital expression. It doesn't explain or even allude to the restraints the Speech Clause imposes. The Department's website advises parents to tell the local school about all cyberbullying, much of which will consist of protected expression. One study of policies at the state level similarly found that states have failed "to give public school officials any guidance on how to apply the definition [of cyberbullying] so as not to run afoul of free speech and other constitutional" constraints.[87]

If school districts have to balance the risk of the federal government suing them or withholding funds (as the Commission recommends) because they failed to protect students from bullying words against the possibility that a silenced student will file a private lawsuit, school districts are likely to ignore speech rights every time.[88]

"Raunchy" Speech, Sexting, and Orwellian "Re-Education"

Sexting by teens has also received a great deal of media attention, perhaps because adults find it so titillating. Varying definitions sweep in a wide range of material: everything from words conveying erotic messages to photos of fully covered provocative poses to "indecent" images that the First

Amendment protects and nudity that remains outside the scope of the obscenity laws. Some of these are legally nuanced and obscure categories in themselves. The First Amendment protects the sexting speaker's rights in school if the transmissions don't violate any state or federal law. Based on legal approaches rather than popular understandings, as I am using the term, a "sexting" communication must contain more than words—it requires photographs and excludes images that violate child pornography or obscenity laws.[89]

The proportion of students in high school or younger who say they have sent or received sexts appears to be much lower than popular opinion would have it. The Pew Research Center's 2009 survey reports that only 4 percent of teenagers between the ages of twelve and seventeen admit they have sent an image of themselves, and 15 percent say they have received a sext. Other surveys report higher participation rates, probably because they include older teenagers and young adults.[90]

Sexting almost always has its genesis off campus. Pictures are taken and transmitted from the relative privacy of a student's home. Other students, however, often open the images on their personal devices while at school. As a result, schools all over the country have disciplined students for sexting when texts spread broadly, receiving intense media coverage. But in reality most sexts are not forwarded to others, and only a tiny fraction of sexters get caught. According to one study, only 3 to 4 percent of sexters say their parents found out, while schools caught and punished 3 percent or fewer.[91]

That doesn't mean sexting is no big deal. When peers who were not the intended recipients see sexted photos (which the same study indicated happened to roughly 20 percent of those who sent photos of themselves), the senders can become the subjects of rumors, harassment, extreme humiliation, and social rejection in the short term. In the longer term, they risk reputational damage if college admissions offices and potential or current employers discover the photos years later.[92]

When schools, sexting, and law enforcement are linked, students have virtually no protections against in-school searches. School officials can search students' belongings without a warrant on very little basis, as long as the search seems "reasonable" when it begins. If schools pass evidence of sexting on to the police, the photos can lead to an adjudication that will place a minor on the registry of sex offenders for up to twenty-five years under federal law.[93] Challenges to school discipline for sexting are just beginning to reach the courts.

Since schools often stumble onto sexts, they have become de facto first responders. As with bullying, many state legislatures and school boards are trying to address the problem while the complex First Amendment law surrounding sexting remains unexamined. At least seventeen states have adopted laws addressing sexting. In contrast to the legislative response to bullying, none seems to require schools to intercept sexts or punish students who exchange them.[94]

Three groups of students occupy distinct legal positions with respect to sexting. The first group consists of students who create and send sexts of themselves from off campus. The second group is made up of the intended recipients; presuming voluntary exchanges of sexts, many students will fall into both the first and second grouping based on a single correspondence. Finally, the third category is made up of students who pass a sext along to people who the original speaker never intended to see the material.

The first group—the student speakers who sext pictures of themselves—are engaging in expressive activity protected by the Speech Clause. Adults may not understand the role and nature of their communications. Social science research suggests that sexting is part of flirting, dating, and courtship for a growing proportion of teenagers.[95] Their youthful indiscretion is best viewed as being part of the essence of youth itself and the search for autonomous definition that leads to adulthood, beyond the scope of the law (but not beyond the reach of parental advice and resolution). The sexter's off-campus speech normally should be immune from school discipline.

An identical analysis covers intended recipients of sexts (the second group of students). They are also engaging in protected speech because the right to speak encompasses the right to receive communications.

In addition to being puzzled and appalled by sexts, adults sometimes confuse modest pictures created in good fun with photos of a very different type. In one egregious case, a group of thirteen-year-old girls in Tunkhannock, Pennsylvania gathered at a friend's home where they posed for photos in bathing suits, in opaque white bras that were at least as modest as many bathing suit tops, or wrapped in towels and sent the pictures to friends. Their school confiscated cell phones belonging to the recipients and turned them over to a county district attorney who threatened to prosecute the girls.

The girls hadn't broken any laws, they hadn't even broken a school rule, but the male prosecutor found the photos "provocative." He offered the girls a plea bargain: They could attend a "re-education program" in which they would be required to write essays acknowledging that what they did was "wrong" or face prosecution. Some of the girls who faced prosecution agreed to the conditions, but three others rejected the Orwellian offer. Those three girls and their parents sought and received a temporary restraining order that barred the district attorney from prosecuting them pending resolution of the First Amendment issues. The photos, the court held, were protected speech and the threatened prosecution appeared to be unlawful retaliation for "refusing to abandon . . . constitutional rights."[96]

I am aware of only one case in which a court has confronted the express question of whether a school can discipline students for sexts created off campus. The case involved "raunchy photos" a group of Indiana girls took of themselves over the summer at a series of slumber parties. Wrapped in towels, they posed with props including "phallic-shaped rainbow colored lollipops." The fully covered girls thought the photos so hilarious that they posted the pictures on various websites to show their friends " 'how funny it was.' "[97]

The school the girls attended punished them for violating the portion of the school code that required all students involved in extracurricular activities to "demonstrate good conduct . . . outside of school . . . including . . . during the summer." Although the pictures didn't contain any information about where the girls went to school, they were banned from team sports. Holding that the expression was protected speech and assuming for argument's sake that the school could punish the students if it met *Tinker*'s rigorous requirements, the judge held that the school had utterly failed to show any risk of campus disruption.[98]

The court smacked down the school's argument that *Fraser* allowed it to punish "lewd, vulgar," and offensive photos "taken inside the privacy of their own homes and . . . published to the internet outside of school," which reached school only through the actions of others. The court also overturned the portion of the code under which the school punished the towel-wrapped teenagers who evoked the bathing beauties of an earlier era. A code that imposes penalties for behavior that "brings discredit or dishonor upon yourself or your school," the court ruled, sweeps too broadly by giving school officials unlimited discretion to penalize students for expressing themselves no matter when or where they do so.[99]

The First Amendment protects the sexting student from school discipline, though her actions expose her to humiliation at the hands of peers who may abuse her trust and misuse her communication. I use the feminine pronoun here intentionally. The repercussions of sexting are usually not gender neutral. Girls are far more likely than boys to suffer reputational damage and school discipline for engaging in sexting activity. Intriguingly, none of the available reports suggests the schools that punish girls for sexting or refer them for prosecution have disciplined the students who received the photos or forwarded them to others. As a matter of social policy, not constitutional law, it makes more sense for schools to try to protect girls who might not have anticipated the unintended consequences of their decision to hit "send" from being shamed in front of their peers rather than to further humiliate them through punishment.

Members of the third group of students implicated in sexting—those who share sexts with people who weren't the intended recipients—violate trust. If they pass photos along to a large group of friends or post them on publicly accessible sites they may be violating privacy laws and engaging in or inciting harassment. Re-senders could be exposing themselves to prosecution if they have the intent required for a criminal act and could also be subject to civil lawsuits by their victims.[100]

In the event that prosecutors and juries in criminal and civil cases treat wide-scale sharing of sexts without the sender's consent as legal violations, they will be confirming that people who transmit this sort of private communication to others are not engaged in protected expression, much as New Jersey became the first state to criminalize "revenge porn" by former intimates in 2004, followed by Alaska and, in 2013, California.[101] If courts rule in the future that schools may discipline sexting that causes material disruption on campus, the disruption should be attributed to the students who distribute the sext widely, not the person who created it—at least if she distributed it to a limited audience.

Vermont provides a useful statutory model for states that wish to regulate teenage sexting. It apportions responsibility equally between sender and recipient by making it an offense for minors to send or possess an "indecent visual depiction" of themselves or another and addresses transmission of photos received from the sexter to other minors. To mitigate the criminalization of voluntary sexting, however, the statute doesn't allow prosecution for a first offense, giving the juvenile court a role in providing wake-up calls to teenagers. The statute envisions that schools may offer education and outreach about the dangers of sexting for "minors, parents, teachers," and others but does not assign schools any role in ferreting out or policing sexting.[102]

The sexter whose photos are shared without her consent has some private legal remedies. She can sue the person who transmits her private communication for tortious "publication of embarrassing private facts," a tort "recognized by some thirty-six states" as of 2010.[103] Schools that elect to educate students about the responsible use of online communications, including sexting, might do well to warn students of the legal risks that accompany turning an "innocent sext" between friends into a tool for humiliation.

Evolving technology may enable users to send a photo that evaporates in a few seconds that could provide some shelter for indiscreet youth. The European Union's recognition in 2014 of a "right to be forgotten," which requires search engines to take down information at the request of individuals unhappy with the material about them on the service, shows the technical capacity exists. California's pathbreaking "eraser law" (effective in 2015) requires social media websites to allow minors to delete potentially embarrassing postings by hitting a button. Beginning in March 2015 several social media platforms voluntarily barred naked photos or agreed to remove such photos if the subject requests that they be deleted.[104] Those developments still leave the onus on the victims whose pictures were circulated without their consent, but they may facilitate the recognition that sexting belongs out of educators' hands.

The extension of school authority over young people who are not even students in their school system would be the ultimate stretch—an absurd but sadly realistic proposition. A decade ago, the superintendent of schools in one suburban town who found her car covered in shaving cream demanded the names of all the teenagers who were standing nearby. One of the boys spoke up to defend the gawking group that had gathered for a closer look at the oddity. The superintendent ordered him to reveal his name and, since the confrontation occurred just after graduation, threatened to revoke his diploma. The crowd truthfully retorted, "[Y]ou can't—he never went to this school." Eyewitnesses told me the superintendent appeared flabbergasted at the notion that any teenager might be exempt from her authority.

The risks to civil liberties have a still more menacing aspect because the spate of delinquency proceedings based entirely on violations of school codes also reaches off-campus expression. Students who poke fun at school officials online can end up in serious trouble even if they haven't broken any laws. In *Snyder*, for example, the principal not only suspended the authors of the fake MySpace page, he also reported them to the police. The girls were lucky. No one pursued charges.

Another girl with an exemplary academic record wasn't as fortunate. She was adjudicated a delinquent solely as a result of posting a similar fictitious MySpace page for a school administrator; she had prominently labeled the site a joke. Because the police had assured her parents that she would be ordered to perform community service, she appeared in juvenile court without a lawyer. Instead, the judge confined her to a for-profit juvenile treatment center. When the Juvenile Law Center, a public interest group in Philadelphia, entered the case to try to secure her release, lawyers unmasked a major scandal. The judge and a colleague were receiving kickbacks for sentencing children to the facility. An investigation that led to the judge's resignation, criminal conviction, and imprisonment received national attention, including in the 2014 documentary *Kids for Cash*.[105] This shameful episode reminds us that violations of student speech rights are intimately tied to a host of systems that deny children the legal protections and liberties to which they are entitled.

Young people engage in many kinds of misbehavior unrelated to school that do not involve the exercise of constitutional liberties: careless driving, riding a bike without a helmet or lights, or staying in a park after dark. I strongly doubt that anyone would propose schools suspend all the students who are seen doing these things. Educators cannot replace parents and civic authority by pursuing children into the streets, malls, and their own homes without violating individual rights.

Nor can educators substitute for criminal authority in responding to criminal harassment, physical attacks, and crimes like rape. Schools are not equipped to conduct criminal investigations or to hold hearings that provide the panoply of legal protections (including the right to an attorney and to challenge the validity of evidence and laws) that are constitutionally required in courtrooms. Victims too have some rights in the justice system that are not usually available in schools (like the rape shield protections against inquiries into the sexual history of a rape victim). Beyond the verified risk that schools may cover up crimes by school heroes (as happened with the football players in Steubenville, Ohio, and at more than one college), it defies logic and the aims of criminal justice to treat schools as the first stop for discipline where serious crimes have occurred. School disciplinarians and judges should think carefully before taking on or permitting such inappropriate roles.

Suppression of off-campus speech threatens democracy as well as the rule of law. If schools intrude into students' off-campus and online lives, and courts allow them to, students will become acclimated to authoritarian scrutiny. Future generations who grow up with minimal expectations that their privacy, autonomy, and communicative rights will be respected may be far less likely to vigorously defend those rights as adults in the face of threats like warrantless mass data mining or intrusion by private firms.

The lesson should be clear: When students don't break the law, their First Amendment freedom to speak, write, or post from home should be beyond the school's purview.

CHAPTER 8

Tinker Rising Like the Phoenix

Evangelicals and LGBTs Allied

At the core of the First Amendment's right to free speech is the right of one student to express a religious viewpoint to another without fear.

—Morgan v. Swanson (5th Cir. 2011) (en banc) (Elrod, J.)

May elementary school students give classmates candy canes with religious messages attached? May high school graduation speakers mention the role God plays in their lives? May students perform "Ave Maria" at graduation? May they hand out leaflets published by a national organization that call abortion "murder"? May students organize daily prayer meetings or proselytize on campus? Must a school permit LGBT students or political conservatives to form a club that meets at school?

The short answer to each of these questions is "it all depends"—on the facts, on the context, and on the court. Schools have blocked each of these kinds of speech, resulting in litigation, and some of these questions have reached federal courts multiple times from school districts across the country on modestly different facts. One judge summed up the reigning confusion in 2010: "The many cases and the large body of literature on this set of issues demonstrate the lack of adequate guidance to enable teachers and principals to determine whether the decisions they make comply with constitutional standards."[1]

Judges routinely use the words "this is not a settled area of law" or the equivalent when asked whether schools must "tolerate" student religious speech. As with so many questions discussed in this book, the Supreme Court has never provided specific guidance on religious speech that emanates directly from students, and the appellate courts do not offer a unified approach. Appellate judge Guido Calabresi, a former dean of Yale Law School not known for his intellectual timidity, regards disputes about student religious speech as invitations "to cut a path through the thorniest of constitutional thickets."[2]

The Fifth Circuit sitting en banc does not share that view. When schools silence students' private, undisruptive, religious speech, the court declared in 2012, they "strike[] at the very heart of the First Amendment."[3]

In this chapter I argue that pure student speech about religion is entitled to the same legal protection accorded all other pure student speech under *Tinker*. My stance should not be misinterpreted as support for what constitutional law scholar and litigator Douglas Laycock has called "[p]ersistent attempts to inculcate religion in some public schools." Impermissible actions favoring religion by school officials have led to numerous lawsuits resulting in judicial opinions that set them straight on the law.[4] Those violations of the Establishment Clause are outside the scope of my discussion of individual speech rights.

In addition to the Speech Clause, the First Amendment includes two clauses guaranteeing religious freedom. The Free Exercise Clause protects the right of each individual to exercise his or her religion, while the Establishment Clause prevents the government from creating an official religion (such as the Church of England), from favoring or disfavoring any religion and, as the Supreme Court has held, from preferring religion to non-religion: The First Amendment "requires the state to be neutral in its relations with groups of religious believers and non-believers."[5]

Cases at the intersection of student speech and religious expression have multiplied exponentially in the past two decades. There were none at all during the 1970s and a handful during the 1980s. During the 1990s they accelerated: Almost one in five of the lawsuits seeking to enforce student speech rights involved student-initiated religious speech. The trend held steady in the first decade of the twenty-first century—20 percent of all student speech litigation involved student religious speech. The percentage would be higher if I counted all the cases since 2000 that centered on speech motivated by religious beliefs, like the anti-gay and anti-abortion speech discussed in earlier chapters.

The explosion of religious speech cases is no accident. Religious activists have concluded that the Speech Clause provides a more promising vehicle for their goals than the Religion Clauses.

Tensions between the Free Exercise and Establishment Clauses and the disparate ways schools have responded to constitutional requirements create a puzzling portrait of religion in public schools. It may seem almost impossible to reconcile two conflicting accounts of the way public schools treat religion. According to the first, schools, in an apparent effort to respect the Establishment Clause, unnecessarily silence personal religious expression, causing evangelical activists associated with Christian conservatives to regard the children of their flock as the most persecuted minority in the country. In the second, schools promote school prayer and Christianity in blatant disregard of Supreme Court rulings, encouraged by some state governments and by Christian culture warriors around the country who seek to reinstate student prayer.[6] Both stories contain elements of the truth.

Some school officials say there is no place for religious expression in school. They are profoundly mistaken. The Constitution doesn't require that schools become religion-free zones. Student-initiated religious expression may come from individuals, from informally coordinated groups, and even from a subset of student clubs that are recognized by the school but not school sponsored. The primary constitutional restriction is that religious exercise or exhortation on campus emanate from students, without prompting, support, or endorsement from teachers or school officials.

The dizzying doctrine that needs to be disentangled in these cases fosters bewilderment. The resulting confusion encourages both sides in disputes to pursue litigation rather than to resolve their differences because they think they might win in court even when legal precedents offer little or no support for their positions.

After a brief overview of the Establishment Clause—providing just enough details to frame discussion of when schools justifiably fear that allowing student religious speech will violate the Constitution—the chapter turns to cases involving what is clearly personal religious expression on campus, showing that schools regularly silence protected student speech about religion. The chapter then looks at more complicated fact patterns, where the lines between personal and official speech are harder to discern. The final section of the chapter turns to the special legal status some clubs initiated by students occupy under the federal Equal Access Act (the "Act"). The Act's authors wanted to protect student religious organizations, but LGBT students soon learned to exploit it. Its operation reveals the continued vitality of the balance *Tinker* struck between protecting student speech rights and heeding societal needs in schools.

The Religion Clauses Summarized

The legal regime governing student speech about religious belief sometimes seems to resemble three-dimensional chess, perhaps with a few rules from backgammon thrown in. Schools that silence students' own religious perspectives often offer the defense that they had to suppress student expression in order to comply with the Establishment Clause. In order to assess that recurrent defense, we need to understand the broad outlines of Establishment Clause jurisprudence.

The Establishment Clause has been the source of much befuddlement and mischief as schools struggle with student religious expression. Like the Speech Clause, the Establishment Clause only restricts the actions of the government and its agents. Many of the Supreme Court's leading Establishment Clause rulings have come in cases involving public schools.

Over the past quarter century, the Supreme Court's decisions have undermined any shared understanding of what the clause means or how courts should resolve controversies about its application. Today, legal scholars and many judges agree that there is "no consensus among the Justices as to the appropriate theory of the Establishment Clause."[7]

Individual Justices and the lower courts use three approaches, sometimes referring to more than one in the same case: (1) a test developed in 1971 in Lemon v. Kurtzman that the Supreme Court has largely discarded but never explicitly rejected; (2) the endorsement test; and (3) the coercion test.

Although by 1995 seven sitting Justices formally questioned the usefulness of the Lemon v. Kurtzman approach to assessing whether government actions violate the Establishment Clause, lower court judges continue to invoke it in cases involving student religious speech. The test has three parts. The first element—whether the government's action has a secular purpose— is critical to decisions about whether schools have permissibly silenced or encouraged student religious expression. The secular purpose need not be the *only* purpose, but there must be one. *Lemon*'s second prong requires the primary effect of the government law or practice to be neutral, in the sense that it "neither advance nor inhibit religion," while the third prohibits "excessive entanglement" between government and religion. Some legal commentators regard *Lemon* as a dead letter, but Kent Greenawalt, a leading scholar of the religion clauses, accurately observes that abandonment of *Lemon* as a "complete test . . . does not mean its various elements are irrelevant."[8]

Lower court judges also often apply two alternative approaches that have never been adopted by a majority of the Court as a substitute for the *Lemon* test but are on display in the opinions of individual Justices and in a sprinkling of majority opinions.

The first—the endorsement test—aims at social and political inclusiveness. Its architect, Justice O'Connor, explained that "government cannot endorse the religious practices and beliefs of some citizens without sending a clear message to nonadherents that they are outsiders."[9] This approach, like *Hazelwood*'s imprimatur requirement, depends on whether observers would believe the government endorsed religion.

Unlike *Hazelwood,* however, the endorsement test imputes knowledge of both facts and context to the observer. Observers cannot be misinformed, as they might be in attributing school sponsorship to student expression. Justice O'Connor elaborated: The "hypothetical observer . . . is presumed to possess a certain level of information that all citizens might not share."[10]

When the endorsement test is used to evaluate the constitutionality of religious speech in schools, it embraces two distinct sets of issues: religious speech by the government or selected by it and religious speech by students who may or may not speak on behalf of the school.

In the first scenario, at issue in the earliest school prayer cases, the government is the speaker or has selected the speech, akin to the speech being the school's own under *Hazelwood.* If the school's own speech is religious or promotes religion, it always violates the Establishment Clause. In the 1960s, the Court handed down a series of opinions holding that school prayer led by teachers, including recitation of the Lord's Prayer and Bible reading, was unconstitutional. Those rulings generated venomous attacks on the Court and recurrent proposals to amend the Constitution to permit school prayer. In subsequent decisions, the Court limited other kinds of official school prayer and the circumstances under which it could be condoned.[11]

In the second context, it is less clear who is speaking or who decided that the content of the speech would include religious perspectives. The correct attribution of ownership of religious expression is key to legal disputes about student religious viewpoints and prayer on campus. The presumption that observers accurately attribute responsibility to the school applies to two separate aspects of the religious speech problem: whether the speakers represent the school or themselves and, if the latter, whether the school appears to endorse the content of the speech.

The coercion test—which religious activists insist on calling the "accommodation approach"—provides another method for assessing Establishment Clause violations. It builds on the premise that "government may not coerce anyone to support or participate in a religion or its exercise" and overlaps with the endorsement approach in its concern for outsiders. Justice Kennedy, who largely developed the coercion approach, used it when he wrote for a five-to-four majority in Lee v. Weisman, decided in 1995. In that case, the Supreme Court held that schools could not invite clergy to deliver nonsectarian prayers at public school graduation ceremonies. The clergy were not given the podium to speak as they wished. Instead, the school district directed them to pray and to do so in a certain (nonsectarian) format. Kennedy reasoned that the prayers inherently though subtly coerced students to give up an important milestone ceremony or passively participate in praying. The Justices are divided about how direct or indirect pressure must be to qualify as coercion. Indeed, the doctrine is so malleable that Kennedy switched sides in *Lee* after drafting an opinion that went the other way, leading to a different five-to-four division.[12]

Given all of the uncertainty about how courts will approach claims that schools have violated the Establishment Clause, school officials have good reason to be confused about where the lines are drawn. In 2001, the Supreme Court expressly reserved for a future controversy the question of whether "a state's interest in avoiding" an actual or cognizable "Establishment Clause violation would justify viewpoint discrimination" against private religious speech.[13]

It is also unclear whether confusion about the law constitutes a defense when a school is sued over an alleged Establishment Clause violation. The Supreme Court has never determined whether a good faith though misguided or unnecessary attempt to comply with the Establishment Clause will get a school off the hook when it violates speech rights. We can think of that common argument as what I call "the well-intentioned but unwarranted" Establishment Clause defense.

Lacking guidance from the Supreme Court, lower courts are divided over whether schools may censor pure student religious speech any time they worry about potential legal exposure to allegations that they violated the Establishment Clause or if the school must show that the Establishment Clause really is implicated.[14] The legitimacy of an administrator's decision to silence a student's religious speech may be undermined if the Establishment Clause does not require the school to prevent the expression. In the absence of bright lines, some school officials have been overzealous in their efforts to avoid Establishment Clause violations at the cost of pure student expression.

Outside of schools, as the Court's composition has become more aggressively conservative, it is increasingly difficult to convince a majority of the Justices that private speech in public spaces violates the Establishment Clause. Justice Alito's arrival created a majority of five Roman Catholics who agree with Justice Scalia that "accommodation" of religious expression by private speakers does not violate the Establishment Clause.[15]

In Town of Greece v. Galloway, a sharply divided Court held five-to-four in 2014 that pervasively Christian prayers at monthly meetings of a town's governing board attended by residents who had business before the board did not violate the Establishment Clause. Arguably, the Court's increasing acceptance of Christian religious speech in public arenas, such as public display of crosses as part of a quasi-civic culture, undermines the defense available to school officials who silence religious speech out of concern about potential Establishment Clause violations.[16]

"You Have to Argue Free Speech to Protect Religious Expression": Personal Religious Expression

The student speech explored in this section concerns religion or the speaker's religious beliefs. It may be a private prayer, a reference to "Jesus Christ," an effort to proselytize, or even a humorous campaign slogan, like "He chose Mary, you should too." The resulting disputes often involve allegations that officials censored student speech precisely because of its religious content and viewpoint. In contrast, in cases like *Nuxoll* authorities justified banning the student's "Be Happy, Not Gay" shirt as necessary to protect the rights of LGBT students. Although they disapproved of Nuxoll's disparaging sentiments, school officials did not censor his shirt on the ground that religious sentiments (whether express or implied) were inappropriate at school.

The central dilemma for school officials is whether student religious speech is truly "private speech endorsing religion" or "attributable to the state" à la *Hazelwood*. Officials must tread carefully as they navigate among First Amendment tests with respect to religious speech. A school would transparently violate Establishment Clause if it proclaimed as truth the school's (or the principal's) position that Christ rose from the dead or that students' lives will be improved if they give themselves over to God or that people and animals are reincarnated after death. If a school asserts ownership of all school publications and claims all the speech those publications contain as the school's own, a decision to publish an autobiographical article about how a student found Christ could raise problems under the Establishment Clause if readers actually regarded the views in the article as the school's. (Remember that some schools have urged courts to treat students' classroom speech as the school's own.) No similar constitutional bar stands in the way of allowing a student to publish, in a school-sponsored journal, any other kind of material that some may consider controversial. This holds true whether the subject is sex, politics, money, or even the world's religions (so long as the contents do not appear to promote or belittle any religious viewpoint).

If the school endorsed or solicited the student's religious expression, the speech likely violates the Establishment Clause, an outcome the school has a strong interest in avoiding.[17] In other circumstances, a student is solely responsible for both the religious expression and its dissemination.

The Supreme Court has emphasized the difference between official or school-sponsored prayer and prayer that originates with students: "Nothing in the Constitution as interpreted by this Court prohibits any public school student from voluntarily praying at any time before, during, or after the school-day."[18] School officials err when they ask whether they *may* permit students to engage in religious speech because if the speech is personal the salient question is whether the school *must* permit it. The answer is yes, on the same terms as any other pure, personal student speech *Tinker* protects.

The constitutional protection accorded personal prayer initiated by students is so robust it's difficult to comprehend why a teacher in upstate New York stopped a kindergarten student from saying this grace over her own snack: "God is good. God is Great. Thank you God for my food." Schools have also suppressed thanks to God in personal yearbook statements and sharing of religious views or experiences with classmates during "show and tell." In another instance, a teacher told an elementary school student she couldn't share her own views about God with her classmates when they talked about their reactions to the 9/11 attacks.[19]

Under the student speech doctrine individual students may pray, discuss religious precepts, or read aloud from religious texts ranging from the St. James version of the Bible to the Koran, the Book of Mormon, the Talmud, the Hindu Upanishads, or L. Ron Hubbard's collected works, so long as they don't materially disrupt the school. In contrast to the Free Exercise Clause, under the Speech Clause it doesn't matter whether the students adhere to the beliefs those texts contain. They may still read them aloud in the cafeteria if they don't disrupt the school day.

Proponents of state-sponsored school prayer have ignored and twisted the Supreme Court's guidance, and misleadingly inflamed their constituencies, by insisting that the Court's decisions—not the mistakes of educators—bar children from praying or expressing religious beliefs at school. They use inflammatory terms like "Hostility to Religious Expression in the

Public Square." At congressional hearings on that topic in 2004, Kelly Shackelford, chief counsel of the conservative Liberty Legal Institute, argued that "religion is being treated as pornography when expressed in public." He charged, "[L]ittle kids get the message. Their religion is treated as a curse word at school. They are taught at an early age, keep your religion to yourself; it is dirty. And that is wrong."[20]

Shackelford is partly correct—schools are wrong when they treat a student's religious expression as inappropriate for sharing with others. He is mistaken, however, when he charges that the Constitution requires or permits schools to censor personal student speech about their religious beliefs. Such exaggeration by those who want to restore official school prayer, who claim that the Supreme Court has turned schools into religion-free zones, has promoted misunderstandings about what the Constitution demands. His own hyperbole has probably made Shackelford's worst fears more likely to be realized.

Despite the complex interaction among these three First Amendment clauses, school officials should not be as puzzled as they claim to be when students express their personal religious beliefs of their own volition. *Tinker* and *Hazelwood*, once understood, greatly simplify the process of separating private student speech from speech that the school encourages or endorses.

If religious speech or prayer is private in the sense that it is the speech of one or more students, it is entitled to protection as long as it is neither school sponsored nor amenable to misinterpretation as having the school's endorsement. This speech is no different from other purely personal expression that happens to take place on campus that the *Hazelwood* majority agreed *Tinker* governs.

One can imagine private religious speech that implicates *Morse*—for example, a Native American student advocating religious observance that includes the use of peyote—but I am not aware of any real controversies involving this scenario. A more remote hypothetical would be a student preaching the gospel in lewd terms that the school could silence under *Fraser*. With these hypothetical exceptions, pure student religious speech is protected unless it threatens material disruption or collides with the rights of others.

Enforceable rights to religious expression became more dependent on the protections of the Speech Clause in the wake of Employment Division v. Smith, a 1990 Supreme Court decision that narrowed free exercise guarantees under the federal Constitution. The Liberty Legal Institute's Shackelford testified, "[T]he only way those of us who practice" in the area of student religious speech "can win now is under the free speech clause, . . . the free exercise clause has been so reduced that you have to argue free speech to protect religious expression."[21]

The relationship between speech and exercise comes to a head periodically in disputes over a clearly personal form of religious expression—attire signaling religious observance, a form of symbolic expression governed by *Tinker*. Many religiously observant people believe that their faith requires them to dress in a particular way. Orthodox Jewish men wear kippahs; as part of modest dress, many Muslim girls cover their heads and sometimes their faces; the Khalsa subgroup of Sikh boys must wear a metal kirpan, or ceremonial knife, at all times, and many also wear long hair and a turban; and some Native American cultures forbid boys to cut their hair.

Where school districts don't allow students to wear hats or boys to have long hair, the religious adherent must seek an exemption from the general rule in order to follow the religious doctrine to which he or she subscribes. If litigation results, Free Exercise rights under the federal Constitution do not require schools to grant exemptions to nondiscriminatory general rules (such as a rule banning all hats and head coverings), though a majority of states do. The law in those states, whether achieved though statute, constitutional amendments, or judicial rulings, restored Free Exercise doctrine to the status that obtained under the First Amendment prior to the 1990 *Smith* decision. In theory, under this approach, the state must grant exemptions from valid laws that infringe on an individual's exercise of religion unless the state can demonstrate a compelling interest in denying the exemption; in practice, courts have rarely granted demands for exceptions.

A speech claim provides a simpler route. If the apparel is analyzed as symbolic speech, lower courts will generally find that students have the right to wear their religion on their sleeves.[22]

Misunderstanding the law, school administrators silence students who want to share their own religious experiences with peers. Officials fear that private speech might confuse or pressure classmates even when most listeners would understand that the views were personal to the speaker. In a talent show, for instance, where each child selected the material he or she wished to perform, a court held that a girl had a right to sing a gospel song even if it would be inappropriate for a teacher to assign that song to a performer or to develop a show that consisted entirely of gospel music.[23]

In another incident, the principal of a school in upstate New York wrongly denied third grader M.B.'s request to distribute literature she had created at home analogizing the discovery of Christ to the joy of finding a lost pet. He worried that other "students might feel pressured to accept and respond to flyers 'offered by a classmate' which might create 'unnecessary divisiveness within the class.'" M.B.'s school thought that students wouldn't understand the origins of the homemade circular, which opened with a clear statement about who was talking: "Hi! My name is [M.B.] and I would like to tell you about my life." It continued, "and how Jesus Christ gave me a new one. . . . This is what he has done for me." Her self-referential examples included her parents' upcoming remarriage ("I will get to see my dad every day"); help learning Bible verses and the piano; and caring "enough about me that He gave me the victory over thinking about something bad that happened to me." When M.B.'s mother sued, a federal court held that the school had violated M B.'s speech rights because no one would have thought the speech was school sponsored. It was all about M.B. and what happened in her life. And the school had not shown any ground under *Tinker* for silencing her expression.[24]

A child is also entitled to share personal opinions with other students in an organized curricular activity unless a risk exists that the audience may think the school has endorsed the student's religious ideas. A first-grade teacher who thought that her students would attribute to the school the Bible story a boy had chosen to read aloud to the class asked the boy to share the story with her outside the class's hearing. A federal court held that she didn't violate the boy's rights by denying him his special moment of sharing. But the doctrine in this area is so undeveloped that the court went on to explain that if the teacher had made the opposite choice, allowing the boy to read the Bible story to the class, she would likely have complied with the law as well.[25]

Justice Alito, dissenting from an en banc decision on related issues in the same controversy when he sat on the Third Circuit, would have held "that public school students have the right to express religious views in class discussion or in assigned work, provided that their expression falls within the scope of the discussion or the assignment."[26] This is not the law, even in the Third Circuit, but it might prove a helpful guideline. It would also be consistent with existing law because, under *Tinker,* repeated nonresponsive statements in class could prove materially disruptive.

Such a rule would not be as easy to administer as it is to state because it would likely lead to litigation over the extent to which religious submissions satisfy academic requirements. Federal courts have already had to resolve disputes about whether a recording of a student singing in church (no matter how beautiful) satisfies the purpose of show-and-tell, which is to learn how to speak (or perform) in front of classmates, and whether a poster largely created by a kindergarten student's mother thanking Jesus for the earth fulfilled the curricular goal of summarizing what the student learned from a class unit on global warming and conservation.[27]

Brittney Kaye Settle, the middle school student who asserted that her freedom to speak was infringed when a teacher refused to accept her research paper on Jesus, lost in court because the teacher had several pedagogically defensible reasons for failing her, as I briefly mentioned in Chapter 4. The lesson aimed to teach students "how to research a topic, synthesize the information they gathered, and write a paper using that information." Contrary to instructions, Settle disregarded the requirement that the teacher approve the topic and did not perform any research.[28]

Settle v. Dickinson County School Board became a rallying point for religious activists who claim it demonstrates hostility to religion. They may be fueled in part by the teacher's testimony that she "just knew that we don't deal with personal religion—personal religious beliefs. It's just not an appropriate thing to do in a public school . . . People don't send their children to school for a teacher to get in a dialogue with personal religio[us] beliefs. They send them to learn to read and write and think. And you can do that without getting into personal religion."[29]

Legal scholar and former appellate judge Michael McConnell charges that the teacher was "uninformed [and] bigoted"; She allowed other students to work on topics including "spiritualism, reincarnation and magic." His argument that "the case would have come out the other way if a racist teacher had forbidden a paper on Martin Luther King Jr., or an anti-communist teacher had forbidden a paper on the evils of capitalism" has surface appeal.[30] However, McConnell minimized the teacher's educational concerns, including her insistence on research, citations, and amenability to criticism.

More important, McConnell failed to fully develop his hypothetical. The proper comparison might be the fraught situation that would result if the African American activist submitted a paper based on what his grandfather told him about Dr. King whose portrait hangs in his family's living room, having failed to read any books, and challenged the failing grade the allegedly racist white teacher gave him. That would not be a close case either.

When speech is louder than an armband—if it involves either speaking or handing something to another student—one important factor in determining whether the religious expression is personal or school sponsored is whether it takes place during structured, curricular, or "non-instructional" time, such as the lunch period or recess. The inquiry overlaps with the mistaken belief that student speech in classrooms meets *Hazelwood*'s definition of school sponsorship (described in Chapter 4), even when it doesn't appear to bear the school's imprimatur.

Informal student-initiated Bible study groups are found on campuses around the country, created by children of all ages. If convened before or after school or at other noninstructional parts of the day, without any faculty involvement or administrative exposure, these groups engage in private speech.[31]

The initial categorization of curricular and noncurricular parts of the school day isn't always as simple as it might sound. Some school districts maintain the entire school day is instructional, especially for the youngest children who are always supervised. If instructional time means the entire school day from the moment the first class starts until the last one is dismissed, students' rights will be constricted. But if it means only the time during which the student speaker is in a class, rights will be greatly expanded.

If a student-initiated Bible study group gathers during recess, the level of First Amendment protection may depend on whether the school treats recess as purely recreational, a time to cut loose, or as a form of physical education. After a parent alleged religious discrimination, the Sixth Circuit in 2012 upheld a verdict for a school that stopped fourth graders from reading and discussing the Bible during recess. The school argued that recess was designed to promote physical activity. Similarly, the minutes between lessons and lunch may be considered instructional in the lower grades if the school maintains that it uses the transition to teach children to listen to the teacher's instructions, line up, and use the bathroom in an orderly fashion.[32]

In the higher grades, geography may raise questions. Does the "locker room" *Tinker* counted as a zone for uninhibited discussion include the rooms in which students change for gym class or football practice, or is the protected zone limited to the lockers where students store their coats and personal gear? We know from human experience that students talk about sex in both—these are also spaces where some of them may talk about God.

Although *Tinker* indisputably governs once religious speech is labeled as student-initiated personal expression, most schools cede the *Tinker* battlefield in religious speech controversies: They rarely assert that the child's expression threatens material disruption. Instead, they concentrate their defense on the position that allowing the child's speech would create the appearance that the school endorsed the child's religious sentiments. As will become clear, designating the boundary between personal religious speech and speech other students may believe to have the school's endorsement can prove very complicated.

When Is Individual Student Speech Not Personal Speech?

Student religious speech that is private because an individual initiates it is not usually private in another meaning of the word, "secluded from the sight or presence of others," or school authorities wouldn't be aware of it. Students' religious expression is often directed to others who have similar beliefs, as in a Bible study or prayer group, or designed to inspire peers to find religious meaning, as when children invite others to church functions, distribute gifts with religious texts attached, or urge peers to find the Lord.

Judges presiding over cases about students' religious expression state what by now should seem axiomatic: "[T]he success of either party rests in large part on the legal standard that is applied to the underlying facts."[33] The initial inquiry into whether the speech is private, personal religious speech or potentially attributable to the school usually proves dispositive because it determines the governing legal standard. Unlike the truly private religious speech *Tinker* protects, if the religious expression occurs in a context that, in *Hazelwood*'s formulation, "students, parents and members of the public might reasonably perceive to bear the imprimatur of the school," the school may restrict it.

A school may lack discretion to choose between censoring and permitting student religious speech if the speech could be attributed to the school. Devoid of clarification on both the limits of school sponsorship and what transgresses the Establishment Clause, some school officials reflexively silence private student speech to avoid any risk that they will be held to account under the Establishment Clause.

The conflicts between a school's interest in avoiding an Establishment Clause violation and student religious speech have generated highly charged community disputes over public customs at high school football games, graduations, and other ceremonies.

Prayer over the loudspeaker at football games reached the Supreme Court in 2000 in Doe v. Santa Fe Independent School District, the Supreme Court's most recent foray into the Establishment Clause and public schools. Three clauses—speech, free exercise, and establishment—coalesced just under the surface of the controversy, although the Court focused squarely on the Establishment Clause challenge and did not rely on the student speech cases in rendering its decision.

Santa Fe High School in Texas, where the vast majority of students are Baptists, had a long-standing tradition in which an elected student "chaplain" led prayer at home football games over a loudspeaker. A trail of litigation over related issues demonstrated that the school promoted and permitted Protestant prayer through a range of actions from allowing the Gideons to distribute Bibles to classroom songs about "Lord Jesus" and prayers by graduation speakers. When two families—one Mormon, the other Roman Catholic—challenged the official prayers in court, the school gradually eliminated all of the practices except for prayer at football games.[34]

In an effort to preserve prayer at football games, the school district adopted a new system for choosing the student speaker as the litigation progressed. The district seized on an approach crafted by Kelly J. Coughlin, an attorney and Christian activist in Houston. Instead of school officials deciding there would be a chaplain and allowing the students to choose that person, the school now held two separate elections. In the first, the students voted yes or no as to whether they wanted prayers at football games; in a second round, they elected the student chaplain who would deliver the prayers during the entire football season. The school originated and administered both rounds of voting.[35]

A six-to-three majority of the Supreme Court rejected the school district's argument that the two-part election transformed school-sponsored prayers into private student speech. The school, not the students, had initiated the prayers in violation of the Establishment Clause.

The school's institutional involvement in formulating the policy, supervising the election, and facilitating the prayer over the school's public address system under faculty supervision made the speech school sponsored. The school had endorsed religion by offering students the loudspeaker for only one viewpoint: religious speech. Coercion was also apparent, Justice Kennedy's opinion for the Court emphasized. The practice threatened to divide the student body and to pressure students who did not share the majority's religious views to chose between the all-important Texas football game and the appearance of participating in prayer.

In many ways the case was a mirror image of *Hazelwood*. The school had promoted and endorsed the speech instead of silencing it and wished to be absolved of accountability instead of asserting control. But *Santa Fe's* discussion of prayer at football games shares the concern that arises under *Hazelwood* about the impact of placing a school's imprimatur where it does not belong.

Even as the *Santa Fe* case was wending its way to the Supreme Court, evangelical Christian activists worried about the outcome. They formulated a backup strategy to secure football game prayer based on speech rights, beginning at Santa Fe High School. Marian Ward, the daughter of a Baptist minister, had became the Santa Fe student chaplain in the fall of 1999 after she returned from a leadership training program for conservative Christian youth in Washington, D.C. Ward wanted to use the microphone to pray despite the Fifth Circuit's injunction barring prayers over the loudspeaker at Santa Fe's games.[36]

Attorney Coughlin represented Ward when she sought and received a temporary restraining order that allowed her to offer a prayer over the loudspeaker at the first football game of the season in 1999, while the case about the selection of the student chaplain awaited resolution by the Supreme Court. Ward claimed that regardless of the Establishment Clause, the Speech Clause permitted her to pray at the football game free from the risk of school discipline. At the first home game of the season, on September 3, 1999, Ward ended her prayer, "In Jesus' name I pray, Amen" to wild applause. She soon became a sought-after speaker at Christian events all over the country, including an event at Pontiac, Michigan's 80,000-seat Silverdome. Today Ward is on the staff of the Campaign for Liberty, an evangelical organization.[37]

Ward's prayer isolated and wounded minorities, the very impact the Supreme Court would later identify as constitutionally problematic. Two weeks after that game, the *Galveston County Daily News* published a letter from Amanda Bruce, a Roman Catholic student at Santa Fe High School, who asked of Ward: "[D]oes she not realize that people out there aren't all Christian? Does she just not care?" Amanda later reported that others supported her view, as revealed in unanticipated "phone calls from people saying, 'Thank you so much.'"[38]

The confirmation Amanda received stood in stark relief to the community's treatment of the anonymous Does who brought the lawsuit. Despite their court-ordered anonymity, rumors abounded about their identity. Someone killed a plaintiff's family dog, and families suspected of being plaintiffs received death threats.

Despite the *Santa Fe* decision, by tradition and silent acquiescence, high school cheerleaders around the country still carry banners proclaiming their

Christian faith. Football players charge through the banners as they run onto the field. Occasionally someone challenges the practice.

Communities sometimes rise up in fury after schools bar cheerleader religious displays. This happened outside Chattanooga, Tennessee, in 2008 where an eight-year tradition of cheerleader banners such as "I press on toward the goal to win the prize for which God has called me in Christ Jesus" ended after a mother who had learned about the First Amendment at evangelical Liberty University pointed out the district's legal jeopardy. When the school ordered the cheerleaders to discard their biblical banners, many of the town's residents turned out at football games bearing their own Christian signs. Calling themselves "Warriors for Christ," the citizens raised the volume of religious speech.[39]

The two sets of signs occupy distinct legal positions. The cheerleaders are engaging in school-sponsored speech, in an organized activity supervised by faculty, with all the indiciae that they bear the school's imprimatur. They are chosen, trained, and supervised by the school and its faculty and generally wear uniforms in the school's colors. The fans are engaging in private speech, even if they do so in numbers so large that the speech may not seem strictly "personal" like a quiet grace before a meal. The same is true of political rallies, but in each instance every individual's speech remains his or her own.

Cheerleaders in Kountze, Texas, challenged the school district's order that they stop displaying Christian messages on run-through banners in 2012. The cheerleaders had been holding up banners for the team to charge through for a number of years, but it is unclear when they first chose religious messages. At the beginning of the 2012–2013 school year, after the public interest group Freedom from Religion Foundation complained, the school district's superintendent ordered principals to restrict cheerleaders to secular messages lest the district offend the Establishment Clause. The high school principal enforced the new policy, he explained, in order to obey the law, even as he personally "commend[ed]" the cheerleaders for "what they are doing." The cheerleaders sued, claiming the speech was their own, not the school's, because they selected the messages.[40]

After the cheerleaders won a preliminary injunction covering the entire school year that allowed them to continue their religious speech, the school district's Board of Trustees concluded that the law did not require the schools to "prohibit messages on banners . . . that display fleeting messages of community sentiment solely because the source or origin of these messages is religious." It expressly rescinded the superintendent's earlier pronouncement, thus resolving the cheerleaders' lawsuit, except for the issue of attorneys' fees. Unfortunately, this left the key legal question the judge had reserved for a later date unexplored: whether the speech on the banners was "governmental speech, student-sponsored [*sic*] speech, or private speech."[41]

Under *Hazelwood*, the speech likely appears to bear the school's imprimatur because cheerleaders have a faculty advisor, are part of organized extracurricular activities run by the school, and wear the school colors, all suggesting that the school is sponsoring or adopting their speech. As I have explained, *Hazelwood*, unlike the analysis of endorsement under the Establishment Clause, does not assume that observers would know that the cheerleaders themselves chose the slogans as they prepared for each game. If the case actually revolved around student speech rights, *Hazelwood* should govern, and the cheerleaders should have lost.

If someone sues the school in the future based on the same facts but seeking to end the cheerleaders' practice and alleging it violates the Establishment Clause, the result would also depend in part on who the court concluded was really speaking. Under the Establishment Clause, if the expression originates with the students, that knowledge would be attributed to observers, and the speech would likely be protected as private religious expression unless the school encouraged the cheerleaders to use the football field to share their spiritual beliefs or the speech is in fact school-sponsored.[42]

Students have a legal right to promote religion, but schools, as agents of the state, violate the Establishment Clause when they prefer any theological position. "Fellow students," one California court succinctly explained with respect to proselytizing, "enjoy constitutional freedoms the [school] district does not."[43]

That students may preach on a public stage where schools can't does not mitigate the harm non-adherents experience. The legal posture—student speech, school-sponsored speech, or community speech—doesn't modulate the hostile message sent to those who believe something different. When the speech all tilts to one viewpoint, the non-adherent understands the message: You are an outsider. Just as with hate speech or bullying, the Constitution offers no easy resolution for implicit verbal attacks on religious minorities if private speakers are the source of the message.

Once again, teachers and school officials may seize teaching moments and engage in constructive interventions. They may permissibly try to temper, discourage, and counter exclusionary messages or underscore that the school and/or the teacher doesn't endorse the idea that non-adherents are going to hell or that they should seek to be saved. Here, the teacher walks on a slender balance beam—the teacher cannot say that the religious speaker is "wrong," only that the view is the speaker's alone.

One of the Kountze cheerleaders offered her own take on the meaning of rights. Referring to people of other faiths, she said, "They can be offended, because that's their right."[44] A teacher, a faculty advisor to the cheerleaders, or the principal would do well to place this comment in the context of how we understand constitutional rights and to try to promote empathy.

But civil society can't always count on school officials to clarify who the student religious speaker represents. Districts like Santa Fe suggest that schools and school districts are among the prime offenders in making some people feel like outsiders. Official religious observance remains pervasive in many school districts despite the strictures the Establishment Clause imposes.[45]

Graduation ceremonies rival athletic events as battlegrounds over religious expression. Some lower courts view all student graduation speeches as school sponsored because the faculty supervises the event, it bears the school's imprimatur, and it is a capstone on the lessons of "discipline, courtesy, and respect for authority."[46]

In other appellate jurisdictions, student use of a platform that the school provides at events like football games and commencement ceremonies may be treated as private speech or be attributed to the school depending on a number of factors. If a school, for example, selects one or more students to speak on neutral grounds (like grades or holding a student government office) and allows the students to choose their topics rather than asking them to pray or to invoke religion, does not suggest a format (such as "benediction"), and neither reviews nor approves the text, the speech will normally be considered private even if it turns out to be religious. Appointing more than one speaker may also make a difference, assuming the multiple speakers present an array of viewpoints. If, on the other hand, the school instructs a student speaker to deliver a benediction, the speech is the school's and is impermissible under the Establishment Clause.[47]

There is one more important variable. The content of the speech may be parsed to determine whether the speaker is sharing her own views and experience or is proselytizing her classmates and their families by asking them to join in her sentiments. School officials can censor personal religious expression that does not appear to be school sponsored if the speech gives the impression that the speaker is imputing her own views to the audience. Sometimes administrators demand textual changes to student speeches when they discover such transgressions before the event, for instance, at rehearsal.

That was one high school's understanding of the setting in which it had silenced a valedictorian's words, but the Supreme Court of Montana saw the facts differently. The court held that the school had violated the girl's speech rights when the principal told her to remove language from her speech or give up her place on the program. The court found that a only small proportion of her speech, "cursory references" to "my faith" to explain what motivated her during high school, could not reasonably be understood as bearing the school's endorsement. Forcing her off the platform was transparent viewpoint discrimination, the court held in 2010.[48]

In contrast, a school may prevent a student speaker from using a commencement platform to deliver what amounts to a sermon, dominated by phrases like "we are all God's children through Jesus Christ['s] death, when we accept his free love and saving grace in our lives" and calling on the audience to "yield to God."[49]

Schools have undisputed authority to penalize students who evade a constitutionally sound process for reviewing the texts of public speakers. For that reason alone, a school can withhold a diploma from a student whose words at graduation differed from the text she submitted for approval, who urged her classmates who didn't "already know" Jesus Christ "personally" to "find out more about the sacrifice He made for you so that you now have the opportunity to live in eternity with Him."[50]

In 2013, the Second Circuit affirmed a ruling that a middle school had not violated a "moving up" ceremony speaker's rights when it told her she could not end with an invocation from the Book of Numbers: "I say to you, may the LORD bless you and keep you; make His face shine upon you and be gracious to you; lift up his countenance upon you and give you peace." The speaker defended her choice by explaining that she had been "taught to give blessings and that it was good to receive blessings from God." The school didn't give ground. It reasoned that the sentence "sounded 'too religious'" and could be perceived as having the school's endorsement. After the student delivered her redacted address (using the text the principal had edited to remove the offending language), she sought vindication in court.[51]

Because the graduation ceremony was an official school function, the court applied *Hazelwood* and merged the endorsement approach to the Establishment Clause with *Hazelwood*'s imprimatur analysis. Although the court found content discrimination in the censorship of the student's closing line, it concluded that blessings can't be understood as anything other than prayer. Blessings from God have no "'real secular analogue.'" They don't offer a permissible religious viewpoint on a secular matter. The school therefore had what the court called a reasonable pedagogical interest in silencing the student's commencement prayer to comply with the Establishment Clause.[52]

Other school districts have blocked student speech without any basis in Establishment Clause concerns. Schools have reportedly prevented students from referring to Jesus in response to questions about Easter and prohibited the phrase "Merry Christmas" in holiday cards children were sending to troops serving overseas.[53]

A substantiated assertion that officials censored student speech to avoid violating the Establishment Clause has two parts. First, there must be a risk that the student's religious expression might be attributed to the school, triggering *Hazelwood*. But that is not enough. For the school's pedagogical concern to be a legitimate ground for silencing student religious expression, most courts agree, the school must justify its apprehension that allowing the expression might transgress the Establishment Clause. Even though it is exceedingly difficult to predict the outcome of Establishment Clause litigation—given the confusion surrounding the legal doctrine—the school should be required to do more than assert a pretextual concern before it can permissibly silence student speech.

Cases arising from disputes over religious music at holiday celebrations, however, reveal that judges generally defer to decisions administrators have already made, whether to allow or to block the performance. Many courts have held that a school's motivation to avoid violating the Establishment Clause is not turned into a sham just because the Constitution doesn't *require* the steps the school took.[54]

For example, even though the Establishment Clause did not require a high school to deny the Wind Ensemble permission to play Franz Biebl's instrumental "Ave Maria" at graduation, the Ninth Circuit held that the decision did not infringe the musicians' expressive rights. Although allowing the students to perform "Ave Maria" would not "necessarily violate the Establishment Clause," the court found that the principal's concern was "reasonable." The court observed that it would not have censured the school had it permitted the performance, and it wouldn't censure the school for blocking the piece.[55] Decisions like this (and the similar waffling seen in the case about whether a first grader had the right to read a Bible story aloud in class) don't offer any guidance to school officials. They perpetuate the likelihood that future lawsuits will be dismissed on the ground that the law was too murky for administrators to understand.

The Ninth Circuit would have been on more solid ground had it enforced its own previous standard, which required a school to show that the expression would appear to be government sponsored or that the religious speech would "impermissibly coerc[e]" those of other beliefs who would appear to be participating "even by their silence."[56]

Neither of these standards would have been likely to justify the school's well intentioned but unwarranted Establishment Clause concerns about an instrumental version of "Ave Maria." The ensemble's performance was slated to be one small part of a broader graduation program. Equally important, the musicians had chosen the piece in their repertoire they thought would show them at their best. The performance guide could have indicated that the players chose the piece and the criterion they used, or a member of the group could have made an announcement to the same effect before the group began to play. Those steps would have satisfied any potential Establishment Clause concerns about endorsement. Finally, the audience at a concert does not seem to be participating in the same way that those who remain silent during a prayer might be said to. The listeners at a classical music performance are not invited to join in, but those listening to a prayer usually are.

The silencing of an instrumental version of "Ave Maria" suggests one sound reason to reject the well-intentioned but unwarranted Establishment Clause defense: Too many cultural works in the fields of music, art, and literature could be censored based on misunderstandings of the law and misplaced fears of violations.

With the Establishment Clause defense laid to one side, the court would be able to focus on the musicians' speech rights, treating the case either as involving pure student speech under *Tinker* (because the students selected "Ave Maria") or as school-sponsored speech if the court concluded *Hazelwood*'s imprimatur requirement was satisfied. When the Establishment Clause and *Hazelwood* overlap in the same dispute, it seems artificial to impute understanding to the audience for purposes of analyzing whether the school appeared to have endorsed religious sentiments but not for evaluating whether the performance was the school's own speech.

To the extent that the high school blocked "Ave Maria" in order to avoid complaints from those of different religions, co-religionists with differing

views, or those who eschew religion, we must ask if that amounts to a reasonable pedagogical concern under *Hazelwood*. Introducing religion to the
calculus doesn't transform the required legal analysis of whether avoidance
of controversy is an acceptable basis for censorship. Disregarding long-
standing doctrine barring censorship grounded in a desire to avoid controversy, some courts have allowed school officials to silence speech that
"sound[s] too religious" and "might offend people" even when it did not
violate the Establishment Clause.[57]

When judges find that avoiding controversy amounts to a legitimate pedagogical concern, they drive a wedge between *Tinker* and the later student
speech cases, removing any trace of continuity. *Tinker*'s statement on avoidance of controversy was a model of clarity: To withstand constitutional
scrutiny, censorship must be premised on "something more than a mere
desire to avoid the discomfort and unpleasantness that always accompany an
unpopular viewpoint." If the desire to avoid controversy were dispositive,
the range of conceivable complaints would reduce school-sponsored speech
to pablum suitable for the sandbox.[58]

The "something" more than mere discomfort required to silence student
speech could be a realistic concern about crossing into a gray area of
Establishment Clause jurisprudence. But if the law is reasonably clear and
allowing the student's religious expression would not suggest either school
sponsorship or endorsement, then avoidance of controversy should not be a
defense when students assert a school trampled on their speech rights.

School officials face an unenviable task when they must determine if pure
student speech about religion appears to bear the school's imprimatur and
if tolerating that expression could violate the Establishment Clause under
doctrine that is murky at best. Still, some situations arise on facts so pristine on either side of the equation that the resolution should be simple—
evangelical cheerleaders in school colors are on one side of the line drawn by
school speech doctrine, students who want to share a personal statement
with a few classmates comparing finding Christ to discovering your lost dog
are on the other.

The Dangers of Proselytizing

The complexities intensify when students move from sharing their own religious experiences to actively proselytizing their peers. A practical consideration renders the job of school officials confronted with campus proselytizers

particularly delicate. Secular speakers generally appear to stumble inadvertently into a single controversy, even if it implicates national controversies and attracts support from national advocacy groups. Students who speak about religion often differ in an important respect. Their goal is to bring religion onto campus, sometimes creating a "gotcha moment," and if they don't get satisfaction, they will be back in court until they do. Parents sometimes ask about rules and then send their young children in to break them. In one case, after the parents vindicated their child's right to hand out religious items in elementary school, they filed a second lawsuit alleging they themselves were prevented from distributing proselytizing literature to other parents during a class gathering.[59]

Older students also push the limits. Alexander Nuxoll didn't only insist on wearing his "Be Happy, Not Gay" shirt. He wanted to hand out pamphlets and engage his peers in discussions about God and abortion throughout the school year. As Judge Posner observed with an implied sigh born of experience, "[F]urther proceedings there will be. [Nuxoll] will not be content with the limited relief we are ordering. This is cause litigation."[60]

Controversies center on all kinds of materials brought from off campus, ranging from newsletters and pamphlets prepared by a local or national religious group to documents students prepared themselves to invitations to religious events to party favors with religious messages.[61] From a legal standpoint, all of these non-school materials are indistinguishable from the underground newspapers that received so much judicial attention in the 1970s.

Many schools require students to seek permission before distributing nonschool materials to more than ten students. Courts have upheld these requirements as long as the rules don't discriminate based on content or viewpoint and as long as the school provides adequate procedural safeguards such as responding quickly, denying permission only when *Tinker* and its progeny justify suppressing the speech, not allowing the decision maker to withhold consent based on subjective assessments about what would be good for the intended audience, and allowing students to appeal an adverse decision.[62]

Schools may limit the mode of distribution by determining how, where, and when students may share materials they import to campus. Students may, for example, be required to leave pamphlets on a distribution table to ensure that peers aren't forced to accept literature they don't want and to avoid practical problems such as excessive litter that might result when students discard paper thrust into their hands.

Courts have compared this prior restraint in schools to the licenses and conditions municipalities may require for parades or demonstrations, which are permissible as long as the decisions are not based on content or viewpoint. The review process allows schools to identify and control potentially disruptive pamphleteering—including religious literature—so long as the school doesn't single out religion (or any other viewpoint, say, Democratic or Tea Party) as inappropriate.

Educators almost never claim that religious material is potentially disruptive, but it can be. Religious speech is not constitutionally privileged if it creates disruption, a question that can be resolved without referring to the content of the expression on the same basis as other speech claims under *Tinker.*

In one unusual case that illustrates the principle, the Tenth Circuit agreed with the trial court that a school district did not offend the Constitution when it refused to allow a religious youth group called Relentless to distribute 2,500 two-inch rubber dolls "designed to be a realistic representation" of a twelve-week-old fetus. Pandemonium resulted when Relentless initially handed out the dolls without having sought the required permission. Students dismembered the dolls' heads, turning them into balls that they tossed around classrooms. Some threw dolls and doll parts onto the ceilings after discovering they would stick. Others used the dolls to plug up toilets. Still other students who may have aspired to become chemists applied hand sanitizer as an accelerant and set the dolls on fire, while another inventive group turned the dolls inside out so they "resembled penises," which they attached to the zippers on their pants.[63]

When Relentless attempted a second distribution of the dolls two weeks later, the school immediately confiscated the rubber fetuses. Applying *Tinker,* the Tenth Circuit concluded that school officials reasonably feared material disruption. The court pointed to several considerations that had nothing to do with content or viewpoint: "proactive contact," the "sheer number of items," and the rubber material that tempted students to disembowel the dolls, use them as projectiles, bounce them, stick them, and set them on fire—a far cry from the passive speech of an armband.[64]

Authorship too sometimes makes a difference. The dolls Relentless distributed came from a national provider, as do many of the other proselytizing materials that reach courts. A school may bar materials prepared by outsiders if it has a good reason, such as wanting students to learn how to write and advocate, even though "adopting the expression of others is a form of speech."[65]

If a school says students may not distribute "written material which is primarily prepared by non-students," then the school must enforce the rule evenhandedly. It can't allow materials prepared by secular organizations but not religious groups. If a school bars a national evangelical anti-abortion pamphlet or doll on that ground, it must also stop students from giving out printed copies of Martin Luther King Jr.'s Letter from Birmingham Jail and the Declaration of Independence and the Supreme Court's *Tinker* decision.

Although schools can prevent students from handing out material written by others, they can't prevent expression supporting national movements. After all, the Tinkers and Christopher Eckhardt chose the dates and form of their protest in conjunction with a national demonstration against the war in Vietnam.

Disputes about what amounts to protected personal speech arise repeatedly over seemingly prosaic events like a child's desire to hand out invitations to an off-campus religious function and children seeking to distribute religiously themed party favors such as "Jesus loves me" pencils and candy canes with Christian messages attached. "Such seemingly innocuous and benign activities as elementary school parties," observes one federal judge, "too often lead to protracted litigation."[66] As innocent as a child's party favor might seem, the issues are hardly benign.

A national organization distributes the candy canes at the heart of several federal court cases. Each cane bears an attachment that explains the candy's religious significance, starting with the assertion that it was created as "a witness to Christ." In summary, the candy is hard "because Christ is the Rock of Ages." The red stripe signifies "the blood Christ shed for the sins of the world" and the marks where the Roman soldiers whipped him.[67]

Sharing of "Jesus pencils" and candy canes bearing "the Legend of the Candy Cane" that tie the treat to the crucifixion requires a complex, but not impossible, analysis unique to each controversy. Much depends on how and where the favors are distributed, who hands them out, and whether something else is given out at the same time. Characterization of holiday parties at school may depend on whether they are described as a class activity and how closely teachers supervise them. Judges may also consider whether gifts with religious content are combined with other presents in one goodie bag or whether all gifts are clearly labeled with the name of the gift giver or handed out by the person who brought them. Some courts also evince an interest in whether the intended recipients are able to decline the materials or feel coerced to accept them

Courts may also ask if items other students brought in appear to have sponsors or celebrate particular views. If a school permits students to distribute pencils with snowmen on them or messages about Justin Bieber, it may not treat pencils celebrating Jesus, Mohammed, Krishna, or Kwanzaa any differently because the government may no more disfavor religion than it may permissibly promote it.[68]

As with secular expression, the more curricular the activity looks, the more likely it is that *Hazelwood* will provide the legal test, giving the religious expression much less protection. If a child offers a religiously themed item for "sale" in "Classroom City," a curricular exercise in which students study how marketplaces work, the school may tell the student the merchandise is unacceptable. On these facts, an appellate court held that the expression was presumptively school sponsored and violated the Establishment Clause.[69] The circumstances of this controversy—tangible religious items for "sale" under class auspices—are distinct from efforts to restrict the ideas available for classroom debate under the guise of school sponsorship discussed in Chapter 4. The potential for confusion about sponsorship of candy canes or pencils bearing messages and distributed during a lesson seems real for the youngest schoolchildren.

Students of all ages still bring invitations from home to give to their classmates, though perhaps they are increasingly likely to publicize events online or by tweeting. The Constitution does not prevent a school from adopting rules designed to promote social sensitivity, as some schools do by requiring students to invite only a small number of students or the entire class to birthday parties. Schools may require that the teacher or the principal consent before students hand out invitations or free tickets to off-campus events at school, just as schools approve other sorts of nonschool materials.

The invitations that schools tend to single out for suppression (at least the ones that reach federal courts) involve religious observance or indoctrination, such as a play or party at a student's church or an invitation to an Easter egg hunt "to have fun and learn the true meaning of Easter."[70] From a school administrator's vantage point, no invitation to a secular event creates the risk that permitting students to invite peers to join in off-campus fun might land her in legal jeopardy. But the specter of the Establishment Clause apparently looms over officials when they are pressed to approve or block distribution of materials about religion, and the resulting disputes repeatedly land in federal courts.

Pencils, candy canes, gift bags, and tickets to church performances all reached the full Fifth Circuit sitting en banc in Morgan v. Swanson in 2011. The Fifth Circuit lamented that the Supreme Court had not provided more specific guidance on "whether *Tinker* or *Hazelwood* governs students' dissemination of written religious materials in public elementary schools, whether at official parties, after school on the 'lawn or sidewalk,' or at unspecified times and in unspecified places during the school day."[71] If the religious sentiments are personal—the speech *Tinker* protects—and cannot be attributed to the state and will not create the appearance of endorsement or involve coercion, the court concluded, the school must allow the speech unless it threatens material disruption.

The facts in *Morgan* echo those in more than a few religious speech cases. Officials at two elementary schools in Plano, Texas, prevented several children from distributing materials including the Legend of the Candy Cane, tickets to a church play about the "passion and crucifixion of Jesus Christ," and pencils inscribed "Jesus loves me." The children and their families described themselves as evangelical Christians whose faith requires "them to 'communicate religious viewpoint ideas to their peers, classmates, and other students,'" to "'introduce . . . classmates . . . to the truth of the Christian faith.'"[72]

The schools' radical posture threatened to undo decades of precedents. The principals claimed that elementary school students do not have any First Amendment rights. Beyond rejecting the very notion of free speech rights for elementary schoolchildren, the school officials asserted that it was "well within the school's ambit of authority" to "specifically restrict distribution of *religious* messages in the classroom" while simultaneously denying they had in fact singled out religious messages for exclusion.[73]

The two principals also asserted a qualified immunity defense, arguing that they were "confused" about what the law required. They contended that some courts had so expanded *Hazelwood*'s reach that it gave them discretion to censor nondisruptive private religious speech. They reasoned that student misimpressions might transform the student expression sufficiently to bring it under school sponsorship.[74]

Morgan reached the en banc court before the facts had been developed through courtroom testimony. The district court had denied a motion to dismiss the claims against the individual defendants who asserted they were immune from suit because the law had not been clear when they acted. The school officials appealed to a panel of the Fifth Circuit, which affirmed the trial court's ruling denying them qualified immunity, and then sought and received en banc review.

The case brought out a veritable all-star cast of lawyers, most unusual for any court except the Supreme Court. Paul Clement, one of the country's most accomplished Supreme Court advocates, argued the case for the parents of the children whose religious speech was silenced at school on behalf of the Liberty Legal Institute. Jay Sekulow of the American Center for Law and Justice, a virtual fixture in these cases, and conservative groups including the Cato Institute, the Christian Legal Society, and the Becket Institute all filed amicus curiae briefs supporting student speech rights on the same side as the Texas affiliate of the American Civil Liberties Union.

Former federal judge, special prosecutor, law school dean, and now chancellor of Baylor University, Kenneth Starr submitted an amicus brief on behalf of the Barnett sisters (whose name the Supreme Court had misspelled as Barnette in the seminal 1943 case). The Barnetts' brief argued that the school district was trying to undermine the core principle of the case that bears their name: that elementary school students have speech rights. Starr also asserted that the Supreme Court had sustained the sisters' right to be free from "religious bigotry."[75]

A majority of the sixteen judges held that the school district had the law wrong on both points.

First, the court reiterated that a principal could not forbid distribution of religious materials based on their content. "At the core of the First Amendment's right to free speech," Judge Jennifer Elrod wrote for the majority, "is the right of one student to express a religious viewpoint to another without fear."[76]

Second, the court clarified that there was no basis for the schools' assertion that the First Amendment had no place in elementary schools. A majority of the judges expressly rebuffed the school district's position that the children whose speech was at issue were too young to have rights. It reaffirmed a larger constitutional norm the Supreme Court had stated repeatedly: "A child, merely on account of his minority, is not beyond protection of the Constitution."[77]

The Fifth Circuit summarized existing doctrine: Neither the Supreme Court nor the Circuit had ever "limited the First Amendment rights of students due to age." "Numerous other circuits," the majority added, "have also rejected claims that the First Amendment does not apply to elementary school students." Judge Easterbrook, for example, writing for the Seventh Circuit in 1993, observed, "[N]othing in the first amendment postpones the right to religious speech until high school." In fact, no appellate court has ever held that elementary schools are liberated from *Tinker*'s strictures.[78]

The Supreme Court had extended school speech rights to the Barnette sisters when they were in elementary school; the youngest Tinker child was eight years old. In 2001, the Court applied free speech principles in holding that public schools may not discriminate against religious groups that want to use a school building for after-school activities because, among other things, in the Court's view, children "ages 6 to 12" could tell the difference between school and an evangelical gathering.[79]

To the extent the question of whether elementary school students have speech rights remained open, the Fifth Circuit appears to have resolved the debate. The next year, one federal district court judge summed up the law: "Although the Supreme Court has not squarely defined the First Amendment rights of elementary school students, and student age is an appropriate consideration, the weight of authority in federal courts of appeal and the district courts" states that *Tinker* applies in elementary schools.[80]

It makes sense that elementary schools have generated many of the disputes that lead to litigation over religious speech. The factors supporting a school's assertion of authority over speech are more likely to be present in schools with younger students. The youngest students are closely supervised, increasing the likelihood that religious expression will occur during a structured activity with an educational purpose. Courts seem to believe that young listeners are likely to misattribute a peer's speech to the school. Reflecting these considerations, more than one appellate court has adopted factors to guide assessments of what student expression is appropriate in an elementary school, "including the type of speech, the age of the locutor and audience, the school's control over the activity in which the expression occurs, and whether the school solicits individual views from students during the activity."[81]

The outcome in *Morgan* should never have been in doubt, but the court still proved receptive to the argument that the law at the intersection of student speech and religious expression had such indistinct contours that no official could fairly be asked to divine its meaning. A different, though overlapping, majority granted the principals qualified immunity.[82]

Dissenting from the grant of qualified immunity, Judge Elrod characterized the principals' position as "extreme: at oral argument, when asked what rights students clearly have regarding religious speech, counsel for the principals replied that he did not know. This is not only unacceptable, it is unreasonable." Since the speech in the case was so clearly the student's personal expression, Elrod wrote, "it is difficult to imagine a case where the law will be sufficiently clear to overcome immunity." In "every case involving religious discourse," the dissenters feared, "schools officials could merely throw their hands up in bewilderment, claim ignorance or confusion, and freely censor private religious speech without consequence."[83]

Some readers may offer myriad cautions in response to the Fifth Circuit's robust view of the right of young children to free speech as a general matter and to personal religious expression at school in particular. As the judicial factors imply, different levels of maturity can affect the nature and extent of rights or support modifications. But this is just another aspect of the context that proves so important in each First Amendment controversy. The Supreme Court has noted the "peculiar vulnerability" of minors that supports differences in legal treatment between minors and adults and among minors at different levels of maturity.[84]

In its earliest pronouncements on state-sponsored school prayer, the Supreme Court was influenced by the Justices' understanding of children's vulnerability to peer pressure and their inclination to eschew nonconformity. As Justice Brennan observed in his influential concurrence in Abington School District v. Schempp, "non-conformity is not an outstanding characteristic of children." He explained that children don't want to be labeled as "'odd balls.'" They may hesitate to call attention to themselves by asking to be excused from devotional exercises.[85] The price of asserting one's own beliefs was simply too high to impose on young children.

School administrators who prohibit proselytization of peers today appear to share these concerns along with those that motivate *Tinker*'s second prong. They say they are protecting the right of listeners to be free from religious zeal during the school day. Other officials have relied on a desire to "avoid subjecting young children to an unsolicited religious promotional message that might conflict with what they are taught at home" to justify silencing personal student religious speech.[86]

School officials who act on this sensitivity when dealing with proselytization among peers may find themselves stymied by speech rights. Reasonable first graders may be less capable than their older siblings of differentiating student speech from the words of a teacher who is an authority figure. Or they may not know how to deflect a classmate's pressure effectively. But, as we have seen repeatedly, if the "rights of others" language means enforceable legal rights, no such right to avoid proselytization at the hands of peers has been recognized, even in public schools.

Adults must recognize that peers will expose children to ideas they have heard at home during casual interactions even if the school blocks organized sharing of views and information. When informal conversation provides the platform, adults have no control over content, just as they cannot control discussions of sex (or television shows some children aren't permitted to watch) on the school bus or in the locker room or cafeteria. Students' discussions, religious pamphleteering in the corridor, and informal prayer meetings are beyond the school's practical or legal reach.

And yet, schools have a great many permissible tools at their disposal to help young children understand who is speaking and to separate personal from official messages. Teachers can intervene constructively by helping students to discern the difference between the curriculum and a peer's personal ideas. Even first graders can understand a teacher's clarification: "These are pencils Jonathan brought from home to share" or "Stephanie is talking about how she experiences the church she attends with her family." Just as with bullying or hate speech, schools can help to mediate expression without trampling protected speech.

Voluntariness is key to analyzing private religious speech in public schools. The first and generally acknowledged aspect of voluntariness concerns the speaker. The speech must truly be private, neither invited nor encouraged with a wink by the school. The second aspect of voluntariness, nascent in a handful of judicial decisions, evinces concern for unwilling listeners. Consistent with both the coercion approach to Establishment Clause dilemmas and the infringement matrix proposed in Chapter 6, the audience should be free to decline proffered religious materials or walk away from the speaker.

A right to express one's own religious views does not necessarily extend to aggressive impingement on others' personal space, as I argued in considering various reformulations of Rachel Zimmer's invocation "you are going to hell." Similarly, students may be ostracized or coerced in the face of organized campaigns like the national "See You at the Pole" student prayer movement if the vast majority of students, or even the most popular, all participate.

The *Morgan* court noted that the religious students had not been disruptive—their peers were free to decline the materials they offered, and invitations to a church event were given only to students who requested them. Despite the captive audience problem that runs through school speech doctrine, a sensible corollary to the right to speak up about religion, implicit in the opinion, would be that atheists, agnostics, Jews, Muslims, Sikhs, and others have as much of a right to decline a religious pamphlet or gift (without being pursued or harangued) as the evangelical has the right to offer it.

If students on the receiving end of religious solicitations from peers don't want to go to the church play, read an anti-abortion magazine, or eat a candy cane labeled as symbolizing the blood of Jesus, they cannot silence the speech, but they can decline the proffered materials or throw them out. Schools can make sure they are free to do so.

Once again, schools may be able to offer some protection against unwelcome peer proselytization by crafting rules that don't rest on content. For example, a rule could require students to respect another student's request to "leave me alone." The rule could address conduct like following peers who are walking away after saying they don't want to listen, potentially reaching harassment as well as preaching.

Unwelcome religious exhortations are no different analytically from group disparagement and other unwelcome ideas discussed in the last three chapters of this book. They are protected unless the school can permissibly regulate them under school speech doctrine.

The Seventh Circuit in 1993 balanced the right of religious students to share their faith with the responsibility of school officials to teach students about what the First Amendment means. Hedges v. Wauconda Community School District involved a constitutional challenge to a school code that the court held had singled out for exclusion from campus "written material . . . of a religious nature" in elementary and middle schools. The court disposed of this rule with "little difficulty. It lumps religious speech with obscenity and libel for outright prohibition."[87]

A revised code adopted during the litigation invoked *Hazelwood* by limiting the ban to religious viewpoints "that students would reasonably believe to be sponsored, endorsed, or given official imprimatur by the school." Testimony at trial revealed that the school imputed a perception of school sponsorship to students whenever they received religious literature from an identifiable faith or other proselytizing materials. Writing for the appellate court, Judge Easterbrook explained that neither the offense other students might take nor their mistaken perceptions of endorsement amounted to permissible grounds for censorship. The court charged schools with an inescapable responsibility for inculcating students with constitutional norms.[88]

Easterbrook emphasized that schools are required to help students understand the foundational principles that govern speech rights. "Schools may explain that they do not endorse speech by permitting it." Too often, Easterbrook wrote in taking Wauconda to task: "School districts seeking an easy way out try to suppress private speech. . . . Dealing with misunderstandings—here, educating the students in the meaning of the Constitution and the distinction between private speech and public endorsement—is, however, what schools are for . . . Yet Wauconda proposes to throw up its hands, declaring that because misconceptions are possible it may silence its pupils, that the best defense against misunderstanding is censorship. What a lesson Wauconda proposes to teach its students! Far better to teach them about the first amendment, about the difference between public and private action, about why we tolerate divergent views. . . . The school's proper response is to educate the audience rather than squelch the speaker."[89]

Unintended Consequences and Unwitting Alliances

As if the taxonomy of school speech and its application to religious speech weren't complicated enough, in 1984 Congress created yet another kind of student speech, which today occupies a transitional space between student speech and the Establishment Clause, neither strictly private nor school sponsored. A deep bipartisan majority passed the Equal Access Act (the "Act") in response to what Congress saw as "widespread discrimination against religious speech in public schools." President Reagan signed the Act into law.[90]

The Act extended to the nation's public secondary schools a doctrine the Supreme Court had created for universities three years earlier in Widmar v. Vincent. *Widmar* held that if public universities open their facilities for use by any student group, the campus may not prevent religious groups from meeting on the same terms. The Court reasoned that such "equal access" didn't promote or endorse religion and therefore did not violate the Establishment Clause.[91] *Widmar* underscores that while the United States does not have a shared official religion, it is a far cry from the insistent secularism of countries like France that discourage any hint of religiosity in public life.

The groups the Act protects must be organized at student initiative and meet voluntarily at school outside of instructional time. The statute requires schools to recognize and facilitate the clubs it governs. Their form and legal status are distinct from the informal Bible study groups discussed earlier in this chapter or from a knitting group that uses lunchtime for craft, though they may exist for Bible study or, in theory, for knitting.

Congressional sponsors understood that the Act could not restrict its scope to faith-based clubs without violating the Establishment Clause. It prohibits discrimination against any student-initiated club "on the basis of the religious, political, philosophical or other content of the speech at such meetings" where the content is not directly related to the curriculum. The Act is triggered when a high school receiving public funds has allowed a single "noncurriculum related student group[]" to meet, unless it can show that the proposed club's activities would "materially and substantially interfere with the orderly conduct of educational activities."[92]

This of course is the essence of the *Tinker* standard. For purposes of my inquiry, it is of little consequence whether the cases arising under the Equal Access Act are decided under the statute or under the student speech doctrine because the test of constitutional offense is identical. As one district court judge explained in 2009, by passing the Act "Congress effectively codified the First Amendment rights of non-curricular student groups."[93] This means all groups that qualify, not just the two I discuss here that have led to the bulk of lawsuits under the Act.

The statute has unwittingly created a strange—if largely de facto—alliance among political and cultural groups not known for seeing the world in similar terms or collaborating on shared goals. The allies include the Liberty Institute and the ACLU, the Rutherford Foundation and national networks of LGBT activists, and similar groups on both sides of the cultural divide. These antithetical pairings find common ground in promoting renewed vitality for *Tinker*'s essential doctrines.

The substantive goals of the two dominant groups that seek campus privileges under federal law could not be more at odds. Religious clubs, almost always composed of evangelical Christians, the statute's presumed beneficiaries and poster children, stand on one side of the divide. Since the late 1990s, clubs promoting tolerance and equal civil rights for LGBTs, often as local chapters of the national group the Gay/Straight Alliance (GSA), have also seized on the safe harbor Congress unwittingly created for them.

Seeking recognition as a club has many advantages over informal gatherings on or off campus. The Act requires that what it calls noncurricular-related clubs function "under the same terms and conditions as other extra-curricular activities," including permission to use the school's announcement systems, to distribute literature, and to promote their activities and goals.[94]

The statute forces schools to tolerate speech they could never permissibly promote. It provides a mechanism for students to broaden the scope of information and ideas available at schools by organizing clubs that center on subjects and viewpoints the curriculum ignores or disfavors. As one judge underscored when applying the Act in 2000, educators may not "act as 'thought police' inhibiting all discussion that is not approved by, and in accord with the official position of, the state."[95]

The Equal Access Act's definition of curricular-related clubs is at odds with *Hazelwood*'s use of a very similar phrase, creating potential for misunderstanding. Under the Act, a school may refuse to recognize all "organizations not directly related to the curriculum," but if it is challenged in court for blocking particular disfavored student organizations, it must convince a federal court that each and every club it has labeled curriculum related actually falls within that definition. Construing the Act in 1988, the Supreme Court in Westside Community Schools v. Mergens held that a school that allowed a scuba diving club and a social service club (which the school had claimed were related to the curriculum) must also permit a Christian club to meet on campus.[96]

Congress intended to restrict the definition of curricular-related clubs so that many groups would fall outside it, triggering the Act and *Tinker*'s protections. *Hazelwood*, in contrast, swept a great many school activities into the realm of school sponsorship, which embraces all activities that "may fairly be characterized as part of the school curriculum, whether or not they occur in a traditional classroom setting, so long as they are supervised by faculty members and designed to impart particular knowledge or skills" to students.[97] The same club may be deemed part of the school curriculum when applying *Hazelwood* but not qualify as curricular related for purposes of the Equal Access Act.

Disputes about schools that refused to recognize religious clubs continued to reach the courts for several years after *Mergens*, but for the past fifteen years the legal action has revolved around Gay/Straight Alliances and similar groups.[98]

Schools have adopted a number of strategies to avoid triggering the Equal Access Act when confronted with applications from student groups that promote dignity for LGBTs. A few schools ventured that a GSA chapter would disrupt the abstinence-only message in the sex education curriculum. Some have asserted that they would rather have no clubs at all than welcome the GSA. Only one school district, however, has ever successfully resisted the formation of a GSA chapter in court; that decision preceded the Supreme Court's 2003 invalidation of laws that criminalize intimate relationships between members of the same sex in Lawrence v. Texas and more recent decisions expressly applying equal protection principles to LGBTs.[99]

However much evangelicals feel beleaguered when religious speech is silenced in school, no episode in the quest for religious speech rights has released the venom and ruthless maneuvering set off when students seek to establish a group promoting gay rights. But in truth everyone whose views remain controversial in the sense that some in a given community perceive the speaker's viewpoint as out of step or too aggressive shares an interest in vibrant protections for freedom of expression.

One of the fiercest clashes erupted in 2002 in Boyd County, a Kentucky school district in the metropolitan area at the intersection of Kentucky, West Virginia, and Ohio. By its own report, the district's only high school had "serious problems" with "anti-gay harassment, homophobia, and use of anti-gay epithets." Two LGBT students had dropped out of school before others sought safety and mutual support in a GSA chapter. Students in an English class had said they "needed to take all the fucking faggots out in the back woods and kill them." Other students regularly tossed epithets at gay classmates.[100]

Informed that the student who began the GSA petition "knew a great deal about legal issues," the principal was eager to approve the club in order to avoid a lawsuit. The superintendent agreed; he also thought it "was the right thing to do."[101]

When word leaked that the GSA was coming, tumult erupted. The student petitioners agreed to wait before formally submitting their application for a club, hoping the objections would die down. Citing safety concerns, the administration urged the students to use pseudonyms in their application, hardly an auspicious beginning for a club about feeling comfortable with one's sexual identity. The students admirably refused: To hide their names would be "defeatist," as the whole point of the group was to raise awareness, "understanding and tolerance."[102]

The school's governing body, known as the Council, consisting of teachers, parents, and the principal, rejected the GSA application three times over two academic years. At its first meeting of the 2002–2003 academic year, the Council approved all of the other twenty applications for clubs, including the Fellowship of Christian Athletes (synonymous with the Bible Club and the Christian Fellow Club) and the Human Rights Club. Aware that the ACLU was tracking the controversy, the Council tabled discussion of the GSA application instead of rejecting the application outright.

One month later, the Council met in a crowded school auditorium where it approved three clubs including, finally, the GSA. When the Council announced its decision the GSA proponents were silent, but the opponents reacted with what the principal described as "open hostility" expressed through "hand gestures, . . . very uncivil body language, . . . loud and angry voices." The principal recalled his fear that someone would get hurt. It was, he testified, "alarming . . . and frightening and disheartening."[103]

One school board member testified that "there was nothing but hatred in that room, and ignorance showed by moms and dads and grandparents. When I left that meeting, I honestly thought . . . yes, a GSA is very much needed in our community, and these people right here needed to be mandated to go to it. It was horrible." Two days later protesters blocked the entrance to the school, shouting, "'If you go inside you're supporting faggots.'" The turmoil mounted as many parents threatened to pull their children out of school.[104]

The school wrote to all the parents in the district to explain that federal law required it to recognize the GSA. To their credit, administrators also voiced concern about the "hostile environment" at the school. The community uproar continued unabated. The same school board member lamented, "[W]e can teach tolerance . . . until we are blue in the face, but if our parents don't teach it to our children also, then it's almost like a losing battle."[105]

Unable to quell the disturbance generated by the anti-GSA hecklers, who were reinforced by local ministers, the school district announced in January 2003 that no clubs of any kind—whether school sponsored or student initiated—would be allowed to meet at the high school. The GSA members complied by moving their meetings off campus.

The Bible Club and three other noncurricular clubs continued to meet at school. When the GSA members finally brought suit under the Equal Access Act, the court found the school had transparently violated federal law.

Infuriated by the school's assertion that it didn't have a clue that the Bible Club had continued to meet in the building, the trial judge announced that he would not "condone" an interpretation of federal law that would allow schools to deny equal access "by burying their heads in the sand and wilfully ignoring student groups, such as the Bible Club, which flagrantly violate those rules."[106]

The judge had just as little patience for the school's fallback position: that the GSA had caused disruption. The *Tinker* standard, the judge pointedly reiterated, is "designed to prevent [school officials] from punishing students who express unpopular views instead of punishing the students who react to those views in a disruptive manner." Legal skirmishes continued even after the court ordered the high school to immediately recognize the GSA chapter.[107]

Elsewhere, officials who recognize that they will have to allow the GSA to meet on campus have tried to avoid community detection by pressuring club founders to change the name to something less identifiable or controversial. In 2010, a federal judge approvingly quoted the testimony of a California student who explained that using the name the "Tolerance Club," as school officials urged, would undermine the whole enterprise. He explained, "To him, 'tolerance' means 'to put up with' in the sense that 'Jews' and 'Blacks' used to be 'put up with' until they were finally 'accepted.'" If he had to change the name, the student summed up, he "'would feel my constitutional rights are useless.'"[108]

Some school administrators perceive a clash of absolutes between student-initiated groups like the GSA and Bible clubs. One school board member who joined a unanimous vote against a GSA application in 1999 commented, "The Bible says we're all sinners, but this, in my opinion, is asking us to legitimize sin."[109]

Since then, the pace of social change in attitudes toward LGBTs has accelerated remarkably. In 2011, popular support for same-sex marriage reached 50 percent for the first time since the Gallup poll began to ask about it, and in 2014, it reached 55 percent. Attitudinal shifts among eighteen- to twenty-nine-year-olds have been most dramatic. Fully 78 percent of respondents in that age group supported same-sex marriage in 2014. Since the presence of a GSA chapter and a sympathetic principal can transform a school environment for LGBT students, the proliferation of GSA chapters may have contributed to that rapid change.[110]

Legal transformation has accompanied social changes. By early 2015 a combination of statutory reforms and lower court decisions have made same-sex marriage legal in the vast majority of states as the Supreme Court considers the constitutionality of state laws that prevent two persons of the same sex from marrying.[111]

Underneath the substance that divides them, organizers of GSA chapters and Christian Bible clubs are united in their battle to exercise expressive rights. Students in both groups have an intimate stake in articulating powerful aspects of their identities, and both seek *Tinker*'s protections, whether under federal statute or the First Amendment. Their parents too, whether cultural and political conservatives, progressives, or libertarians, share common ground when local schools stifle their children's ability to express ideas they hold dear.

Lest the episodes I've been discussing have not sufficiently conveyed the fragility of democratic pluralism, that fragility is underscored by the behavior of even the self-proclaimed defenders of constitutional norms. Proponents of tolerance are not immune from the temptation to inhibit student speech.

Hudson High School in Massachusetts, one of only eleven schools across the country enrolled in the "First Amendment Schools" program that promotes understanding of the "rights and responsibilities of citizenship," silenced Christopher Bowler when he decided to start a chapter of the Conservative Clubs of America at the school in 2004. The High School Conservative Clubs aim to foster "the pillars of the Bible, patriotism and conservative beliefs as balance to the mostly 'liberal' viewpoint of teachers."[112]

Bowler obtained permission to start a club, found a faculty advisor, and put up posters announcing the first meeting. The posters shared the address for the national group's website, which in turn featured a link to five graphic videos showing extremist Muslims beheading captives under the banner "Islam: A Religion of Peace?" When the school became aware of the website's content, it pulled down all of the posters and blocked access to the website on school computers on the basis that graphic violence violated the school's rules.[113]

It seems teachers took offense at other aspects of the website, which included calls to substitute the American flag wherever the rainbow flag appeared, a rallying cry for the right to bear arms, and a purportedly humorous "12-Step Liberal Recovery Program." The school allowed the club to meet but deprived it of the normal means of publicity within the school, diminishing its opportunity to recruit members.[114]

After the Rutherford Institute filed a lawsuit alleging that the school had censored the club's posters and won the first skirmish in court, the school agreed to revise its policies to expressly prohibit censorship "on the basis of political viewpoint."[115] To do otherwise violated the Constitution, as a school that considered itself a haven for First Amendment rights should have known.

Similarly, in 2002, a public high school in Ann Arbor, Michigan, home to one of the country's leading public universities, excluded a student member of the Pioneers for Christ club from participating in a panel on "Religion and Homosexuality" during the school's "diversity week." Tolerance went only so far. The school would not countenance religious views that homosexuality was "unacceptable." When the religious student sued, the judge asked rhetorically, what does diversity mean if "a school may promote one view of diversity over another"? Condemning the "unsettling" "practice of one-way diversity," the judge reminded officials in *Tinker*'s words, "schools may not be enclaves of totalitarianism." The essence of diversity does not turn on how LGBTs are treated as much as on "tolerance of different, perhaps 'politically incorrect,' viewpoints in the public schools."[116]

The distinction between excluding the voice of tolerance and censoring a more orthodox viewpoint is illusory. An effort to inculcate tolerance doesn't excuse censorship. As the judge in the Ann Arbor case reflected, "[T]here is no end to the mischief that can be done in the name of good intentions."[117]

Conclusion

Living Liberty

> It is most important that our young become convinced that
> our Constitution is a living reality, not parchment preserved
> under glass.
>
> —Shanley v. Northeast Independent School District (5th Cir. 1972)

We are nearing the end of our journey through the morass of student speech rights. En route, we have delved into the foundational cases, scrutinized many facets of expressive freedom, and unraveled legal doctrines. Along the way, we have encountered enormous discrepancies between the legal doctrine and students' common experience that schools curtail their right to express themselves. In concluding, I step back from the details of disputes, cases, and circuit splits to remind readers why sustaining student speech rights matters and then turn to how various constituencies can help stem the rampant constitutional violations that plague our schools.

Our democracy rests on a belief that "we the people" remains meaningful and that every voice matters. For some, that entails citizens representing a multitude of perspectives whose dialogue influences law and policy. Others hold a less robust vision of citizenship, and of the habits of speech it requires, that might be satisfied by a higher voter participation rate or more positive responses to pollsters' queries about faith in government. One need not subscribe to any single ideal of democracy, however, to agree that an educational system that promotes pluralist democratic values, celebrates political and civil rights, and transmits the capacity to participate in civic life will, at a minimum, help to preserve democracy for future generations.

Even before the advent of widely available free schools, Americans expected educators to prepare the young for citizenship. Such preparation was widely understood as essential to a successful democracy.

Recently, however, a more instrumental philosophy has dominated public debate about educational policy, evidenced in the contemporary focus on testable skills and economic competition. The prominence accorded practical skills has narrowed the educational agenda, squeezing transmission of the norms of liberty and civic engagement from a significant position on the educational agenda. The common core standards, promulgated by the nation's governors and chief educational officers in 2010, do not even mention the public schools' role in preserving democracy.[1]

These developments reinforce the many incentives that lead educators to value order over what they fear will become the chaos of free expression and to enforce a legal regime that emphasizes obedience instead of balancing rules and rights. It can be hard to strike the constitutionally required balance in school, but the First Amendment mandates that educators strive to achieve that delicate equilibrium.

Many life skills—like tying shoelaces, shooting baskets, and parallel parking—require practice. More complex competencies like learning to think critically, to speak thoughtfully and effectively, to engage with those who have different views, and to exercise rights responsibly develop through frequent exposure and usage. Some students—like Matthew Fraser who became a debate coach and Marian Ward who prayed at the Santa Fe football game—find their life's work in their early struggle to speak. Others may be trying ideas on for size, articulating positions they will later abandon. They may learn from the counterarguments others offer or from the harm they cause others, especially if teachers and other school personnel help them interpret events. All of this is part of growing up. In constitutional terms this experimentation is not only about free expression; it is part of the quest for autonomy, for a meaningful life reflecting one's own individual values.

Inculcating the norms of citizenship can be approached in several ways. One method—rote recitation of abstract principles and drilling patriotic values that demands or imputes acceptance of shared viewpoints—violates *Barnette*'s precepts. Instead, I stress the process of exercising rights: of learning by doing.

The approach I have in mind—"living liberty"—has two reciprocal components. Schools must provide good models by respecting rights, as *Barnette* made clear, because we "are educating the young for citizenship." Schools teach rights best by honoring them, by modeling a government that means what it says about individual liberty, thus creating an environment in which liberty can flourish. Students for their part learn rights by living them in a respectful setting.

As an extra dividend, recent research refutes the notion that sounder discipline and more deference to those in charge are prerequisites for effective learning. Instead, less authoritarian environments promote mutual respect between educators and those they seek to educate. School environments characterized by respect for students yield higher academic achievement and reduced disciplinary problems.[2]

Teenagers quoted throughout this book understood the link between freedom of expression and citizenship: the signers of a petition protesting abusive treatment at the hands of a coach; journalists who pushed back at the authoritarian schools that normally prudent federal judges have compared to "'Stalinism,'" "enclaves of totalitarianism," and "societies in which everyone lives in fear"; and puzzled students who asked about the peers removed from class, "Why didn't they have speech rights?" Reflecting many years later on the case that bears his family's name, John Tinker observed, "We can't have a democracy without kids learning in school what freedom and democracy are all about."[3]

When Constance A. Flanagan, an expert on human development, asked high school students, "What does democracy mean to you?" they corroborated what many young people engaged in the struggle for expression believe. Students talked about "'freedom'" or "'my freedom.'" They talked about responsibilities including tolerance and social cohesiveness. And they talked about individual rights: "'freedom of speech, freedom of choice, and just about every one can have some kind of rights'"; "'To me, democracy means equal rights for all. It means freedom of speech and opinion.'" They also understood the deliberative process and the importance of listening: "'having the right to express your opinions & going w[ith] the majority of opinion.'" These views of citizenship know no boundaries of partisanship or viewpoint. Students also understood freedom has limits: "'[P]eople are free to decide what they want as long as they aren't hurting other people.'"[4]

Although many young people demonstrate that they have sufficient capacity to exercise rights (and many adults may not), one important question remains: Does the right to expression in school belong to the child or the parents? This issue almost never arises in courts for practical reasons. Minors generally cannot access the courts without an accompanying adult, who is usually a parent, and there are virtually no school speech cases in which a judge has appointed another adult as a guardian ad litem to pursue the constitutional claim. In the overwhelming majority of cases, parents and child are aligned against the school. And as we have seen, in most of the disputes that turn on deeply held political, cultural, or religious beliefs, the young are expressing perspectives they picked up at home.

Yet parents and children don't always agree. Rebelling against family belief systems is a normal part of adolescent development. Teenagers, in particular, may find a different God or a different way of practicing religion than their parents or may oppose a war their parents support, all manifested in expression on campus. Some parents may disagree with what their children say but nonetheless defend their children's right to speak without penalty. Others may not be willing to support expression that offends them against school authorities. LGBT students whose parents regard their identity as sinful or a breach of the natural order may be closeted at home or lack adult support to challenge illegal restrictions on clothing proclaiming gay pride or cross-dressing at the prom.

Close parsing of the cases shows that although courts seldom confront controversies in which the parents defer to the school's silencing of protected speech, the right belongs to the individual regardless of age. Not one of the many hundreds of school speech cases so much as hints to the contrary.

Only one case, decided by the Eighth Circuit in 2008, considered the issue at all as far as I am aware. The court held that the Florida legislature could choose to support parents' dominion over their children by requiring that schools honor written parental requests that children be excused from reciting the pledge—regardless of the child's preference—and that a student who did not want to recite the pledge must have written permission from a parent. The state can protect parental rights, the court reasoned, even at the cost of restricting some students' speech rights because "a parent's right to interfere with the wishes of his child is stronger than a public school official's right to interfere on behalf of the school's own interest."[5] The court implicitly accepted the principle that the speech right belongs to the student but permitted a legislative judgment allowing the parent to supervise or control the exercise of the right to stand. Absent such a statute, the speech right is the young person's, even if a minor can't find a way to enforce that right without parental assistance.

Too many educators and judges refuse to recognize that the young are not only citizens in training; some of them are already contributing to society, and they can vote in local elections in at least two Maryland communities. People all over the world praise Malala Yousafzai, the seventeen-year-old Pakistani who received the Nobel Peace Prize in 2014 two years after the Taliban tried to assassinate her because she insisted on staying in school.

But in the United States, we often treat our own fifteen-year-olds as lacking capacity to explore or form consequential ideas.

During the same week in which the Nobel Committee awarded the Peace Prize to Yousafzai, two groups of students—one in Hong Kong and one in the suburbs outside Denver, Colorado—stood up to be counted on important issues. In Hong Kong, students courageously demonstrated for more meaningful democratic elections; the seventeen-year-old leader and others were arrested, capturing international attention.

In Colorado, hundreds of students walked out of school to march and demonstrate against proposed curricular changes that aimed to drill students in perceived patriotic values. A school board member had demanded that the district promote "'patriotism, essentials and benefits of the free enterprise system, respect for authority, and respect for individual rights.'" Respect for authority alone would not suffice: "Materials," she urged, "should not encourage or condone civil disorder [or] social strife."[6]

These young people were not "punks," as one FOX News commentator charged. They understood what was at stake. The heart of the proposal would deprive students of the chance to learn about the very tools of democracy the demonstrators were putting to work. Seventeen-year-old Sarena Phu told a crowd of hundreds at a rally that "most great social changes in American history—from women's suffrage to civil rights—were accomplished through protest and civil disobedience." True, the students disrupted education and, even under *Tinker*, they risked punishment because they caused four of the district's schools to shut down. But they had the support of the teachers' union, the PTA board, and many members of the community, which had one year earlier given conservatives control of the school board. Toni Johnson Boschee, a mother who joined the student-led demonstration, spoke in words reminiscent of *Barnette*'s challenge to "village tyrants": "'This is tyranny in slow motion . . . We all need to stand up and raise our voices.'" One young man, channeling John Tinker's dismay that the school board president would not talk with him, told the school board, "You appear to have no respect for us . . . Thank you for your lesson in civil disobedience." The board ultimately backed down.[7]

If American schools stamp out curiosity and convince students that disagreement with those in power is unacceptable and that questioning is frowned on, it may not be easy to stimulate and restore these traits when they are needed for success in adulthood. Some young people may stop experimenting with half-formed ideas that might get them in trouble. Students who are punished for expressing their ideas may get the message that they must yield to authority. Without support, those students may also learn that authorities prevail because it is impossible or too difficult to challenge those in power, no matter how arbitrary their rules and decisions. History, as Justice Jackson underscored in *Barnette,* amply illustrates that learning passivity in response to authoritarianism paves the way to antidemocratic regimes.

Given the high stakes for democracy and individual fulfillment, educators and courts should ensure that young people have reason to believe that the entire Constitution, including the Speech Clause, is "a living reality, not parchment preserved under glass," as the Fifth Circuit exhorted in Shanley v. Northeast Independent School District. The *Shanley* opinion, you may recall, berated a school board that disregarded the "very existence" of the First Amendment by, among other things, purporting to control students' speech rights everywhere and, in modern terminology, "24/7."

How then do we convince students that the speech rights the Constitution promises them are not a sham? In short, what is to be done to restore and guarantee vital speech rights in our schools, and by whom?

Throughout, I have offered examples of constructive interventions to problematic episodes involving student expression. I have emphasized the distinction between censoring or punishing speech and using protected but ill-advised, inappropriate, or offensive speech as the basis for teaching about norms of respect and civility in public discourse. Consistent with constitutional limitations, these lessons can take the form of private discussions with individual students or public discussions with a whole class, a grade level, or the student body and can even bring in parents and community groups if the grievances the speech generates seem to require dialogue with a broader audience.

The principal in Novato, California, who earned a judge's praise for convening a public dialogue about anti-immigrant speech, also preempted a second potential controversy. While Andrew Smith's lawsuit about the aftermath of his "Immigration" column was pending, he drafted another provocative editorial, this time on affirmative action. The principal reached out to the local branch of the ACLU and, following its advice that the opinion was protected speech, allowed the school paper to publish Smith's second column.[8] Anticipating potential legal issues and a timely consultation with the lawyers most likely to challenge censorship helped clarify the legal issues.

Similarly, when a school responds appropriately to an employee's violation of a student's rights and takes steps to avoid a recurrence, it may not be held to account in court. The school district that Daniel Glowacki sued after his teacher ejected him from the classroom for refusing to modify his stance toward LGBTs responded decisively to the violation of Glowacki's expressive rights. It reprimanded the teacher, required him to undergo additional training in constitutional rights, and amended its anti-bullying training to clarify the limitations the Speech Clause imposes—all before the Glowackis filed their lawsuit. Because the school acted to prevent future incidents, the judge found that no legal remedies were needed to avoid violations of student speech rights in the future. The court denied the family's request that the district pay nearly $125,000 in attorneys' fees and costs because the district's policies emerged "unscathed" from the litigation. The judge observed that the incident itself, not the litigation, "may have created a teachable moment for those involved," which the district used to full advantage.[9] The message to school officials: You can avoid damages if you make it right.

A willingness to admit error can save school districts a lot of money; the lawsuits discussed in this book cost losing school districts amounts ranging from the tens of thousands of dollars up to $1 million in damages as well as attorneys' fees and costs for both sides. That calculation omits the time administrators, other personnel, and school board members spent defending against the lawsuit. Litigation is most easily avoided by respecting constitutional rights from the outset, but schools that fail to meet their constitutional obligations will find that remedial measures such as making amends and heading off the risk of future violations are the next best solution.

Schools systems accomplish several important goals when they are flexible enough to apologize for wrongfully infringing speech rights and when they are willing to retract penalties that turn out not to have been warranted. They alleviate some of the pressure on officials who sometimes must make split second decisions in response to perceived risks of serious disruption or violence. And they provide a model of reasoned discourse. By behaving reasonably instead of asserting arbitrary raw power, they likely increase respect for authority as well.

The ultimate goal is for schools to avoid infringing protected student expression in the first instance. As I have emphasized, there is no reason to expect laypeople who lack legal training to be able to understand the intricacies of First Amendment doctrine. On the other hand, it makes little sense for graduate schools of education to sidestep the crucial task of preparing future school administrators and teachers to remain within the bounds of school speech law.

All schools of education should offer at least an introductory overview of student speech rights that covers the categories of student speech and the

BEFORE YOU SILENCE STUDENT SPEECH

Identify the type of speech:

PURE[1]	**SCHOOL SPONSORED**[2]	**UNPROTECTED**[3]
The student's own speech	Appears to be school's own speech	Lewd, pro-drug, threatening, inciting violence or defamatory

May NOT censor unless:	**May censor**	**May censor and punish**
1. You reasonably anticipate material disruption, or 2. Speech collides with the legal rights of others	for a "legitimate pedalogical reason"	unless pro-drug speech is "political"

References:
1. Tinker v. Des Moines, 393 U.S. 503 (1969)
2. Hazelwood Sch. Dist. v. Kuhlmeier, 484 U.S. 260 (1988)
3. Bethel Sch. Dist. v. Fraser, 478 U.S. 675 (1986). Morse v. Frederick, 551 U.S. 393 (2007).

legal standards that govern each group so that educators are prepared before they confront an urgent situation. Ideally, courses covering this subject matter should be available to all students preparing for a career in teaching and would be required for those who aspire to administrative positions. At their best, such courses would go beyond the taxonomy to emphasize why freedom of speech in schools is essential to preserving democracy and intellectual inquiry.

Law schools could do a better job of preparing students to counsel educators about student speech rights. Many of the leading legal textbooks assigned to law students in constitutional law survey courses do not present any of the student speech cases or any discussion of the special standards that obtain in schools. The current edition of the book that I myself assign in my class on the constitutional amendments no longer includes student speech rights as a topic.[10]

Perhaps more significant, it seems that some attorneys who represent school districts don't always take the "counselor" part of their job description to heart. Lawyers play many roles, including defending the choices their clients make. But before that, they have opportunities to sensitize their clients to the spirit as well as the letter of the law: "Have you considered other ways of handling this problem?" or "the law allows you to do that, but doesn't require you to" and "I might be able to defend that action, but it may be a bit too close to the line and might attract a lawsuit, which you could lose at great expense." Clients often appreciate this kind of advice, which reflects understanding of their broader enterprise.

If all school administrators had at least a rudimentary understanding of the law that governs student speech, they would be positioned to take advantage of a modest suggestion I offer for principals, teachers, and school board members. Because school personnel often need to respond quickly when confronted with potentially disruptive or dangerous speech, I propose that each principal's office prominently post a diagram (see chart on page 294) that shows the basic outlines of school speech doctrine as the law exists today.

This poster would serve the same purpose in emergencies as the ubiquitous Heimlich maneuver diagrams on the walls of establishments that serve food. The diagram will help school officials classify the speech properly in the school speech taxonomy and then direct them to the constitutional constraints on their ability to censor or punish that kind of student speech. The chart has a limited scope. It is designed to remind administrators of basic concepts, the student speech taxonomy, and the tests that apply. It does not define terms and is not meant to replace consultation with the school district's attorneys.

Because it captures the current legal regime, the chart does not incorporate specific proposals for reform offered in most of the chapters of this book. I won't repeat those specific suggestions here. Instead, I build on them by focusing on what some particular state actors and other constituencies could do to reduce the rampant infringement of student expression and, if they are so inclined, to enhance legal protections for student speech.

Federal agencies, most notably the Departments of Justice and Education and the Commission on Civil Rights (and parallel agencies in state governments), which currently give short shrift to student's expressive rights when tackling problems like bullying, should immediately revise their advisory publications and regulations to explain the potential conflicts between efforts to control hurtful speech and First Amendment rights. A brief nod to a potential legal problem is not enough and may signal that the First Amendment is not really something to worry about. School districts can encourage agencies to provide more careful analysis by requesting answers to hard questions about contradictions in the law beyond the current notation that the First Amendment might pose a problem as schools try to comply with federal and state requirements.

Federal constitutional, statutory, and common law merely establish the minimum rights to which students are entitled. States, localities, school districts, and individual campuses can all elect to offer greater protection to student speech than the federal Constitution requires, presuming that no other regulation prevents them from doing so. As we have seen, California, among other states, already provides statutes and judicial rulings that make the post-*Tinker* Supreme Court decisions all but irrelevant in the state. In addition, since 2008, California has protected teachers who stand up for student speech rights (for example, faculty members who advise student publications or direct student plays) from retaliation by their employers.[11] These statutes offer models for legal reform in other jurisdictions.

Localities too can raise the floor that supports student rights. Among other things, they can exercise their discretion by choosing not to use all of the censorship powers the student speech doctrine gives them. The Constitution does not require schools to punish remarks that may be sexually suggestive but are not obscene (like Matthew Fraser's extended metaphor)—it only allows them to. Similarly, just because a school can identify a pedagogical rationale for silencing school-sponsored student expression doesn't mean, as a matter of policy or pedagogy, that the school *must* censor the material. Sometimes a better lesson would flow from allowing controversial expression to appear and then helping students to discuss it or sharing the school's considerations in deciding whether to let the speech be aired.

Parents and other citizens play important roles too on both sides of the battle over student speech. I have described numerous incidents in which one parent or a small group of parents or outside activists convinced schools to suppress controversial speech. Those individuals often have a disproportionate impact on how schools treat speech because it seems easier in the short run to placate them than to risk a broader controversy in the community. So we need to honor the individuals in these disputes who stood up for constitutional rights: the young people who demanded to be heard and the adults who backed them up against schools and school boards and in court. These proponents of civil liberty include average citizens pushed too far, local and national activists, and attorneys who volunteer to represent the young people and their families.

The decisions of the Supreme Court are not self-executing. If they were, the speech infringements that led to numerous "easy cases" would never have occurred. And we would never know about the infringements if the students and their families had not fought on behalf of all of us, as judges repeatedly note when they award attorneys' fees to students who prevail in speech cases.

I harbor the hope that parents and other adults who read this book might be inspired to remind their school systems about the importance of school as a training ground for citizenship and to urge their local educators to honor student rights. It can be much more effective to begin the conversation as a matter of preferred policy instead of waiting for a highly charged censorship episode when school officials may be motivated to defend decisions they have already made. Citizen engagement on the side of more speech provides a counterweight to the voices demanding censorship of ideas that might upset some people. And by supporting a generous reading of student rights, engaged advocates of free speech also provide a model for the community's young people about the potential to influence events.

There is no reason other than inertia (and perhaps a lack of awareness of the threats to free expression) for the battle over school speech to be dominated by the censorious. The pressing demands of contemporary school and curricular reform provide an opportunity to use district-wide conversations about the future to add the exercise of free speech to the educational agenda. Parents don't have to take over the school board, as a challenger did in Juneau, Alaska, after *Morse*, to make a difference.

Finally, the discrete group of lawyers who serve as judges have often avoided rendering difficult decisions. Some have been too timid, too deferential, or too ready to admit defeat in the face of confusing and incomplete instructions from above to fulfill their obligations to state the law and enforce it when it comes to controlling educators who abuse their powers. Throughout, I have criticized numerous courts that abdicated by failing to identify the governing doctrine, accepting government claims without probing them sufficiently, or taking account of extraneous prejudicial material, such as national fears about school shootings or the rise of bullying. And we have also seen judges whose holdings are careful and correct, who treat cases involving students with the seriousness to which all constitutional claims are entitled.

Among the characteristics separating these two groups of judges is the level of deference they show to professional educators and whether they treat school officials the same way they treat other experts who present their opinions in court. In areas of law that usually require expert testimony, such as torts or antitrust, each side generally has at least one expert—so the judge can't just defer. But in litigation over school speech rights, the same educator who silenced or punished the student is treated as the expert on education, entitled to substantial or unlimited deference under every category in the taxonomy of rights except for the pure speech *Tinker* governs.

There is nothing so difficult or incomprehensible about school speech doctrine that judges must defer to the experts who run schools any more than they must defer to engineers in complex tort litigation or to economists in antitrust litigation where the judge or jury must choose between competing expert interpretations. A judge who can apportion causality among multiple corporate tort-feasors or assess market power in antitrust cases surely has the intellectual heft to examine the reasons a school gives for apprehending material disruption, review the pedagogical rationale for censoring school-sponsored speech, or assess whether an observer could be misled into thinking that a spirited rebuke of school policies or a comment during a classroom debate appeared to bear the school's own imprimatur.

Judges would also be well advised to exercise their equitable powers when schools impose seriously disproportionate penalties on students for speech code violations. They need not fear that occasionally weighing in on egregious injustice would turn the federal courts into a national school board. There are hundreds of litigated school speech cases, not thousands, and they don't all involve disproportionate penalties.

Appellate court judges have additional responsibilities—above all not to shy from clarifying the law and sketching out answers to the myriad unresolved questions the Supreme Court is unlikely to ever consider. School officials, teachers, students, and lawyers, as well as district court judges, all await the guidance only courts can provide (including on some of the big doctrinal issues, like the line between conduct and expression or what the Establishment Clause really means and when religious speech by a student represents his or her school).

Schools especially need more concrete advice from the lower courts about how to craft a school code that respects student rights, provides adequate notice of what speech is susceptible to discipline, and preserves sufficient administrative discretion. Further articulation of the lines that separate protected expression from speech that can be regulated in school without violating student rights is largely up to the courts, which will ultimately gauge the permissibility of efforts to encapsulate the legal rules (including those I have offered here should schools adopt them).

The approach to student speech embodied in this book is consistent with existing law. I have drawn on the robust vision of rights that animated *Barnette* and *Tinker* while remaining true to the balance set out in *Tinker* and staying within the confines imposed later by *Fraser, Hazelwood,* and *Morse.*

The essential principles set out in *Barnette* and *Tinker* endure. They are not confined in the annals of history to opinions by liberal Justices like Brennan, Marshall, and Fortas. Despite retrenchment by the Supreme Court starting in the 1980s, Justices from the centrist Stevens to the conservative Alito have repeatedly affirmed a steadfast and nuanced vision of student expressive rights.

Many lower court judges—again from every point on the political and philosophical spectrum—have explicitly linked the realization of student speech rights to transmitting democratic habits and the skills that foster citizenship. As Judge Frank Easterbrook explained, educators must take advantage of the teaching moments unavoidably generated by protected speech because schools are obligated to explain why the Constitution safeguards expression some people may not want to hear. If schools cannot teach the foundations of speech rights and help students distinguish private from official speakers, he ruminated, "then one wonders whether the . . . schools can teach anything at all." To Easterbrook, the bottom line could not be simpler: "[E]ducating the students in the meaning of the Constitution [is] what schools are for."[12] Nothing could be more indispensable to the union we continually strive to perfect.

Appendix:
The Federal Judicial Circuits

The map on the following page shows the locations of the Federal Circuit Courts of Appeals and the states that fall within the jurisdiction of each Circuit Court.

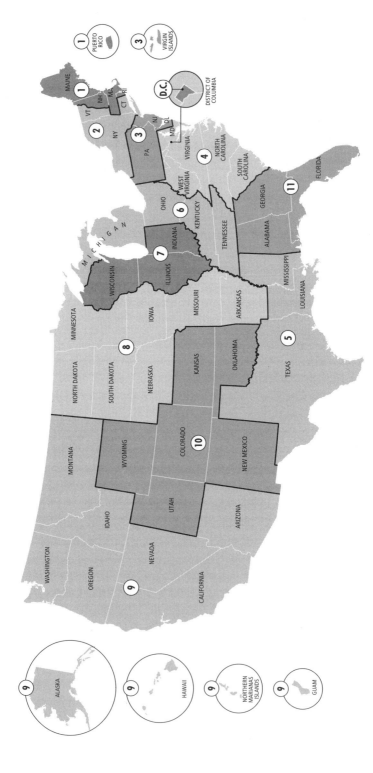

Courts of Appeals designated 1 to 11 on the map are known by their numerals. For example, "1" means the Court of Appeals for the First Circuit, and so forth. "D.C." designates the Court of Appeals for the District of Columbia.

Notes

A note for readers on citations to court decisions:

The endnotes adapt legal citation form for judicial opinions. The abbreviations to the F. Supp. series refer to the volumes containing District Court (trial level) opinions; F., F.2d, and F.3d report appellate court opinions; and U.S. refers to Supreme Court opinions, except for the most recent, which appear as S. Ct.

State court opinions are published in a variety of reporters; the state is indicated in parentheses. Other citation forms, such as citations to electronic services Westlaw or Lexis, indicate that opinions have not been published.

Introduction

1. "Long Island Student Suspended for Fictional Video about Bullying," www.foxnews.com (accessed 3/11/14).
2. Griggs v. Fort Wayne Sch. Bd., 359 F. Supp. 2d 731 (N.D. Ind. 2005); Guiles v. Marineau, 461 F.3d 320 (2d. Cir. 2006). These cases are analyzed in Chapter 5. All the incidents mentioned in the Introduction will be discussed, with references, in later chapters.
3. Michael W. McConnell, "Equal Treatment and Religious Discrimination," *Equal Treatment of Religion in a Pluralistic Society*, ed. Stephen Monsma and J. Christopher Soper (Grand Rapids: Eerdmans Publishing Company, 1998), 38.
4. Vincent Blasi and Seana V. Shiffrin, "The Story of West Virginia State Board of Education v. Barnette: The Pledge of Allegiance and the Freedom of Thought," *Constitutional Law Stories*, ed. Michael C. Dorf (New York: Foundation Press, 2004), 433, 455. See Amy Gutman, *Democratic Education* (Princeton: Princeton University Press, 1987); Stephen Macedo, *Diversity and Distrust: Civic Education in a Multicultural Democracy* (Cambridge, MA: Harvard University Press, 2000); Eamonn Callan, *Creating Citizens: Political Education and Liberal Democracy* (Oxford: Oxford University Press, 1997); Rob Reich, *Bridging Liberalism and Multiculturalism in American Education* (Chicago: University of Chicago Press, 2002); and James E. Fleming and

Linda B. McClain, *Ordered Liberty: Rights, Responsibilities and Virtues* (Cambridge, MA: Harvard University Press, 2013).

5. Stephen Breyer, *Active Liberty: Interpreting Our Democratic Constitution* (New York: Random House, 2005), 46–47.

6. Michael Walzer, *On Toleration* (New Haven: Yale University Press, 1997), 71–72.

7. Cohen v. California, 403 U.S. 15,22 (1971) (quoting Baumgartner v. United States, 322 U.S. 665, 673–674 (1944)).

8. West Virginia State Bd. of Educ. v. Barnette, 319 U.S. 624, 637 (1943).

1. Think as You Will and Speak as You Think

1. West Virginia State Bd. of Educ. v. Barnette, 319 U.S. 624 (1943); Tinker v. Des Moines Indep. Cmty. Sch. Dist., 393 U.S. 503 (1969).

2. Zechariah Chafee, Jr., *Free Speech in the United States* (Cambridge, MA: Harvard University Press, 1941), 3; Schenck v. United States, 249 U.S. 47 (1919); Debs v. United States, 249 U.S. 211 (1919); Frohwerk v. United States, 249 U.S. 204 (1919) (all authored by Justice Holmes).

3. Abrams v. United States, 250 U.S. 616 (1919).

4. Ibid., 628, 630 (Holmes, J., dissenting).

5. Ibid.

6. Gitlow v. New York, 268 U.S. 652, 666 (1925).

7. Whitney v. California, 274 U.S. 357, 375, 377 (1927) (Brandeis, J., concurring), rev'd in part; Brandenberg v. Ohio, 395 U.S. 444 (1969).

8. Whitney v. California, 274 U.S. at 375–376 (Brandeis, J., concurring).

9. Stromberg v. California, 283 U.S. 359 (1931); Near v. Minnesota, 283 U.S. 697, 716 (1931).

10. Near v. Minnesota, 283 U.S. 697, 713 (1931).

11. West Virginia v. Barnette, 319 U.S. 624.

12. Minersville Sch. Dist. v. Gobitis, 310 U.S. 586, 591, 596 (1940); West Virginia v. Barnette, 319 U.S. 624.

13. Minersville Sch. Dist. v. Gobitis, 310 U.S. at 592, n. 2; Brief for Petitioner at 11–12, Minersville Sch. Dist. v. Gobitis, 310 U.S. 586 (1940) (No. 690); Brief of the Committee on the Bill of Rights, of the American Bar Association as Amici Curiae at 16–17, Minersville Sch. Dist. v. Gobitis, 310 U.S. 586 (1940) (No. 690); Brief for ACLU as Amici Curiae at 28–29, Minersville Sch. Dist. v. Gobitis, 310 U.S. 586 (1940) (No. 690).

     In *Gobitis*, a father who had enrolled his expelled children in private school sought injunctive relief ordering the public schools to accommodate the family's position and reinstate them. The posture of *Barnette* differed. In *Barnette*, parents and children faced prosecution.

14. Minersville Sch. Dist. v. Gobitis, 310 U.S. at 601 (Stone, J., dissenting).

15. Brief of the Committee on the Bill of Rights, of the American Bar Association, as Friends of the Court at 24, West Virginia v. Barnette, 319 U.S. 624 (1943) (No. 591).

16. ACLU, *Jehovah's Witnesses and the War* (New York: ACLU, 1943), 28–29; West Virginia v. Barnette, 319 U.S. at 629; Appellees' Brief at 81–84, West Virginia v. Barnette, 319 U.S. 624 (1943) (No. 591); see also Richard J. Ellis, *To the Flag: The Unlikely History of the Pledge of Allegiance* (Lawrence: University Press of Kansas, 2005), Chapter 4.

17. Appellees' Brief at 11, West Virginia v. Barnette, 319 U.S. 624.

18. The stage had been set for reversal even earlier, when, in a most unusual development, three Justices who had signed the majority opinion in *Gobitis* joined Harlan Stone—the sole dissenter in that case who had since become Chief Justice—in using an intervening case to announce their view that *Gobitis* had been "wrongly decided." Jones v. Opelika, 316 U.S. 584, 624 (1942) (Murphy, J., Black, J., and Douglas, J., dissenting).

19. Harry Kalven, Jr., *A Worthy Tradition: Freedom of Speech in America* (Jamie Kalven, ed., New York: Harper & Row 1989), 81.

20. West Virginia v. Barnette, 319 U.S. at 635, 630, 631, 633.

21. Ibid., 633, n. 13; Appellees Brief at 19–20, West Virginia v. Barnette, 319 U.S. 624. In Wooley v. Maynard, 430 U.S. 705, 715 (1977), the Court reiterated that the First Amendment protects against coerced speech.

22. West Virginia v. Barnette, 319 U.S. at 634–635.

23. Ibid., 633 (relying on Stromberg v. California, 283 U.S. 359 (1931)), 634. Justice Murphy expressly agreed that the "right of freedom of thought and of religion . . . includes both the right to speak freely and the right to refrain from speaking," West Virginia v. Barnette, 319 U.S. at 645 (Murphy, J., concurring).

24. West Virginia v. Barnette, 319 U.S. at 641, 642; Texas v. Johnson, 491 U.S. 397, 415 (1989).

25. West Virginia v. Barnette, 319 U.S. at 642.

26. Ibid., 637.

27. Ibid., 638; Minersville v. Gobitis, 310 U.S. at 598.

28. Letter from Robert H. Jackson to Armistead Brown (July 13, 1943), Robert Jackson Papers, Library of Congress, Box 127, folder 11.

29. Tinker v. Des Moines Indep. Cmty. Sch. Dist., 393 U.S. 503 (1969).

30. Police Dep't of Chicago v. Mosley, 408 U.S. 92, 95 (1972); R.A.V. v. St. Paul, 505 U.S. 377, 382 (1992).

31. Terminiello v. Chicago, 337 U.S. 1 (1949); Cox v. Louisiana, 379 U.S. 536 (1965).

32. Chaplinsky v. New Hampshire, 315 U.S. 568 (1942); Brandenberg v. Ohio, 395 U.S. 444 (1969) (decision announced three months after *Tinker*); Watts v. United States, 394 U.S. 705 (1969); Roth v. Ohio, 378 U.S. 184 (1964). The Court articulated the current standard in Miller v. California, 413 U.S. 15 (1973). See Reno v. ACLU, 521 U.S. 844, 872–873 (1997); Brown v. Entertainment Merchants Ass'n, 131 S. Ct. 2729, 2744 (2011).

33. Cox v. New Hampshire, 312 U.S. 569 (1941); Kovacs v. Cooper, 336 U.S. 77 (1949).

34. Thomas I. Emerson, *The System of Freedom of Expression* (New York: Random House, 1970), 719.

35. Ibid.
36. United States v. Kent, 383 U.S. 541 (1966).
37. Application of Gault, 387 U.S. 1, 4 (1967).
38. Ibid., 26.
39. Tinker v. Des Moines, 258 F. Supp. 971, 972 (S.D. Iowa 1966); Alexander Meiklejohn, *Free Speech and Its Relation to Self-Government* (New York: Harper Brothers Publishers, 1948).
40. Doreen Rappaport, *Tinker vs. Des Moines: Student Rights on Trial* (New York: HarperCollins Publishers, 1993), 20.
41. Joint Appendix at 8, 10, Tinker v. Des Moines, 393 U.S. 503 (1968) (No. 21).
42. Brief for Petitioners at 6, Tinker v. Des Moines, 393 U.S. 503 (1969) (No. 21).
43. Brief for Respondents at 32–33, Tinker v. Des Moines, 393 U.S. 503 (1969) (No. 21); Tinker v. Des Moines, 393 U.S. at 505.
44. Brief for Respondents at 22, Tinker v. Des Moines, 393 U.S. 503.
45. Tinker v. Des Moines, 393 U.S. at 507.
46. Brief of the Committee on the Bill of Rights, of the American Bar Association, as Friends of the Court at 13, West Virginia v. Barnette, 319 U.S. 624 (1943) (No. 591).
47. Tinker v. Des Moines, 393 U.S. at 511.
48. Brief for Respondents at 10, Tinker v. Des Moines, 393 U.S. 503; Tinker, 393 U.S. at 509, n. 3, 512–513 (quoting Keyshian v. Bd. of Regents, 385 U.S. 589, 603 (1967)).
49. Tinker v. Des Moines, 393 U.S. at 515 (Stewart, J., concurring); Ginsberg v. New York, 390 U.S. 629 (1968); Laura Kalman, *Abe Fortas: A Biography* (New Haven: Yale University Press, 1990), 55.
50. Tinker v. Des Moines, 393 U.S. at 508.
51. Ibid., 510.
52. Ibid., 506, 511.
53. Ibid., 508–509 (quoting Burnside v. Byars, 363 F.2d 744, 749 (5th Cir. 1966)). See also Blackwell v. Issaquena Cnty. Bd. of Educ., 363 F.2d 749 (5th Cir. 1966). The Tinkers' brief urged adoption of this standard. Sheldon v. Fannin, 221 F. Supp. 766, 775 (D. Az. 1963) (case governed by *Barnette*, students "not disorderly" and "did not materially disrupt" education); West Virginia v. Barnette, 319 U.S. at 630.
54. Milk Wagon Drivers Union of Chicago v. Meadowmoor Dairies, 312 U.S. 287, 301–302 (1941) (Black, J., dissenting).
55. Brown v. Louisiana, 383 U.S. 131, 139 (1966). See also ibid., 133 (Fortas, J.).
56. Ibid.,165, 168 (Black, J., dissenting) quoted in Brief for Respondents at 25, Tinker v. Des Moines, 393 U.S. 503.
57. Morse v. Frederick, 551 U.S. 393, 422 (2007) (Thomas, J., concurring).
58. Tinker v. Des Moines, 393 U.S. at 522, 517–518 (Black, J., dissenting).
59. Joint Appendix at 30, Tinker v. Des Moines, 393 U.S. 503 (No. 21).
60. Brief for Petitioners at 3, Tinker v. Des Moines, 393 U.S. 503.

61. Roger K.Newman, *Hugo Black: A Biography* (New York: Pantheon Books, 1994), 392.

62. Tinker v. Des Moines, 393 U.S. at 525 (Black, J., dissenting).

63. Ibid.

64. Ibid., 525–526 (Black, J., dissenting).

65. Ibid., 525; "Page Proof of Justice Black's Dissent," undated, Abe Fortas Papers, Yale University Manuscripts and Archives, Box 79, Folder 1669.

66. Newman, *Hugo Black*, 592.

67. "Supreme Court Opens Pandora's Box," *The Lemoore [California] Advance*, February 27, 1969, 2, and Lance W. Goldenberg (age seventeen) to Fortas (March 16, 1969), both in Fortas Papers, Box 80, Folder 1670. See also David Lawrence, "Is Treason Permissible as Merely Free Speech?" *U.S. News & World Report*, March 10, 1969, Fortas Papers, Box 80, Folder 1671.

68. Shapiro v. Thompson, 394 U.S. 618, 634 (1969); Richard H. Fallon Jr., "Strict Judicial Scrutiny," *University of California Los Angeles Law Review* 54 (2007): 1267, 1282. Previously referred to as *exacting scrutiny*, Buckley v. Valeo, 424 U.S. 1, 16 (1976), the phrase *strict scrutiny* first appears in a Supreme Court opinion in a case involving the Speech Clause in 1978, First Nat'l Bank of Boston v. Bellotti, 435 U.S. 765, 787, n. 24 (1978).

69. Gerald Gunther, "The Supreme Court, 1971 Term – Foreword: In Search of Evolving Doctrine on a Changing Court: A Model for a Newer Equal Protection," Harvard Law Review 86 (1972): 1, 8.

70. Jim Newton, *Justice for All: Earl Warren and the Nation He Made* (New York: Penguin Group, 2006), 502–503.

71. Ibid., 505.

2. A Taxonomy of School Censorship Takes Form

1. Brief of Student Press Law Center et al., Hazelwood v. Kuhlmeier, 484 U.S. 260 (1988) (No. 86–836), 1987 WL 864177, at *19 (quoting Jack Nelson, *Captive Voices: The Report of the Commission of Inquiry into High School Journalism* (Schocken Books, 1974), 42), *8, n. 3 (collecting cases).

2. Hazelwood Sch. Dist. v. Kuhlmeier, 484 U.S. 260, 281 (1988) (Brennan, J., dissenting).

3. William Martin, *With God on Our Side: The Rise of the Religious Right in America* (New York: Broadway Books, 1966), 133 (quoting columnist Elmer Fike).

4. Goss v. Lopez, 419 U.S. 565, 579, 580–581, 583 (1975); Ingraham v. Wright, 430 U.S. 651 (1977); Valerie Strauss, "The Answer Sheet: 19 States Still Allow Corporal Punishment in School," *Washington Post*, September 18, 2014, www.washingtonpost.com/blogs/answer-sheet/wp/2014/09/18/19-states-still-allow-corporal-punishment-in-school (accessed 10/16/14).

5. New Jersey v. T.L.O., 469 U.S. 325, 343 (1985); Vernonia Sch. Dist. 47J v. Acton, 515 U.S. 646 (1995); Bd. of Educ. of Indep. Sch. Dist. No. 92 of Pottowatomie Cnty. v. Earls, 536 U.S 82 (2002).

6. David L. Hudson, Jr., *Let the Students Speak! A History of the Fight for Free Expression in American Schools* (Boston: Beacon Press, 2011), 86.

7. Bethel Sch. Dist. No. 403 v. Fraser, 478 U.S. 675, 687 (1986) (Brennan, J., concurring).

8. Ibid., 678.

9. Hudson, *Let the Students Speak,* 90 (quoting William Coats).

10. Bethel v. Fraser, 478 U.S. at 678.

11. Ibid., 680 (quoting Fraser v. Bethel Sch. Dist. No. 403, 755 F.2d 1356, 1363 (9th Cir. 1985)).

12. Brief of Respondents, Bethel Sch. Dist. No. 403 v. Fraser, 478 U.S. 675 (1986) (No. 84–1667), 1986 WL 720451, at *6, 16, 26.

13. Bethel v. Fraser, 478 U.S. 686 (quoting Tinker v. Des Moines Indep. Cmnty. Sch. Dist., 393 U.S. 503, 526 (Black, J., dissenting)).

14. Ibid., 681 (quoting Charles Beard and Mary Beard, *New Basic History of the United States* (Garden City NY: Doubleday, 1968), 228), 682, 683, 685.

15. Ibid., 680–685.

16. John Stewart Mill, *On Liberty* (New York: Dover Publications, 2002); Ginsberg v. New York, 390 U.S. 629, 650 (1968) (Stewart, J., concurring).

17. Harry Kalven, Jr., *A Worthy Tradition: Freedom of Speech in America,* (Jamie Kalven, ed., New York: Harper & Row, 1988), 55; e.g., Brown v. Entertainment Merchants Ass'n, 131 S. Ct. 2729 (2011); Reno v. ACLU, 521 U.S. 844 (1997); Ashcroft v. ACLU, 535 U.S. 564 (2002); Sable Communications, Inc. v. FCC, 492 U.S. 115 (1989).

18. Cohen v. California, 403 U.S. 15, 21 (1971); Bolger v. Youngs Drug Products Corp., 463 U.S. 60, 72 (1983).

19. Bethel v. Fraser, 478 U.S 695 (Stevens, J., dissenting).

20. Ibid., 695 n. 5.

21. Ibid., 687.

22. Ibid., 687–688 (Brennan, J., concurring).

23. Ibid., 690.

24. Ibid., 696 (Stevens, J., dissenting).

25. Morse v. Frederick, 551 U.S. 393, 404 (2007).

26. Jeffrey Kahn, "Ronald Reagan Launched Political Career Using the Berkeley Campus as a Target," June 8, 2004, www.berkeley.edu/news (accessed 7/1/13).

27. Quoted in Jonathan Zimmerman, *Whose America? Culture Wars in the Public Schools* (Cambridge, MA: Harvard University Press, 2002), 182.

28. David L. Shapiro, "Mr. Justice Rehnquist: A Preliminary View," *Harvard Law Review* 90 (1976): 293, 294; William H. Rehnquist, "Robert H. Jackson, A Perspective Twenty-Five Years Later," *Albany Law Review* 44 (1980): 533, 535; Laura K. Ray, "A Law Clerk and His Justice: What William Rehnquist Did Not Learn from Robert Jackson," *Indiana Law Review* 29 (1996): 535, 574.

29. Ronald T. Hyman, "Educational Beliefs of Supreme Court Justices in the 1980s," *West's Education Law Reporter* 59 (May 24, 1990): 285, 286.

30. Hazelwood Sch. Dist. v. Kuhlmeier, 484 U.S. 260 (1988).

31. Kulhmeier v. Hazelwood Sch. Dist., 607 F. Supp. 1450, 1457–1458 (E.D. Mo. 1985), aff'd 795 F.2d (8th Cir. 1986), rev'd 484 U.S. 260 (1988).

32. Reply Brief for the Petitioners, Hazelwood v. Kuhlmeier, 484 U.S. 260 (1988) (No. 86–836), 1987 WL 864174, at *18. But see Hazelwood v. Kuhlmeier, 484 U.S. at 271–272, and 484 U.S. at 285–286 (Brennan, J., dissenting).

33. Brief and Motion of American Society of Newspaper Editors et al., Hazelwood v. Kuhlmeier, 484 U.S. 260 (1988) (No. 86–836), 1987 WL 864178, at *8–9.

34. Motion for Leave to File and Brief of Amici Curiae NOW Legal Defense Fund et al., Hazelwood Sch. Dist. v. Kuhlmeier, 484 U.S. 260 (1988) No. 86–836, 1987 U.S. S. Ct. Briefs LEXIS 1134, at *21–22.

35. See Hudson, *Let the Students Speak,* 93–102.

36. Brief for the Petitioners, Hazelwood Sch. Dist. v. Kuhlmeier, 484 U.S. 260 (1988) (No. 86–836), 1987 WL 864172, at *13, 33; Kulhmeier v. Hazelwood, 607 F. Supp. 1450, 1466–1467 (E.D. Mo. 1985).

37. Kuhlmeier v. Hazelwood Sch. Dist., 795 F.2d 1368, 1373 (8th Cir. 1986).

38. Ibid., 1370.

39. Ibid., 1371 n. 2.

40. "Too hot for Hazelwood," *St. Louis Globe Democrat*, February 9, 1985 (Weekend Section), 5, cited in Brief of Student Press Law Center, Hazelwood v. Kuhlmeier, at *9.

41. Hazelwood v. Kuhlmeier, 484 U.S. at 262.

42. Ibid., 271.

43. Ibid.

44. Joint Appendix at 10, Tinker v. Des Moines, 393 U.S. 503 (1968) (No. 21).

45. Tinker v. Des Moines, 511; Keyishian v. Bd. of Regents, 385 U.S. 589, 603 (1967).

46. Hazelwood v. Kuhlmeier, 484 U.S. at 271.

47. Bd. of Educ., Island Trees Union Free Sch. Dist. No. 26 v. Pico, 457 U.S. 853, 863–864 (1982).

48. Hazelwood v. Kuhlmeier, 484 U.S. at 270–271.

49. Ibid., 271.

50. Ibid.

51. Ibid., 273, 270, 271 n. 4, citing Bethel v. Fraser, 484 U.S. at 271–272 n. 4, quoting Tinker v. Des Moines, 478 U.S. at 526 (Black, J., dissenting).

52. "Danny" [Danny Ertel] to Justice Blackmun, memorandum dated Nov. 20, 1987, Harry A. Blackmun Papers, Manuscript Division, Library of Congress, Washington, DC, Box 494, Folder 5.

53. Justice Stevens to Justice White, Nov. 20, 1987, Thurgood Marshall Papers, Manuscript Division, Library of Congress, Washington, DC, Box 442, Folder 6 (if you make these changes "you will garner my vote"); "Danny" [Danny Ertel] to Justice Blackmun, memo dated Nov. 20, 1987; Hazelwood v. Kuhlmeier, 484 U.S. at 273.

54. Turner v. Safley, 482 U.S. 78, 99, 98, 100 (1987) (O'Connor, J.). See James E. Ryan, "The Supreme Court and Public Schools," *Virginia Law Review* 80 (2000): 1335, 1358, n. 2; Aaron H. Caplan, "Freedom of Speech in Schools and Prisons," *Washington Law Review* 85 (2010): 71, 80 ("debunking" the connection).

55. Seth Stern and Stephen Wermiel, *Justice Brennan: Liberal Champion* (Boston: Houghton Mifflin Harcourt, 2010), 444.

56. Ibid., 291, 285-286.

57. Ibid., 288. Detailed descriptions of the articles are included in the district court's opinion following an evidentiary hearing. Kuhlmeier v. Hazelwood Sch. Dist., 607 F. Supp. 1450, 1457–1460 (E.D. Mo. 1985), rev'd, 484 U.S. 260 (1988).

58. Class 3-Watkins, Hillside School, to Justice Blackmun, January 20, 1988, Harry Blackmun Papers, Manuscript Division, Library of Congress, Washington, DC, Box 494, Folder 6 E.

59. Hazelwood v. Kuhlmeier, 484 U.S. at 281 (Brennan, J., dissenting).

60. Personal communication from Douglas K. Mertz, June 9, 2014.

61. Frederick v. Morse, No. J 02–008 CV(JWS), 2003 WL 25274689, at *5 (D. Alaska May 27, 2003).

62. Frederick v. Morse, 439 F.3d 1114, 1124 (9th Cir. 2006), vacated, 551 U.S. 393 (2007).

63. Morse v. Frederick, 551 U.S. 393 (2007).

64. Layshock v. Hermitage Sch. Dist., 496 F. Supp. 2d 587, 595 (W.D. Pa. 2007), aff'd in part on rehearing en banc, 650 F.3d 205 (3d Cir. 2011), cert. denied sub nom Blue Mtn. Sch. Dist. v. J. S., 132 S. Ct. 1097 (2012). Frederick Schauer, "Abandoning the Guidance Function: Morse v. Frederick," *Supreme Court Review* (2007): 205, 207.

65. The Justices clearly did not believe that the banner appeared to bear the school's imprimatur or could be treated as school sponsored. If they had, the Court would have applied *Hazelwood*. See Frederick v. Morse, 557 U.S. at 405.

66. Ibid., 406.

67. Lee Epstein, Christopher M. Parker, and Jeffrey A. Segal, "Do Justices Defend the Speech They Hate? In-Group Bias, Opportunism, and the First Amendment," American Political Science Association Annual Meeting Paper 5 (August 6, 2013), papers.ssrn.com/sol3/papers.cfm?abstract _id=2300572 (using *Morse* as an example in a comprehensive statistical study).

68. Vernonia Sch. Dist. 47J v. Acton, 515 U.S. 646 (1995); Bd. of Educ. of Indep. Sch. Dist. No. 92 of Pottawatomie Cnty. v. Earls, 536 U.S. 822 (2002).

69. Bethel v. Fraser, 478 U.S. at 682 (citing New Jersey v. T.L.O., 469 U.S. at 340–342); Hazelwood v. Kuhlmeier, 484 U.S. at 266 (same); Morse v. Frederick, 551 U.S. at 406 (citing Vernonia v. Acton, 515 U.S. at 655–656, New Jersey v. T.L.O., 469 U.S. 325, 340 (1985), and Pottawatomie v. Earls, 536 U.S. at 829–830).

70. Schauer, "Abandoning the Guidance Function," 209.

71. Morse v. Frederick, 551 U.S. at 422 (Alito, J., concurring).
72. Ibid., 402–403 and 422 (Alito, J., concurring).
73. Ibid., 445 n. 8. (Stevens, J., dissenting).
74. National Conference of State Legislatures, "State Medical Marijuana Laws," (January 28, 2015), http://www.ncsl.org/research/health/medical-marijuanalaws.aspx (accessed February 25, 2015).
75. Douglas K. Mertz, "My Turn: Another Look at the 'Bong Hits' Case," JuneauEmpire.com, July 6, 2007, www.juneauempire.com (accessed 6/9/14).
76. Nuxoll v. Indian Prairie Sch. Dist. No. 204, 523 F.3d 668, 673–674 (6th Cir. 2008) (Posner, J.).
77. Doninger v. Niehoff, 642 F.3d 334, 354 (2d. Cir. 2011).
78. Schauer, "Abandoning the Guidance Function," 212, 212 n. 25 (quoting Morse v. Frederick, 394).
79. Morse v. Frederick, 551 U.S. at 403.
80. Aaron H. Caplan, "Visions of Public Education in Morse v. Frederick," *Journal of Educational Controversy* 3, no. 1 (2008): 11. Loyola Legal Studies Papers No. 2008=23 (accessed 6/6/14).
81. Ibid., 9; Morse v. Frederick, 551 U.S. at 411 (Thomas, J., dissenting).
82. Mark Choate, quoted in James C. Foster, *Bong Hits 4 Jesus: A Perfect Constitutional Storm in Alaska's Capital* (Fairbanks: University of Alaska Press, 2011), 204.
83. Foster, *Bong Hits 4 Jesus,* 207–209.

3. Dissing and Discipline

1. Saxe v. State College Sch. Dist., 240 F.3d 200, 214 (3d Cir. 2000) (Alito, J.).
2. S. G. v. Sayreville Bd. of Educ., 333 F.3d 417 (3d. Cir. 2003), cert. denied, 540 U.S. 1104 (2004).
3. U.S. Department of Education, *Guiding Principles: A Resource Guide for Improving School Climate and Discipline* (Washington, DC: U.S. Department of Education, 2014), 3, 12.
4. Wisniewski ex rel. Wisniewski v. Bd. of Educ., 494 F.3d 34, 37 (2d Cir. 2007); "Arresting Development: Addressing the School Discipline Crisis in Florida," report prepared by Florida State Conference NAACP Advancement Project and the NAACP Legal Defense Fund and Educational Fund (2006); "Education on Lockdown: The Schoolhouse to Jailhouse Track," NAACP Advancement Project (2005), 13; Layshock v. Hermitage Sch. Dist., 412 F. Supp. 2d 502, 505 (W.D. Pa. 2006), aff'd in part on rehearing en banc, 650 F.3d 205 (3d Cir 2011), cert. denied sub nom Blue Mtn. Sch. Dist. v. J.S., 132 S. Ct. 1097 (2012).
5. Rebecca W. Cohen, "Reframing the Problem: New Institutionalism and Exclusionary Discipline in Schools," *Journal of Educational Controversy* 7 (2013), www.wce.wwu.edu (accessed 6/6/14); Catherine Y. Kim et al., *The School-to-Prison Pipeline: Structuring Legal Reform* (New York: New York University Press, 2010).

6. U.S. Department of Education, *Guiding Principles,* i; Jason P. Nance, "Student Security and Race," *Emory Law Journal* 63, no. 1 (2013).

7. "Keeping Kids in School and Out of Court: Report and Recommendations," *New York City School–Justice Partnership Task Force* (May 2013), 2, 4, 10; "Breaking Schools' Rules: A Statewide Study of How School Discipline Relates to Students' Success and Juvenile Justice Involvement," *Council of State Governments Justice Center* (2011); Layshock v. Hermitage Sch. Dist., 412 F. Supp. 2d 502 (W.D. Pa. 2006) (alternative placement with disturbed, disruptive students).

8. U.S. Department of Education, *Guiding Principles,* iii, 11. Responding to similar concerns about the high numbers of students referred to courts for minor infractions of school codes, in 2013 the State of Texas stripped police officers posted at public schools of the power to charge students with a Class C misdemeanor for offenses including disorderly language. Jody Serrano, "School Officers Can No Longer Issue On-Campus Citations," *The Texas Tribune,* August 29, 2013, http://www.texastribune.org/2013/08/29/class-disruption-cases-head-principals-office-not-/ (accessed 3/14/15).

9. Chongmin Na and Denise Gottfredson, "Police Officers in Schools: Effects on School Crime and the Processing of Offending Behaviors," *Justice Quarterly* (October 3, 2011).

10. In re Amir X. S., 639 S.E. 2d 144, 147–148, 150 (S.C. 2006), cert. denied, 551 U.S. 1132 (2007).

11. Shoemaker v. State, 38 S.W.3d 350 (Ark. 2001).

12. Ibid.; "Arresting Development," 31, 39, 43.

13. Bethel Sch. Dist. v. Fraser, 478 U.S. 675, 678, 685 (1986).

14. Saxe v. State College Area Sch. Dist., 240 F.3d 200, 213 (3d Cir. 2001) (Alito, J.); see Wildman v. Marshalltown Sch. Dist., 249 F.3d 768, 771 (8th Cir. 2001); Doe v. Perry Cmty. Sch. Dist., 316 F. Supp. 2d 809, 838 (S.D. Iowa 2004).

15. Muller v. Jefferson Lighthouse Sch., 98 F.3d 1530, 1540 (7th Cir. 1996), cert. denied, 520 U.S. 1156 (1997); Bethel v. Fraser, 478 U.S. at 681.

16. Cohen v. California, 403 U.S. 15, 21, 24–26 (1971). "Indecency doctrine" allows the Federal Communications Commission (FCC) to regulate indecency on broadcast media that hold public licenses to the airways. It offers the only narrow exception to the principle that the Constitution protects indecent speech —at least outside of schools. The FCC and the Supreme Court premise this exception primarily on the need to protect small children from exposure to indecent language such as the "seven words" you can never say on [broadcast] television. FCC v. Pacifica Foundation, 438 U.S. 726, 751–752 (1978) (Appendix) (Transcript of George Carlin's "Filthy Words").

17. Thomas v. Bd. of Educ., Granville Cent. Sch. Dist., 607 F.2d 1043, 1057 (2d Cir. 1979) (Newman, J., concurring) cert. denied, 444 U.S. 1081 (1980) (quoted in, among other places, Bethel v. Fraser, 478 U.S. at 682–683).

18. Posthumus v. Bd. of Educ., 380 F. Supp. 2d 891 (W.D. Mich. 2005); Smith v. Mount Pleasant Pub. Sch., 285 F. Supp. 2d 987, 989 (E.D. Mich. 2003).
19. Tinker v. Des Moines, 393 U.S. at 506; Hazelwood Sch. Dist. v. Kuhlmeier, 484 U.S. at 281 (Brennan, J., dissenting).
20. Poling v. Murphy, 872 F.2d 757, 761 (6th Cir. 1989), cert. denied, 493 U.S. 1091 (1990).
21. Henerey v. St. Charles, 200 F.3d 1128, 1136–1137 (Wolle, J., dissenting); Carey v. Population Servs. Int'l., 431 U.S. 678 (1977); Henerey, 200 F.3d at 1133.
22. Phillips v. Oxford Separate Mun. Sch. Dist., 314 F. Supp. 2d 643, 648 (N.D. Miss. 2003). See also Posthumus v. Bd. of Educ., 380 F. Supp. 2d at 901; Henerey v. St. Charles, 200 F.3d at 1133; Poling v. Murphy, 872 F.2d at 761.
23. Poling v. Murphy, 872 F.3d at 759–761. See also Doninger v. Niehoff, 527 F.3d 41, 46 (2d Cir. 2008).
24. Poling v. Murphy, 872 F.3d at 761, 766.
25. Ibid., 765–766 (Merritt, J., dissenting).
26. Cohen v. California, 403 U.S. 15, 27 (1971) (Blackmun, J., dissenting).
27. Poling v. Murphy, 872 F.2d at 758; Morse v. Frederick, 551 U.S. at 435 (Stevens, J., dissenting).
28. Kicklighter v. Evans Cnty. Sch. Dist., 968 F. Supp. 712 (S.D. Ga. 1997).
29. Ibid., 712, 714, 714 n. 2.
30. Ibid., 714–715.
31. Ibid.; "Arresting Development," 10, 44, 48, 50; "Education on Lockdown," 23–25.
32. Kicklighter v. Evans Cnty. Sch. Dist., 968 F. Supp. at 718.
33. Wooley v. Maynard, 430 U.S. 705, 714 (1977) (quoting West Virginia State Bd. of Educ. v. Barnette, 319 U.S. 624, 637 (1943)).
34. Paul Levinson, "The Flouting of the First Amendment," paullevinson .blogspot.com (accessed 5/26/09).
35. Sullivan v. Houston Indep. Sch. Dist., 333 F. Supp. 1149, 1163 n.16 (S.D. Tex. 1971), rev'd, 475 F.2d 1071 (5th Cir. 1973).
36. Ibid., 333 F. Supp. 1149.
37. Posthumus v. Bd. of Educ., 380 F. Supp. 2d at 895, 902.
38. Peter Jamieson, "ACLU Defends Student Who Called Teacher 'Douche Bag' on Facebook," blogs.sfweekly.com (accessed 11/8/11); Andy Thibault, "Defense Crumbles as Students Weather Cross-Examination," ctnewsjunkie.com (accessed 8/23/07). Expert testimony on *fuck* was offered in Sullivan v. Houston Indep. Sch. Dist., 333 F. Supp. at 1165.
39. Bethel Sch. Dist. v. Fraser, 478 U.S. at 689 n. 2 (Brennan, J., concurring). Edward Wyatt, "More than Ever, You Can Say That on Television," *New York Times*, November 14, 2009, A-1.
40. Wildman v. Marshalltown Sch. Dist., 249 F.3d 768, 770–771 (8th Cir. 2001).
41. Pinard v. Clatskanie Sch. Dist. 6J, 467 F.3d 755, 760 (9th Cir. 2006).
42. Ibid., 760.

43. Ibid., 763.
44. Acevedo v. Sklarz, 553 F. Supp. 2d 164, 170 (D. Conn. 2008); Posthumus v. Bd. of Educ., 380 F. Supp, 2d at 902.
45. O'Brien v. United States, 391 U.S. 367 (1968); Texas v. Johnson. 491 U.S. 397 (1989). Eugene Volokh, "Speech as Conduct: Generally Applicable Laws, Illegal Courses of Conduct, 'Situation-Altering Utterances,' and the Uncharted Zones," *Cornell Law Review* 90 (2005): 1277, 1339 n. 317.
46. Lowery v. Euverard, 497 F.3d 584, 588 (6th Cir. 2007), cert. denied, 555 U.S. 825 (2008).
47. Volokh, "Speech as Conduct," 1284; Kent Greenawalt, *Speech, Crime, and the Uses of Language* (New York: Oxford University Press, 1989).
48. Anderson v. Milbank Sch. Dist. 25–4, 197 F.R.D. 682 (D. S.D. 2000); Fed. R. Evid. 803(2).
49. FCC v. Fox Television Stations, 556 U.S. 502, 543–544 (2009) (Stevens, J., dissenting).
50. Paye v. Gibraltar Sch. Dist., No. 90CV7044DT, 1991 U.S. Dist. LEXIS 16480 at *4 (E.D. Mich. 1991).
51. Keyishian v. Bd. of Regents, 385 U.S. 589, 603 (1967); Evans-Marshall v. Bd. of Educ., 428 F.3d 223, 229 (6th Cir. 2005); Evans-Marshall v. Bd. of Educ., 428 F.3d at 235 (Sutton, J., concurring); Pickering v. Bd. of Educ., 391 U.S. 563 (1968); Karen C. Daly, "Balancing Act: Teachers' Classroom Speech and the First Amendment," *Journal of Law & Education* 30 (2001): 1; Kramer v. New York City Bd. of Educ., 715 F. Supp. 2d 335 (E.D.N.Y. 2010); Garcetti v. Ceballos, 547 U.S. 410, 421 (2006).
    Circuits that routinely apply *Hazelwood* to teachers' classroom speech include the First, Second, Seventh, Eighth, Tenth, and Eleventh.
    A minority of circuit courts apply the Supreme Court's more restrictive standard for analyzing official speech of public employees, reasoning that "teachers do not speak on matters of public concern when they follow a school-mandated curriculum." Kramer v. Bd. of Educ., 715 F. Supp. 2d at 354.
52. Lacks v. Ferguson Reorganized Sch. Dist. R-2, 936 F. Supp. 676, 678 (E.D. Mo. 1996), rev'd, 154 F.3d 904 (8th Cir. 1998), cert. denied, 526 U.S. 1012 (1999); Kramer v. New York City Bd. of Educ., 715 F. Supp. 2d at 343–345.
53. Lacks v. Ferguson, 936 F. Supp. 2d 676.
54. www.cissylacks.com (accessed 6/26/14).
55. Lacks v. Ferguson, 154 F.3d at 908–910 (McMillian, J., dissenting from denial of rehearing en banc).
56. Ibid., 909–911.
57. Ibid., 147 F.3d at 721–722 (8th Cir. 1998) (Arnold, J.).
58. Hosford v. Sch. Comm. of Sandwich, 659 N.E.2d 1178 (Mass. 1996).
59. Ibid., 1179–1180, 1183.
60. Ibid., 1179–1180, 1182–1183; Tinker v. Des Moines, 393 U.S. at 506.
61. Miller v. California, 413 U.S. 15, 23 (1973). Bd. of Educ., Island Trees Union Free Sch. Dist. No. 26 v. Pico, 457 U.S. 853 (1982).

62. Kramer v. New York City Bd. of Educ., 715 F. Supp. 2d at 364; Hosford v. Sch. Comm. of Sandwich, 659 N.E.2d at 715; Trachtman v. Anker, 563 F.2d 512, 517–519 (2d Cir. 1977).

63. Behymer-Smith v. Coral Acad. of Science, 427 F. Supp. 2d 969, 971 (D. Nev. 2006).

64. Ibid., 972.

65. Bethel v. Fraser, 478 U.S. at 68. Hazelwood v. Kuhlmeier, 484 U.S. at 267.

66. Compare Henerey v. St. Charles, Sch. Dist., 200 F.3d 1128, 1132 (8th Cir. 1999); Hosford v. Sch. Comm. of Sandwich, 659 N.E.2d at 1181; Muller v. Jefferson Lighthouse Sch., 98 F.3d at 1536; and Nuxoll v. Indian Prairie Sch. Dist. No. 204, 523 F.3d 668, 672 (7th Cir. 2008) with Boroff v. Van Wert City Bd. of Educ., 220 F.3d 465 (6th Cir. 2000).

67. Posthumus v. Bd. of Educ., 380 F. Supp. 2d at 901.

68. Ibid., 899.

69. Morse v. Frederick, 551 U.S. 393, 425–426 (2007) (Breyer, J., concurring in judgment and dissenting in part).

70. Posthumus v. Bd. of Educ., 380 F. Supp. 2d at 899, 901. See also S.G. v. Sayreville Bd. of Educ., 333 F.3d 417 (3d. Cir. 2003) (applying *Fraser* to the suspension of a kindergarten student for violating a rule against "playing guns" using his fingers and words), cert. denied, 540 U.S. 1104 (2004); Chief Justice Roberts, however, regards the power of schools to consider content under *Fraser* an open question. Frederick v. Morse, 551 U.S. at 404–405.

71. Poling v. Murphy, 872 F.2d at 765 (Merritt, J., dissenting).

72. Anderson v. Milbank Sch. Dist. 25–4, 197 F.R.D. at 684, 687, 689 (citing Henerey v. St. Charles, 200 F.3d at 1135; Poling v. Murphy, 872 F.2d at 762; and other cases that applied *Hazelwood*).

73. Poling v. Murphy, 872 F.2d at 762.

4. School-Sponsored Speech

1. West Virginia State Bd. of Educ. v. Barnette, 319 U.S. 624, 637 (1943).

2. Brief for Petitioner, Morse v. Frederick, 551 U.S. 393 (2007) (06-278) at 24.

3. Hazelwood Sch. Dist. v. Kuhlmeier, 484 U.S. 260, 273 (1988).

4. Morse v. Frederick, 551 U.S. 393, 423 (2007) (Alito, J., concurring).

5. Desilets v. Clearview Reg'l Bd. of Educ., 647 A.2d 150 (N.J. 1994); Hazelwood Sch. Dist. v. Kuhlmeier, 484 U.S. 260, 271 (1988).

6. Hazelwood v. Kuhlmeier, 484 U.S. at 271.

7. Peck v. Baldwinsville Cent. Sch. Dist., 426 F.3d 617, 630 (2d Cir. 2005) (quoting Fleming v. Jefferson Cnty. Sch. Dist. R-1, 298 F.3d 918, 932 (10th Cir. 2002)) (omitting internal quotations and adding emphasis); Hazelwood Sch. Dist. v. Kuhlmeier, 484 U.S. at 271. See Martha McCarthy, "Post-Hazelwood Developments: A Threat to Free Inquiry in Public Schools," *Education Law Reporter* 81 (1993): 685, 691–692.

8. Susan Hodara, "Communities; Irvington Bans V-Word in Play's Ad," *New York Times*, March 3, 2002; Diana Jean Schemo, "In Small Town, 'Grease' Ignites a Culture War," *New York Times*, February 11, 2006.

9. Interview with Wilton High School drama teacher Bonnie Dickinson, Wilton, Connecticut (June 7, 2009).

10. E.g., Boring v. Buncombe Cnty. Bd. of Educ., 136 F.3d 364 (4th Cir. 1998).

11. Island Trees Bd. of Educ. v. Pico, 457 U.S. 853 (1982).

12. Schemo, "In Small Town, 'Grease' Ignites a Culture War."

13. Ibid.

14. Ibid.

15. Ibid.

16. Ibid.

17. Ibid.; Hodara, "Communities; Irvington Bans V-Word."

18. Tinker v. Des Moines Indep. Cmty. Sch. Dist., 393 U.S. 503, 508, 509 (1969); Fleming v. Jefferson Cnty. Sch. Dist. R-1, 298 F.3d 918, 925–926 (10th Cir. 2002) (collecting cases); West Virginia v. Barnette, 319 U.S. at 637.

19. See, e.g., Rachel Smolkin, "Cities without Newspapers," *American Journalism Review* 31 (June–July 2009): 16, 18.

20. "About the Student Press Law Center," www.splc.org (accessed 7/8/09); "Newseum Presents 1st Annual Courage in Student Journalism Awards," www.freedomforum.org (accessed 7/2/09).

21. 42 U.S.C. § 1988 (b)(2012); e.g., Smith v. Novato Unified Sch. Dist., 59 Cal. Rptr. 3d 508, 511 n. 2 (Cal. Ct. App. 2007), cert. denied, 552 U.S. 1184 (2008).

22. Tyler J. Buller, "Subtle Censorship: The Problem of Retaliation against High School Journalism Advisors and Three Ways to Stop It," *Journal of Law and Education* 40 (2011): 609; Scott Kauffman, "WI School Officials Seize Control over Student Paper after 'Rape Culture' Article Appears," March 12, 2014, www.rawstory.com (accessed 3/14/14); Tanvi Kumar, "The Rape Joke: Surviving Rape in a Culture that Won't Let You," *Cardinal Columns*, February 2014, www.cardinalcolumns.org (accessed 3/14/14).

23. Mike Hiestand, "Wooster Decision Clarifies Censorship Guidelines," National Scholastic Press Association, www.splc.org, February 26, 2003 (accessed 3/5/14).

24. Draudt v. Wooster City Sch. Dist. Bd. of Educ., 246 F. Supp. 2d 820 (N.D. Ohio 2003).

25. Transcript of Testimony, Christopher Eckhardt at 14, Tinker v. Des Moines, On Writ of Certiorari to the Eighth Circuit (No. 1034); Jean Strouse, *Up Against the Law: The Legal Rights of People Under 21* (New York: New American Library, 1970), 28–29.

26. E.g., Casey Banas, "Unpublished Story Divides Teens, School Article on Sex Case Sparks Debate," *Chicago Tribune*, October 3, 1997; Mark Goodman, "Student Journalism after Hazelwood," files.asne.org/kiosk /editor/julyaugust/goodman.htm (accessed March 4, 2015); "Newseum

Presents 1st Annual Courage in Student Journalism Awards"; personal communication from former student journalist Joanna Roberts regarding Mamaroneck High School (New York).

27. Mark Goodman, "Hazelwood School District v. Kuhlmeier: A Complete Guide," 2 s3.amazon.aws.com/cdn.getsnetworks.com/spl/pdf/HazelwoodGuide .pdf (accessed March 4, 2015). Heistand, "Wooster Decision Clarifies Censorship Guidelines."

28. Desilets v. Clearview Regional Bd. of Ed., 647 A.2d 150 (N.J. 1994), aff'g 630 A.2d 333 (N.J. Super. App. Div. 1993).

29. Ibid., 630 A.2d at 340, 338; 647 A.2d at 154.

30. Dean v. Utica Cmty. Sch., 345 F. Supp. 2d 799 (E.D. Mi. 2004). The plaintiff in the lawsuit over the diesel exhaust died in 2002, and the school district settled with the family for an undisclosed amount.

31. Ibid., 803.

32. Ibid.; David L. Hudson, Jr., *Let the Students Speak! A History of the Fight for Free Expression in American Schools* (Boston: Beacon Press: 2011), 103.

33. Dean v. Utica Cmty. Sch., 345 F. Supp. 2d at 801–804.

34. Ibid., 813.

35. Ibid., 800, 804, 808 (quoting Harry S. Truman, Special Message to the Congress on the Internal Security of the United States, August 8, 1950).

36. The states include Arkansas, California, Colorado, Iowa, Kansas, Massachusetts, Oregon, Pennsylvania, and Washington. www.splc.org (accessed 6/12/14). Cal. Educ. Code § 48907 (1983) (West 2011).

37. "Students Censored, but Issue Lives On," *New York Times,* September 7, 1997; "School Newspaper in Illinois Revives Debate over Censorship," *New York Times,* September 28, 1997.

38. Ibid.; Rick Pearson, "Edgar Vetoes Student Newspaper Bill," *Chicago Tribune,* August 11, 1997.

39. Cal. Educ. Code § 48907 (quoted and discussed in Smith v. Novato Unified Sch. Dist., 59 Cal. Rptr. 3d 508, 515–516 (Cal. Ct. App. 2007).

40. Lopez v. Tulare Joint Union High Sch. Dist., 40 Cal. Rptr. 2d 762, 767–768 (Cal. Ct. App. 1995).

41. Lopez v. Tulare, 40 Cal. Rptr. 2d at 770. (emphasis in original), quoted in Smith v. Novato Unified Sch. Dist., 59 Cal. Rptr. 3d at 516.

42. Madeline Halpert and Eva Rosenfeld, "Depressed, but Not Ashamed," *New York Times,* May 22, 2014, A29.

43. Ibid.

44. Hazelwood v. Kuhlmeier, 484 U.S. at 280 (Brennan, J., dissenting) (quoting Tinker v. Des Moines, 393 U.S. at 511).

45. Ibid., 484 U.S. at 271.

46. McCarthy, "Post-Hazelwood Developments," 685, 685.

47. Meyer v. Nebraska, 262 U.S. 390, 402 (1923). See Johanns v. Livestock Mktg. Ass'n, 544 U.S. 550, 553 (2005); Rosenberger v. Rector and Visitors of Univ. of Va., 515 U.S. 819, 833 (1995). The Eleventh Circuit has held that the law governing school-sponsored speech applies to curricular decisions as

well as student speech. The court sustained a school board's decision that an English textbook was "immoral" because it included excerpts from Aristophanes's *Lysistrata* and Chaucer's *The Miller's Tale* as a legitimate pedagogical decision. Virgil v. School Bd. of Columbia Cnty., Fla., 862 F.2d 1517 (11th Cir. 1989).

48. Diane Ravitch, *The Language Police: How Pressure Groups Restrict What Students Learn* (New York: Vintage Books, 2004), 141.

49. Griswold v. Driscoll, 625 F. Supp. 2d 49 (D. Mass. 2009).

50. Legal Services Corp. v. Velazquez, 531 U.S. 533, 541–542 (2001) (quoting Bd. of Regents v. Southworth, 529 U.S. 217, 235 (2000)).

51. Tinker v. Des Moines, 393 U.S. at 506; Garcetti v. Caballos, 547 US 410, 425 (2006).

52. Kirkland v. Northside Indep. Sch. Dist., 890 F.2d 794, 795–796 (5th Cir. 1989); Mayer v. Monroe Cnty. Cmty. Sch. Corp., 474 F.3d 477, 478 (7th Cir. 2007); Miles v. Denver Pub. Sch., 944 F.2d 773, 774 (10th Cir. 1991); Lee v. York Cnty. Sch. Div., 484 F.3d 687 (4th Cir. 2007); Weingarten v. Board of Educ. of City Sch. Dist. of City of New York, 680 F. Supp. 2d 595 (S.D.N.Y. 2010).

53. Ward v. Hickey, 996 F.2d 448, 452 (1st Cir. 1993); Edwards v. Aguillard, 482 U.S. 578 (1987); Epperson v. Arkansas, 393 U.S. 97 (1968); Kitzmiller v. Dover Area Sch. Dist., 400 F. Supp. 2d 707 (M.D. Pa. 2005); Edward Humes, *Monkey Girl: Evolution, Education, Religion and the Battle for America's Soul* (New York: ecco Books, 2007), 53–56; Peloza v. Capistrano Unified Sch. Dist., 37 F.3d 517, 522 (9th Cir. 1994).

54. Bd. of Educ. of Jefferson Cnty. Sch. Dist. R-1 v. Wilder, 960 P. 2d 695, 717 (Colo. App. 1996) (en banc) (Hobbs, J., dissenting). See also Karen C. Daly, "Balancing Act: Teachers' Classroom Speech and the First Amendment," *Journal of Law and Education* 30 (2001): 1.

55. Mayer v. Monroe Cnty. Cmty. Sch. Corp., 474 F.3d 477 (7th Cir. 2007).

56. Ibid., 478; Amy Goodman and David Goodman, *Standing Up to the Madness: Ordinary Heroes in Extraordinary Times* (New York: Hyperion, 2008), 154.

57. Mayer v. Monroe Cnty. Cmnty. Sch. Corp., No. 1:04-CV-1695-SEB-VSS, 2006 WL 693555, at *12, *2 (S.D. Ind. 2006), aff'd, 474 F.3d 477 (7th Cir. 2007).

58. Mayer v. Monroe Cnty. Cmty. Sch. Corp., 2006 WL 693555, at *2, 3; interview with child development expert David Moshman, professor of educational psychology, University of Nebraska–Lincoln, June 13, 2013.

59. Mayer v. Monroe Cnty. Cmty. Sch. Corp., 474 F.3d at 479 (Easterbook, J.); Garcetti v. Caballos, 547 US 410 (2006); Connick v. Myers, 461 U.S. 138 (1983); Pickering v. Bd. of Educ., 391 U.S. 563 (1968); Kirkland v. Northside Indep. Sch. Dist., 890 F.2d 794, 797–800 (5th Cir. 1989); Evans-Marshall v. Bd. of Educ. of the Tipp City Exempted Village Sch. Dist., 624 F.3d 332, 337–344 (6th Cir. 2010); Cockrel v. Shelby Cnty. Sch. Dist., 270 F.3d 1036 (6th Cir. 2001).

60. Mayer v. Monroe Cnty. Cmty. Sch. Corp., 474 F.3d at 479–480.

61. Lee v. York Cnty. Sch. Div., 484 F.3d 687, 695 (4th Cir. 2007); Daly, "Balancing Act," 26 n. 135 (citing Kirkland, 890 F.2d at 801; Boring, 136 F.3d at 370–371).
62. Tinker v. Des Moines, 393 U.S. at 511.
63. Ibid., 512, 513 (emphasis added).
64. Frederick v. Morse, 551 U.S. 393, 445, 448, 447 (2007) (Stevens, J., dissenting) (quoting Tinker v. Des Moines, 393 U.S. at 508–509).
65. Hazelwood Sch. Dist. v. Kuhlmeier, 484 U.S. at 279–280 (Brennan, J., dissenting) (quoting West Virginia State Bd. of Educ. v. Barnette, 319 U.S. at 637).
66. Frederick v. Morse, 551 U.S. at 428 (Breyer, J., concurring in part and dissenting in part).
67. Settle v. Dickson Cnty. Sch. Bd., 53 F.3d 152, 158 (6th Cir. 1995) (Batchelder, J., concurring).
68. DeNooyer v. Livonia Pub. Sch., 799 F. Supp. 744, 751 (E.D. Mich. 1992) (citing Duran v. Nitsche, 780 F. Supp. 1048, 1054 n. 8 (E.D. Pa. 1991)); Hazelwood Sch. Dist. v. Kuhlmeier, 484 U.S. at 271; ibid., 283 (Brennan, J., dissenting).
69. Interview with David Moshman, June 13, 2013. See Denooyer v. Livonia Pub. Sch., 12 F.3d 211, at *2 (6th Cir. 1993) (unpub.), cert. denied, 511 U.S. 1031 (1994).
70. When schools display or publicize student curricular work, they may change the status of the speech in the Court's taxonomy. But this is the exception rather than the rule. For example, schools periodically post artwork or essays prominently where other students and members of the community can see them. The student's product might appear to be "school sponsored" even if every student in the class is represented in the display. A prominent disclaimer explaining that the views are the student's own would prevent misattribution, but the law doesn't require schools to take that step. Denooyer v. Livonia Pub. Sch., 12 F.3d 211, at *3. See Fleming v. Jefferson Cnty. Sch. Dist R-1, 298 F.3d 918 (10th Cir. 2002); Bannon v. Sch. Dist. of Palm Beach Cnty., 387 F.3d 1208, 1214 (11th Cir. 2004).
71. DeNooyer v. Livonia Pub. Sch., 12 F.3d 211, at *3.
72. Peck v. Baldwinsville Cent. Sch. Dist., 426 F.3d 617 (2d Cir. 2005); O.T. v. Frenchtown Elementary Sch. Dist. Bd. of Educ., 465 F. Supp. 2d 369 (D. N.J. 2006); DeNooyer v. Livonia Pub. Sch., 12 F.3d 211; Duran v. Nitsche, 780 F. Supp. 1048, 1050 (E.D. Pa. 1991), order vacated, appeal dismissed, 972 F.2d 1331 (3d Cir. 1992).
73. Martin H. Redish and Kevin Finnerty, "What Did You Learn in School Today? Free Speech, Values Inculcation, and the Democratic-Educational Paradox," *Cornell Law Review* 88 (2002): 62, 78–79, 80.
74. Hazelwood v. Kuhlmeier, 484 U.S. at 286–287, 288 (Brennan J., dissenting).
75. Frederick v. Morse, 551 U.S. at 437 (Stevens, J., dissenting).
76. C.H. v. Oliva, 226 F.3d 198, 210 n. 4 (3d Cir. 2000) (Alito, J., dissenting). Justice Alito observed that the Supreme Court had vacillated between

treating viewpoint discrimination as unconstitutional per se wherever it occurs and (more recently) suggesting that viewpoint discrimination may be upheld if it survives strict scrutiny.

77. C.H. v. Oliva, 226 F.3d at 210 (citing Lamb's Chapel v. Ctr. Moriches Union Free Sch. Dist., 508 U.S. 384, 394–395 (1993)).

78. Alison Leigh Cowan, "Play about Iraq War Divides a Connecticut School," *New York Times,* March 24, 2007, B1.

79. C.H. v. Oliva, 226 F.3d 198 (3d Cir. 2000) (reh'g en banc).

80. Geoffrey Stone, "Free Speech in the Twenty-first Century: Ten Lessons from the Twentieth Century," *Pepperdine Law Review* 36 (2009): 273, 285; Bryan R. Warnick, *Understanding Student Rights in Schools: Speech, Religion, and Privacy in Educational Settings* (New York: Teachers College Press, 2013), 17–22; Robert Post, "Between Governance and Management: The History and Theory of the Public Forum," *UCLA Law Review* 34 (1987): 1713,1809.

81. Schall v. Martin, 467 U.S. 253, 265 (1984).

82. Warnick, *Understanding Student Rights in Schools*, 84–87.

83. See Bannon v. Sch. Dist. of Palm Beach Cnty., 387 F.3d 1208, 1215, 1215 n. 4 (citing Searcey v. Harris, 888 F.2d 1314, 1315, 1325 (11th Cir. 1989)). Three circuits have expressly held that *Hazelwood* does not absolve schools of the obligation to maintain viewpoint neutrality. See Morgan v. Swanson, 659 F.3d 359, 379 n. 82 (5th Cir. 2011) (summarizing split).

84. Peck v. Baldwinsville Cent. Sch. Dist., 426 F.3d 617, 633 (2d Cir. 2005) (original emphasis).

85. Bd. of Educ., Island Trees Union Free Sch. Dist. No. 26 v. Pico, 457 U.S. 853, 857, 870–874, 880 (1982) (plurality op.).

86. Dean v. Utica Cmty. Sch., 345 F. Supp. 2d at 804.

5. Unsettled Waters

1. Griggs v. Fort Wayne Sch. Bd., 359 F. Supp. 2d 731 (N.D. Ind. 2005).

2. Guiles v. Marineau, 461 F.3d 320 (2d Cir. 2006).

3. Griggs v. Fort Wayne, 359 F. Supp. 2d 731; Guiles v. Marineau, 461 F.3d 320.

4. Holloman v. Harland, 370 F.3d 1252 (11th Cir. 2004); Gregory L. Peterson et al., "Recollections of West Virginia State Board of Education v. Barnette," *Saint John's Law Review* 81 (2007): 755, 792.

5. Tamar Lewin, "High School Tells Student to Remove Antiwar Shirt," *New York Times*, February 26, 2003, A12.

6. Morse v. Frederick, 551 U.S. 393, 430 (2007) (Breyer, J., concurring in judgment and dissenting in part).

7. Texas v. Johnson, 491 U.S. 397, 403 (1989); Spence v. Washington, 418 U.S. 405, 408 (1974); Ward v. Rock Against Racism, 491 U.S. 781 (1989). West Virginia State Bd. of Educ. v. Barnette, 319 U.S. 624, 633 (1943) (citing Stromberg v. California, 283 U.S. 359 (1931)); Tinker v. Des Moines Indep. Cmty. Sch. Dist., 393 U.S. 503, 505 (1969).

8. Spence v. Washington, 418 U.S. at 410; Texas v. Johnson, 491 U.S. at 404.

9. Brandt v. Bd. of Educ. of Chi., 420 F. Supp. 2d 921 (N.D. Ill. 2006).

10. Tinker v. Des Moines, 393 U.S. at 507–508.

11. Jo B. Paoletti, *Sex and Unisex: Fashion, Feminism and the Sexual Revolution* (Bloomington, IN: University of Indiana Press, 2015), 129.

12. Dempsey v. Alston, 966 A.2d 1 (N.J. Super. Ct. App. Div. 2009); Bar-Navon ex rel. Bar Navon v. Brevard Cnty. Sch. Bd., No. 07–15639, 2008 WL 3822612 (11th Cir. Aug. 15, 2008); Bear v. Fleming, 714 F. Supp. 2d 972 (D. So. Dak. 2010); Isaacs v. Bd. of Educ. of Howard Cnty., 40 F. Supp. 2d 335 (D. Md. 1999).

13. Spence v. Washington, 418 U.S. 405; Texas v. Johnson, 491 U.S. 397; Doe ex rel. Doe v. Yunits, No. 001060A, 2000 WL 33162199 (Mass. Super. Oct. 11, 2000); Zalewska v. Cnty. of Sullivan, N.Y., 316 F.3d 314 (2d Cir. 2003).

14. Bear v. Fleming, 714 F. Supp. 2d 972 (D. So. Dak. 2010); Betenbaugh ex rel. A.A. v. Needville Indep. Sch. Dist., 701 F. Supp. 2d 863 (S.D. Tex. 2009); Defoe v. Spiva, 625 F.3d 324 (6th Cir. 2010).

15. United States v. O'Brien, 391 U.S. 367, 377 (1968); Spence v. Washington, 418 U.S. 405. See, for example, Chalifoux v. New Casey Indep. Sch. Dist, 976 F. Supp. 659, 665–666 (S.D. Tex. 1997); John Hart Ely, "Flag Desecration: A Case Study in the Roles of Categorization and Balancing in First Amendment Analysis," *Harvard Law Review* 88 (1975): 1482.

16. Simone Robers et al., *Indicators of School Crime and Safety: 2012* (Washington, DC: U.S. Department of Education, Bureau of Justice Statistics, 2013) (NCES 2013–2036), viii.

17. "Don't Shake Down Kids over 'Harlem Shake,'" www.ncac.org (accessed 12/23/13); Nick Abrams, "Mitch McConnell's Team Makes Harlem Shake Video," *Huffington Post,* March 6, 2013; Charlene Gubash, "How the Harlem Shake Is Being Used to Push for Change in Egypt," *NBC News,* March 1, 2013.

18. Nguon v. Wolf, 517 F. Supp. 2d 1177 (C.D. Cal. 2007).

19. See, e.g., Saxe v. State Coll. Area Sch. Dist., 240 F.3d 200 (3d Cir. 2001); Requa v. Kent Sch. Dist., 492 F. Supp. 2d 1272, 1280 (W.D. Wa. 2007); C.H. v. Bridgeton Bd. of Educ., No. 09–5815, 2010 WL 1644612 (D. N.J. Apr. 22, 2010); Porter v. Ascension Parish Sch. Bd., 393 F.3d 608 (5th Cir. 2004); Hazelwood Sch. Dist. v. Kuhlmeier, 484 U.S. at 281 (Brennan, J., dissenting).

20. C.H. v. Bridgeton, 2010 WL 1644612, at *6; Barr v. Lafon, 538 F.3d 554, 564 (6th Cir. 2008), cert denied, 538 U.S. 817 (2009) (citing Guiles v. Marineau, 461 F.3d at 325); Harper v. Poway Unified Sch. Dist., 445 F.3d 1166, 1176–1177 (9th Cir. 2006), vacated on other grounds, 548 U.S. 1262 (2007).

21. K.A. v. Pocono Mountain Sch. Dist, 2012 Westlaw 715304 (M.D. Pa. 2012) *2, aff'd 710 F.3d 99, 105 (3d Cir. 2013).

22. Guiles v. Marineau, 461 F.3d at 326 ; Ponce v. Socorro Indep. Sch. Dist., 508 F.3d at 772 (citing Schenck v. United States, 249 U.S. 47, 52 (1919),

quoting *Morse*, 127 U.S. at 425 (Alito, J., concurring) (reversing district
court ruling based on *Tinker*)); Boim v. Fulton Cnty. Sch. Dist., 494 F.3d at
984, discussing school shootings at length and suggesting that *Morse*
instructs deference to school administrators. Johnson v. New Brighton Area
Sch. Dist., No. 06–1672, 2008 WL 4204718 (W.D. Pa. 2008) (*Morse* allows
a school to punish a student's use of the word *Columbine* to protect other students from harm—applying an amalgam of *Tinker, Watts, Morse,* and
"fighting words" cases).

23. Guiles v. Marineau, 461 F.3d at 330.
24. Erwin Chemerinsky, "Students Do Leave Their First Amendment Rights at
the Schoolhouse Gates: What's Left of *Tinker?,*" *Drake Law Review* 48
(2000): 527, 546; See M.A.L. v. Kinsland, 543 F.3d 841 (6th Cir. 2008);
Palmer v. Waxahachie Indep. Sch. Dist., 579 F.3d 502, 509 (5th Cir. 2009),
cert. denied, 130 S. Ct. 1055 (2010); Bar-Navon v. Brevard Cnty. Sch. Bd.,
290 Fed. Appx. 273, 277 (11th Cir. 2008); Jacobs v. Clark Cnty. Sch. Dist.,
526 F.3d 419, 431–432 (9th Cir. 2008); Castorina v. Madison Cnty. Sch.
Bd., 246 F.3d 536, 548 (6th Cir. 2001).
25. Bd. of Airport Comm'rs of City of Los Angeles v. Jews for Jesus, 482 U.S.
569, 574, 571, 576–577 (1987).
26. "No. 21-Tinker" n.7 (undated draft), Abe Fortas Papers, Yale University
Manuscripts and Archives, Box 79, Folder 1667.
27. Morse v. Frederick, 551 U.S. at 405, 406. Compare Defoe v. Spiva, 625 F.3d
324, 332 (6th Cir. 2010) (*Morse* does not alter *Tinker*'s applicability) with
Defoe v. Spiva, 625 F.3d at 339–340 (Rogers, J., concurring) (*Morse* supports
barring speech where the state has a compelling interest even in the absence
of a threat of disruption; here, barring racial intolerance is "reasonable").
28. Boroff v. Van Wert City Bd. of Educ., 220 F.3d 465, 470 (6th Cir. 2000)
(citing Hazelwood v. Kuhlmeier, 484 U.S. at 266); Defoe v. Spiva, 625 F.3d
at 342 (Rogers, J., concurring).
29. Lowry v. Watson Chapel Sch. Dist., 540 F.3d 752, 760, 765 (8th Cir. 2008),
cert. denied, 555 U.S. 1212 (2009). "ACLU Victorious in Texas Black
Armband Case," www.aclu.org (accessed 12/20/13). The Sixth Circuit has
applied a standard higher than *Hazelwood* but less stringent than *Tinker* to
school dress codes, Castorina v. Madison Cnty. Sch. Bd., 246 F.3d 536, 548
(6th Cir. 2001), while the Eighth Circuit has required schools to show an
anticipation of substantial disruption. B.W.A. v. Farmington R-7 Sch. Dist.,
554 F.3d 734, 739–741(8th Cir. 2009). See also Barr v. Lafon, 553 F.3d 463,
465 (6th Cir. 2009) (Boggs, J., dissenting from denial of rehearing en banc).
30. Laura Hibbard, "'All the Cool Girls Are Lesbians' T-shirt Sparks
Controversy at Massachusetts School," *Huffington Post,* March 13, 2012.
31. M. Alex Johnson, "'Lesbians Are Cool' T-shirt Puts Massachusetts School
in National Spotlight," *NBCNews.com* (accessed 8/3/13); Seth Grody,
"Connecticut Teen Has Anti-Gay T-shirt Approved by High School,"
www.huffingtonpost.com, February 26, 2013.
32. "Let Students Wear Their Speech," *Des Moines Register,* May 2, 2005, A10.

33. Doninger v. Niehoff, 642 F.3d 334 (2d Cir. 2011) (granting qualified immunity).
34. Defoe v. Spiva, 650 F. Supp. 2d 811 (E.D. Tenn. 2009); Lowry v. Watson Chapel Sch. Dist., No. 5:06CV00262, 2007 WL 3002073 (E.D. Ark. 2007).
35. Terminiello v. Chicago, 337 U.S. 1, 37 (1949) (Jackson, J., dissenting).
36. Virginia v. Black, 538 U.S. 343, 359 (2003) (citing Watts v. United States, 394 U.S. 705, 708 (1969)) (per curiam).
37. In re Douglas D., 626 N.W.2d 725, 739 (Wis. 2001); Virginia v. Black, 538 U.S. at 343.
38. Watts v. United States, 394 U.S. 705 (1969).
39. United States v. Dinwiddie, 76 F.3d 913, 925 (8th Cir. 1996) (Arnold, J.); United States v. Bagdasarian, 652 F.3d 1113, 1123 (9th Cir. 2011) (quoting United States v. Sutcliffe, 505 F.3d 944, 951–952 (9th Cir. 2007). See Doe v. Pulaski, 306 F.3d at 627–629 (describing cases that satisfy the true threats standard).
40. Andrews v. State, 930 A.2d 846, 854 n. 30 (Del. 2007).
41. Elonis v. United States, 575 U.S. __, No. 13–983, slip op. at 15 (U.S. June 1, 2015) (Roberts, C. J.) (federal criminal liability is premised on the defendant having the requisite mental state); Virginia v. Black, 394 U.S. at 360. The Elonis opinion clarified for the nine circuits that had held otherwise that true threat doctrine requires subjective intent. The majority opinion did not address Elonis's free speech claims or the government's argument that recklessness suffices to find criminal liability under the applicable federal statute.
42. See In re A.S. v. A.S., 626 N.W.2d 712 (Wis. 2001); People ex rel. C.C.H., 651 N.W.2d 702 (S.D. 2002); Cox v. Warwick Valley Sch. Dist., 654 F.3d 267 (2d Cir. 2011) (Jacobs, C. J.).
43. Yanosky v. St. Tammany Parish Sch. Bd., No. 08–5047, 2010 WL 1254586 (E.D. LA 2010); Brandenberg v. Ohio, 395 U.S. 444 (1969) (per curiam); Cox v. Warwick Valley Central Sch. Dist., 654 F.2d 267 (2d Cir. 2011).
44. D.J.M[ardis] v Hannibal Pub. Sch. Dist. #60, 647 F.3d 754 (8th Cir. 2011).
45. Ibid.; Lovell v. Poway Unified Sch. Dist., 90 F.3d 367, 369 (9th Cir. 1996); Jones v. State, 64 S.W.3d 728, 733–734 (Ark. 2002).
46. The standards of proof and procedural protections vary greatly as do the penalties a school or the state's delinquency or criminal law apparatus may impose. See Diane Heckman, "Just Kidding: K–12 Students, Threats and First Amendment Freedom of Speech Protection," *West's Education Law Reporter* 259 (2010): 381, 404–407; Mardis v. Hannibal Pub. Sch. Dist., 684 F. Supp. 2d at 1115–1116.
47. Porter v. Ascension Public Sch. Dist., 393 F.3d 608, 617 (5th Cir. 2004), cert. denied, 393 F.3d 609 (2005); Wisniewski v. Bd. of Educ. of Weedsport Cent. Sch. Dist., 494 F.3d 34, 36 (2d Cir. 2007) (police concluded it was a "joke"); Doe v. Pulaski, 306 F.3d at 634 (Arnold, J., dissenting); Doe v. Pulaski, 306 F.3d at 636 (McMillian, J., dissenting).
48. Mardis v. Hannibal Pub. Sch. Dist., 684 F. Supp. at 1122–1124; Wisniewski v. Bd. of Educ., 494 F.3d at 34, 36; LaVine v. Blaine Sch. Dist., 257 F.3d 981 (9th Cir. 2001); Wisniewski v. Bd. of Educ., 494 F.3d 34.
49. Neal v. Efurd, Civ. No. 04–2195 (W.D. Ark. Feb. 18, 2005) (unpublished).

50. Cuff v. Valley Cent. Sch. Dist., 559 F. Supp. 2d 415, 422 (S.D.N.Y. 2008); LaVine v. Blaine Sch. Dist., 257 F.3d 981; Wisniewski v. Bd. of Educ., 494 F.3d 34; Ponce v. Socorro Indep. Sch. Dist., 432 F. Supp. 2d 682; Boim v. Fulton Cnty. Sch. Dist., 494 F.3d 978; Boman v. Bluestem Unified Sch. Dist. No. 205, No. 1034, 2000 WL 433083 at *2 (D. Kan. 2000).
51. Roberts v. State, 78 S.W.3d 743, 746 (Ark. Ct. App. Div. IV 2002).
52. Porter v. Ascension Parish Sch. Bd., 393 F.3d 609, 618, n.33, 619–620 (5th Cir. 2004) (granting qualified immunity), cert denied, 393 F.3d 609 (2005).
53. Boman v. Bluestem Unified Sch. Dist., 2000 WL 297167 (D. Kan. 2000); Sarah Boman,'Who Killed My Dog,' Art on Trial: The Arts, the First Amendment, and the Courts," www.tjcenter.org/ArtonTrial/threats.html. (accessed March 7, 2015).
54. Boman v, Bluestem Unified Sch. Dist., *2.
55. Ibid., *4.
56. Ibid., *2.
57. Ibid., *2 n. 2.
58. This is a fairly conservative estimate, based on a Westlaw Next search for "Columbine /p shoot shooting & school" which yielded 163 cases on December 9, 2013. Eleven additional cases are generated from the same search run from that date through December 31, 2014 on March 10, 2015. On March 13, 2015 a Westlaw Next search of "da (aft 1998) & school & columbine "Virginia tech" yielded 442 cases; Adding "& speech" reduced the number to 146. The list of over 400 opinions includes some in which references to school shootings by students, teachers or prosecutors are part of the evidence in the case.
59. Boim v. Fulton Cnty. Sch. Dist., 494 F.3d at 983–985.
60. Mardis v. Hannibal Pub. Sch. Dist. #60, 684 F. Supp. 2d at 1122 (citing Doe v. Pulaski, 306 F.3d at 626, n.4); Ponce v. Socorro Indep. Sch. Dist., 432 F. Supp. 2d 682, 686 n. 4, 696 n. 9 (W.D. Tex. 2006), vacated, 508 F.3d 765 (5th Cir. 2007). If the subjective intent required in Elonis v. United States, 575 U.S. __, (2015), applied to schools, the penalties in all of these cases and others would have been reversed.
61. Ponce v. Socorro Indep. Sch. Dist., 432 F. Supp. 2d at 686 n. 4, 696 n. 9.
62. Ibid., 702.
63. Ponce v. Socorro Indep. Sch. Dist., 508 F.3d at 771–772 (quoting Doe v. Pulaski Cnty. Special Sch. Dist., 306 F.3d 616, 626 n. 4 (8th Cir. 2002); Frederick v. Morse, 127 U.S. at 425 (Alito, J., concurring).
64. Robers et al., *Indicators of School Crime and Safety*, 7, 98.
65. Wisniewski v. Bd. of Educ., 494 F.3d at 38 (2007) (Newman, J.).
66. Doe v. Pulaski Special Sch. Dist., 306 F.3d at 634 (Heaney, J., dissenting) (en banc).
67. Wisniewski v. Bd. of Educ., 494 F.3d 34.
68. Holloman v. Harland, 370 F.3d 1252 at 1271–1272 (11th Cir. 2004) (internal citations omitted).
69. J.S. v. Blue Mountain Sch. Dist., 650 F.3d 915, 930 (3d Cir. 2011) (en banc), cert. denied, 132 S. Ct. 1097 (2012); Cox v. Warwick Valley Cent. Sch.

Dist., 2010 WL 6501655, at *14; Dariano v. Morgan Hill Unified Sch. Dist., 822 F. Supp. 2d 1037, 1042 (N.D. Cal. 2011) (citing Karp v. Becken, 477 F.2d 171, 174 (9th Cir. 1973)), aff'd, 745 F. 3d 354 (9th Cir. Feb. 27, 2014), amended by 767 F. 3d 764 (9th Cir. 2014), cert. denied, 83 U.S.L.W. 3762 (U.S. March 30, 2015) (No. 14-720).

70. Tinker v. Des Moines, 393 U.S. at 508, 509 (quoting Burnside v. Byars, 363 F.2d 744, 749 (5th Cir. 1966)). Due to a reorganization of the federal courts in 1980, portions of the Fifth Circuit became part of a new Eleventh Circuit, and all Fifth Circuit rulings prior to that time are binding in the current Eleventh Circuit.

71. Tinker v. Des Moines Indep. Cmty. Sch. Dist., 393 U.S. at 508, 514. The Supreme Court in *Tinker* recognized that organized demonstrations on campus might be inherently disruptive, though it made clear that disapproval of demonstrations *without more* did not suffice to justify outlawing them. Ibid., 509 n. 3.

72. Burnside v. Byars, 363 F.2d 744 (5th Cir. 1966); Blackwell v. Issaquena Cnty. Bd. of Educ., 363 F. 2d 749 (5th Cir. 1966); e.g., DeFabio v. East Hampton Union Free Sch. Dist., 623 F.3d 71, 78 (2d Cir. 2010); Gillman v. Sch. Bd. for Holmes Cnty., Fla., 567 F. Supp. 2d 1359 (N.D. Fla. 2008).

73. Jonathan Rieder, *Gospel of Freedom: Martin Luther King, Jr.'s Letter from Birmingham Jail and the Struggle that Changed a Nation* (New York: Bloomsbury Press, 2013), 114.

74. Ibid.; Andrew Young at Harvard University's W. E. B. DuBois Research Institute, Cambridge, MA (March 7, 2013).

75. Kristi L. Bowman, "The Civil Rights Roots of Tinker's Disruption Tests," *American University Law Review* 58 (2009): 1129, 1134–1135.

76. Burnside v. Byars, 363 F.2d 744 (5th Cir. 1966); Blackwell v. Issaquena Cnty. Bd. of Educ., 363 F. 2d 749 (5th Cir. 1966).

77. Burch v. Barker, 861 F.3d 1149, 1153 (9th Cir. 1988); John E. Taylor, "Tinker and Viewpoint Discrimination," *University of Kansas City Law Review* 77 (2009): 569.

78. Blackwell v. Issaquena Cnty. Bd. of Educ., 363 F. 2d 749, 751, 751 n.2 (5th Cir. 1966).

79. Ibid., 751 n. 3.

80. Burnside v. Byars, 363 F.2d at 747 n. 5, 748.

81. Ibid., 749.

82. Norton v. Discipline Comm. of East Tenn. State Univ., 419 F.2d 195, 209 (1969) (Celebrezze, J., dissenting) (discussing Blackwell v. Issaquena Cnty. Bd. of Educ., 363 F.2d 749).

83. Brown v. Cabell Cnty, Bd. of Educ., 714 F. Supp. 2d 587, 590 (S.D. W. Va. 2010); Madrid v. Anthony, 510 F. Supp. 2d 425 (S.D. Tex. 2007); Pangle v. Bend-Lapine Sch. Dist., 10 P. 3d 275, 286–287 and 10 P. 3d at 289, 290–291 (Armstrong, J., dissenting in part) (vulgarity in an underground newspaper does not threaten disruption).

84. Heinkel v. Sch. Bd. of Lee Cnty., 194 Fed. Appx 604, 609–610 (11th Cir. 2006); Planned Parenthood v. Danforth, 428 U.S. 52 (1976); Bellotti v.

Baird, 443 U.S. 622 (1979); Ayotte v. Planned Parenthood, 546 U.S. 320 (2006).

85. Gillman v. Sch. Bd. for Holmes Cnty., Fla., 567 F. Supp. 2d at 1372–1373.
86. J.C. v. Beverly Hills Unified Sch. Dist., 711 F. Supp. 2d 1094, 1117–1119 (C.D. Cal. 2010); J.S. v. Blue Mountain Sch. Dist. 650 F.3d 915 (3d Cir. 2011) (en banc); T.V. v. Smith-Green Cmty. Sch. Corp., 807 F. Supp. 2d 767, 772, 782–783 (N.D. Ind. 2011).
87. Gillman v. Sch. Bd., 567 F. Supp. at 1372–1373.
88. B.H. v. Easton Area Sch. Dist., 827 F. Supp. 2d 392, 407–408 (E.D. Pa. April 12, 2011) (determining it would have been unreasonable for school officials to conclude that the breast cancer awareness bracelets are lewd or vulgar under the *Fraser* standard); aff'd, B.H. v. Easton Area Sch. Dist., 725 F.3d 293 (3d Cir. 2013) (en banc); K.J v. Sauk Prairie Sch. Dist., No. 11-cv-622-bbc, 2012 U.S. Dist. LEXIS 187689, at *2 (D. Wisc. Feb. 6, 2012) (slip op); J.A. v. Fort Wayne Cmty. Sch., No. 1:12-CV-155JVB, 2013 WL 4479229, at *1 (N.D. Ind. Aug. 20, 2013).
89. B.H v. Easton Area Sch. Dist., 827 F. Supp. 2d at 408; B.H. v. Easton Area Sch. Dist., 725 F.3d at 321.
90. B.H. v. Easton Area Sch. Dist., 827 F. Supp. at 408–409.
91. B.H. v. Easton Area Sch. Dist., 725 F.3d at 321.
92. Griggs v. Fort Wayne Sch. Bd., 359 F. Supp. 2d at 746, 747 n.14.
93. Guiles v. Marineau, 461 F.3d at 321, 326: Griggs v. Fort Wayne Sch. Bd., 359 F. Supp. 2d at 746; the majority of circuits (Third, Fourth, Fifth, Sixth, Eighth, Ninth, Tenth, and Eleventh) would apply *Tinker,* though the Seventh also consults *Hazelwood.*
94. Guiles v. Marineau, 461 F.3d at 331.
95. K.J. v. Sauk Prairie Sch. Dist., 2012 U.S. Dist. LEXIS 187689, *4.
96. Guiles v. Marineau, 461 F.3d at 329, 330.
97. Burch v. Barker, 651 F. Supp. 1149, 1155 (W.D. Wash. 1987).

6. Words that Harm

1. Nixon v. Northern Local Sch. Dist. Bd. of Educ., 383 F. Supp. 2d 965, 974 (S.D. Ohio 2005).
2. Hazelwood Sch. Dist. v. Kuhlmeier, 484 U.S. at 289 (Brennan, J., dissenting); J.C. v. Beverly Hills Unified Sch. Dist., 711 F. Supp. 2d 1094, 1122–1123 (C.D. Cal. 2010); Nuxoll v. Indian Prairie Sch. Dist., 523 F.3d 668, 670 (7th Cir. 2008); Sypniewski v. Warren Hills Reg'l Bd. of Educ., 307 F.3d 243 (3rd Cir. 2002), cert. denied, 538 U.S. 1003 (2003).
3. Slotterback v. Interboro Sch. Dist., 766 F. Supp. 280, 289 n. 8 (E.D. Pa. 1991); J.C. v. Beverly Hills, 711 F. Supp. 2d at 1123.
4. Aaron H. Caplan, "Free Speech and Civil Harassment Orders," *Hastings Law Journal* 64 (2013): 781, 785, 786 n. 21.
5. Ibid.; e.g., Mass. Gen. Laws Ann. § 43A (West 2010); State v. Vaughn, 366 S.W.3d 513 (Mo. 2012).

6. Caplan, "Free Speech and Civil Harassment Orders," 791; e.g., Iowa Code Ann. § 708.7 (West, Westlaw through February of 2015 Regular Session); N.Y. Penal Law § 240.30 (McKinney Supp. 2015) (including intent to "annoy" and perception of race, color, and so on); James C. McKinley Jr., "Times Sq. Spider-Man Is Cleared in Assault, but Fined for Foul Language," *New York Times,* June 19, 2014, A22; People v. Golb, 15 N.E.3d 805 (N.Y. 2014) (overturning as "unconstitutionally vague and overbroad" Penal Law § 240.30,(1) which defines harassment as "any communication that has the intent to annoy").

7. Payne v. Worthington Sch., No. C2–99–830, 2001 WL 506509 (S.D. Ohio 2001) (no school liability). See also Distiso v. Town of Wolcott, 352 Fed. Appx. 478 (2d Cir. 2009); Abeyta v. Chama Valley Indep. Sch. Dist., 77 F.3d 1253 (10th Cir. 1996); Marcum v. Bd. of Educ. of Bloom-Carroll Local Sch. Dist., 727 F. Supp. 2d 657, 663 (S.D. Ohio 2010).

8. Jeremy Waldron, *The Harm in Hate Speech* (Cambridge, MA: Harvard University Press, 2012).

9. R.A.V. v. St. Paul, 505 U.S. 377 (1992).

10. Nat Hentoff, "Multicultural Contempt for Free Speech," *The Nat Hentoff Reader* (Cambridge, MA: De Capo Press, 2001), 70; Elena Kagan, "When a Speech Code Is a Speech Code: The Stanford Policy and the Theory of Incidental Restraints," *University of California Davis Law Review* 29 (1996): 957, 968; Corry v. Leland Stanford Junior Univ., No. 740309 (Cal. Super. Ct. Feb. 27, 1995); Waldron, *The Harm in Hate Speech;* Kagan, "When Speech Code Is a Speech Code," 957.

11. Saxe v. State College Area Sch. Dist., 240 F.3d 200, 202 (3d Cir. 2001) (Alito, J.).

12. Ibid., 203.

13. Ibid., 204, 208, 209.

14. Ibid., 209–210, 218–223.

15. Ibid., 217.

16. Jack Balkin, "Free Speech and Hostile Environments," *Columbia Law Review* 99 (1999): 2295.

17. Neuqua Valley High School in Naperville, Illinois (quoted in Nuxoll v. Indian Prairie Sch. Dist., 523 F.3d 668, 670 (7th Cir. 2008)).

18. Chaney Hall, "Sticks and Stones May Break My Bones but Will the Law Ever Protect Me? Ensuring Educational Access through Federal Prohibition of Peer-on-Peer Harassment," *Children's Legal Rights Journal* 29 (2009): 42, 48–49.

19. Texas v. Johnson, 491 U.S. 397 (1989); R.A.V. v. St. Paul, 505 U.S. 377 (1992).

20. Pierce v. Soc'y of Sisters of the Holy Names of Jesus and Mary, 268 U.S. 510, 535 (1925).

21. Schroeder v. Hamilton School Dist., 282 F.3d 946, 955 (7th Cir. 2002) (Manion, J.).

22. School systems periodically argue the deferential review of *Fraser* or *Morse* should apply because allowing hateful expression on campus would undermine

the school's civics lessons about diversity; judges usually reject the argument. See, e.g., Denno v. Sch. Bd. of Volusia Cnty., 218 F.3d 1267, 1274 (11th Cir. 2000); Hardwick v. Heyward, 711 F.3d 426 (4th Cir. 2013).

23. Palmore v. Sidoti, 466 U.S. 429, 432 (1984).
24. E.g., Smith v. Tammany Parish Sch. Bd., 448 F.2d 414 (5th Cir. 1971); Augustus v. Sch. Bd. of Escambia Cnty., 361 F. Supp. 383 (N.D. Fla. 1973), modified by 507 F.2d 152 (5th Cir. 1975); Melton v. Young, 465 F.2d 1332 (6th Cir. 1972); Banks v. Muncie Cmty. Sch., 433 F.2d 292 (7th Cir. 1970).
25. West v. Derby, 23 F. Supp. 2d 1223, 1232 (D. Kan. 1998), aff'd 206 F.S3d 1358 (10th Cir.), cert. denied, 531 U.S. 825 (2000); Denno v. Sch. Bd. of Volusia Cnty., 218 F.3d 1267, 1285 (11th Cir. 2000); B.W.A. v. Farmington R-7 Sch. Dist., 554 F.3d 734, 736–738, 736 n. 2 (8th Cir. 2009), aff'g B.W.A. v. Farmington R-7 Sch. Dist., 508 F. Supp. 2d 740 (E.D. Mo. 2007).
26. B.W.A. v. Farmington R-7 Sch. Dist., 554 F.3d at 736–738, 736 n. 2.
27. Ibid., 736–738, 738 n.6.
28. Ibid., 740, 741.
29. Ibid.
30. Hardwick v. Heyward, 711 F.3d 426, 438 (4th Cir. 2013).
31. Bragg v. Swanson, 371 F. Supp. 2d 814, 827 (W.D. W.Va. 2005); Castorina v. Madison Cnty. Sch. Bd., 246 F.3d 536, 541 (6th Cir. 2001).
32. Doninger v. Niehoff, 527 F.3d 41 (2008); DeFabio v. East Hampton Union Free Sch. Dist., 623 F.3d 71 (2d Cir. 2010).
33. Madrid v. Anthony, 510 F. Supp. 2d 425, 436 (S.D. Tex. 2007).
34. Terminiello v. Chicago, 337 U.S. 1, 4 (1949).
35. Morse v. Frederick, 551 U.S. 393, 425 (2007) (Alito, J., concurring).
36. Zamencik v. Indian Prairie Sch. Dist. No. 204, 636 F.3d 874, 880 (7th Cir. 2011) (Posner, J.).
37. DeFabio v. East Hampton Union Free Sch. Dist., 623 F.3d at 74.
38. Ibid., 469.
39. Ibid., 471.
40. Ibid.
41. Ibid., 480.
42. Ibid. (quoting Doninger v. Niehoff, 527 F.3d at 51–52).
43. Ibid., 482.
44. Dariano v. Morgan Hill Unified Sch. Dist, 767 F.3d 764, 766, 769 (9th Cir. 2014) (O'Scannlain, J., dissenting from denial of rehearing en banc), cert. denied, 83 U.S.L.W. 3762 (U.S. March 30, 2015) (No. 14-720).
45. Ibid., 772.
46. Smith v. Novato Unified Sch. Dist., 59 Cal. Rptr.3d 508, 516 (Cal. App. 1 Dist. 2007), cert. denied, 552 U.S. 1199 (2008). The subsequent ruling by the Ninth Circuit in Dariano v. Morgan Hill Unified Sch. Dist., 767 F.3d 764, calls this basic principle into question.
47. Smith v. Novato Unified Sch. Dist., 59 Cal. Rptr.3d at 521.
48. Ibid., 512–513.

49. Ibid., 513, 524.
50. Ibid., 513, 524.
51. Ibid., 520, 523.
52. Bragg v. Swanson, 371 F. Supp. 2d 814, 827 (W.D. W.Va. 2005); Castorina v. Madison Cnty. Sch. Bd., 246 F.3d at 541. Denno v. School Bd. of Volusha Cnty., 182 F.3d 780, 782–784 (11th Cir. 1999). Subsequently, the circuit considered the claim as raising issues that could be resolved under *Fraser*. Denno v. School Bd. of Volusha Cnty., 218 F.3d 1267 (11th Cir. 2000).
53. Bethel v. Fraser, 478 U.S. at 683; see also Hardwick v. Heyward, 711 F.3d 426, 441 (4th Cir. 2013) (finding the school dress code incorporated *Tinker* and *Fraser* standards); Muller v. Jefferson Lighthouse Sch., 98 F.3d 1530, 1539 (7th Cir. 1996) (quoted with approval by Denno v. Sch. Bd. of Volusia Cnty., 218 F.3d 1267, 1272–1273 (11th Cir. 2000)), also citing, among others, Scott v. School Bd. of Alachua Cnty., 324 F.3d 1246, 1248–1249 (11th Cir. 2003) (quoting Denno, 218 F.3d at 1273) (citing West v. Derby, 23 F. Supp. 2d 1223, 1233–1234 (D.Kan. 1998), aff'd 206 F.3d 1358 (10th Cir. 2000) (quoting *Fraser*)).
54. B.W.A. v. Farmington, 508 F. Supp. 2d at 748 (*Fraser* is inapplicable as the flag is "not patently offensive"); Barr v. Lafon, 538 F.3d 554, 569 n. 7 (6th Cir. 2008) cert. denied, 558 U.S. 817 (2009); Brown v. Cabell Cnty. Bd. of Educ., 714 F. Supp. 2d 587, 593, 593 n.2 (S.D. W.Va. 2010).
55. Barr v. Lafon, 538 F.3d at 560 (deposition of county school director).
56. Scott v. Sch. Bd. of Alachua Cnty., 324 F.3d 1246, 1249 (11th Cir. 2003) (emphasis added).
57. Defoe v. Spiva, 566 F. Supp. 2d 748, 754, 755 (E.D. Tenn. July 10, 2008).
58. Barr v. Lafon, 538 F.3d at 567–568.
59. Sypniewski v. Warren Hills Reg'l Bd. of Educ., 307 F.3d 243, 250, 257, 258, 263, 264, 265 (3d Cir. 2002).
60. Cohen v. California, 403 U.S. 15, 21 (1971).
61. Hardwick v. Heyward, 711 F.3d 426 436–437 (4th Cir. 2013), cert. denied, 134 S. Ct. 201 (2013).
62. Ibid., 439.
63. Randall Kennedy, *Nigger: The Strange Career of a Troublesome Word* (New York: Pantheon Books, 2002).
64. John M. Coski, *The Confederate Battle Flag: America's Most Embattled Emblem* (Cambridge, MA: Harvard University Press, 2005), 300.
65. Denno v. Sch. Bd., 218 F.3d at 1285 (Forrester, J., concurring in part and dissenting in part) (dissenting from grant of qualified immunity in the light of clear law); Hardwick v. Heyward, 711 F.3d 426 (collecting cases).
66. Defoe v. Spiva, 674 F.3d at 507 (Boggs, J., dissenting).
67. Ibid., 507–508 (Boggs, J., dissenting) and Defoe v. Spiva, 625 F.3d at 337 (Rogers, J., concurring).
68. Nixon v. Northern Local Sch. Dist. Bd. of Educ., 383 F. Supp. 2d 965, 967 (S.D. Ohio 2005).

69. U.S. Dep't of Education, Office for Civil Rights, Dear Colleague Letter: Harassment and Bullying (2010), 2 n. 8, http://www2.ed.gove/about/office /list/ocr/letters/colleague-2010.pdf (accessed 3/7/15); "Protections against Discrimination and Harassment: The Law Is On Your Side," data.lambdalegal .org (accessed 12/31/13). See Dena T. Saco et al., "An Overview of State Anti-Bullying Legislation and Other Related Laws," *The Kinder and Braver World Project: Research Series* (February 23, 2012), 5, Table 5; U.S. Department of Education, Questions and Answers on Title IX and Sexual Violence, April 29, 2014, B-1, B-2, www.ed.gov (accessed 5/8/14).

70. Harper v. Poway Unified Sch. Dist., 445 F.3d at 1176, 1178 (9th Cir. 2006), vacated on other grounds, 549 U.S. 1262 (2007). California law protects students from harassment based on sexual orientation. CAL. EDUC. CODE §§ 200, 201 (2012).

71. Nuxoll v. Indian Prairie Sch. Dist., 523 F.3d 668, 669–670 (7th Cir. 2008), reversing Zamecnik v. Indian Prairie Sch. Dist. No. 204 Bd. of Educ., 619 F. Supp.2d 517, 526 (N.D. Ill. 2007).

72. Nuxoll v. Indian Prairie Sch. Dist., 523 F.3d at 674.

73. Zamecnik v. Indian Prairie Sch. Dist. No. 204 Bd. of Educ., No. 07 C 1586, 2007 WL 1141597 (N.D. Ill. Apr. 17, 2007), at *11, rev'd and remanded sub nom. Nuxoll ex rel. Nuxoll v. Indian Prairie Sch. Dist., No. 204, 523 F.3d 668 (7th Cir. 2008).

74. Nuxoll v. Indian Prairie Sch. Dist., 523 F.3d at 676.

75. American Amusement Machine Ass'n v. Kendrick, 244 F.3d 572 (7th Cir. 2001); Nuxoll v. Indian Prairie Sch. Dist., 523 F.3d at 674–675.

76. Nuxoll v. Indian Prairie Sch. Dist., 523 F.3d at 671.

77. Ibid., 674.

78. Ibid., 671, 674.

79. Ibid., 672.

80. Ibid., 671–672, 674.

81. Ibid., 676 (Rovner, J., concurring) (citation omitted).

82. Ibid., 678–679 (Rovner, J., concurring).

83. Ibid., 679 (Rovner, J., concurring), quoted with approval in Zamencik v. Indian Prairie Sch. Dist. No. 204, 636 F.3d 874, 880 (7th Cir. 2011) (Posner, J.).

84. Nuxoll v. Indian Prairie Sch. Dist., 523 F.3d at 680 (Rovner, J., concurring).

85. Zamenick v. Indian Prairie Sch. Dist. No. 204, 636 F.3d 874 (7th Cir. 2011).

86. Ibid., 876, 877 (Posner, J.); See Richard A. Posner, *Reflections on Judging* (Cambridge, MA: Harvard University Press, 2013).

87. Baskin v. Bogan, 766 F.3d 648 (7th Cir.) (Posner, J.), cert. denied, 135 S.Ct. 316 (2014).

88. Nuxoll v. Indian Prairie Sch. Dist., 525 F.3d at 671 (citing R.A.V. v. St. Paul, 505 U.S. 377, 386 (1992)).

89. R.Z. v. Carmel Clay Schools, 868 F. Supp. 2d 785 (S.D. Ind. 2012).

90. Ibid., 785, 788.

91. Ibid., 789

92. Ibid., 790.

93. Ibid., 789; Depo. of Sherri Zimmer at 54:11–55:7, Zimmer v. Carmel Clay Schs., No. 1:10-cv-01117-WTL-DKL, Doc. 51–40 (Sup. Ct. Ind. Nov. 7, 2011).

94. R.Z. v. Carmel Clay Schools, 868 F. Supp. 2d at 799, 790.

95. Nuxoll v. Indian Prairie Sch. Dist., 525 F.3d at 675 (discussing the line dividing harassment and wounding speech); Glowacki v. Howell Pub. Sch. Dist., No. 2:11-cv-15481, 2013 WL 3148272, at *8 (E.D. Mich. 2013).

96. Blackwell v. Issaquena Cnty. Bd. of Educ., 363 F.2d at 751, 751 n. 2 (emphasis in original).

97. Cohen v. California, 403 U.S. 15 (1971); Bolger v. Youngs Drugs Products Corp., 463 U.S. 60 (1983).

98. "Bullying," www.violence preventionworks.org (accessed 1/3/14).

99. Saxe v. State College Area Sch. Dist., 240 F.3d at 206.

100. Nabozny v. Podlesny, 92 F.3d 446, 451–452 (7th Cir. 1996); Emily Bazelon, *Sticks and Stones: Defeating the Culture of Bullying and Rediscovering the Power of Character and Empathy* (New York: Random House, 2013), 165.

101. "Bullying," www.nlm.nih.gov (accessed 12/29/13); Elizabeth Kandel, *Bullying and Cyberbullying: What Every Educator Needs to Know* (Cambridge, MA: Harvard University Press, 2013), 17; Rachel Dinkes et al., "Indicators of School Crime and Safety," *National Center for Education Statistics* (2009), Table 11.2.

102. Bazelon, *Sticks and Stones.*

103. DeShaney v. Winnebago Cnty. Dep't of Soc. Services, 489 U.S. 189, 213 (1989) (Blackmun, J., dissenting). See also Estate of Carmichael v. Galbraitih, No. 3:11-CV-0622-D, 2012 WL 4442413 (N.D. Tx. 2012).

104. Title IX, Education Amendments of 1972, § 901 (a) as amended, 20 U.S.C.A. §§ 1681(a), 1687. See, e.g., Nabozny v. Podlesny, 92 F.3d 446; W. v. Fairport Central Sch. Dist., 927 F. Supp. 2d 76 (W.D. N.Y. 2013); Bazelon, *Sticks and Stones,* 151–152. For state statutes, see Dean T. Sacco et al., "An Overview of State Anti-Bullying Legislation and Other Related Laws," *The Kinder & Braver World Project* (February 23, 2012), cyber.law .harvard.edu.

105. Nabozny v. Podlesny, 92 F.3d 446; Bazelon, *Sticks and Stones,* 151.

106. Davis v. Monroe Cnty. Bd. of Educ., 526 U.S. 629 (1999).

107. Ibid., 631.

108. Ibid., 651–652.

109. Fitzgerald v. Barnstable Sch. Comm., 555 U.S. 246, 249 (2009).

110. Davis v. Monroe Cnty. Bd. of Educ., 526 U.S. at 660, 676–678 (Kennedy, J., dissenting).

111. Bazelon, *Sticks and Stones,* 298.

112. Kirby v. Loyalsock Tp. Sch. Dist., 837 F. Supp. 2d 467, 472 (M.D. Pa. 2011).

113. Ibid.; Alan S. Goodwin to Students, email dated August 28, 2013 (Walt Whitman High School, Bethesda, MD) (on file with author); La Junta Junior/Senior High School Student Handbook & Planner, 2012–2013, La Junta, Colorado, at 8.

114. U.S. Dep't of Education, Office for Civil Rights, Dear Colleague Letter: Harrassment and Bullying (2010), 2, n.8; U.S. Dep't of Education, Office for Civil Rights, Dear Colleague Letter: First Amendment (2003), http://www2 .ed.gov/about/offices/list/ocr/letters/colleague-201010.pdf (accessed 3/7/15).

115. "Peer to Peer Violence and Bullying: Examining the Federal Response," *U.S. Commission on Civil Rights* (2011), 145–146 (dissent and Rebuttal of Commissioners Gaziano and Kirasanow).

116. Brown v. Bd. of Educ., 347 U.S. 483 (1954); "Don't Say Poo Poo Heads," *American Libraries Magazine,* July 13, 2011. The next year, the boy's mother persuaded the school board to remove a popular children's book containing the term from the school's library.

117. Anti-Bullying Bill of Rights Act, 2010 N.J. Laws 1319 (codified as amended in scattered sections of N.J. Stat. Ann. Tit. 18A); N.J. Stat. Ann. § 18A:37-13.2 & 37-14 (West 2013).

118. Davis v. Monroe Cnty. Bd. of Educ., 526 U.S. at 651.

119. T.K. v. New York City Dep't of Educ., 779 F. Supp. 2d 286, 317 (E.D. N.Y. 2011).

120. U.S. Dep't of Education, Office for Civil Rights, Dear Colleague Letter: Bullying of Students with Disabilities (2014), 6, http://www2.ed.gov/about/ offices/list/ocr/letters/colleague6201410.pdf (accessed 3/7/15).

121. Zeno v. Pine Plains Cent. Sch. Dist., 702 F.3d 655 (2d Cir. 2012).

122. Ibid., 667, 672. *Zeno* didn't involve any claims about free speech, but it could have. Imagine that the school district had silenced the bullies instead of ignoring them and the bullies had asserted their right to speak. If a court found the bullying speech did not amount to fighting or threatening words and was protected, though low value, speech, the school would presumably have asserted that *Tinker* allowed it to punish the bullying speech. It could argue that although there was no schoolwide material disruption, the bullying speech collided with Zeno's right to an education by materially disrupting his learning environment.

123. Zeno v. Pine Plains Cent. Sch. Dist., 702 F.3d at 660, 669.

124. For a useful guide to resources, see Bazelon, *Sticks and Stones,* 326 ff. For responses based on social science research, see Elizabeth Englander, *Bullying and Cyberbullying: What Every Educator Needs to Know* (Cambridge MA: Harvard University Press 2013); The Southern Poverty Law Center's periodical on teaching tolerance is available on line at www.splccenter.org.

125. "Prevention of Bullying Related Morbidity and Mortality," www.aacap.org (accessed 12/31/13) (Policy Statement Approved June 2011); Saxe v. State College Area Sch. Dist., 240 F.3d at 212; Harper v Poway, 445 F.3d at 1171 (applying *Tinker* and expressly not reaching the rights of others question, n. 28 at 1183–1184); Harper v. Poway, 445 F.3d at 1192, 1193–1194, 119 n. 7, 1196, n. 8 (Kozinski, J., dissenting).

126. Glowacki v. Howell Public Schools, No. 2:11-cv-15481, 2013 WL 3148272 (E.D. Mich. 2013).

127. Ibid., *3.
128. Ibid., *8.
129. Ibid.
130. Ibid., *9.
131. Ibid., *4.

7. Off-Campus Taunts and Online *Sans-Gêne* Speech

1. Guevarra v. Seton Medical Center, No. C-13–2267 CW, 2013 WL 6235352 (N.D. Cal. Dec. 2, 2013).
2. Deborah Ahrens, "Schools, Cyberbullies, and the Surveillance State," *American Criminal Law Review* 49 (2012): 1669, 1674; Catherine Smith, "School Ban Would Crack Down on Sexting—Even in the Home," *Huffington Post,* June 21, 2010.
3. Amici Curiae Brief of Nat'l Sch. Boards Ass'n et al., Blue Mountain Sch. Dist. v. Snyder, 650 F.3d 915 (3d Cir. 2011) (No. 11–502), 2011 WL 5254664, at *3; Bell v. Itawamba Cnty. Sch. Bd., 774 F.3d 280, 319 (5th Cir. 2014) (Barksdale, J., concurring in part and dissenting in part), en banc review granted, No. 12-60264, 2015 BL 47831 (5th Cir. Feb. 19, 2015) (distinction is "obsolete").
4. Ibid.; Brown v. Entm't Merch.'s Ass'n, 131 S. Ct. 2729, 2765–2766 (Breyer, J., dissenting); Layshock v. Hermitage Sch. Dist., 650 F.3d 205, 221(3d Cir. 2011) (Jordan, J., concurring); Gia E. Barboza, "The Behavioral, Socio-Legal and Institutional Antecedents of Peer Harassment and Bullying in School: How Do Legal Norms Interact with the Multiple Contexts of Childhood Aggression?," *Criminal Law Bulletin* 45, Art. 8 (2009) (Internet use for purposes of "harassment or intimidation" has "outstripped existing school conduct codes and have left school officials unsure about how far their authority to regulate it extends"); Winnie Hu, "Bullying Law Puts New Jersey Schools on Spot," *New York Times,* August 30, 2011, A1; Kathleen McGrory, "Cyberbullying Proposals Win Support, Raise Legal Questions," *Miami Herald,* March 21, 2013.
5. Amici Curiae Brief of Nat'l Sch. Boards Ass'n et al., Blue Mountain Sch. Dist. v. Snyder, 2011 WL 5254664, at *13.
6. R.S. v. Minnewaska Area Sch. Dist. No. 2149, 894 F. Supp. 2d 1128, 1139 (D. Mn. 2012).
7. Morse v. Frederick, 551 U.S. 393, 401 (2007) (Roberts, J.) (citing Porter v. Ascension Parish Sch. Bd., 393 F.3d 608, 615 n. 22 (5th Cir. 2004)).
8. Brown v. Entm't Merchants Ass'n, 131 S. Ct. 2729 (2011) (Scalia, J.); Ginsberg v. New York, 390 U.S. 629, 639–640 (1968).
9. Ginsberg v. New York, 390 U.S. at 639, quoting Prince v. Massachusetts, 321 U.S. 158, 166 (1944).
10. Ibid.; Troxel v. Granville, 530 U.S. 57, 65 (2000) (O'Connor, J., plurality op.).
11. Pierce v. Soc'y of Sisters, 268 U.S. 510 (1925).

12. See Bell v. Itawamba Cnty. Sch. Bd., 859 F. Supp. 2d 834 (N.D. Ms. 2012) (summarizing cases and applying to penalty for a YouTube posting), aff'd 774 F.3d 280, en banc. review granted, reversed, 774 F.3d 280 (5th Cir. 2014), en banc review granted, No. 12-60264, 2015 BL 47831 (5th Cir. Feb. 19, 2015).

13. Phillip Buckley, "Subjects, Citizens, or Civic Learners? Judicial Conceptions of Childhood and the Speech Rights of American Public School Students," *Childhood* 2, no. 2 (2013): 226–241.

14. Thomas v. Bd. of Educ. Granville Cent. Sch. Dist., 607 F.2d 1043, 1044-1045 (2d. Cir. 1979).

15. Expressly rejected in J.S. v. Blue Mountain, 650 F.3d 915, 933, (3d Cir. 2011) (en banc), cert. denied, 132 S. Ct. 1097 (2012).

16. Lander v. Seaver, 32 Vt. 114, 120 (1859).

17. "The State of the First Amendment: 2012," First Amendment Center, www.firstamendmentcenter.org (accessed 1/18/14), 5.

18. Danielle Keats Citron, *Hate Crimes in Cyberspace* (Cambridge, MA: Harvard University Press, 2014), 243, citing McAfee Digital Deception Study 2013:Exploring the Online Disconnect between Parents & Pre-teens, Teens and Young Adults, May 28, 2013, http://www.mcafee.com/us/resources/reports/rp-digital-deception-survey-pdf.?culture=en-us&affd=0&cid=122416.

19. Bruce C. Hafen, "Developing Student Expression through Institutional Authority: Public Schools as Mediating Structures, " *Ohio State Law Journal* 48 (1987): 663, 694, 705.

20. Ibid., 707.

21. Anne Profitt Dupre, *Speaking Up: The Unintended Costs of Free Speech in Public Schools* (Cambridge, MA: Harvard University Press, 2009), 253; see also Kay S. Hymowitz, "Tinker and the Lessons from the Slippery Slope," *Drake Law Review* 48 (2000): 547.

22. Klein v. Smith, 635 F. Supp. 1440, 1441–1442 D. Me. 1986); Thomas v. Granville, 607 F.2d at 1051.

23. Shanley v. Northeast Indep. Sch. Dist., 462 F.2d 960, 964 (5th Cir. 1972).

24. Ibid., 964, 965 n. 1.

25. Ibid., 964, 966 n. 2, 967, 964.

26. Ibid., 964, 966 n. 2, 967.

27. Ibid., 974.

28. Thomas v. Granville, 607 F.2d at 1050, 1050 n. 13 (2d. Cir. 1979).

29. Ibid., 1051; see also Klein v. Smith, 635 F. Supp. at 1441–1442, 1051, 1051 n. 15.

30. Klein v. Smith, 635 F. Supp. 1440, 1441, 1441 n. 4.

31. Ibid., 1441–1442, 1441 n. 3. Compare Fenton v. Stear, 423 F. Supp. 767, 769 (W.D. Pa. 1976) (not citing *Tinker* and viewing the term *prick* as fighting words).

32. Klein v. Smith, 635 F. Supp. at 1442.

33. Thomas v. Granville, 607 F.2d at 1052 n. 17.

34. Amici Curiae Brief of Nat'l Sch. Boards Ass'n et al., at 4, Blue Mountain Sch. Dist. v. Snyder, 650 F.3d 915 (3d Cir. 2011) (No. 11–502).

35. Peter Jamieson, "ACLU Defends Student Who Called Teacher 'Douche Bag' on Facebook," *SF Weekly Blog*, January 31, 2011; ACLU of Louisiana, "ACLU Cases as of May 2011, Wallace v. East Baton Rouge Parish School Board," www.laaclu.org (accessed 9/4/11); Doe v. West Baton Rouge Parish Sch. Bd., Complaint, 3:11-cv-712 (M.D. La. Nov. 1, 2011); R.S. v. Minnewaska Area Sch. Dist. No. 2149, 894 F. Supp. 1128, 1133 (D. Mn. 2012).

36. R.S. v. Minnewaska Area Sch. Dist., 894 F. Supp. 2d at 1133; Evans v. Bayer, 684 F. Supp. 2d 1365, 1367 (S.D. Fl. 2010).

37. "Minnesota Teen Sues School District, Police Chief after Suspension over Tweet," June 18, 2014, www.foxnews.com (accessed 6/24/14); Laura Fosmire, "At Least 20 Ore. Students Suspended Because of Tweet," www.usatoday.com (accessed 6/24/14).

38. Emily Bazelon, *Sticks and Stones: Defeating the Culture of Bullying and Rediscovering the Power of Character and Empathy* (New York: Random House, 2013), 28 (citing Dan Olweus).

39. Evans v. Bayer, 684 F. Supp. 2d at 1373.

40. J.S. v. Bethlehem Area Sch. Dist., 807 A.2d at 852; J.S. v. Blue Mountain, 650 F.3d at 946–947, 946 n. 3 (Fisher, J., dissenting); Layshock v. Hermitage Sch. Dist., 650 F.3d at 220–222 (Jordan, J., concurring); Schroeder v. Hamilton Sch. Dist., 282 F.3d 946, 950 (7th Cir. 2002).

41. Schroeder v. Hamilton School District, 282 F. 3d 946.

42. Doninger v. Niehoff, 594 F. Supp. 2d 211, 223 (D. Ct. 2009), aff'd in part, rev'd in part, 642 F.3d 334 (2d Cir. 2011).

43. Shanley v. Northeast Indep. Sch. Dist., 462 F.2d at 974.

44. J.S. v. Bethlehem Area Sch. Dist., 807 A.2d 847 (Pa. 2002).

45. J.C. v. Beverly Hills Sch. Dist., 711 F. Supp. 2d at 1098-1099, 1108. See also Wynar v. Douglas Cnty. Sch. Dist., 728 F.3d 1062, 1068–1070 (9th Cir. 2013) (listing and summarizing cases); J.S. v. Bethlehem, 807 A.2d at 852; O.Z. v. Bd. of Trustees of the Long Beach Unified Sch. Dist, No. CV 08–5671 ODW, 2008 WL 4396895, at *1–2 (C.D. Ca. 2008); see Shanley v. Northeast Indep. Sch. Dist., 462 F. 2d at 974; J.C. v. Beverly Hills, 711 F. Supp. 2d at 1103–1106 (discussing other cases).

46. Karl Taro Greenfield, "My Daughter's Homework Is Killing Me," *The Atlantic*, September 18, 2013, 80, 87.

47. Interview with Wilton High School teacher Bonnie Dickinson, June 7, 2009, Wilton, Connecticut; Allison Leigh Cowan, "Play about Iraq War Divides a Connecticut School," *New York Times*, March 24, 2007.

48. Amy Goodman and David Goodman, *Standing Up to the Madness: Ordinary Heroes in Extraordinary Times* (New York: Hyperion, 2008), 160.

49. Doninger v. Niehoff, 642 F.3d 334.

50. Ibid.,351; Bethel Sch. Dist. No. 403 v. Fraser, 478 U.S. 675, 685 (1986).

51. Doe v. Pulaski, 306 F.3d 616 (8th Cir. 2002); D.J.M. v. Hannibal Pub. Sch. Dist. No. 60, 647 F.3d 754, 765–766 (8th Cir. 2011); Wynar v. Douglas Cnty. Sch. Dist., 728 F.3d 1062 (9th Cir. 2013); Wisniewski v.

Bd. of Educ., 494 F.3d 34 (2d Cir. 2007); Doninger v. Niehoff, 642 F.3d 334.

52. Doe v. Pulaski, 306 F.3d 616; D.J.M., 647 F.3d at 765–766 (discussed in R.S. v. Minnewaska Area Sch. Dist. 894 F. Supp. 2d at 1139 (D. Mn. 2012)); Wynar v. Douglas Cnty. Sch. Dist., 728 F.3d 1062.

53. Wynar v. Douglas Cnty. Sch. Dist., 728 F.3d at 1069. However, this approach confronts judges with an unacknowledged dilemma. In order to assess whether a school can invoke *Tinker* with respect to off-campus speech, a court must first hear the school's allegations about threatened disruption. It reverses the normal order of judicial inquiry by requiring the court to "peek at the merits" before deciding a jurisdictional question. The judge must consider the nature of the alleged disorder in order to determine whether the school district had any authority over the off-campus speech.

54. Layshock v. Hermitage Sch. Dist., 650 F.3d 205, 217 n. 16, 208 (3d Cir. 2011) (en banc) (McKee, C. J.); J.S. v. Blue Mountain, 650 F.3d at 921.

55. Layshock v. Hermitage Sch. Dist., 650 F.3d at 216.

56. Somini Sengupta, "Warily, Schools Watch Students on the Internet," *New York Times,* October 29, 2013, A1.

57. J.S. v. Blue Mountain, 650 F.3d at 933.

58. Ibid., 936 (Smith, J., concurring) (joined by, among others, McKee, J., who authored court's en banc opinion in *Layshock* issued on the same day). A panel of the Fifth Circuit agreed that *Tinker* does not govern off campus speech and that such speech even when posted online is not subject to school discipline. Bell v. Itawamba Cnty. Sch. Bd., 774 F.3d 280.

59. Matot v. C.H., No. 6:13-cv-153-MC, 2013 WL 5431586, at *2 (D. Or. Sep. 26, 2013) (quoting U.S. v. Nosal, 676 F.3d 854, 862 (9th Cir. 2012)).

60. Finkel v. Daubert, 906 N.Y.S.2d 697 at *1–2, 3 (N.Y. Sup. Ct. 2010).

61. Schroeder v. Hamilton Sch. Dist., 282 F.3d 946, 952–953 (7th Cir. 2002) (citations omitted).

62. D.C. v. Harvard-Westlake Sch., 98 Cal. Rptr. 3d 300, 304 (Cal. Ct. App. 2009).

63. Danielle Citron, *Hate Crimes in Cyberspace*, 85–90, 137–139.

64. Alan S. Goodwin to Students, August 28, 2013 (Walt Whitman High School, Bethesda, MD) (e-mail on file with author).

65. J.C. v. Beverly Hills Unified Sch. Dist., 711 F. Supp. 2d at 1098.

66. Ibid., 1111, 1117; Wynar v. Douglas Cnty. Sch. Dist., 728 F.3d at 1069.

67. Kowalski v. Berkeley Cnty. Schools, 652 F.3d 565 (4th Cir. 2011), cert. denied, 132 S. Ct. 1095 (2012).

68. Ibid., 571–574.

69. Ibid., 571–573.

70. Ibid., 576, 577.

71. R.S. v. Minnewaska Area Sch. Dist. 894 F. Supp. 2d at 1133–1134.

72. Ibid.; "ACLU-MN Settles Facebook Case with Minnewaska School
    District: Minnewaska Agrees to Strengthen Privacy Protections," March 25,
    2014, www.aclu.org/technology-and-liberty-mn-settles-facebook-case
    -minnewaska-school-district (accessed 5/20/14). The ACLU received half
    of the money paid in damages to cover the costs of litigation and support
    its work on student privacy.
73. Riley v. California, 134 S. Ct. 2473, 2484 (2014).
74. Ibid., 2489.
75. R.S. v. Minnewaska Area Sch. Dist., 894 F. Supp. 2d at 1140.
76. Ibid.
77. John P. Martin, "Lower Merion District's Laptop Saga Ends with $610,000
    Settlement," www.philly.com, October 12, 2010 (accessed 6/24/14); CBS
    News, *Report: No Spying in Pa. School Laptops Case,* May 3, 2010, www.cbsnews
    .com/news/report-no-spying-in-pa-school-laptops-case (accessed 6/24/14).
78. Sameer Hinduja and Justin W. Patchin, "State Sexting Laws: A Brief
    Review of State Sexting Laws and Policies," www.cyberbullling.us (accessed
    1/15/14); "State Cyberbullying Laws: A Brief Review of State Cyberbullying
    Law and Policies", http://www.cyberbullying.us/Bullying-and-Cyberbullying
    -Laws.pdf (accessed 3/8/15); "Policies and Laws," http://www.stopbullying
    .gov/laws/ (accessed 3/8/15).
79. N.J.S.A. 18A:37–15–3 (effective September 1, 2011); NJ St 18A:37–14
    (effective September 1, 2011); 2007 NJ Sess. Law Serv. Ch. 129 (SENATE
    993 (WEST)); Jeanette Rundquist, "Anti-bullying Law Prompts More
    Appeals, Students, Parents Fighting to Keep Charges Off School Records,"
    The Express Times, April 26, 2013, News p. B!.
80. Rundquist, "Anti-bullying Law".
81. CAL EDUC. CODE § 32261(a) (West Supp. 2012); CAL. EDUC. CODE
    § 48900(r)(1) (West Supp. 2014).
82. Ibid.
83. Justin W. Patchin, "Cyberbullying Laws and School Policy: A Blessing or a
    Curse?," cyberbulling.us (accessed 11/5/13).
84. People v. Marquan M., 24 N.Y.3d 1 (N.Y. 2014).
85. "Peer-to-Peer Violence and Bullying: Examining the Federal Response,"
    U.S. Commission on Civil Rights (2011), 76, 87.
86. Ibid., 150, 151.
87. "Cyberbullying: Recognizing the Signs and Reporting the Problem,"
    www.justice.gov (accessed 1/10/14); Naomi Harlin Goodno, "How Public
    Schools Can Constitutionally Halt Cyberbullying: A Model Cyberbullying
    Policy That Considers First Amendment, Due Process, and Fourth Amend-
    ment Challenges," *Wake Forest Law Review* 46 (Fall 2011): 641, 655.
88. "Peer-to-Peer Violence," 152.
89. If the subject of a photo is coerced into posing and the photo is porno-
    graphic, schools must report what they have discovered to child welfare
    authorities for investigation and possible prosecution. Juveniles have been

prosecuted for enticing their peers to pose and for creating and transmitting photos that violate federal law. It is less clear whether the minors who pose and sext are vulnerable to prosecution for their role in creating child pornography, although that is surely not the law's intent and few prosecutors appear to pursue such charges. Anupah Chander, "Youthful Indiscretion in an Internet Age," *The Offensive Internet*, eds. Saul Levmore and Martha C. Nussbaum (Cambridge, MA: Harvard University Press, 2010), 129; Elizabeth Kandel Englander, *Bullying and Cyberbullying: What Every Educator Needs to Know* (Cambridge, MA: Harvard Education Press, 2013), 90.

90. Amanda Lenhart, "Teens and Sexting: How and Why Minor Teens Are Sending Sexually Suggestive Nude or Nearly Nude Images via Text Messaging," *Pew Internet and American Life Project* (2009); Kelly Talon, "Addressing Sexting in Schools," *Children's Legal Rights Journal* 30 (2010): 1.

91. Compare Jeff R. Temple et al., "Teen Sexting and Its Association with Sexual Behaviors," *Archives of Pediatrics & Adolescent Medicine* 166 (2012): 828–833; Kimberly J. Mitchell et al., "Prevalence and Characteristics of Youth Sexting: A National Study," *Pediatrics* 129 (2012): 13–20; Amanda Lenhart et al., "Teens, Adults & Sexting: Data on Sending/Receiving Sexually Suggestive Nude or Nearly Nude Photos by Americans," www.pewinternet.org (accessed 1/15/14); Elizabeth Kandel Englander, *Bullying and Cyberbullying*, 90.

92. Englander, *Bullying and Cyberbullying*, 90.

93. New Jersey v. T.L.O., 469 U.S. 325, 336 (1985); Board of Education v. Earls, 515 U.S. 646 (2002); Adam Walsh Child Protection and Safety Act of 2006, Pub. L. 109–248, 120 Stat. 587 (2006); An Act Relating to Expanding the Sex Offender Registry, Act of June 1, 2009. Ch. 58 §4, 2009 Vt. Acts & Resolves 552, 554–555 (codified at VT. STAT. ANN, tit. 13, § 2802b (2009). But see In re J.B., CP-67-JV-0000726–2010 (Pa. Ct. Common Pleas, York County Nov. 4, 2013) (ruling Pennsylvania's Sexual Offender Registration and Notification Act unconstitutional as it applies to juveniles).

94. Hinduja and Patchin, "State Sexting Laws"; Talon, "Addressing Sexting."

95. Temple et al., "Teen Sexting," E3–E4.

96. Miller v. Skumanick, 605 F.Supp.2d 634, 638, 640 (M.D. Pa. 2009); Miller v. Mitchell, No. 3:09CV540, 2010 WL 1779925 (M.D. Pa. 2010).

97. T.V. v. Smith-Green Cmty. Sch. Corp., 807 F. Supp. 2d 767, 771–773 (N.D. Ind. 2011).

98. Ibid.,

99. Ibid., 779, 787.

100. Chander, "Youthful Indiscretion," 126 (citing MSNBC story).

101. N.J. Stat. § 2C:14–9 (West 2005); ALASKA STAT. § 11.61.123 (2012); Act of June 28, 2014, ch. 71 § 125, 2014 Cal. Legis. Serv. 1691, 1835 (amending CAL. PENAL CODE § 647(j)(4)). See Danielle Keats Citron and Mary Anne Franks, "Criminalizing Revenge Porn." Wake Forest Law Review 49.2 (2014), 345.

102. 2009 Vermont Laws No. 58 (S. 125) §§ 4, 5 (2009); Temple et al., "Teen Sexting," E5.

103. Chander, "Youthful Indiscretion," 129.

104. Case C-131/12, Google Spain SL, Google Inc. v Agencia Española de Protección de Datos (AEPD), Mario Costeja González, curia.europa.eu /juris/documents.jsf?num=C-131/12 (May 13, 2014). CAL. BUS. & PROF. CODE §§ 22580–22582 (West Supp. 2014) (operative January 1, 2015); Associated Press, "Reddit, Google crack down on posting nude pics: Change comes after hackers posted nude photos of Jennifer Lawrence, other celebrities to social media," CBCnews, February 24, 2015, http://www .cbc.ca/news/technology/reddit-google-crack-down-on-posting-nude-pics -1.2970523 (accessed 3/8/15).

105. "In re J.V.R.," *Juvenile Law Center,* www.jlc.org; *Kids for Cash* (SenArt Films 2014).

8. *Tinker* Rising Like the Phoenix

1. Pounds v. Katy Indep. Sch. Dist., 730 F. Supp. 2d 636, 638 (S.D. Tex. 2010).

2. Gilio v. Sch. Bd. of Hillsborough Cnty., 905 F. Supp. 2d 1262, 1274 n. 23 (M.D. Fla. 2012). Peck v. Baldwinsville Cent. Sch. Dist., 426 F.3d 617, 620 (2d Cir. 2005) (Calabresi, J.).

3. Morgan v. Swanson, 659 F.3d 359, 396 (5th Cir. 2011) (Elrod, J.).

4. Douglas Laycock, "High-Value Speech and the Basic Educational Mission of a Public School: Some Preliminary Thoughts," *Lewis & Clark Law Review* 12 (2008): 111, 124.

5. Everson v. Bd. of Educ., 330 U.S. 1, 18 (1947).

6. See, e.g., Kim Severson, "Mississippi Tells Public Schools to Develop Policies Allowing Prayers," *New York Times,* March 16, 2013, A13; Tex. Educ. Code §§ 25.151–25.156 (West 2007); "Gov. Perry Signs School-children's Religious Liberty Bill," www.christianattorney.com (accessed 1/27/14); "Religious Viewpoints Anti-Discrimination Act," *Office of the Governor Rick Perry,* www.governor.state.tx.us (accessed 1/27/14); Kent Greenawalt, *Does God Belong in Public Schools?* (Princeton: Princeton University Press, 2005), 37; Santa Fe Indep. Sch. Dist. v. Doe, 530 U.S. 290, 295 (2000); Lisa Graybill et al., "At the Mercy of the Majority: Attacks on Religious Freedom in Texas Public Schools in the Decade after Santa Fe v. Doe," *ACLU of Texas,* September 12, 2012, 24. See also Chandler v. James, 985 F. Supp. 1094, 1100 (M.D. Ala. 1997) ("it is uncontroverted" that prayer and Bible reading continue in district classrooms); Lane v. Sabine Parish Sch. Bd., Complaint, No. 5:14-cv-00100-EEF-KLH (W.D. La., filed Jan. 22, 2014) (alleging same).

7. Erwin Chemerinsky, "A Fixture on a Changing Court: Justice Stevens and the Establishment Clause," *Northwestern University Law Review* 106 (2012): 587, 592.

8. Lemon v. Kurtzman, 403 U.S. 602, 612 (1971); Kent Greenawalt, *Religion and the Constitution Vol. 2: Establishment and Fairness* (Princeton: Princeton University Press, 2008), 160.
9. Cnty. of Allegheny v. ACLU, 492 U.S. 573, 627 (1989) (O'Connor, J., concurring).
10. Capitol Square Review and Advisory Bd. v. Pinette, 515 U.S. 753, 780 (1995) (O'Connor, J., concurring).
11. Engel v. Vitale, 370 U.S. 421 (1962); Sch. Dist. of Abington Twp., Pa. v. Schempp, 374 U.S. 203 (1963); Wallace v. Jaffree, 472 U.S. 38 (1985); Lee v. Weisman, 505 U.S. 577 (1992); Santa Fe Indep. Sch. Dist. v. Doe, 530 U.S. 290 (2000).
12. Lee v. Weisman, 505 U.S. 577, 587 (1992); Bruce Allen Murphy, *Scalia: A Court of One* (New York: Simon & Schuster, 2014), 200–201.
13. Good News Club v. Milford Cent. Sch., 533 U.S. 98, 113 (2001).
14. Compare Widmar v, Vincent, 454 U.S. 263, 270–271 (1981) with Rosenberger v. Rector, 515 U.S. 819, 837–846 (1995) and Locke v. Davey, 540 U.S. 712, 725 (2004). Doe v. Duncanville Indep. Sch. Dist., 994 F.2d 160, 165 (5th Cir. 1993); Nurre v. Whitehead, 580 F.3d 1087, 1096–1098 (9th Cir. 2009), cert. denied, 130 S. Ct. 1937 (2010); Nurre v. Whitehead, 580 F.3d at 1101–1102 (Smith, J., dissenting in part).
15. Chemerinksy, "A Fixture on a Changing Court," 600; Capitol Square Review v. Pinette, 515 U.S. at 770 (Scalia, J.) (plurality opinion); Lee v. Weisman, 505 U.S. at 640–642 (Scalia, J., dissenting).
16. Town of Greece v. Galloway, 134 S. Ct. 1811 (2014); Salazar v. Buono, 559 U.S. 700 (2010).
17. Santa Fe Indep. Sch. Dist. v. Doe, 550 U.S. 290, 302 (2000), quoting Bd. of Educ. of Westside Cmty. Schs. v. Mergens, 496 U.S. 226, 250 (1990) (O'Connor, J., plurality opinion) (quoted in Doe v. Sch. Dist. of City of Norfolk, 340 F.3d 605, 610 (8th Cir. 2003)).
18. Santa Fe Indep. Sch. Dist. v. Doe, 550 U.S. at 313.
19. Frank J. Murray, "Federal Court Hears Lawsuit over Kindergarten Christian," *Washington Times,* April 12, 2002 (cited in "Statement of Hiram S. Sasser III before United States Commission on Civil Rights," www.eusccr.com (accessed 1/21/14), 11); Pounds v. Katy Indep. Sch. Dist., 517 F. Supp. 2d at 906 n. 3.
20. *Beyond the Pledge of Allegiance: Hostility to Religious Expression in the Public Square before the Subcommittee on the Constitution, Civil Rights and Property Rights of the Committee on the Judiciary, United States Senate,* 108th Cong. 30 (2004) (statement of Kelly Shackelford, chief counsel of the Liberty Legal Institute, Plano, Texas).
21. Employment Div., Dep't of Human Resources v. Smith, 494 U.S. 872 (1990); *Beyond the Pledge of Allegiance,* 34–35.
22. E.g., Chalifoux v. New Caney Indep. Sch. Dist., 976 F. Supp. 659 (S.D. Tx. 1997); Alabama and Coushatta Tribes of Tex. v. Big Sandy Indep. Sch. Dist., 817 F. Supp. 1319 (E.D. Tx. 1993).

23. O.T. v. Frenchtown Elementary Sch. Dist. Bd. of Educ., 465 F. Supp. 2d 369 (D. N.J. 2006).
24. M.B. v. Liverpool Cent. Sch. Dist., 487 F. Supp. 2d 117, 128–129 (N.D. N.Y. 2007).
25. C.H. v. Oliva, 990 F. Supp. 341 (D. N.J. 1997), aff'd, 166 F.3d 1204 (3d Cir. 1998), aff'd, 195 F.3d 167 (3d Cir. 1999), aff'd, 226 F.3d 198 (3d Cir. 2000) (evenly divided en banc court).
26. C.H. v. Oliva, 226 F.3d at 210 (Alito, J., dissenting).
27. DeNooyer v. Livonia Pub. Sch., 799 F. Supp. 744 (E.D. Mich. 1992); Peck v Baldwinsville Cent. Sch. Dist., 426 F.3d 617.
28. Settle v. Dickinson Cnty. Sch. Bd., 53 F.3d 152, 153 (6th Cir.), cert. denied, 516 U.S. 989 (1995). See also Peck v. Baldwinsville Cent. Sch. Dist., 426 F.3d at 621–624.
29. Michael W. McConnell, "Equal Treatment and Religious Discrimination," *Equal Treatment of Religion in a Pluralistic Society,* eds. Stephen V. Monsma and J. Christopher Soper (Grand Rapids: William B. Eerdmann Publishing Co., 1998), 39; Settle v. Dickinson Cnty. Sch. Bd., 53 F.3d at 154.
30. McConnell, "Equal Treatment," 39.
31. Morgan v. Swanson, 659 F.3d at 387–388.
32. Whitson v. Knox Cnty. Bd. of Educ., 468 Fed. Appx. 532 (6th Cir. 2012).
33. A.M. v. Taconic Hills Cent. Sch. Dist., 2012 WL 177954, at *3 (N.D. N.Y. 2012), aff'd, 510 Fed. Appx 3 (2d. Cir. 2013), cert. denied, 134 S. Ct. 196 (2013).
34. Doe v. Santa Fe Indep. Sch. Dist., 168 F.3d 806 (5th Cir. 1999).
35. Nathan Koppel, "New Reading on School Prayer," *Texas Law* 15 (September 20, 1999): 1.
36. Liz Stevens, "Marian's Prayer—When Marian Ward Bowed Her Head before a High School Football Game, She Became a Symbol for a Raging National Debate," *Fort Worth Star-Telegram* (TX), April 2, 2000, Life 1; Santa Fe Indep. Sch. Dist. v. Doe, 171 F.3d 1013 (5th Cir. 1999), aff'd, 530 U.S. 290 (2000).
37. Stevens, "Marian's Prayer"; Colbert I. King, "School-Sanctioned Prayer Is Used as a Cultural Weapon," *Sacramento Bee,* July 1, 2000, B7; "Marian Ward," *Campaign for Liberty,* www.campaignforliberty.org (accessed 2/8/14); Pamela Colloff, "They Haven't Got a Prayer," *Texas Monthly,* November 2000.
38. Stevens, "Marian's Prayer."
39. Robbie Brown, "Barred from Field, Religious Signs Move to Stands," *New York Times,* October 27, 2009, A14.
40. Matthews v. Kountze Indep. Sch. Dist., 2014 WL 1857797 (Tex. App. May 8, 2014); Manny Fernandez, "Cheerleaders with Bible Verses Set Off a Debate," *New York Times,* October 4, 2012, A14.
41. Matthews v. Kountze Indep. Sch. Dist., 2014 WL 1857797 (Tex. App. May 8, 2014); Complaint, Matthews v. Kountze, Ninth District of Texas at Beaumont, NO. 09–13–00251-CV, 4, 10, 19–20; Kountze ISD's Notice of

Accelerated Appeal, No. 53526 (356th Judicial Dist. of Hardin Cnty., Tx. May 28, 2013); Matthews v. Kountze Indep. Sch. Dist., Order on Plaintiffs' Application for Temporary Preliminary Injunction, No 53526 (Dist. Ct. Hardin County Tx., 356th Judicial District, Oct. 18, 2012); Miriam Rozen, "Texas Supreme Court May Hear Kountze ISD Cheerleader Case," *Texas Lawyer*, October 21, 2014, www.texaslawyer.com/id.=1202674102443 /Texas-Supreme-Court-May-Hear-Kountze-ISD-Cheerleader-Case?slreturn=20150215135…(accessed 3/15/15).

42. An amicus brief filed by Americans United and joined by other religious liberty organizations raised the Establishment Clause arguments in the Texas appellate court. As the case lingered for resolution of attorneys' fees, in March 2015 the Texas Supreme Court agreed to revisit the substantive issues, which the lower courts had dismissed as moot. Americans United, "Kountze Independent School District v. Matthews," (updated March 12, 2015), https:www.au.org./our-work/legal/lawsuits/Kountze-independent -school-district-v.matthews. (accessed 3/15/15).

43. Perumal v. Saddleback Valley Unified Sch. Dist., 243 Cal. Rptr. 545, 565 (Ct. App. 4th Dist. Div. 3 1988).

44. Fernandez, "Cheerleaders with Bible Verses."

45. E.g., Graybill et al., "At the Mercy of the Majority."

46. Corder v. Lewis Palmer Sch. Dist., 566 F.3d 1219, 1228 (10th Cir.), cert. denied, 558 U.S. 1048 (2009), quoting Fleming v. Jefferson Cnty. Sch. Dist. R-1, 298 F.3d at 925. Hazelwood governs graduation in the Third, Ninth, and Tenth Circuits. Brody v. Spang, 957 F.2d 1108, 1122 (3d Cir. 1992); Nurre v. Whitehead, 580 F.3d 1087, 1095 (9th Cir. 2009), cert. denied, 130 S. Ct. 1937 (2010); Corder v. Lewis Palmer Sch. Dist. No. 38, 566 F.3d at 1229.

47. See Kent Greenawalt, *Does God Belong in Public Schools?*, 48; Adler v. Duval Cnty. Sch. Bd., 112 F.3d 1475 (11th Cir. 1997); "Guidance on Constitutionally Protected Prayer in Public Elementary and Secondary Schools," U.S. Department of Education, February 7, 2003; Lassonde v. Pleasanton Unified Sch. Dist., 320 F.3d 979, 983 (9th Cir. 2003); Cole v. Oroville Union High Sch. Dist., 228 F.3d 1092 (9th Cir. 2000); A.M. v. Taconic Hills, 2012 WL 177954; Peck v. Baldwinsville, 426 F.3d at 633; Corder v. Lewis Palmer Sch. Dist., 566 F.3d 1219.

48. Griffith v. Butte Sch. Dist. No. 1, 244 P.3d 321 (Mt. 2010).

49. Cole v. Oroville Union High Sch. Dist., 228 F.3d 1092, 1097 (9th Cir 2000); Corder v. Lewis Palmer Sch. Dist., 566 F.3d at 1233.

50. Corder v. Lewis Palmer Sch. Dist., 568 F. Supp. 2d at 1241.

51. A.M. v. Taconic Hills Cent. Sch. Dist., 510 Fed. Appx. at *7–*9.

52. Ibid., *8–*9, quoting Bronx Household of Faith v. Bd. of Educ., 650 F.3d 30, 38 (2d Cir.), cert. denied, 132 S. Ct. 816 (2011).

53. "Religious Viewpoints Anti-Discrimination Act," *Office of the Governor Rick Perry*, www.governor.state.tx.us (accessed 1/27/14); Tex. Educ. Code

§§ 25.151–25.156; "Gov. Perry Signs Schoolchildren's Religious Liberty Bill."

54. See Stratechuk v. South Orange-Maplewood Sch. Dist., 587 F.3d 597 (3d Cir. 2009).

55. Nurre v. Whitehead, 580 F.3d at 1096; Lassonde v. Pleasanton Unified Sch. Dist., 320 F.2d 979, 983 (9th Cir. 2003).

56. Lassonde v. Pleasanton Unified Sch. Dist., 320 F.3d at 983.

57. A.M. v. Taconic Hills, 2012 WL 177954, at *5.

58. Ibid; Tinker v. Des Moines, 393 U.S. at 509; C.H. v. Oliva, 226 F.3d 198, 214 (3d Cir. 2000) (Alito, J., dissenting).

59. Morgan v. Swanson, 748 F.3d 241 (5th Cir. 2014).

60. Nuxoll v. Indian Prairie Sch. Dist. No. 204, 523 F.3d 668, 676 (7th Cir. 2008) (Posner, J.).

61. Rivera v. East Otero Sch. Dist. R-1, 721 F. Supp. 1189, 1191 (D. Colo. 1989); see also Hedges v. Wauconda Cmty. Unit Sch. Dist. No. 118, 9 F.3d 1295, 1296–1297 (7th Cir. 1993); Thompson v. Waynesboro Area Sch. Dis., 673 F. Supp. 1379, 1380–1381 (M.D. Pa. 1987).

62. Hedges v. Wauconda Cmty. Sch. Dist., 9 F.3d 1295; Heinkel v. Sch. Bd. of Lee Cnty., Fla., 194 Fed. Appx. 604 (11th Cir. 2006); Freedman v. Maryland, 380 U.S. 51, 59 (1965); M.B. v. Liverpool Cent. Sch. Dist., 487 F. Supp. 2d 117, 145 (N.D. N.Y. 2007); Rivera v. East Otero School Dist., 721 F. Supp. at 1197.

63. Taylor v. Roswell Indep. Sch. Dist., 713 F.3d 25, 41–43 (10th Cir. 2013).

64. Ibid., 36–38.

65. Hedges v. Wauconda Cmty. Sch. Dist., 9 F.3d at 1302.

66. Morgan v. Swanson, 659 F.3d 359, 411 (5th Cir. 2011) (en banc) (summarizing cases), cert. denied, 132 S. Ct. 2740 (2012); Pounds v. Katy Indep. Sch. Dist., 730 F. Supp. 2d at 638.

67. Morgan v. Swanson, 659 F.3d at 366, 366 n. 7 (collecting cases); see also Curry v. Hensiner, 513 F.3d 570 (6th Cir. 2008); Walz v. Egg Harbor Twp. Bd. of Educ., 342 F.3d 271 (3d Cir. 2003); Westfield High Sch. L.I.F.E. Club v. City of Westfield, 249 F. Supp. 2d 98 (D. Mass. 2003).

68. See Morgan v. Swanson, 659 F.3d at 384; Peck v. Upshur Cnty. Bd. of Educ., 155 F.3d 274, 275–276 (4th Cir. 1998).

69. Curry v. Hensiner, 513 F.3d 570.

70. Gilio v. Sch. Bd., 905 F. Supp. 2d at 1267. See also Morgan v. Swanson, 659 F.3d 359; K.A. v. Pocono Mountain Sch. Dist., 2011 WL 5008358.

71. Morgan v. Swanson, 659 F.3d at 376 (Benavides, J.).

72. Ibid., 365.

73. Ibid., 367, 367 n. 10.

74. Ibid., 414 (Elrod, J.).

75. Brief of Amici Curiae Gathie Barnett Edmonds and Marie Barnett Snodgrass at 3, Morgan v. Swanson, 659 F.3d 359 (5th Cir. 2011) (No. 09–40373), 2011 WL 2179540, at *3 (C.A. 5) (Appellate Brief).

76. Morgan v. Swanson, 659 F.3d at 396 (Elrod, J.).

77. Ibid.

78. Ibid., 421; Hedges v. Wauconda Cmty. Sch. Dist., 9 F.3d at 1298.

79. Good News Club v. Milford Cent. Sch., 533 U.S. 98, 118 (2001).

80. Morgan v. Swanson, 659 F.3d at 404–407, 405 n. 12, 407 n 21 (Elrod, J.) (collecting and distinguishing cases); Gilio v. Sch. Bd., 905 F. Supp. 2d at 1272.

81. Walz v. Egg Harbor Twp. Bd. of Educ., 342 F.3d at 278, quoted with approval in Curry v. Hensiner, 513 F.3d at 578–579.

82. Morgan v. Swanson, 755 F.3d 757, 763 (5th Cir. 2014) (Benavides, J., concurring).

83. Morgan v. Swanson, 659 F.3d at 421 (Elrod, J., dissenting).

84. Bellotti v. Baird, 443 U.S. 622, 634 (1979) (citing In re Gault, 387 U.S. 1, 13 (1967)).

85. Sch. Dist. of Abington Twp., Pa. v. Schempp, 374 U.S. 203, 289, 289 n. 68, 291–292 (1963) (Brennan, J., concurring), quoting Illinois v. Bd. of Educ. of Sch. Dist. No. 71, 333 U.S. 203, 227 (1948) (Black, J.).

86. Morgan v. Swanson, 659 F.3d at 380, quoting Curry v. Hensiner, 513 F.3d at 579.

87. Hedges v. Wauconda Cmty. Sch. Dist., 9 F.3d at 1296–1297.

88. Ibid., 1296–1298.

89. Ibid., 1299, 1300.

90. 20 U.S. C. § 4071 (a), (c)(3).

91. Widmar v. Vincent, 454 U.S. 263 (1981).

92. 20 U.S.C. § 4071 (b) (2012); 20 U.S.C. § 4071(c)(4) (2012).

93. Gay-Straight Alliance v. School Bd. of Nassau, 602 F. Supp. 2d 1233, 1235 (M.D. Fla. 2009).

94. Krestan v. Deer Valley Unified Sch. Dist. No. 97, 561 F. Supp. 2d 1078, 1086 (D. Ariz. 2008), quoting Prince v. Jacoby, 303 F.3d 1074, 1082 (9th Cir. 2002).

95. Colin v. Orange Unified Sch. Dis., 83 F. Supp. 2d 1135, 1141 (C.D. Cal. 2000).

96. Bd. of Educ. of Westside Cmty. Schools v. Mergens, 496 U.S. 226 (1990). Since *Mergens,* many lower courts have refused to accept school districts' characterization of clubs as curricular related. East High Gay/Straight Alliance v. Bd. of Educ. of Salt Lake City Sch. Dist., 81 F. Supp. 2d 1166, 1168 (D. Utah 1999); Pope v. East Brunswick Bd. of Educ., 12 F.3d 1244 (3d Cir. 1993); Colin v. Orange Unified Sch. Dist. 83 F. Supp. 2d 1135 (C.D. Cal 2000); Boyd Cnty. High Sch. Gay Straight Alliance v. Bd. of Educ. of Boyd Cnty., Ky., 258 F. Supp. 2d 667 (E.D. Ky. 2003).

97. Hazelwood v. Kuhlmeier, 484 U.S, at 271.

98. East High Gay/Straight Alliance v. Bd. of Educ. of Salt Lake City Sch. Dist., 81 F. Supp. 2d at 1168; East High Gay/Straight Alliance v. Bd. of Educ. of Salt Lake City Sch. Dist., 30 F. Supp. 2d 1356 (D. Utah 1998); East High Sch. Prism Club v. Seidel, 95 F. Supp. 2d 1239, 1243, 1244 (D. Utah 2000).

99. Caudillo v. Lubbock Indep. Sch. Dist., 311 F. Supp. 2d 550, 558 (N.D. Tex. 2004); Gonzalez v. Sch. Bd. of Okeechobee Cnty., 571 F. Supp. 2d 1257, 1269 (S.D. Fla. 2008); Gay-Straight Alliance Yulee v. Sch. Bd. of Nassau Cnty., 602 F.Supp. 2d 1233, 1235 n. 2 (M.D. Fla. 2009); "School Bans All Non-academic Clubs to Avoid Approving Gay-Straight Alliance," *LGBTQ Nation,* February 28, 2011, www.lgbqtnation.com (accessed 2/3/14); Lawrence v. Texas, 539 U.S. 558 (2003); Windsor v. United States, 133 S. Ct. 2675 (2013).

100. Boyd Cnty. High Sch. Gay Straight Alliance v. Bd. of Educ. of Boyd Cnty., Ky., 258 F. Supp. 2d 667, 670 n. 1, 671 (E.D. Ky. 2003).

101. Ibid., 670 n. 1, 671.

102. Ibid., 671.

103. Ibid., 673.

104. Ibid., 673, 674.

105. Ibid., 673.

106. Ibid., 686.

107. Ibid., 690; Morrison v. Bd. of Educ. of Boyd Cnty., 419 F. Supp. 2d 937 (E.D. Ky. 2006), rev'd, 507 F.3d 494 (6th Cir. 2008), vacated and aff'g district court's opinion, 521 F.3d 602 (6th Cir. 2008), cert. denied, 555 U.S. 1171 (2009).

108. Gay-Straight Alliance v. School Bd. of Nassau, 602 F. Supp. 2d at 1236 n. 6 (quoting Colin v. Orange Unified Sch. Dist., 83 F. Supp. 2d at 1148); Colin v. Orange Unified Sch. Dist., 83 F. Supp. 2d at 1147.

109. Colin v. Orange Unified Sch. Dist., 83 F. Supp. 2d at 1148–1149.

110. "Same-Sex Marriage Support Reaches New High at 55%," May 21, 2014, www.gallup.com (accessed 7/14/14); James O'Higgins-Norman et al., "Addressing Homophobic Bullying in Second-Level Schools," (The Equality Authority 2010), 16, http://www.equality.ie/Files/Addressing%20 Homophobic%20in%20%Second%20Level%20Schools.pdf (accessed 7/18/14).

111. Human Rights Campaign, "Maps of State Laws & Policies," www.hrc.org /state_maps (accessed 3/8/15); DeBoer v. Snyder, 772 F.3d 388 (6th Cir. 2014), cert. granted, 135 S. Ct. 1039 (2015) (consolidating cases including Obergefell v. Hodges).

112. Bowler v. Town of Hudson, 514 F. Supp. 2d 168, 172 n. 3 (D. Mass. 2007); "First Amendment Victory: Mass. School Agrees to Settle Free Speech Lawsuit and Amend Practices to Protect Conservative Student Expression," *The Rutherford Institute News,* May 29, 2008, www.rutherford.org (accessed 2/3/14).

113. Bowler v. Town of Hudson, 514 F. Supp. 2d at 171-173.

114. Ibid., 173-175.

115. "First Amendment Victory," *The Rutherford Institute News.*

116. Hansen v. Ann Arbor Pub. Schools, 293 F. Supp. 2d 780, 783 (E.D. Mich. 2003).

117. Ibid., 803.

Conclusion

1. See Rob Reich, *Bridging Liberalism and Multiculturalism in American Education*, (Chicago: University of Chicago Press 2002), 218; Common Core State Standards Initiative, released June 2, 2010, www.corestandards.org (accessed 3/8/15).

2. Bryan R. Warnick, *Understanding Student Rights in Schools: Speech, Religion, and Privacy in Educational Settings* (New York: Teachers College Press, 2013), 84, 87–88.

3. Quoted in David Hudson, *Let the Students Speak! A History of the Fight for Free Expression in American Schools* (Boston: Beacon Press, 1995), 67.

4. Constance A. Flanagan, *Teenage Citizens: The Political Theories of the Young* (Cambridge, MA: Harvard University Press, 2013), 96, 101–102.

5. Frazier v. Winn, 535 F. 1279, 1285 (8th Cir. 2008)

6. Karen Tumulty and Lyndsey Laytin, "The Culture Wars Come to a Colo. History Course," *Washington Post,* October 6, 2014, A1.

7. Charles C. Haynes, "Inside the First Amendment," *The Morning Sun,* October 11, 2014, KS Opinion, 5; Colleen Slevin, "Colorado School Board Vote Doesn't Appease Critics," Associated Press, October 4, 2014; Tumulty and Laytin, "The Culture Wars"; Denisa R. Superville, "Amid Backlash, Colo. Board Rethinks U.S. History Review," *Education Week,* October 8, 2014.

8. Smith v. Novato Unified Sch. Dist., 59 Cal. Rptr. 3d 508, 513–514 (Cal. Ct. App. 2007), cert. denied, 552 U.S. 1184 (2008).

9. Glowacki v. Howell Public Sch. Dist., 2013 WL 5203885 (No 2:11-cv-15481 Sept. 16, 2013), aff'd 2014 WL 2109310 (6th Cir. May 20, 2014).

10. Michael Stokes Paulsen et al., *The Constitution of the United States,* Second Edition (St. Paul, MN: Thompson Reuters/Foundation Press, 2013).

11. CAL. EDUC. CODE § 66301 (f) (West 2012).

12. Hedges v. Wauconda Sch. Dist., 9 F.3d 1295, 1300, 1299 (7th Cir. 1993) (Easterbrook, J.).

Acknowledgments

I began work on this book as a Member of the School of Social Science at the Institute for Advanced Study in Princeton in 2008–2009. It is hard to imagine a better environment for pursuing the life of the mind, and I am deeply indebted to the Institute far beyond its financial support. I also thank the colleagues who participated in that year's seminar on social norms and cooperation, especially Barry O'Neill and Rick Schweder, as well as the members of the seminar convened by Joan Scott for their comments and camaraderie. I very much appreciate the encouragement I received from Eric Maskin (who convened the 2008–2009 group), Danielle Allen, Joan Scott, and Michael Walzer. Special thanks are due to the excellent reference librarians at the Institute (who, among other things, refuse to abandon the card catalogue) and Donne Petito, who kept everything running.

During 2008–2009, I received sabbatical funding from George Washington University Law School, which over the course of this project generously provided me with summer research grants, research assistance, and other institutional support. I thank the deans who led the school while I was writing this book, especially Interim Dean Gregory Maggs and Dean Blake Morant. Faculty colleagues, especially the friends who kept me laughing, provided a warm community.

Mary Kate Hunter, reference librarian at George Washington University Law School, has helped at every stage, always with an eye to detail and generosity of spirit, even sending me material on snow days as deadlines loomed. I have been fortunate to have excellent and devoted research assistants: Lauren Birzon, Averie Maldanado, Elizabeth Szabo, and Alisa Yasin, as well as Michael Lanning and Lindsey Strang, who all contributed in important ways. Students in my classes have both supported and challenged my ideas, and shared pertinent anecdotes, enriching the project along the way.

I thank those who generously commented on all or part of the manuscript. Naomi Cahn and Ira (Chip) Lupu each read the entire manuscript and offered thoughtful editorial suggestions, large and small. Danielle Citron and Linda McClain pushed me in helpful ways. My former students Melissa Colangelo and Elizabeth Szabo, who went on to work in children's rights and education law, commented on a draft. Each of them, along with anonymous outside readers for Harvard University Press, helped improve the manuscript.

For their encouragement at the outset, I thank Martha Minow, Carol Sanger, and Barbara Woodhouse. Reaching further back, I owe intellectual debts to Burke Marshall and Owen Fiss, who mentored me at Yale Law School in constitutional law generally and First Amendment law in particular. Both powerfully influenced my understanding of reading, teaching, and writing about the Constitution.

I received helpful feedback when I presented portions of this book at the annual meetings of the American Political Science Association and the Southeastern Association of Law Schools, and at faculty workshops at Rutgers School of Law–Camden, Tulane Law School, and George Washington University Law School. Exchange with the other participants in the Seminar on Education, Democracy, and Justice, convened at the Institute for Advanced Study in 2009–2010 by Danielle Allen and Rob Reich, enriched my work.

A special note of gratitude goes to my good friends Stephen Kling and Nancy Miller. Stephen, a graphic designer, executed and helped me conceptualize the chart "Before You Silence Student Speech," which appears in the book's conclusion. Nancy offered sage advice over the years.

Michael Aronson, my editor at Harvard University Press, had faith in this project from its inception, helped me define its scope, and offered nuanced editorial suggestions from beginning to end. It was a gift to work with Mike. He read and responded to every word in the manuscript, even reviewing some chapters more than once. I thank the S. M. Bessie Fund for supporting publication of this book, and Kathleen Drummy and Donna Bouvier, among others at the Harvard University Press, who helped with the final product. Thanks are also due to Isabelle Lewis, who designed the map in the Appendix.

I am grateful to friends and extended family—scattered all over the country and beyond—for their indulgence during my long periods of immersion in this project. I thank them all. But I must single out my brother-in-law Eric Rieder. He read every word of the manuscript with a former journalist's eye and a practicing lawyer's habit of questioning—and generously responded to all manner of follow-up questions.

My father, Alexander I. Ross, who arrived in the United States as a teenager in 1940, transmitted to me his fervent belief in the promise of pluralist democracy, his precise use of the English language, and the confidence that comes from being loved and cared for. I miss him every day.

This book is dedicated to my husband, Jonathan Rieder. He is my lifelong companion, my foremost champion, and, to my great benefit, one of the best editors I have ever known. For roughly twenty-eight years, we have shared spirited conversations with our son, Daniel Ross-Rieder, who—while unwavering in his affection—never lets me venture an opinion I cannot defend. Together, they created the loving home base that made my work possible.

Index